Rod Heikell

The Gift of a Sea

A Short History of Yachting in the Mediterranean

Taniwha Press UK

www.taniwhapress.com

Published by the Taniwha Press UK

www.taniwhapress.com

Facebook TaniwhaPress

British Library Cataloguing in Publication Data

Heikell, Rod

Title *The Gift of a Sea: A Short History of Yachting in the Mediterranean*

Type Non fiction. Sailing. Yachting history. Yacht charter. Superyachts. Mediterranean. Egypt. Greece. Turkey. Croatia. Italy. Malta. France. Spain. Gibraltar.

1st edition 2019

ISBN 978-0-9954699-5-2

All photos © by Rod and Lucinda Heikell except where © is otherwise named.

The publisher has checked all URLs for accuracy at the time of printing, but has no responsibility for the continued existence or the content of websites cited in the book.

Edited by Shelagh Aitken www.editorproofreader.co.uk

Printed and bound by Biddles Books, King's Lynn, Norfolk PE32 1SF

For all those who love to sail on this sea,
especially for my wife, Lucinda.

I have loved the Mediterranean with passion, no doubt because I am a northerner like so many others in whose footsteps I have followed. I have joyfully dedicated long years of study to it – much more than all my youth. In return, I hope that a little of this joy and a great deal of Mediterranean sunlight will shine from the pages of this book. Ideally perhaps one should, like the novelist, have one's subject under control, never losing it from sight and constantly aware of its over-powering presence... The reader who approaches this book in the spirit I would wish will do well to bring with him his own memories, his own vision of the Mediterranean to add colour to the text and to help me conjure up this vast presence, as I have done my best to do.

Fernand Braudel in the preface to the 1st edition of *The Mediterranean and the Mediterranean World in the Age of Philip II, 1949*

TABLE OF CONTENTS

PREFACE

In 1976–77 I sailed the 20 ft *Roulette*, an old hard chine plywood boat with a dodgy engine and little else down to Greece. No electrics, a steering compass, a few charts, cotton sails and a certain naivety about wind, weather and sea. *Roulette* sailed to St Malo and then through the Brittany canals to the Bay of Biscay where we coast-hopped down to Bordeaux. The Garonne Canal and Canal du Midi provide a short-cut to the Mediterranean coast of France and a lot of sightseeing along the way. From here *Roulette* crossed to Corsica, Italy and finally to Greece. So what happened on the way to the Mediterranean? I was 27 in 1976 when we set off from England, sure that this little voyage was to be an interstice before I returned to New Zealand and some 'proper job'. You could call it escaping. I prefer to think of it as something of a pilgrimage, though the object of the pilgrimage was obscure. Something happened on this voyage so that bit by bit I fell in love with this life and with the Mediterranean.

Over the years I've collected scraps of information, old postcards and any books pertinent (or nearly so) to sailing in the Mediterranean. In the past I've written small chunks of the history of yachting in the Mediterranean and a few articles. Now it's time to expand on that after some forty odd years of sailing around and an intimacy with the recent history of the subject.

This history is not, and cannot be, a definitive history of yachting in the Mediterranean. For starters, it is by a native English speaker who, while he has some conversational French and Greek, is not equipped to translate papers on the subject from any of the languages spoken around the Mediterranean. Rather, it is an attempt to bring together the disparate sources in English on yachting in the Mediterranean. Consequently it has an inbuilt bias from the start. Thankfully a lot of the papers and literature covering this area are in English or have been translated into English at some time.

It would be tempting to elaborate on some methodological procedure and an angle on schools of historical thinking on the subject. While I have tried to be as rigorous and objective as possible with my sources, if I adhere to any system, it is to history as 'stamp collecting': get the collection together, order into countries, sub-order into periods and subjects, until you have something along the lines of a Linnaean classification and a historical timeline. Then you can take a look at the causes and effects of why things ended up the way they have. I have included references to the sources in footnotes and in the bibliography so that my interpretation of a period in the history can be checked, but we are talking about all sorts of sources; some of them have an obvious bias from the start. If you have been employed in an industry to produce a paper on promoting yachting tourism in a country, it is unlikely you will have too many negatives in it. Hopefully I have applied a little objectivity to this bias and sorted out the obvious twaddle in some of the papers sponsored by those with interests in the tourism industry, various NGOs and a few university faculties.

I am not trying to belittle the efforts and some of the conclusions in these papers on yachting in the Mediterranean, particularly in the present, but after spending forty years sailing and writing about yachting in the Mediterranean, I have a sense of place for the sea and how it has changed over time. Even worse, I have become a historical artefact. In Turkey a young manager of a marina asked me if I could sign one of my books for him. When he arrived with a first edition that was published thirty-five years ago, I was horrified and immediately assured him I would get him a new edition. He told me that it had taken him some time to find this old first edition and he wanted it so he could see what the area looked like before he was born. The old black-and-white photographs and the hand-drawn plans showed what the coast looked like before all the marinas were built and the shoreside facilities developed. I'm not sure if I was that impressed at being an artefact so soon, but when I glanced over the plans and photos and text, I could see what he meant. The modern history of the coast and yachting activity was laid out in the changes over thirty-five years and the ten editions of the book.

Rod Heikell, Cowes and Greece 2019

FOREWORD

One afternoon, more than five million years ago, the earth shrugged its shoulders for a moment and gave birth to the Middle Sea. Its crustal plates clunked and bent and ripped open a tiny gap in the mountain range that connected Europe to Africa. The Atlantic Ocean poured through the breach of what was to become the Straits of Gibraltar. It was the most spectacular flood in the earth's history, the force of a thousand Amazon rivers, in a huge water ramp, soon several miles wide. It foamed over a cliff, itself nearly a mile high, to fill the dried-up basin beyond. Within two years, the flickering of an eyelid in geological terms, the Mediterranean as we know it now had become the navel of the world.

It's a pond when you compare it to the great expanses of proper oceans. But it's been the crossroads of our planet, the cradle of mankind and the cockpit of his civilization. It has the climate where we could thrive and learn and think. The sea was the key to it all, though. The sea and its sailors, exploring, trading, conquering; taking technologies and philosophies from the inland sea to every corner of the globe.

For those of us who ply its waters for pleasure today, crossing (or so we fancy) the wakes of Odysseus in Homer's wine-dark sea, Themistocles turning back the Persians at Salamis, John of Austria saving Europe from the Turk at Lepanto, and those centuries from Blake, through the glorious Nelson to Cunningham when it was an English lake, it's history as much as wind that fills our sails.

That's just one of the reasons why Rod Heikell is our guide of guides, why his pilot books, well-thumbed, heavily annotated and limp in places from spilled coffee and wine, are our bibles. For decades now, he's explored nearly every creek and bay around the great circle of the Mediterranean's crinkly coastline. He knows where best to hide from the Mistral and the Bora, the Scirocco and the dread Meltemi. He tells us where we can safely anchor and where we have to be careful – 'not everywhere good holding' will one day be the title of my Booker-shortlisted novel. He has the best places to stop and watch the world go by over a glass of Retsina or Villa Dolucca. He has a cosmopolitan enthusiasm for the peoples of the littoral, their customs and their cultures. And he is a sailor with a hinterland. He has a wonderful sense of the continuity of life, of how we connect with those who've sailed these waters before, from the Lycians with their taste for memorialised death, to the Victorian English aristocrats in yachts the size of warships and their appetite for cultural plunder.

Wherever we who play at sailors go around the Med today, from the scruffiest liveaboard to the grandest pink-panted, double-breasted, Rolex-flashing superyacht sultan, we – or our partners – ask: 'what does Heikell say about this place?'

He says it with wit. He says it with style. He's one of us, really, except that he knows what he's talking about. In the sailors' pantheon, he's 'Rod the God', omniscient but fun, the ideal companion as we sail the loveliest of seas.

Michael Buerk

ACKNOWLEDGEMENTS

Numerous people helped me with the recent history of yachting and others made suggestions and edited portions of the text on the earlier history of yachting in the Mediterranean. Numbers of those involved in yacht charter, particularly the flotilla story, and in the superyacht business, provided help and photos of these earlier days. Many of the photos and illustrations in this book are my own or by Lucinda Heikell or are from original editions and papers in my collection. Where the photos are from other sources this is cited in the caption to the photo or illustration.

Of the many who helped with this book I would like to thank the following. If I have forgotten anyone my apologies for such carelessness. Michael Buerk who kindly wrote the Foreword and who loves to sail his yacht on this sea. Mike Cox who was operations manager for the Yacht Cruising Association and Sunsail. Barrie and Heidi Neilson who own and operate Flotilla Sailing Holidays. Chris and Shan Blunt who worked on flotillas and later on superyachts. Steve Clarke-Lens for his account of 4000 miles in a Wayfarer dinghy. Chris Geankoplis for his account of his youthful trip in a Lightning dinghy. Nic the Greek for his account and photos of Aristotle Onasis in the Ionian and the visit to Skorpios all those years ago. Joe and Robin Charlton in Levkas. Richard Kouvaras at Greek Sails. Kerr Whiteford and Chrissy Cansdell. Hasan Kacmaz for enthusiasm and good cheer. Jules Sanders for encouragement and wine. To Kadir Kir (KK) for his wonderful aerial photos. Harry Potts for stories of superyacht life. Penny Minney for checking the text on *Crab* and for photos. Professor Maria Fusaro at Exeter University for help with the Janet Cusack paper. Robert McCabe for old photos in the Mediterranean. Jonathan Beard for guidance around the museums in Istanbul. The Naval Museum in Istanbul. Ertugrul Duru for his tour of the Rahmi M Koc Museum in Istanbul. The Museum of Naval History in Malta and the Malta Tourism Authority. Cowes Classic Boat Museum. The Bodleian Library at Oxford University. To Dave Selby for optimism and insight and curiosity. To Imray, Laurie, Norie and Wilson who have published many of my other books and for permissions to use maps and plans.

Thanks to my wife Lucinda who offered encouragement and read and re-read sections of the book. Finally my thanks to Shelagh Aitken who edited the book into what you see before you.

Tower of Winds from the 1st century CE in Plaka in Athens reminding the citizens of Athens what the weather will be when the wind blows from a certain direction and what it will be like for those on the sea.

INTRODUCTION

Defining just what a 'yacht' is in a history of this sort throws up all sorts of problems. We know where the word comes from though not exactly why. *The Oxford Companion to the Ships and the Sea* has this derivation.

YACHT, from the Dutch *jacht* (p.p. of *jachten*, to hurry, to hunt), originally a vessel of state, usually employed to convey princes, ambassadors or other great personages from one kingdom to another. (Falconer, *Marine Dictionary* 1771); later any vessel propelled by either sail or power used for pleasure and not plying for hire.

Peter Kemp *The Oxford Companion to Ships and the Sea* OUP 1976 p 947

Jachts are thought to have originally been small fast ships to act as escorts to larger naval ships and to pursue smuggling craft around the waters of Holland. *Jachts* were adopted by Dutch royalty as vessels of state and fitted out sumptuously to accommodate royalty and other persons of note. The richer merchants and lesser nobles also commissioned *jachts* for their own use and these were often used in parades of sail around the home waters of Holland.

The word yacht, from the Dutch *jacht*, was introduced into the English language by Charles II who happened to be in Holland when he was restored to the throne in 1660. The Dutch presented him with the gift of a 100 ton *jacht*, the *Mary*, which was subsequently sailed back to England. By 1771 when Falconer's *Marine Dictionary* was published, the word 'yacht' was in common use for sailing craft fitted out for pleasure and state occasions by the royals and rich merchants and lesser nobles in England. It was not until the later years of the 19th century that the word was used to describe more humble

Charles II's *jacht Royal Escape* from a painting by William van der Velde the Younger.

craft sailed for pleasure by ordinary mortals who did not belong to the ranks of rich gentlemen or royalty.[1]

Although the word 'yacht' was newly minted for use in the 17th and 18th centuries, the idea of a 'yacht' as a vessel of state goes back millennia. In the book of Ezekiel in the Old Testament there is a description of a ship that is evidently for formal occasions and not for rufty-tufty trade on the seas.

Thy borders are in the midst of the seas, thy builders have perfected thy beauty. They have made all thy ship boards of fir trees of Senir: they have taken cedars from Lebanon to make masts for thee. Of the oaks of Bashan have they made thine oars; the company of the Ashurites have made thy benches of ivory, brought out of the isles of Chittim. Fine linen with broidered work from Egypt was that which thou spreadest forth to be thy sail; blue and purple from the isles of Elishah was that which covered thee.

Ezekiel, Chapter XXVII, St James version of the *Bible*.

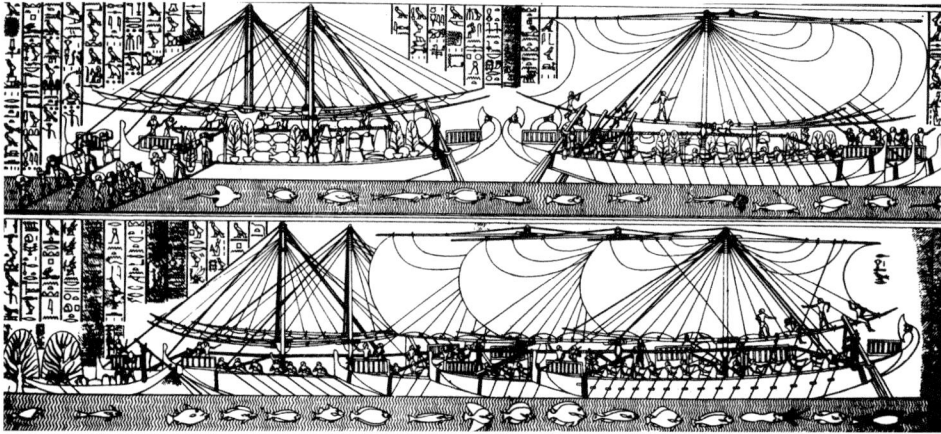

Egyptian ships relief c.1500 BCE from Lionel Casson *Ships and Seamanship in the Ancient World.*

Around 2500 BCE the Pharaoh Cheops had a royal barge built that was buried with him in the Great Pyramid at Giza. Later, the Ptolomies and notably Cleopatra had royal barges used for state occasions. We know little about yachts of any sort during the Greek period, but royal yachts pop up again in the Roman era with, amongst others, the royal barges of the demented Caligula which he used for mock battles and orgiastic parties. The Roman era also throws up our first modest yachtsman, someone who was not of royalty or a man of note within the state, but a poet with a deft line in witty and

1   Peter Kemp *The Oxford Companion to Ships and the Sea* OUP, 1976 p 947

often rude couplets. Catallus left us numerous poems describing his love for his boat and of his voyages in and around the Adriatic and Aegean and they tell us that he experienced much of what yachtsmen of more modest means experience today.[2]

In the Medieval Age there is little on yachting in the Mediterranean, though it is likely there were royal yachts of some sort in the Imperial courts of Byzantium and the Holy Roman Empire. In the Ottoman Empire there were at least ornate *kaikis* to ferry nobles around and for the occasional picnic. The Maritime City states of Venice, Amalfi, Pisa and Genoa staged regattas with small, ornate oared galleys, with the regatta in Venice starting in 1315. The present-day regatta using eight-oared boats reviving the Medieval competition was started after WWII in which each of the once great Medieval maritime city-states enters a boat.

It is not really until the beginning of the 19th century that we again get reliable accounts of yachting in the Mediterranean. The English are about, and Shelley and Byron have yachts built to sail around La Spezia on the Italian coast. Others sail down from England and across from the USA to the Mediterranean in large yachts to explore the mysteries and culture of the countries dotted around the inland sea. Some of these, like the American newspaper magnate Gordon Bennett, Jr are eccentric to say the least. Others are somewhat more restrained, leaving interesting if rather bland accounts of cruising the Mediterranean. In 1895 the Earl of Cavan sailed the 200 ton schooner, *Roseneath*, the length of the Mediterranean and wrote of his experiences in *With the Yacht, Camera, and Cycle in the Mediterranean*.

In the Edwardian era more yachts began to make the voyage to the Mediterranean and although many of these were still in the category of little ships, there were numbers of smaller yachts under twenty tons as well. Between the wars the redoubtable MacPherson sailed his 40 ft yacht *Driac* down and around the Mediterranean and later took the 32 ft *Driac II* to the Mediterranean and beyond. Still, most of the yachts cruising the Mediterranean were larger craft and it was popular to combine a shooting and yachting expedition: woodcock and deer in Albania, wildfowl in Greece,

2   In the translation by Peter Whigham his boat is described as a yacht. Transl. Peter Whigham *The Poems of Catullus* Penguin, 1966.

boar in Turkey, and even the odd lion in North Africa, though it was advised these were by now scarce.

After the Second World War an increasing number of small yachts began to cruise the Mediterranean. Small yachts had been shown to be capable of extended voyages with the exploits of Humphrey Barton in *Vertue XXVI* and Adlard Coles in *Cohoe*. The Mediterranean had its own unsung heroes with the voyages of George Millar in the 48 ft *Truant* and the more relaxed cruises of Ernle Bradford in his Dutch *botter Mother Goose* after the war. Right up until the Sixties a voyage to the Mediterranean was an adventure equal to a voyage to the South Seas or the Caribbean, not in distance and days at sea, but in the sense of adventure that offered excitement and the unknown. The western Mediterranean was barely known and the eastern Mediterranean little visited at all.

In the late Sixties and into the Seventies the number of charter boats began to gradually increase. At first most of these were yachts, large and small, with a skipper and crew, but smaller boats for adventurous bareboat charter also began to make an appearance. In the 1970's the Yacht Cruising Association put the first flotilla yachts in Greece. The concept of flotilla sailing was an immediate success and flotilla holidays spread to other parts of Greece, Yugoslavia, Turkey, Italy, France, Spain and eventually back to England from whence the idea had originated. More and more private yachts began to cruise around the Mediterranean and, in a sense, it had become the playground of northern Europe.

We are still left struggling with the definition of 'what is a yacht'? The etymology of the word from the Dutch is of little help because the word has been used in so many contexts that over time different definitions have emerged. Various yachting writers have defined it as a craft of 30- or 40- or 50 ft and others as a boat on which crew are employed to sail it. None of these definitions is helpful. The one constant in these definitions is that it is a boat used for pleasure. That means it can be powered by sail or engine or both. In times gone by the engine of a bank of rowers could supplant sail power. It is usually a boat with a cabin where there are a few home comforts and somewhere to sleep. That would exclude sailing dinghies, except I include a chapter in this book on small boat exploits in the Mediterranean made in open-decked boats which, with the addition of a cockpit tent and some camping gear, were cruised for

The rise of flotillas in the 1970's: sailing holidays for everyman. Sailing Holidays Ltd.

extended periods.[3] It certainly includes some small decked boats, and many of us have sailed down and around the Mediterranean in modest craft under 20 ft (6 metres).[4] Many of the early definitions exclude 'boats for hire', but that would exclude charter yachts of which there are a lot in the Mediterranean.[5] In the end any definition is bursting at the seams with exceptions and old definitions need to be re-employed and the definition of yachts and yachting left a lot looser.

3   Chapter 14, Small Yacht Exploits in the Mediterranean
4   Rod Heikell *The Accidental Sailor* Taniwha Press, 2013
5   Peter Heaton *Yachting: A History* Batsford, 1955 p 17

For much of this short history we are mostly talking about cruising yachts, although inevitably there is some crossover between cruising yachts which race as well as cruise. There are also yachts used for state occasions like the royal barges of the ancient Egyptians up to the yachts of republics and royalty. In the modern era it includes everything from pocket cruisers and open-decked boats to yachts the size of a small cruise ship. Most histories of yachting and the definition of 'what a yacht is' have not dwelt on the origins of sailing for pleasure in the Mediterranean and have concentrated on the origins of yachting in Britain or the USA.[6]

Inevitably there is some overlap and the history of yachting in northern Europe has influenced and been influenced by the history of yachting in the Mediterranean. A book like this one extends the timeline to cover much earlier periods in which neither the word 'yacht' nor the concept of 'yachting' existed in northern Europe, but did so in the Mediterranean. Hopefully this history will round off the history of yachting in general and give us a bit more of a clue as to why people spend so much time messing about on the sea for pleasure.

In the end, the exact definition of what a yacht is doesn't need to be spelled out as succinctly as some might like. It doesn't matter that much whether you call it a yacht, a sailboat, a motorboat, a private vessel, a little ship or, horror of horrors, a self-propelled watercraft. Perhaps it's better to treat the term with a bit of humour as Kim Kavin does here:

Can you call the boat you own right now a yacht? If any more than three of these five items are true, you pass the test:

1. You refer to your boat as 'she' rather than 'it'

2. Maintenance and upgrades are done by someone else

3. You deduct the loan payments by considering the boat as a second home

4. Etiquette and clean feet are more important to you on board than on dry land

5. Gawkers from the dock often say 'Nice yacht', with a straight face

Kim Kavin www.boats.com/on-the-water/when-is-a-boat-also-a-yacht/#

---

6   Heaton *Yachting: A History*; Douglas Phillips-Birt *The History of Yachting* Stein & Day, 1974; Mike Bender *A New History of Yachting* Boydell Press, 2017

You may not appreciate such levity, but at least it clears the air of long-winded exclusion clauses and lets me get on with the business of detailing what I know of the history of yachting in the Mediterranean.

The Mediterranean: A bit about the sea

Compared to the Atlantic, it looks like a backwater creek running inland from the ocean. But it exerts a pull way beyond its geographical scale on all of us. For some, it is a place where the sun shines from an azure sky, over an anchorage with a few pastel-coloured fishermen's houses ashore. For others, the virtual absence of tides removes at a stroke a complication of sailing that has bedevilled them for years. It is warm spray over the bows, from a blue sea. It is a sea stretching from the Occident to the Orient, a sea surrounded by a variety of countries and cultures that have played a significant part in shaping our own history. For the archaeologist it is a goldmine full of ancient artefacts. Whatever the images are, they exercise a powerful pull on us to visit this sea and sail around it.[7]

In the Atlantic and Pacific Oceans the thing that stands out is the large tracts of water between the land and islands. The trade wind belt, the doldrums and the Sargasso Sea, the breeding grounds for hurricanes, the Humboldt current and the Gulf Stream, the roaring forties: the interaction of wind and water defines these oceans and much of the character of the bordering lands. To make sense of the Mediterranean you have to turn this feature inside out and look at the land as defining the sea, the largest and most important inland sea in the world, although small in size and volume compared to the oceans. To those who cruise on the waters of the Mediterranean, it is this feature, the land which surrounds the sea and the islands dotted about it, which gives the sea its appeal.

At its longest the Mediterranean is 3700 kilometres (2300 miles) from Gibraltar to Iskenderun; and at its widest, with a bit of a dog-leg, it is 1800 kilometres (1100 miles) from Trieste at the top of the Adriatic to the Gulf of Sirte in Libya. The surface area is 2.96 million square kilometres (1.46 million square miles). Of importance to the yachtsman is its long coastline, enormously increased by the long peninsula of Italy, the much-indented

7   For more detail see Rod Heikell *Mediterranean Cruising Handbook* Imray, 2012; Ernle Bradford *The Mediterranean: Portrait of a Sea* Harcourt Brace Jovanovich, 1971.

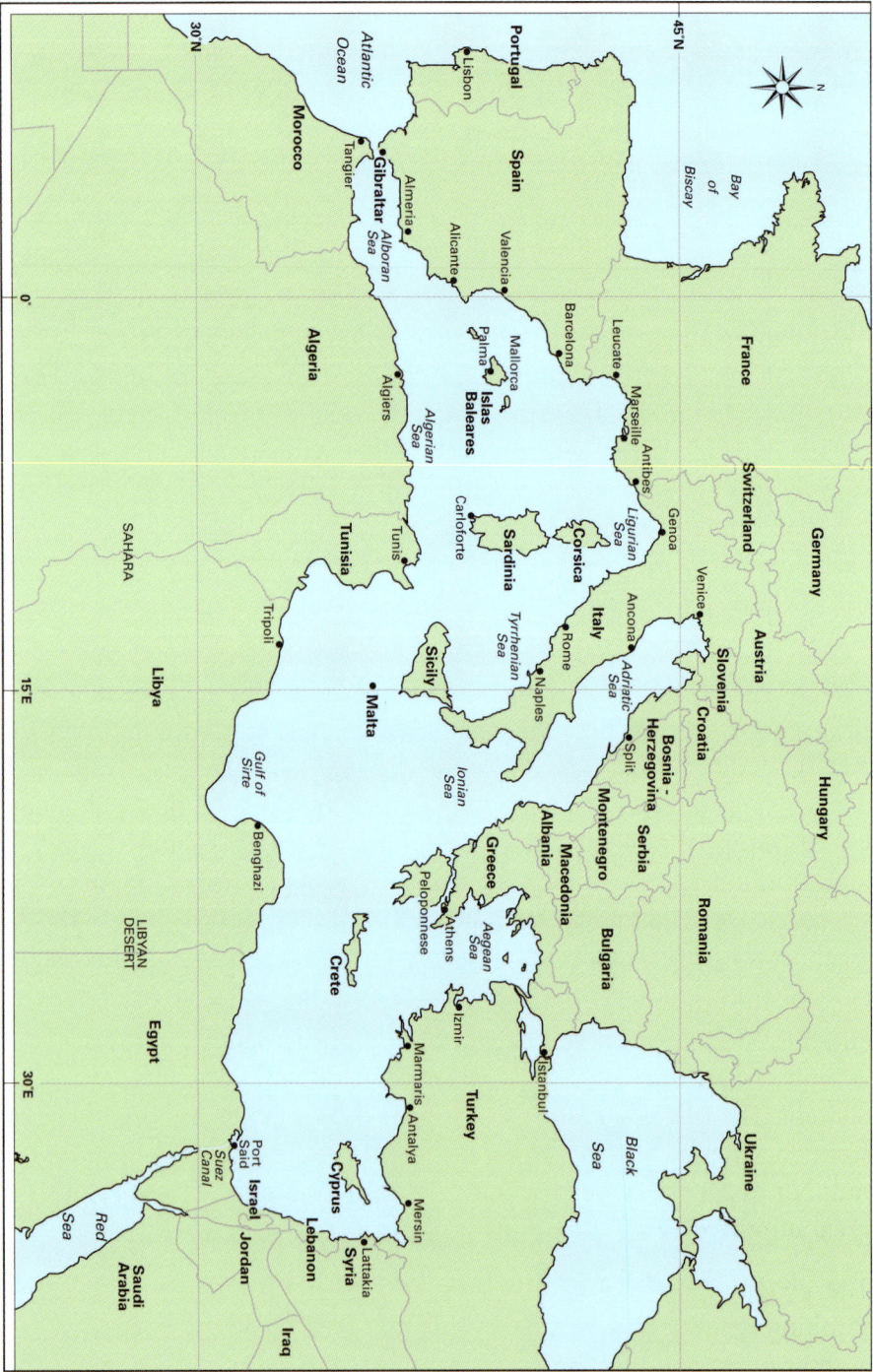

The Mediterranean. Courtesy of Imray

coastlines of countries like Greece and Turkey, and the myriad islands. Apart from the well-known larger islands like Mallorca, Corsica, Sardinia, Sicily, Evia, Crete and Cyprus, there are thousands of others of all shapes and sizes down to small uninhabited rocks. The complex outline of the mainland and the islands makes it virtually impossible to calculate a figure for the total length of coastline, but some idea of just how large this would be can be gained from the fact that Sardinia's coastline is over 1100 miles and Sicily's over 1400 miles.

The Mediterranean is not only small but comparatively shallow in comparison to the oceans. Its area is about 1/140th of the total sea area of the world, but its volume is a mere 1/355th. The mean depth is 1500 metres and even its greatest depth, at 4600 metres southwest of Cape Matapan in Greece, is only slightly more than the mean depth of the Atlantic. There is a paradox here because although the Mediterranean is not deep in oceanographic terms, to yachtsmen it is. There are often depths of 50 metres right up to the coast in many places, so that one of the delights is being able to sail close to the shore and sightsee without running aground. The virtual absence of tides means that the depth changes little.

If we look at the Mediterranean in cross-section, a feature that stands out is the ridges separating the basins. The principal ridge at Gibraltar, between the Atlantic and the western Mediterranean, is 320 metres down; that between Sicily and Tunisia 400 metres; in the Bosphorus the sill is only 40 metres deep. These features are important not just geologically but for the character of the sea as well. The shallow ridge between the Atlantic and the western basin shuts out the effect of the Atlantic tides, and as the volume of water in the Mediterranean is comparatively so small, the gravitational pull of the sun and the moon does not generate great tidal range. Salinity in the eastern basin is higher than in the western basin where Atlantic water decreases the salt content. The ridges containing the western and eastern basins tend to confine some marine life to these areas, especially the smaller species, so that a large number of Mediterranean species are not found elsewhere, or at least not in great numbers.

The geographical picture is a partial view of the Mediterranean that the thinking visitor will want to fill in with the peoples and cultures around it. Such a description and history would be difficult to fit into a large book without skimping here and there, and there are plenty of sources in which to find out more.[8] What I can do here is paint a broad canvas with the Mediterranean in the centre. This thin gash between the continents has historically separated completely different worlds, and it still does. The divisions may be blurred by the political boundaries defining the twenty-one countries now surrounding the Mediterranean, but the overall picture is there, and it takes something like the Arab Spring and fundamentalist Islam, or the partitioning of Cyprus in 1974, to bring these wider divisions to the surface.

The Mediterranean straddles the Occident and the Orient; taking Italy as a dividing line, everything to the west is the Occident and to the east the Orient. This is made immediately obvious in the cuisine of the two regions. In the west thick soups, oven-baked dishes and rich sauces predominate, whereas in the east cold starters, spicy grilled kebabs and meatballs, and simple salads are the mainstay of the diet. In the 19th and early 20th centuries the division was still an accepted one referred to in travel books of the era. In *Eothen*, which means 'from the east', A. W. Kinglake describes his journey through Greece, Turkey, Cyprus and the Levant in 1835 as an 'Oriental tour'.[9] Most other travel writers of the period similarly described the eastern Mediterranean as 'the Orient'.

After the Second World War the division between Occident and Orient was used less, as parts of the Orient apparently became Occidental, though anyone who visits the countries in the eastern Mediterranean soon understands that under the western surface an Oriental heart still beats. From this broad division between west and east, it is useful to reconsider the Mediterranean as a whole and this time carve it into 'three huge, thriving civilizations, three major modes of thinking, believing, eating, drinking and living' (Braudel). These divisions exist intact not only in the present but can be traced through the convoluted history of the Mediterranean from very early on. And from this inland sea the impact of the three civilizations stretches thousands of miles, across the oceans on either side of the Mediterranean, and permeates

8   I recommend David Abulafia *The Great Sea: A Human History of the Mediterranean* Penguin 2014, or the older but still wonderful Fernand Braudel *The Mediterranean and the Mediterranean World in the Age of Philip II* BCA, 1949/1992.
9   A. W. Kinglake *Eothen: or Traces of travel brought home from the East* Century 1844/1982

through to the cultures on the continents to the north and south.[10]

The first of these is the western culture corresponding to the Occident. It is the Christian world, formerly the Roman Catholic world, with Rome at the hub. As such it spread north to split into the Protestant church and its myriad offspring, and from there Catholic and Protestant together migrated to the New World and colonised it. So much of our current mythology — the Protestant ethic, the idea of progress as a good and worthy object, of converting those in faraway lands to our western ideals — evolved from the old Latin universe centred in Rome. In Europe it can be difficult to see this, but in America the imported religious underpinning of western ideals is more obvious.

The Occident anchored to the Roman Catholic Church. Erice in Sicily.

The second division is the Greek Orthodox world. Until quite recently western historians paid scant attention to Byzantium and its legacy; indeed, few of us comprehend the extent today of the Orthodox church and fewer still its antecedents. From Greece, the Orthodox church covers the Balkan peninsula, Bulgaria, Serbia, Croatia, Romania, and north up to the vastness of Russia. The barrier of the Eastern Bloc disguised its extent, but after the Velvet Revolutions in the Eastern Bloc in the late 1980's and early 1990's, the Orthodox church came to centre stage again and any traveller to the region will tell you

The Greek Orthodox world visible all through Greece and with variations to the north as far as Russia.

10   Tom Holland *In the Shadow of the Sword: The Battle for Global Empire and the End of the Ancient World* Little Brown, 2012 provides the historical antecedents to this world.

that it is very much alive and on the ascendant. Until the Ottoman Turks over-ran Constantinople in 1453, the Orthodox church, then the Holy Roman Empire in the east, was the most powerful and most civilized part of the old world. Since then Orthodoxy has been without a centre although not without power. In Cyprus the tension between the Greek Orthodox community and the Turkish Muslim community would end in conflict and the eventual partition of the island.

To the Orient where the call to prayer from the minaret orders the day.

Islam is the third slice of the Mediterranean, starting at Turkey on the eastern end of the Mediterranean and running around its southern shores to Morocco. It extends from there into Africa, across the Indian Ocean to Indonesia, the Philippines and to the islands in the Melanesian archipelago. The effect of Islam on the Mediterranean was considerable when the Ottoman Empire held sway over all of Greece, the Balkans, and threatened Italy and Malta. From North Africa the Arab invasions of Spain introduced Islam at the western end of the Mediterranean. The legacy of Islam was not just the obvious cultural influences as seen in cuisine, music and dress, but also on agriculture, with the introduction of new species and methods of irrigation, in science and in architecture, influences which spread throughout the Catholic and Orthodox worlds and remained after the Turks and Arabs left. One of our most popular beverages, coffee, was one of lslam's legacies to the west.

From these three divisions further sub-divisions can be made. Some are a part of one of the major civilizations, others combine parts of them. The Levant brings together the Orthodox islands close to Asia Minor and stretches down this coast to include Syria, Lebanon and across to Cyprus. The Maghreb pulls together Tunisia, Algeria and Morocco, reflecting their interlocked history and cultural roots. The Balkans include northern Greece, Bulgaria, Romania and the Dalmatian coast as an area with much history and culture in common. In the Occidental half of the Mediterranean it is more difficult today to pick out the larger patterns that once shaped the history of these countries, although regional differences are fiercely defended as in Sicily or the Catalan states.

No other region has experienced such a concentrated and lengthy period of building up civilizations and demolishing others; from the very first hunters and gatherers in the Mesopotamian valley through the Egyptians, Hittites, Assyrians, Minoans and Mycenaeans, Greeks, Romans, Arabs, Byzantines, Franks, Ottomans, Venetians and Genoese, the Papal States, the Spanish, French, British and Russians, to the First and Second World Wars and the division of the Mediterranean into the twenty-one countries around its shores today.

The geography and the cultural history have a lot to do with why those of us who sail around the shores of the Mediterranean value it so much more than anywhere else we have sailed. That history involved trade under sail over millennia, trade that shaped the history of the Mediterranean and gave rise to its great civilizations. The sea also played a major part in military conquests and, once a war had been won, in policing the peace. Getting about on the water was faster and safer than getting about on the land, and from the ancient Greeks up to the European powers fighting it out in the 19th century, power was displayed on the water whether through military might or trade. Intermingled with this life on the water are the remnants of accounts of sailing for pleasure, and though the sources are scarce, it is this same sea and its wind and weather that has shaped yachting on its waters and shapes this book.

Most people picture the Mediterranean as a deep blue sea ruffled by the occasional zephyr blowing out of an azure sky. The reality can come as something of a shock: it blows in the Mediterranean, and at times it can blow too much. In the Aegean the meltemi blows through July and August with some ferocity, often at Force 6 to 7 for days on end.[11] Those ashore welcome the cooling wind and watch the yachts bucking at anchor, but the yachtsman curses the same wind shrieking through his rigging and prays for it to die

11   See Rod Heikell *Mediterranean Cruising Handbook* Imray, 2012 Chapter 12, Wind and Weather

down, especially if he is going north. At the other end of the Mediterranean the levanter hurtles through the Straits of Gibraltar, making it difficult even for ships going east to get through, and causing eddies over the Rock that complicate aircraft landings. The next day it is calm, and bewildered yachtsmen at either end of the Mediterranean get ready to motor out onto a mill-pond.

But if there are strong winds in the Mediterranean, and calms too, they are predictable for the most part. The beginning and end of the meltemi in the Aegean, its strength and direction, has been plotted since antiquity. Our meltemi (from the Turkish, meaning bad-tempered) and the ancients' etesians (from the Greek *etios*, meaning annual), were used by the plump merchant ships to sail south, where they waited until the autumn southerlies to come north again.[12] Many of the big merchant fleets of the Middle Ages were prohibited to leave harbour at certain times of the year, until the bad winter weather had gone. The renowned Genoese admiral Prince Doria used to say, 'In the Mediterranean, there are three ports: Cartagena, June, and July'.[13] In the western Mediterranean the sea breeze reigns supreme and small ships could safely tramp along the coast, 'buying one's butter at Villefranche, vinegar at Nice, oil and bacon at Toulon'.[14]

The spices once so prized in the Occident are still there. Spice stall in Turkey.

The idea that the Mediterranean summer is one of light zephyrs on a calm sea is a confusion concerning the predictable patterns of the season. A settled summer where thermal winds predominate does not mean a summer without strong winds. The blue sea can be quickly covered with whitecaps and steep seas whipped up by a wind blowing out of a clear azure sky. It comes as a constant surprise to the yachtsman from northern Europe just how much wind there can be and in most of the sources from the 18th century on, there

12   This is the conventional thesis on trading in Greek and Roman times, but see Heikell *Sailing Ancient Seas* Taniwha Press, 2015, Appendix 1 Could Ancient Ships Sail to Windward?
13   Quoted in Braudel *The Mediterranean and the Mediterranean World in the Age of Philip II* p 191
14   Braudel *The Mediterranean and the Mediterranean World in the Age of Philip II* p 65

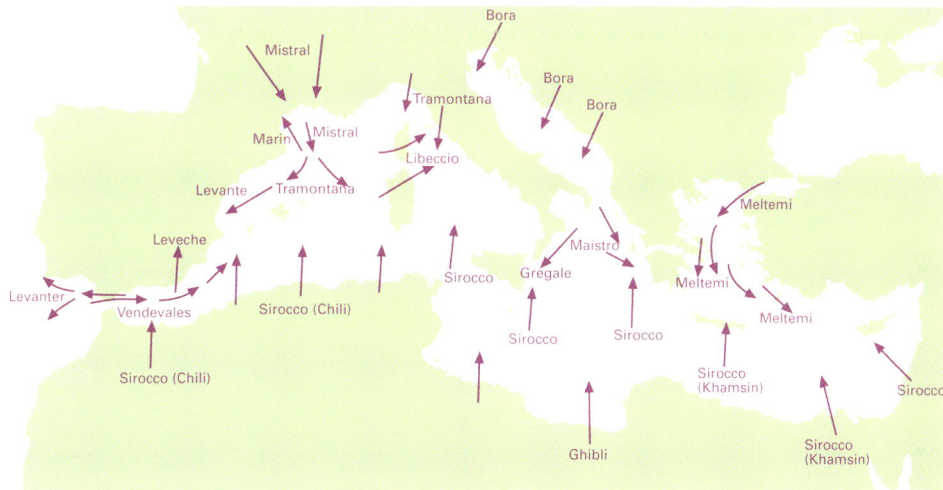

Locally named winds in the Mediterranean.
Map from *Mediterranean Cruising Handbook* 6th ed.

are often references to windy corners of the sea and of how a wind will pop up out of nowhere and catch the unwary yachtsman by surprise.

The contrast between summer and winter is difficult for the northern mind to imagine and, as Braudel points out, 'the early Orientalist painters created an enduring false impression with their glowing palettes'.[15] Today holiday companies create similar impressions with their glossy colour photographs of winter sun. Braudel goes on to describe the fortunes of one Fromentin, a 19th century traveller escaping south to what he fondly believed was a mild, sunny winter in the Mediterranean. In October 1869, Fromentin, leaving Messina by boat, noted, 'grey skies, cold wind, a few drops of rain on the awning. It is sad, it could be the Baltic'. Earlier, in February 1848, he had fled towards the Sahara from the persistent grey mists of the Mediterranean winter: 'there was no interval that year … between the November rains and the heavy winter rains, which had lasted for three and a half months with hardly a day's respite'. All natives of Algiers must, at one time or another, have had occasion to see newcomers aghast at the torrential downpours over the city.[16]

In spring and autumn the climate hovers between the Atlantic and Sahara influences. In the spring the Sahara effect works its way west and north,

15   Braudel *The Mediterranean and the Mediterranean World in the Age of Philip II* p 172
16   Braudel *The Mediterranean and the Mediterranean World in the Age of Philip II* p 172

bringing sun and warmth to the European shores. In the autumn the Atlantic influence is more violent as depressions swerve down through the Mediterranean, bringing gales and rain deep into the eastern region with little warning after the soporific summer. For most yachts sailing in the Mediterranean the summer season is the settled season, though yachts do sail deep into autumn, and some start in the early spring. These seasonal patterns have been observed and noted by commentators and sailors alike for aeons, and throughout history wind was synonymous with weather for most people.

Under the shadow of the Acropolis in Athens stands the remarkable Tower of Winds. Built in the first century BCE by the Macedonian astronomer Andronikos of Kyrrhos, the octagonal tower is remarkable for a number of reasons. On each of the eight marble sides there is a relief of a winged figure representing the wind that blows from that direction. What is most remarkable is that each of the eight sides of the tower faces the cardinal and half-cardinal points of the compass, although the compass in its most rudimentary form was not introduced from the east until over a thousand years later. Moreover, the figures depicting the wind fly around the tower in an anticlockwise direction, which is the direction in which any cyclonic system entering the Mediterranean also revolves, with the winds of a depression following the same pattern and sequence as that shown on the tower.

Each of the figures represents a season: Boreas, the violent and cold north wind, represented by a bearded old man wrapped in a thick mantle with the folds being plucked by the wind; Notios, the south wind, a sour-looking figure, empties an urn, implying rain and sultry weather; Lips, represented by a figure pushing the prow of a ship, signifies the wind that is unfavourable for ships leaving Athens; and so the winds signifying the eight seasons are portrayed revolving around this remarkable tower, reminding the citizens of Athens what the weather will be when the wind blows from a certain direction and what it will be like for those on the sea.[17]

While it is true that some people can travel without seeing what is all around them, I doubt that many of them will be reading this book. While there are a few who sail to the Mediterranean because it is sunny and the beer is cheap, they are in the minority: most people who sail there want to know something

---

17   Heikell *Sailing Ancient Seas,* Appendix 5 An Anomaly: The Tower of Winds

about the countries and cultures around its shores, to get a feel for its history, to feel the heave of a sea that has so defined our own history and culture. I can only recommend that you read some of the excellent histories of the Mediterranean, some of which I have mentioned in the footnotes to this chapter, and then when you are sitting in the sun with a glass of something local, that you spend an idle hour or two reflecting on this great inland sea.

The figures on the Tower of Winds in Athens.

Khufu ship in the Giza Solar Ship Museum. Wiki Commons Ovedc.

1 EGYPT

Herodotus put his finger on it: 'Egypt', he wrote, 'is the gift of the Nile.' He was referring to the fact that the Nile provided water for agriculture, for the people, and for construction in a country where it rains little. The annual flooding of the Nile deposited silt all along the margins of the river for agriculture, and the river itself provided water to irrigate the crops. The silt that flowed into the Mediterranean proved to be a rich fishing ground as it is to this day. It was also a principal arterial route for river transportation running approximately north to south and it is no surprise that many of the cities of ancient Egypt are dotted along its length. Passage was made easy by the fact that the prevailing wind blows from the north so a simple squaresail would suffice to take boats upstream. Downstream when coming south to north the current of the river and oars provided propulsion power. Mother nature had provided the perfect juxtaposition of forces to propel craft along the river, and so it is no accident that the Nile provided a handy transportation link to and from the Mediterranean, serving the royal cities along the way.

It's thought that the first boats were made of bundles of papyrus reeds bound together with hemp and sailed and paddled up and down the Nile. Thor Heyerdahl believed such papyrus boats could cross oceans and his Ra expeditions and the Tigris expedition proved they were surprisingly capable craft.[1] Archaeological evidence suggests that wooden boat-building techniques were known as long ago as 3500 BCE and probably earlier. What is surprising is the sophistication of the techniques used in these wooden boats. The Abydos boats from around 2675 BCE utilise mortice and tenon joints in the

Model of ancient Egyptian boat in the British Museum. Eyesonmilan Shutterstock.com

planking and also use different types of wood, including cedar from Lebanon.[2]

1   Thor Heyerdahl *The Tigris Expedition: In Search of Our Beginnings* Flamingo, 1993; Heyerdahl *The Ra Expeditions* George Allen & Unwin, 1971
2   David O'Connor *Boat Graves and Pyramid Origins* Penn University, 2005

We have lots of information on the boats from pictures painted in tombs and petroglyphs on royal monuments, and there are numerous accounts describing the ancient boats, large and small, and detailing cargoes, dimensions and voyages made. In addition, over twenty ancient Egyptian boats have been excavated. The Khufu ship, used as a Pharaonic royal barge or yacht, is one of the most famous and dates back to 2500 BCE. Historical accounts leave us in no doubt that other boat-building was not only for commercial transportation, but also for the pleasure of the royal dynasties.

Early accounts

Many of the oldest boats excavated are evidently funeral boats, solar boats used to sail and transport luxuries to the afterworld. That they were used as royal yachts is almost certain and in the *Story of the Turquoise Pendant*, the third story in the Westcar Papyrus dating to the beginning of the Middle Kingdom, (around 2040 BCE), the account could easily be transferred to the present day and some oligarch's superyacht cruising the fleshpots of the Mediterranean.[3] In the account, the son of Khufu is advised by the chief priest Djadjamankh to go sailing to alleviate his boredom.

Then Djadjamankh said to him, 'Oh, may your Majesty go to the lake of the palace, and man a ship with all beautiful women from inside your palace. The heart of your majesty will be cheered by seeing them row a trip back and forth and seeing the beautiful reeds of your lake and seeing its beautiful fields and water banks. Your heart will be gladdened by this so I will arrange a rowing trip.'

'Let there be brought to me twenty oars of ebony plated with gold, their handles of sandalwood plated with electrum. Let there be brought to me twenty women with beautiful bodies, well developed breasts, who have braided, and who have not yet given birth. And let me be brought to me twenty nets and give these nets to these women after their clothes have been taken off'. All was done as his majesty commanded. Then they rowed back and forth and the heart of his majesty was gladdened by seeing them row.

Tales from the Westcar Papyrus Story of the Turquoise Pendant Translation Mark-Jan Nederhof and A. M. Blackman 1988/2008

The passage from the book of Ezekiel in the Old Testament quoted in the Introduction is interesting in that it mentions Tyre and the construction of what is evidently a royal pleasure yacht built of quite exotic materials. The book of Ezekiel is reckoned to be late 6th century BCE, and at the time it is likely the Egyptians had adopted Phoenician boat-building methods or had

---

3   *Westcar Papyrus* Transl. Mark-Jan Nederhof and A. M. Blackman, 1988/2008

boats constructed by the Phoenicians. Certainly, they were using Lebanese cedar well before this date as both the Khufu ship and other ships use cedar, which does not grow in Egypt, in the construction.

Much later we have the numerous accounts of Cleopatra and her royal barge on which she invited Antony, where he fell prey to her evident charms. I'll deal with Cleopatra later, but for now we have Plutarch's description of the event:

> ...she came sailing up the river Cydnus in a barge with gilded stern and outspread sails of purple, while oars of silver beat time to the music of flutes and fifes and harps.[4]

There are also the accounts of the huge pleasure-vessels *Isis* and *Thalamegus*, built by Ptolemy Philopator (around 222 BCE) that probably went nowhere, but were used more as status symbols by Ptolemy, a floating tribute moored on the Nile as evidence of his wealth and power.

> Ptolemy Philopator built one of forty banks of oars, which had a length of two hundred and eighty cubits, and a height, to the top of her stern, of forty-eight; she was manned by four hundred sailors, who did no rowing, and by four thousand rowers, and besides these she had room, on her gangways and decks, for nearly three thousand men-at arms. But this ship was merely for show; and since she differed little from a stationary edifice on land, being meant for exhibition and not for use, she was moved only with difficulty and danger.

Plutarch's *Lives (Life of Demetrius)* translated by Dryden/Clough 1859

There is speculation that these vessels were catamarans, though the likelihood is that the size is apocryphal. The length of two hundred and eighty cubits equates to around 420 ft and the height of forty-eight cubits to 72 ft. The longest wooden ship on record in recent times, at 450 ft, was the *Wyoming*, built in Maine in 1909. Once launched the hull tended to flex and she constantly took on water until she eventually sank in 1924. Given boat-building methods in 200 BCE it is unlikely the *Isis* or *Thalamegus* could have gone anywhere, given the loads on the hull or hulls.

Apart from written accounts, we also have models of boats from the tomb of Tutankhamun, (died around 1323 BCE), including at least one of what is likely a pleasure boat for sailing up the Nile. Various models were found by Howard Carter in his 1922 excavation and the tomb and the models were all in wonderful condition. The model of the 'pleasure boat' even had a red linen sail still intact.

4   Plutarch's *Lives* translated by Dryden/Clough, 1859

The burying of the model boats and the full-size boats in royal tombs or nearby, as at Abydos, (2675 BCE), and the Khufu ship (c.2500 BCE), are interpreted archaeologically as solar ships, representations of the real thing for transportation to the afterlife. The ships often point west so they could follow the sun and the sun-god Ra across the sky,

Ship model from the Middle Kingdom, (1991–1778 BCE), found in a tomb dedicated to Djehutynakht. Wiki Commons Marcus Cyron.

and transport not just the resurrected royal, but also the things he might need in the afterlife including gifts of food and precious spices, metals and other offerings to the gods. In the case of the Khufu ship there is evidence it was used in the water, presumably on the Nile, and as such is not just a token for the afterlife but was also used in earnest in real life by Khufu.

Construction techniques

The construction of these boats was the shell first method whereby the hull was constructed joining the planks edge to edge and then adding framing inside to strengthen the hull. No outside keel was laid and pictures of the boats show one or more short masts carrying a hawser from bow to stern to stop the hull distorting under load (a hogging truss). These craft were likely of sewn construction with the planks sewn together, a method still used in a few places in the Indian Ocean to this day as iron is scarce in the region.[5] The boats also showed considerable sophistication in the carpentry techniques of the mortice and tenon joints used to join timbers together. In the case of the Khufu

Sewn boat in the Kerala backwaters in India.

5   Heikell *Sailing Ancient Seas* p 91

ship these are not fastened and the whole ship was found in segments that were then re-assembled.

The wood used varied. Early boats used the local acacia which does not grow straight and true, so that small sections of wood were joined together, as Herodotus describes it, 'like bricks'. Mortice and tenon joints aligned the 'bricks' so the construction could be sewn together. Unusually, and probably because the boats were dis-assembled for transportation overland, the mortice and tenon joints were not pegged.

Their boats with which they carry cargoes are made of the thorny acacia, of which the form is very like that of the Kyrenian lotos, and that which exudes from it is gum. From this tree they cut pieces of wood about two cubits in length and arrange them like bricks, fastening the boat together by running a great number of long bolts through the two-cubit pieces; and when they have thus fastened the boat together, they lay cross-pieces over the top, using no ribs for the sides; and within they caulk the seams with papyrus. They make one steering-oar for it, which is passed through the bottom of the boat; and they have a mast of acacia and sails of papyrus.

Herodotus, Book 2: *The Landmark Herodotus* ed. B. Strassler Quercus, 2008[6]

Spinning sisal rope in the Kerala backwaters. Similar techniques were likely used in ancient Egypt.

Royal pleasure boats and funerary boats built by royalty could afford to use imported Lebanese cedar as early as 2500 BCE, with the Khufu ship constructed almost entirely of cedar. The planks were made watertight with lengths of papyrus hammered into the seams as a form of caulking.

The boats were rigged with a simple square sail that early on had a spar top and bottom and later just a top spar with the bottom loose-footed. Pictograms show a bi-pole mast on early boats, although a single spar of cedar soon became the norm. The rigging and ropes were of palm coir and possibly later of flax. Coir ropes are still made in the traditional way in India and Sri Lanka.[7] Sails

6   A new excavation of a vessel in Egypt using exactly these techniques has recently been found. Dalya Alberge *Observer* 17 March 2019.

7   Heikell *Sailing Ancient Seas* p 91

were likely of flax or possibly linen in the case of the royal boats, although papyrus is also mentioned.[8]

On the Nile and on sea voyages the boats were at first paddled with the paddlers sitting on the side-decks. Later, oars were used with a simple rope loop through the gunwale for a rowlock. This must have been hard work as the rowers would likely have had to stand to pull the oar through the water before bringing it back for the next stroke. There is no indication the rowers had benches as on later oared galleys. Herodotus makes the following interesting comments on navigation on the Nile.

These boats cannot sail up the river unless there be a very fresh wind blowing, but are towed from the shore: down-stream however they travel as follows: they have a door-shaped crate made of tamarisk wood and reed mats sewn together, and also a stone of about two talents weight bored with a hole; and of these the boatman lets the crate float on in front of the boat, fastened with a rope, and the stone drag behind by another rope. The crate then, as the force of the stream presses upon it, goes on swiftly and draws on the 'baris' (for so these boats are called), while the stone dragging after it behind and sunk deep in the water keeps its course straight. These boats they have in great numbers and some of them carry many thousands of talents' burden.

Herodotus, Book 2 *The Landmark Herodotus* ed. B Strassler Quercus 2008

While numbers of early boats were probably constructed in Egypt where they certainly had the requisite carpentry skills, later, after c.1000 BCE, it is likely sea-going ships were constructed in Tyre and nearby ports by Phoenician shipwrights. Cleopatra's royal barge was almost certainly a solid and seaworthy craft if it was to voyage safely from Alexandria to Tarsus, a voyage of nearly 500 nautical miles over a changeable and often dangerous sea.

The Khufu ship

In 1954 a boat pit was discovered next to Cheops Pyramid at Giza near Cairo. Several boat pits had already been uncovered here, but this fourth pit contained a complete, dismantled boat with much of it intact including the wooden hull, framing, superstructure and ropes for the rigging.[9] It took ten years of painstaking reconstruction to reassemble the ship which now sits in the Solar Boat Museum next to the Cheops Pyramid. It is most likely a ship

8   Herodotus Book 2; Lionel Casson *Ships and Seamanship in the Ancient World* John Hopkins, 1971 pp 19–20
9   Nancy Jenkins *The Boat Beneath the Pyramid* Thames and Hudson, 1980

constructed for Pharaoh Khufu (Cheops) around 2600 BCE and dismantled and buried next to the pyramid for his journey across the sky to the afterlife.

The Khufu ship in the Giza Solar Ship Museum. Wiki Commons Ovedc.

The ship measures in at 43.6 m (143 ft) long and 5.9 m (19.5 ft) across the maximum beam. It has been rightly described as a masterpiece of wooden construction using Lebanese cedar (though this is disputed by some sources) worked by skilled carpenters. It is thought the ship was built to be dismantled or it would have been too large for the boat pit it was found in, possibly in a previously built pit. Planks were fitted together using mortice and tenon joints although these were not pegged, possibly intentionally so the boat could be dismantled to transport it overland. The planks of the hull were held together in a sewn construction and the superstructure features a lavish cabin and shelter, probably adorned with mats and curtains.

It was originally thought the boat was purely ceremonial, a solar ship to take Khufu across the sky to the afterlife. However, during the reconstruction it was discovered that the ship had been used in the water, presumably the Nile. The question arises as to whether it was used solely as a funeral ship or as a pleasure boat prior to Khufu's death. Given that the pharaohs liked to take treasured possessions with them on their voyage to the afterlife, it is feasible that the ship was used as a pleasure boat before being disassembled and stored in the pit. It probably didn't travel very far as it has no provision for a mast or sails and only six long oars were found, two of which would be for the steering oars at the stern. Nonetheless it could have ben towed up the Nile and drifted back down again as described by Herodotus. Or it may have just been a status symbol as described in the account where the priest Djadjamankh advises the son of Khufu to raise his spirits by going on a little cruise with a boatload of beautiful women – '… and man a ship with all beautiful women from inside your palace.'[10]

As I mentioned earlier, it reminds me of the present age where a few of the super-rich fill a superyacht with attractive women to gladden their hearts.

Cleopatra

It's difficult to sort out the truth about Cleopatra when so much has been written about her and her relatively short life as a key player in the political events that shaped the Roman Empire in the decades leading up to the Common Era. Was she a temptress or star-crossed lover, politico or pawn, goddess or harlot? What we do know is that she enticed Julius Caesar into her bed and then later ensnared his protégé, the man's man, the rabble-rousing Mark Antony. It is the meeting of Cleopatra and Antony in Tarsus that interests us. Shakespeare waxes lyrical on the meeting, but it is Plutarch who gives us a description closer to the event in his *Life of Antony*.

The Meeting of Antony and Cleopatra. Sir Lawrence Alma-Tadema 1884. Wiki Commons.

Crossing the Mediterranean to Cilicia, where Antony then was, she came up the River Cydnus in a vessel, the stern whereof was gold, the sails of purple silk, and the oars of silver, which gently kept time to the sound of music.

She placed herself under a rich canopy of cloth-of-gold, habited like Venus rising out of the sea, with beautiful boys about her, like cupids, fanning her; and her women, representing the

10 *Westcar Papyrus* Transl. Mark-Jan Nederhof and A. M. Blackman

Nereids and Graces, leaned negligently on the sides and shrouds of the vessel, while troops of virgins, richly drest, marched on the banks of the river burning incense and rich perfumes, which were covered with an infinite number of people, gazing on in wonder and admiration. The Queen's success with Antony was answerable to her expectations.

Plutarch's *Lives (Life of Antony)* translated by Dryden/Clough 1859

Around 41 BCE Antony summoned Cleopatra to Tarsus, where he had taken up residence, to order her to collect and pay taxes to his Eastern Roman Empire. Cleopatra was in Alexandria and subsequently set off for Tarsus, situated in the modern Mersin-Adana province of Turkey near the Syrian border. As mentioned above, this is a voyage of nearly 500 miles across the southeastern corner of the Mediterranean, a voyage not to be undertaken lightly.[11] We have no idea of the size of the ships that set off, and there would likely have been more than one, but the sort of galley favoured by the Romans at the time was the Liburnian, a galley around 100 ft (30.5 metres) long with a beam of around 16–18 ft (5 metres) and a minimal draft of 3–4 ft (1 metre). It had two banks of rowers, around twenty on each side, and carried a squaresail that would be used when the wind was aft of the beam.[12] This does to some extent conform to Plutarch's description of the galley and to that of Shakespeare, who basically versified Plutarch's account.

The galley or galleys that carried Cleopatra from Alexandria to Tarsus would have been accompanied by a small fleet of ships carrying supplies for the trip. These would likely have been tubby 'round ships' of the type that carried mixed cargoes around the coast. The 'round ships' could be anything from 45 ft (14 metres) to 80-odd ft (25 metres) and were principally sailing boats with a squaresail and an artemison, the latter a small stubby mast at the bows for balance and windward ability. They were not designed to be rowed and would have used a few oars either side to

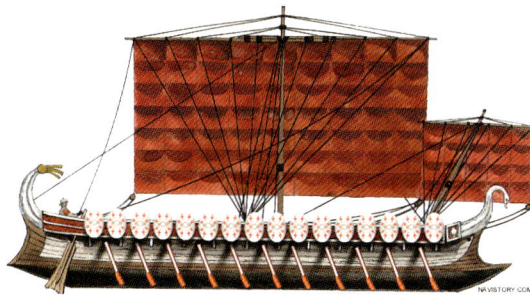

Liburnian galley, possibly of the type used by Cleopatra to sail to Tarsus in. Wiki Commons.

11   Rod & Lucinda Heikell *Turkish Waters & Cyprus Pilot* Imray, 2013 pp 313–344
12   Lionel Casson *Ships and Seamanship in the Ancient World* John Hopkins, 1971 pp 141ff

get in and out of harbours and anchorages.[13] The galleys and auxiliary ships would have been manned by professional crews, possibly Phoenician, or other experienced captains and crew familiar with the sea area and the landfall at the mouth of the Cyndus River.

The Cyndus River (ancient Cyndus, contemporary Berdan) winds down through the river flat that extends from the high land behind. Today it meanders back and forth much like the Menderes, the ancient Meander, its namesake on the Turkish Aegean coast. The river mouth has silted since ancient times so there is a shallow bar at the seaward entrance in common with other ancient river ports like Ephesus and Caunos. A Liburnian galley with its shallow draft would have been able to get up the river, though it is likely that it stopped before Tarsus itself so that Cleopatra could get everything ready for her rhapsodic approach along the river. Antony was smitten by the Egyptian queen and when she summoned him to the royal barge he didn't hesitate. It wasn't long before he had decided to accompany her back to Alexandria where the Bacchanalian tryst of the two lovers was celebrated by all and sundry and became the stuff of legend.

… he suffered her to hurry him off to Alexandria. There, indulging in the sports and diversions of a young man of leisure, he squandered and spent upon pleasures that which Antiphon calls the most costly outlay, namely, time. For they had an association called The Inimitable Livers, and every day they feasted one another, making their expenditures of incredible profusion.

Plutarch's *Lives (Life of Antony)* translated by Dryden/Clough 1859

It was all to end in 31 BCE with the Battle of Actium off the modern-day town of Preveza in the Greek Ionian where this Roman soap opera came to a tragic end. While the battle progressed, Cleopatra ordered her royal galley and the Egyptian fleet to flee southwards and Antony, 'like a doting mallard', followed, abandoning his men to defeat by Octavius' army. The story ends badly with Antony and Cleopatra committing suicide and Octavius ordering the progeny of Cleopatra from both her union with Julius Caesar and Antony to be put to the sword.

13   Heikell *Sailing Ancient Seas* p 134

The Death of Cleopatra. Reginald Arthur 1892. Roy Miles Gallery.

The Siren Vase. British Museum.

2 GREECE

There is surprisingly little on pleasure boating in the huge pantheon of Greek literature. You would have thought some of them could have taken some time off from working out the basics of modern fiction, putting together competing philosophical schools we still dwell on today, working out the circumference of the earth and establishing the history of the known world, as well as laying down the basics of science and mathematics, to describe the simple pleasures of sailing for the fun of it. But 'NO'. There is little written down or depicted to go on.

It has been argued that *The Odyssey* is the schema for much of the fiction written through the ages. The tale of the weary warrior attempting to return home after the fall of Troy against all the odds is not only an epic plot, but also has subplots aplenty. It might be thought irreverent to look askance at *The Odyssey* and ask a few questions about events along the way,[1] and I'm not going to pursue this somewhat tenuous line of enquiry too far, but you can get the feeling that we have a boat-load of men stopping for longer than might be necessary on the journey back to Ithaca. Out of a ten-year voyage they spend a year dallying with Circe and her willing handmaidens, Odysseus spends seven years with the delectable Calypso on her island, and when nearly home has time for an all-singing-and-dancing party on Scheria where he tells his story before his eventual return to Ithaca.

On a more substantive level, one of the earliest depictions in Greece of boats used in a procession or rally is the 'Ship Frieze' found at Akrotiri on the island of Thira. The settlement at Akrotiri was overwhelmed by earthquakes and the eruption of Thira in the Minoan Bronze Age, around 1625 BCE, and the friezes in the houses were preserved when a layer of volcanic ash covered the settlement. The friezes are remarkable for their detail and state of preservation, none more so than the large 'Ship Frieze' occupying one wall of a house. It was supposed for a while that it represented a voyage between different parts of the Minoan Empire, possibly around the Aegean or between Thira and Crete

1   There are a lot of variants on the theme, but see Margaret Atwood's *The Penelopiad*, Lyndsey Clarke's *The Return from Troy* and J. C. Graeme's *My Name is No One*. Even a contemporary film such as the Coen brothers' *O Brother, Where Art Thou?* is based on *The Odyssey*.

or Libya, but recent papers suggest it was likely the representation of a local waterside festival or nautical ceremony on Thira itself.[2]

Akrotiri ship procession frieze. Wiki Commons.

The boats depicted look superficially similar to Egyptian boats of the period, much like the Khufu ship with a pronounced 'banana' shape to the hull. All of the boats have paddlers or rowers, steering oars at the stern, and several have a stubby mast. One even has a sail up and no paddlers. They also have 'cabins' (*ikria*) with cloth shades for the passengers or dignitaries in them. It seems likely that the frieze does depict a nautical ceremony of some sort, perhaps even a race, but to try and extract more meaning pertaining to pleasure boats would be unrealistic.

There is one other mention of boat races from the ever-pedantic geographer Pausanias who tramped around Greece in the first century CE collecting material for his encyclopaedic *Description of Greece*. At Ermioni in the Saronic he observes the following:

Near the latter is a temple of Dionysus of the Black Goatskin. In his honour every year they hold a competition in music, and they offer prizes for swimming-races and boat-races.

Pausanias [2.35.1] XXXV

Apart from those scanty references we are left with Homer and *The Odyssey*, a gift that has influenced many to up-sticks and sail away.

The gift of *The Odyssey*

If there is one thing we can be sure of it is that *The Odyssey* has been a well-spring for inspiring voyages in small boats to parts of the world where there is a sense of excitement and danger removed from the mundane.[3] The idea of pitting oneself against all that the gods and man can throw at you and

2   Thomas F. Strasser *Location and Perspective in the Theran Flotilla Fresco*, Journal of Mediterranean Archaeology 23(1), 2010, pp. 3–26
3   J. R. L. Anderson *The Ulysses Factor* Hodder & Stoughton, 1970

come through it, battered and bloody but unbowed, is the sort of story we all like to think we can tell about ourselves. Most of us are familiar with at least the bare bones of *The Odyssey* and it's not surprising that the impetus of the epic is a defining feature of modern life. Even if you can't relate exactly what happens, I'll bet you know the outline story and empathise with Odysseus and his struggle to get home against the odds.

The Iliad is a different book to *The Odyssey*. It is more of a descriptive history of the power and trade of the emerging Greek culture, a book that is peopled by a whole pantheon of heroes on both sides, of the battle for Troy, of Achilles and Hector and Agenor and Patroclus. It has its subplots with the menace of Agamemnon and the cunning of Odysseus and of course the elopement of Paris with Helen, daughter of Zeus and Leda, and wife of Menelaus. At its centre is the battle for Troy, widely believed to be a battle for territory and trade routes to the Black Sea, and the entanglement of the gods and mortals in the whole affair. *The Odyssey* is a follow-on from *The Iliad*, a different sort of poem of the story of one man and his battle against the gods and mortals, of a man battling against the odds stacked against him in the real world and against his own weakness and folly in how he copes with what he is up against, to return to Ithaca and his Penelope.

It was *The Odyssey* that fuelled my first voyage down to the Mediterranean. At the age of thirteen we had some sort of geography-history project to do at school, a sort of scrapbook where you pasted in bits cut out from source material and drew maps and commented on the geographical location of the history. For reasons long lost in the mists of time I got to do *The Odyssey*, complete with maps of Greece and the locations mentioned in the book. This was in an era where you sent off for pictures, maps and anything else useful by post, a strange and unusual concept for today's smartphone generation, and then used scissors and paste to put the project together in the scrapbook.

Somehow this project lodged in my young psyche, though it would be a good few years later before I let it loose. In 1976 I sailed an old plywood 20 footer called *Roulette* from the south of England to Greece.[4] There was no academic or metaphysical impetus to making the voyage, more some residue of a folk memory of that school project on *The Odyssey*. These days the little craft that I

4   Heikell *The Accidental Sailor*

sailed down would be banned from leaving the Solent. The engine rarely worked, the sails were old and cotton except for a terylene storm jib I had made, and the sole navigation tools were a grid-bearing compass and some charts marked 'Not For Navigation'. *Roulette* was so low on the water you could trail your hand in the sea when sitting in the cockpit.

The Siren Vase. British Museum.

There is a connection between simple, even unsuitable, small ships, that would-be voyagers take to sea, and nowhere in *The Odyssey* is this more evident than the 'raft' that Odysseus builds on Calypso's island for his voyage home. I say 'raft' when it is evident from the text that it is not a raft, but a roughly built half-decker constructed with mortice and tenon joints and looking much like small flat-bottomed traders of the time.

…When she had shown him the place where the trees were tallest the gracious goddess went home, and Odysseus began to cut down the trees. He worked fast and felled twenty in all and lopped their branches with his axe, then trimmed them in a workmanlike manner and with a line made their edges straight. Presently Calypso brought him boring-tools. With these he drilled through all his planks, cut them to fit each other, and fixed this flooring together by means of dowels driven through the interlocking joints, giving the same width to his raft as a skilled shipwright would choose in rounding out the hull for a broad-bottomed trading vessel. He next put up the decking, which he fitted to ribs at short intervals, finishing with long gunwales down the sides. He made a mast to go in the raft, and constructed a half-deck and a rudder to keep it on its course. And from stem to stern he fenced its sides with plaited osier twigs and a plentiful backing of brushwood, as some protection against the heavy seas. Meanwhile the goddess Calypso had brought him cloth with which to make the sail. This too he skilfully made; then lashed the braces, halyards and sheets in their places on board. Finally he dragged it down on rollers into the bright sea.

The Odyssey Penguin Transl. E. V. Rieu 1946, pp. 68–69

Not only does Calypso provide the materials for his 'raft', she also promises a fair wind from the west and gives him the information he needs to navigate to Ithaca.

It was with a happy heart that the noble Odysseus spread his sail to catch the wind and skilfully kept the raft on course with the rudder. There he sat and never closed his eyes in sleep, but kept them on the Pleiads, or watched the late-setting Bootes slowly fade, or the Great Bear, sometimes called the Wain, which always wheels round in the same place and looks across at Orion the Hunter with a wary eye. It was this constellation, the only one which never sinks below the horizon to bathe in Ocean's Stream, that the wise goddess Calypso had told him to keep on his left hand as he sailed across the sea. So for seventeen days he sailed on his course, and on the eighteenth there came into view the shadowy mountains of the Phaeacians' country, which jutted out to meet him. The land looked like a shield laid on the misty sea.

The Odyssey Penguin Transl. E. V. Rieu, pp. 69–70

Just as he is about to reach land and be within touching distance of Ithaca, Poseidon causes a storm of such magnitude that his craft is overwhelmed, and he is fortunate to be washed up on the beach of Scheria. This is the fear any sailor has, that the wind and sea will overwhelm him even when it looks like a safe landfall is nigh. It is this visceral shudder that gives meaning to *The Odyssey* in a way the armchair reader does not understand. Adam Nicolson in *The Mighty Dead: Why Homer Matters* writes of how, as he helmed a yacht in the Irish Sea in a building breeze, with his copy of *The Odyssey* wedged next to him, he began to understand that this was not about the geographical voyage, but about an inner geography, about our own personal voyage 'through the fears and desires of a man's life'.[5] This is how the flawed Odysseus reaches out to us, though I think we can make too much of discussing Odysseus and forget *The Odyssey*.

There are aspects of Odysseus' character that we can choose to dislike but still overlook in our assessment of the ragged hero. He is on his way home to his beloved queen Penelope, yet he spends an awful lot of time womanising.

A Reading from Homer. Sir Lawrence Alma-Tadema 1884. Philadelphia Museum of Art. The George W. Elkins Collection, 1924.

5   Adam Nicolson *The Mighty Dead: Why Homer Matters* William Collins, 2015

After a year with Circe and her comely handmaidens it takes one of his men to raise the question of their return to Ithaca. Odysseus seems in no hurry. He raids various tribes along the way to get provisions for the trip back. The first place he raids is the land of the Cicones, commonly placed in northern Greece, and hardly on the direct route home to Ithaca. The prevailing winds here are from the north and northeast so getting to the land of the Cicones is not on their route. He has the arrogance to steal the cattle of the sun god Helios despite a prophecy that he will lose all his men. The list goes on and on and yet, somehow, we can accommodate the contradictions of our hero and antihero.

Except for the end. However much we excuse or empathise with Odysseus, however much we are drawn into the contradictions of the man, I for one cannot handle his behaviour when he arrives back in Ithaca. Perhaps he needed to kill all the suitors and their entourage who had made merry with the hospitality of the island kingdom. Perhaps. But to hang the dozen handmaidens, his own, who had pleasured the suitors in his absence, is not something I can exculpate Odysseus from. This seems a cold-blooded revenge that my Odysseus should not have carried out.

What then is the gift of *The Odyssey*? It is the gift of a voyage to strange lands, to secret places, a voyage of geography and inner geography, of pleasures and fears, of tests and triumphs, of despair and joy. It is the gift of the voyage that the old poet of Alexandria, Cavafy, captures in his poem *To Ithaca*.

…Keep Ithaka always in your mind.
Arriving there is what you are destined for.
But do not hurry the journey at all.
Better if it lasts for years,
so you are old by the time you reach the island,
wealthy with all you have gained on the way,
not expecting Ithaka to make you rich.

Ithaka gave you the marvellous journey.
Without her you would not have set out.
She has nothing left to give you now.

And if you find her poor, Ithaka won't have fooled you.
Wise as you will have become, so full of experience,
you will have understood by then what these Ithakas mean.

C. P. Cavafy, *Collected Poems* Transl. Edmund Keeley and Philip Sherrard, Ed. George Savidis. Princeton University Press, 1992

Advances in Construction Techniques

Between 1984 and 1994 Dr George Bass and the underwater archaeology team from INA, the Institute of Nautical Archaeology based in Bodrum, excavated what is now believed to be the oldest known shipwreck.[6] Known as the Ulu Burun wreck after the cape on the Turkish coast where it was excavated, the approximately 50 ft round ship has pushed back the dates for

The Ulu Burun replica in Turkey.

6   N. Fawcett & J. C. Zietsman Uluburun – *The Discovery and Excavation of the World's Oldest Known Shipwreck* Akroterion 46 (March, 2012)
http://akroterion.journals.ac.za/pub/article/view/116

ship construction methods by several centuries. From the pottery found on board the date of the wreck can be established to be around the 14th century BCE. What is interesting is that parts of the keel and ribs were found which indicate that this ship was constructed using the 'inside out' method whereby the keel and ribs are constructed first and then planked over, as opposed to the 'shell first' method used to build Egyptian and other earlier ships. The 'inside-out' method means a sturdier and more seaworthy hull is created. Not surprisingly this method of construction soon superseded the 'shell first' method to become the norm for shipbuilding in the Mediterranean.

The diversity of the origins of the cargo on the Ulu Burun ship is staggering. The copper ingots probably came from Cyprus, the glass and the amphorae from the Canaanites in what are now Israel and the Lebanon. Tin ingots found on board may have originated in Afghanistan. A vase is of Mycenaean origin. Unworked ivory may have come from Syria or North Africa. Most incredibly of all, amber beads found on board are of a type of amber originating in the Baltic. From wrecks like this it is necessary to revise the limits of the known trading world and accept that goods travelled greater distances, more frequently, than was previously thought. The Ulu Burun ship carried a cargo from the four corners of the ancient world and quite possibly a crew of mixed nationalities. The excavation and analysis of the finds has pushed back our ideas of the extent of trade in the ancient world to more than 3300 years ago, as well as giving us a window onto the ships and the men and the cultures of the times.

As I mentioned in the previous chapter, the sort of craft that accompanied Cleopatra on her voyage from Alexandria to Tarsus was surely something sturdier than the Nile boats commonly depicted and was probably a boat along the lines of the Ulu Burun ship. These round ships became the norm for trading around the Mediterranean for centuries with only a few small modifications, as will be seen in the Roman era.

Reconstruction of the Ulu Burun ship in Bodrum Underwater Archaeology Museum.

Mosaic showing fishermen in the Villa Romana del Casale in Sicily. Wiki Commons.

3 ROME

The Roman Emperor Caligula showed the same predilection for royal pleasure craft as had the Egyptians. Some commentators suggest that the huge craft (the longest was some 70 metres (240 ft) long) were built by the demented Caligula to demonstrate to the Ptolemaic rulers of Egypt that anything they could do, he could do better. In this case we have not just written evidence,

but the wrecked ships themselves, or at least photos of the excavated hulls.[1] Benito Mussolini had the lake in which they sank drained and the hulls recovered.

All of this is a long way from the poems of Catullus and his loving descriptions of his little yacht and the voyages he made in it.[2] It's a bit like parking your own modest cruiser next to a superyacht where the size of the tender on the superyacht is bigger

Petroglyph of a Roman ship c.1st century CE. Wiki Commons.

than your own craft. Here Catullus and Caligula are parked alongside each other in time; Catullus died around 54 BCE while Caligula was dispatched by his own Praetorian guard in 41 CE, though their characters and experiences are polar opposites.

Caligula

There are few Roman emperors that get as much bad press as Caligula. Hardly anyone in the Roman world had anything good to say about him and all of them went out of their way to describe his demented and cruel ways when he ruled as emperor. His proper title was Gaius Julius Caesar Augustus Germanicus, but he acquired the nick name Caligula, 'Little Boots', when as a boy he would march with his father's troops in Germany in little boots just like the soldiers' boots. When crowned emperor on the death of Tiberius he immediately had his brother killed, and a few others as well, to ensure no one challenged his accession. Caligula immediately set about spending the Roman coffers on lavish games until after a brief seven months of rule he fell ill and emerged from

1   https://rarehistoricalphotos.com/caligula-nemi-ships-1932/
2   *The Poems of Catullus* Transl. Peter Whigham Penguin, 1966

his illness as a monster. He insisted he be treated as a god, was thought to have had incestuous relationships with his sisters, often dressed as a woman, and in his gladiatorial shows fed live criminals to the wild animals in the Coliseum. His appetite for lavish projects was unsurpassed and there was little he would not do for his own amusement. One of these projects was to build several huge ships on Lake Nemi just inland from Rome.

Caligula had two ships built, though there is mention of a third, and for a long time the descriptions of the craft were thought to be much exaggerated. The first ship was said to be 70 metres (230 ft) long with a beam of 20 metres (66 ft). The second ship was 73 metres long with a beam of 24 metres (79 ft).

He also built Liburnian galleys with ten banks of oars, with sterns set with gems, particoloured sails, huge spacious baths, colonnades, and banquet-halls, and even a great variety of vines and fruit trees; that on board of them he might recline at table from an early hour, and coast along the shores of Campania amid songs and choruses.

Suetonius *The Lives of the Twelve Caesars (Caligula)*

Why Caligula had these large ships built on such a small lake is something of a mystery. Lake Nemi is the old caldera of a volcano, around 1.2 km wide by 1.8 km long. It is just 33 metres deep. For the Romans the lake was sacred

Caligula's Nemi ship 1929. Photographer unknown. Rarehistorialphotos.com.

to Diana, goddess of the hunt and of nature, and as such desecration of a place sacred to the gods was prohibited. Pliny the Younger argued that the ships built here were temples to Diana[3] and not floating pleasure palaces at all. While the largest ship did have a temple to Diana, it's unlikely the sole purpose of the ships was to honour the goddess. In fact, the unhinged Caligula was said to recline outside on moon-lit nights and call to Diana to join with him.

3   Pliny the Younger *Litterae* VIII-20

Unusually, here we have not just the scribblings of commentators on Caligula from around this time, but also the pleasure ships themselves. After Caligula was assassinated, he was succeeded by Claudius who is believed to have had the ships intentionally sunk in the lake. Local fishermen and others familiar with the location of the wrecks looted bits and pieces of the ships and their treasure. In 1446, Cardinal Prospero Colonna, with the help of several engineers, located the wrecks lying in 18 metres (60 ft) and, with a pontoon bridge and floating crane, attempted to bring the ships to the surface. He had little success though he did discover that the ships were made of cedar and sheathed in lead. The latter was common practice for sea-going vessels to protect them against teredo worms eating the wooden hulls, but was of little use in a fresh water lake where the teredo doesn't live.

Over the next three centuries there were several more attempts to salvage the ships which largely resulted in them being damaged without the hulls being lifted. Further damage was inflicted on Caligula's ships by the local fishermen and others who dredged up whatever they could get from the wrecks. In 1895 an antiques dealer, Eliseo Borghi, employed professional divers to investigate the ships and retrieve artefacts. They retrieved statues, marble pillars, mosaics and pottery. They also reported that the hulls were built of cedar and sheathed in lead fastened with copper nails and the decks adorned with beautiful glass mosaics.[4] Some of the finds were bought by the government and others 'disappeared' as artefacts are inclined to do. At the turn of the century the wrecks were again investigated by a naval engineer, Comendatore Vittorio Malfatti, who charted the positions of the wrecks and after some research, concluded the only way to retrieve them intact would be to lower the lake level so they could then be removed.

Benito Mussolini attending the inauguration of the Museum of Nemi (Il Museo delle Navi Romane). Rarehistorialphotos.com.

4   https://historybecauseitshere.weebly.com/roman-emperor-caligula-and-his-legendary-lake-nemi-ships.html

Three decades later Benito Mussolini, Il Duce, put the plan to retrieve the ships into action. Il Duce had an abiding interest in the Roman Empire and wanted to re-establish Italy as a great European power that would once again rule large swathes of Europe and North Africa. He had grand plans to restore the glory of Rome and somehow the Nemi ships of Caligula tickled his aspirations. Mussolini employed naval engineers, archaeologists and private contractors

Italians viewing Caligula's royal barge after excavation. Rarehistorialphotos.com.

to work on the project and drain the lake. The local farmers knew of a Roman irrigation tunnel; this was cleared and with the aid of powerful pumps the level of the lake was reduced to expose the first ship in 1931 and it was moved to the shore. After numerous setbacks, including a mud landslide

Caligula's royal barge in the Nemi Museum around 1932. Rarehistorialphotos.com.

that partially damaged the second ship, it too was finally exposed and recovered in 1932.

Ashore Mussolini had a museum constructed to house the two ships and display the numerous artefacts recovered from the excavation. There are old black and white photos of the excavation and museum that bear out the jottings of Suetonius and others. These were vast ships, although it is unlikely they went very far, if anywhere, on the tiny lake. Sadly, the museum and the ships were destroyed in the Second World War when Allied aircraft bombed the building and its contents. Any remaining artefacts were looted during or after the war and today little remains except some one-fifth scale models of the ships and a few recovered artefacts.

Catullus

What of lesser mortals in this era of grandiose royal pleasure craft? It is likely that there were rich aristocrats around who either had sailing yachts constructed or converted one of the small tubby trading boats for pleasure use. The problem is that nobody wrote about it, or if they did, it was lost as happened to so many ancient works. That is, except for one important exception. The first concrete reference we have of sailing for pleasure comes from the Roman poet Catullus.

Catullus is not widely read today, but in his time he instigated something of a revolution in poetic circles, writing lyrical and passionate poems with a gut feeling to them, pungent epigrams that can still shock, and poems of descriptive verse that are both evocative and accurate.[5] He was born around 84 BCE and died at an early age in 54 BCE. Catullus began writing when he was fifteen or sixteen, but the period describing his yachting endeavours occurred a few years before his death. His brother died in the Troad and Catullus went to visit his grave. While he was in Bithynia, on the Asiatic shores of the Black Sea, he decided, for whatever reasons, to have a yacht built.

Catallus from the cover of the Penguin edition translated by Peter Whigham 1966.

near Cytorus
before you were a yacht
you stood
part of some wooded slope
where the leaves speak continuously in sibilants together.
Pontic Amastris
Cytorus
– stifled with box-wood –
these things
my boat affirms
are common knowledge to you both.

He calls his yacht a 'bean-pod boat' and in common with most boat owners asserts 'that she's been the fastest piece of timber under oar or sail afloat'. The sailing boats of this period looked much the same over a thousand-year period – short and broad double-enders, a twenty-metre boat would have had

5   All quotations of Catullus' poems are from *The Poems of Catullus* Transl. Peter Whigham Penguin, 1966.

a beam of around six metres and carried a square sail on a stubby mast with a short foremast, the *artemion*. Essentially, they were not too far removed from the double-ended *caique*, the *trehandiri*, seen in Greece today. The sail was set on a yard nearly twice as long as the mast, the yard itself being constructed from two saplings lashed together and with a sheet from either end led back to the steering oars. In strong winds the sail could be reefed by brailing it upwards to the yard. Some of these boats also carried a small sail, the *artemion*, on a short fore-mast, and in very strong winds this would have been the only sail up. It also aided stability downwind and would have helped the boat get to weather compared to a simple square sail. In effect it operated here like a sort of proto-foresail.[6] These boats could be rowed for short periods in a calm or into harbour, but they were not anywhere near as fast under oars as the sleek galleys of the time.

In his yacht Catullus sailed out of the Black Sea, through the Bosphorus and Dardanelles, into the Aegean. Here he sailed to Rhodes and then across the Aegean and through the Cyclades and probably around the Peloponnesus where he turned north to sail up the Adriatic to the river Po.

Call as witness
the rough Dalmatian coast
the little islands of the Cyclades
Colossan Rhodes
the savage Bosphorus
the unpredictable surface of the Pontic Sea.

He then sailed up the Po river and the Mincio to Lake Garda where he describes her lying under his villa at Sirmio on the lake.

Finally,
no claim on the protection of any sea god
on the long voyage up to this clear lake.
These things have all gone by.
Drawn up here fathering quiet age.

Catullus was not just a passenger on these trips. In various poems he accurately describes the winds, navigation, storms, and his boat, in a manner only someone intimately acquainted with the sea could do. In this fragment he describes the afternoon breeze getting up in the Aegean.

6   See Heikell *Sailing Ancient Seas* Appendix 1,

Zephyr
flicks the flat water into ridges
with a morning puff,
the sloped waves
loiter musically,
later the wind rises
& they rise,
they multiply
they shed the sun's sea purple as they flee.

And in this fragment reveals an awareness of the basics of navigation by the times of sunrise and sunset and the appearance of certain stars.

Who scans the bright
machinery of the skies
& plots the hours of star-set & star-rise,
this or that planet as it earthward dips,
the coursing brightness of the sun's eclipse.

Catullus died at Sirmio with his yacht drawn up on the shore of Lake Garda when he was only thirty years old. For over a thousand years his poetry was lost until the codex was discovered, so the story goes, wedging a wine barrel in Verona at the end of the thirteenth century. How many more works have been lost describing innocent pleasures on the water in those long-ago times is something we will never know. Catullus himself would no doubt have made further voyages had he lived longer – he had that hunger to break loose and go travelling that a yachtsman needs.

Now spring bursts
with warm airs
now the furor of March
skies
retreats under Zephyrus...
and Catullus will forsake
these Phrygian fields
the sun-drenched farm-
lands of Nicaea
& make for the resorts of
Asia Minor,
the famous cities.
Now, the trepidation of
departure
now lust of travel,
feet impatiently urging him
to be gone.
Good friends, good-bye.

Roman ship from 1st century CE. Wiki Commons.

Imperial *kaiki* off Eminonu in Istanbul. Painting by Allon in *The Caique*.

4 THE MIDDLE AGES AND THE RENAISSANCE

There is very little written on pleasure yachts in the Middle Ages and the Renaissance.[1] It is likely that in Byzantium, Venice, Genoa and other centres of wealth in the intervening period, the aristocracy and rich eccentrics had sailing boats constructed and sailed them for pleasure, but there are no records of adventures such as those of Catullus. The closest we come is in the maritime processions staged annually by some of the states that dominated the Mediterranean. Numerous powerful maritime nations, including Genoa, Pisa, Amalfi and Venice, held annual celebrations that combined a religious ceremony blessing the sea and all it had brought to their city state and a day of celebration on the water.

Although not strictly pleasure yachts, there are also other instances of boats used for ceremony or pleasure. The first dates from around 1000 CE, the *bucentaur*, the state barge used in the Venetian Marriage of the Sea festival. Perhaps the most illustrative are the Ottoman *kaikis* used to ferry nobles and notables across the Bosphorus and for picnics around the Golden Horn. The last mention is a modern re-invention involving galley races, started in 1956, using rowing galleys from a design of around 1200 CE.

The *bucentaur*

Every year on Ascension[2] the Venetian state held a ceremony, the Marriage of the Sea, to celebrate the blessings that sea-borne trade in the Mediterranean had bestowed on the city state. It must be remembered that for centuries Venice controlled many of the trade routes in the eastern Mediterranean, built massive forts to guard routes that are still there to this day, and profited hugely from them. The wealth garnered by the merchants plying the sea is what gave Venice her wealth and power. So it is not surprising that the Doge himself should acknowledge this relationship between the sea and Venice in the Marriage of the Sea ceremony.

---

1 Roughly from the fall of the Roman Empire in the West (5th century) to the fall of Constantinople in 1453. The Renaissance revival of European art and literature occurred in the 14th–16th centuries.
2 The fortieth day of Easter.

… when each Ascension Day the Doge went out in his bucintoro to wed the sea, it was in a morganatic way the universal ocean that he was marrying, in a more intimate and particular sense the Adriatic was his bride.

Jan Morris *The Venetian Empire Penguin*, 1980 p 136

Jan Morris mentions here that he went out in a *bucintoro*, one of the flat-bottomed barges employed around the lagoons of Venice. In fact, the ship he went out in was far grander than a modest barge. The *bucentaur* was first thought to be used around 1000 CE, though the first real accounts are from the early 14th century and from paintings including one by Canaletto of the last Venetian *bucentaur*.[3] The last, and grandest, of the *bucentaurs* was burnt on the orders of Napoleon after he had taken Venice in 1797.

The Departure of the Bucentaur Towards the Lido. Francesco Guardi 1768. Wiki Commons.

This last *bucentaur*[4] was an ornate barge gilded in gold and with statues, including inevitably the Lion of St Mark, adorning the deck. It was 35 metres (115 ft) long and, from the painting by Canaletto and others, looked decidedly top heavy. It was not intended to go to sea and was rowed around the lagoon by 168 oarsmen with the Doge seated under a purple canopy at the stern. The Doge would cast a golden wedding ring into the sea symbolising the marriage of the state and the sea. Presumably after that there was much feasting and celebrating on Ascension Day.

The last *bucentaur* was set on fire on Napoleon's orders only after the gold leaf and statuary had been stripped from it. Recently there has been a project to rebuild this *bucentaur* and moor it in Venice as a symbol of the bygone power of the city.[5] Given its ornate and somewhat garish looks it will be interesting

3   *Bucintoro at the Molo on Ascension Day.* Original by Canaletto in the Dulwich Picture Gallery, London, UK
4   https://en.wikipedia.org/wiki/Bucentaur
5   https://www.independent.co.uk/news/world/europe/venetian-dream-boat-ship-of-fools-sails-again-801237.html

to see how it will sit amongst the modern pleasure yachts of the rich that frequent the Venetian lagoons today.

Ottoman *kaikis*

When the Ottomans finally took Constantinople from the Byzantines, they discovered the easiest way to get around the waters dividing Europe and Asia was on oared *kaikis*.[6] In fact the only way to get from the European side to the Asian side was by boat. For the nobles of the court the *kaikis* soon evolved into finely painted and ornamented craft that signified the rank of the noble, with the finest reserved, not surprisingly, for the sultan. Rich merchants soon emulated the royal craft and had their own ornate *kaikis* built to ferry their owners around and for pleasure trips visiting the *yalis*, the private mansions, dotted around the shores of the Bosphorus.

A number of these *kaikis* have been restored and rebuilt and are on show in the Martime Museum in Istanbul. The size of the *kaikis* varies from around 20 ft (6 metres) to the imperial *kaiki* of the sultan, measuring in at 130 ft (40 metres).

Lengths of the barges may be gauged from the twenty-nine state *caiques* which have been preserved at the Maritime Museum in Istanbul. The smallest is the 5.2 metre Excursion Caique with four oars. The fourteen-oared *caique* of 1910 is 15.2 metres in length. The two twenty-eight oared caiques built for Sultan Abdulmejit I (1839–1861) extend thirty-two metres. Surpassing all is the great Kadirga of the late sixteenth century, at forty metres. This large galley may have been intended for longer journeys, as from Istanbul to Gallipoli or Nicaea.

Width of the caiques is from 1.2 metres to 2.4 metres, with the exception again of the Kadirga at 5.7 metres due to its wide outriggers. Heights of the hulls averaged approximately two metres.

Douglas S Brookes *The Turkish Imperial State Barges* The Mariner's Mirror Vol 76 (1990) p 41

While the *kaikis* had the utilitarian purpose of getting from one place to another, mostly from the European side across the Bosphorus to the Asian side, they were also used for pleasure excursions around the shores of the Bosphorus. There are numerous paintings of the *kaikis* anchored around the Bosphorus and Golden Horn, often with parties of women on board

---

6   *Kaiki* is the Turkish term for what we transliterate as *caique*, a generic term for the various local craft plying the waters of the eastern Mediterranean. It is related to the French *caique* and Italian *carrico*, but the origin is likely the Turkish *kaiki* or *kayik*. See Celik Gulersoy *The Caique* Istanbul, Kitapligi 1991, pp 9–10.

supervised by a eunuch keeping an eye on things and especially on the men manning the oars.[7] The larger *kaikis* that these excursions were made on often had an open mini-kiosk near the stern that could be curtained off for privacy and it was here that the parties of women on a picnic would sit on cushions, out of sight of the rowers. These mini-kiosks were ornate affairs decorated with mother-of-pearl, gold leaf and delicate fretwork, with benches on which cushions and carpets were arranged to sit on.

Ottoman *kaikis* in the Maritime Museum in Istanbul. Shutterstock.

While parties of women would usually seek out some secluded spot for a picnic away from the public gaze, the men, by contrast, cruised the shores, stopping frequently at the *yalis* of friends and acquaintances to go ashore to eat and drink. These were well organised affairs where the owners of the houses would arrange for music in their gardens and spread tables under torchlight with the best in food and drink. Moonlight excursions were particularly popular and a number of poets and scribes wrote of moonlit excursions around Istanbul. When the fashion for such excursions started is less well documented.

Just when it first became fashionable to go boating along the Bosphorus in the moonlight isn't clear. Some historians date it to the reign of Sultan Selim II (1566–1574), who acquired a reputation for debauchery. Villages dotted the shoreline here and there, and summer houses belonging to the wealthy became popular as the Ottoman sultans built small palaces or

7   Gullersoy's book, *The Caique*, has numerous watercolours and etchings of these excursions.

hunting lodges along the water. Others date these moonlight boating excursions to a later period such as the so-called Lale Devri (Tulip Period) between 1718 and 1730.

Niki Gamm *Sailing by the moon on the Ottoman Bosphorus* Hurriyet, August 23, 2014

The person in charge of the imperial *caiques* was, strangely enough, the Bostancı Başı, the head gardener of the royal palace at Topkapi. The post was originally one of caring for the palace gardens, but over time came to include all the parks and gardens in Istanbul and then the shoreline of the city. In time his responsibilities expanded to the imperial *kaikis* and by the end of the 18th century he was responsible for 2500 staff. His remit covered the care and maintenance of the *kaikis* and the planning and construction of the boathouses and landing places around the shoreline. Despite his high position he was apparently still required to take the helm of the sultan's *kaiki* whenever it went out. [8]

Ottoman *kaiki* on a picnic trip on the Golden Horn.
Illustration in Celik Gulersoy *The Caique*.

8   Gamm *Ottomans sail in style on the Bosphorus* Hurriyet January 21 2012

These beautiful boats were overtaken in the 20th century by steam and then the diesel engine. With the demise of the Ottoman Empire in 1920 and the foundation of the modern Turkish republic under Kemal Ataturk, the *kaikis* were no longer built, though fortunately examples of the craft were kept and can be seen in the collection in the Istanbul Maritime Museum.

The galley races of the city states

In the late 1940's, two admirers of the four old city states, Francesco Amodio of Amalfi and Mirro Chiaverini of Pisa, hit upon the idea of a historical festival celebrating the old maritime republics. At its centre would be a rowing regatta in galleys modelled on those used in Medieval times. In 1955 the idea was officially recognised and a regatta panel set up incorporating the four Medieval maritime republics: Amalfi, Pisa, Genoa and Venice. The rowing regatta is held every year around June in one of the four cities.[9]

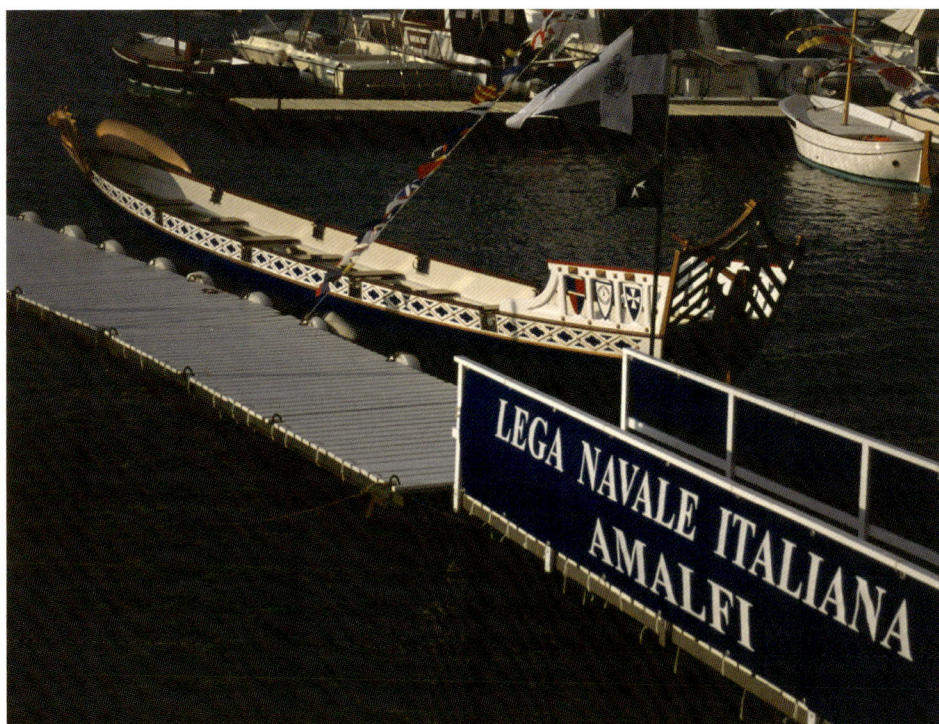

Galley replica ready for racing in Amalfi.

9   http://tangoitalia.com/campania/historical-regatta-of-the-maritime-republics-of-italy-amalfi-genoa-pisa-and-venice/

The galleys are modelled on a 12th century design with ornate features including a figurehead and a small poop deck with a carved sternpost where the helmsman sits. The galleys all have distinctive colours according to the city state they represent. The galley from Amalfi is blue, from Pisa red, from Genoa white and from Venice green.[10] There are just eight rowers to propel a galley that is 8 metres (26 ft) long and weighs around three-quarters of a ton over a 2000 metre (1.25 mile) long course.

I was in Amalfi a few years ago when the festival was on and the galleys are an amazing sight – all gilt, carved wood and impeccable paint jobs, with everyone wandering around in Medieval costumes sporting banners and flags from one of the four cities. The galleys and the costumes transformed the place into an old maritime state again and the atmosphere hinted at a past where pomp and ceremony and power were the norm in Amalfi. The galleys are cumbersome craft that take some effort to row and, not surprisingly, the oars are manned by young, well-muscled men who train for months before the race. The rowers and the team looking after the boats are immensely proud of the galleys; when they come out of the water of an evening, much time is spent lovingly cleaning and polishing the craft. At the end of the festival they are transported back to the city they represent until their next appearance in one of the other cities.

While they are not strictly pleasure craft as such, the galleys, built from a design of around 1200 CE, at least give us some idea of what celebrations on the water in Medieval times could have been like. While it is likely that a rich merchant or noble would have had his own personal galley to ferry him around and take the family and friends for a little tour on the water and the odd picnic afloat, there is little written down, painted or sketched to go on. What these replica galleys bring to us is a notion of what it all looked like at the time when there is so little else to glean any information from.

10   https://www.italianeventplanners.com/blog/that-s-italia/item/262-historical-reenactment-that-features-colorful-16th-century-boats.html

Sketch presumed to be of the *Bolivar* and the *Don Juan*, the yachts of Byron and Shelley. The sketch was found in Shelley's notebook and may be by his friend Williams. Bodleian Library.

5 THE ROMANTIC POETS IN THE MEDITERRANEAN

In the 18th century Samuel Johnson opined that 'The grand object of travelling is to see the shores of the Mediterranean', and for the young Romantic poets of the early 19th century the remark, throwaway or not, was taken to heart. The tangled history of Percy Bysshe Shelley and George Gordon Byron, more commonly abbreviated to just Lord Byron, and their self-imposed exile to Italy was to end in tragedy and death.[1] Shelley drowned off the shores of the western coast of Italy in 1822, Byron died in the fever-ridden swamps of Missalonghi in Greece two years later. The two deaths are intimately bound up with the sea and the rivalry between the two poets, each vying to best the other, not only in verse, but also in their prowess on the water.

Lord Byron.
Coloured engraving.
Wiki Commons.

The reasons for the pilgrimage to Italy were not simply to do with an exploration of the shores of the Mediterranean along the lines of a Grand Tour. Byron had a troubled relationship with his native land and travelled extensively on the continent before returning in 1811. By this time he was as famous for his verse as for his exploits abroad. He was profligate in his lifestyle, spending far more than he had, and bedded numbers of women including his half-sister Augusta. In 1815 he married Anabella Leigh, a rich heiress, as much to settle his debts as to quash rumours of his incestuous relationship with Augusta and his other sexual escapades. By 1816 he had decided to go abroad once more and took a villa on the shores of Lake Geneva. It was here he met Shelley and his future wife Mary.

Shelley was also a self-imposed exile for some of the same reasons as Byron. He had little money and had fled England, leaving substantial debts. Shelley, though still married, eloped to Lake Geneva with Mary Godwin, whom he

1   Daisy Hay *Young Romantics: The Shelleys, Byron and Other Tangled Lives* Bloomsbury, 2011

married soon after in 1816. Byron and Shelley spent much time together and with the added intellectual input of John Keats and Mary Shelley, the makeshift salon produced a literary outpouring of poems and novels. One evening, while reciting German ghost stories, Byron challenged the group to write a ghost story of their own. Mary wrote the basis of what was to become *Frankenstein (The Modern Prometheus)* at the age of nineteen.

It was on Lake Geneva that Shelley and Byron first went sailing. They hired a boat and spent days cruising the shores of the lake. Shelley had already sailed on the Thames and the Rhine,

Percy Bysshe Shelley by Alfred Clint.
Wiki Commons.

and the inference from this was that his abilities were limited to calm inland waterways. In fact, lake and river cruising has its own perils and the chance of strong winds ripping down mountain valleys and raising dangerous seas that can endanger small craft is ever-present. We can be sure that Shelley was not the most experienced sailor when he arrived in Lerici in 1822, but whatever he was not, we can be sure that sailing on the sea was a deep passion for the poet, a passion that is written large throughout his poetry. So is a deep melancholy and the recurring fatalism that presaged his death.

Unfathomable Sea! whose waves are years,
Ocean of Time, whose waters of deep woe
Are brackish with the salt of human tears!
Thou shoreless flood, which in thy ebb and flow
Claspest the limits of mortality!

And sick of prey, yet howling on for more,
Vomitest thy wrecks on its inhospitable shore;
Treacherous in calm, and terrible in storm,
Who shall put forth on thee,
Unfathomable Sea?

Time Percy Bysshe Shelley[2]

2   https://www.poetryfoundation.org/poems/45141/time-56d224858f450

Italy

In April 1822 Shelley moved from his apartment near Pisa to the Villa Magni in the hamlet of San Terenzo in the Bay of La Spezia. Even today San Terenzo sits resolutely apart from the other resorts around the bay and it isn't difficult to imagine the isolation and sense of wildness that attracted Shelley here in 1822. Today the villa sits back from the sea, but in 1822 it was right on the sea's

Villa Magni in San Terenzo in the Bay of La Spezia. Wiki Commons.

edge. Now it is a grand, well-kept building, but in Shelley's time it was described as abandoned and hardly fit for habitation. The bottom of the villa was used to store boats and equipment. Upstairs there were four rooms where Percy and Mary, and their friends the Williams, installed themselves. Mary recorded that she hated the place while Percy was infatuated. He loved the proximity to the sea and the sound of it breaking on the shore right outside the house.

Prior to moving there Byron and Shelley had come up with a plan for each of them to acquire or build a yacht to sail on the waters of the bay. It seems to have been one of those plans that materialises out of an evening conversation and several bottles of wine, though of course Edward Trelawney takes credit for planting the idea after a visit to Leghorn (Livorno). He may well have. He was certainly instrumental in organising the project and commissioned a retired naval captain residing in Genoa to build the boats.

Sketch of Trelawney by Severn. Wiki Commons.

I wrote to an old naval friend, Captain Roberts, then staying at Genoa, a man peculiarly fitted to execute the order, and requested him to send plans and estimates of an open boat for Shelley, and a large decked one for Byron… I rode on to Genoa, and settled with Captain Roberts about building the boats. He had already, with his usual activity, obtained permission to build them in the government dock-yards, and had his plans and estimates made out.

Trelawney Chapter X *Recollections of the Last Days of Shelley and Byron*

Much of what we know of events comes from *Recollections of the Last Days of Shelley and Byron,*[3] published some thirty-five years afterwards. Trelawny, as noted by most critics, is a teller of tales and a notoriously unreliable witness. He is forever 'bigging himself up', intent on showing that anything Byron can do, he can do better. Byron in an aside once said of Trelawney that 'he could not tell the truth to save his life'. While Trelawney's *Recollections* leave

Sketch presumed to be of the yachts of Byron and Shelley found in Shelley's notebook. The sketch may be by his friend Williams. Bodleian Library.

much to be desired, they are the most detailed account we have of someone who was in Lerici at the time and knew something of Shelley and his boat.

The yacht that Shelley had built was a small half-decked craft that is often said to be modelled on an American schooner. In fact, Trelawney states that, although they visited an American clipper in Leghorn, the yacht that was built was from a model that Shelley's friend, Edward Williams, had supplied.

Williams had brought with him, on leaving England, the section of a boat as a model to build from, designed by a naval officer... so the boat was built according to his cherished model. When it was finished, it took two tons of iron ballast to bring her down to her bearings, and then she was very crank in a breeze, though not deficient in beam. She was fast, strongly built, and Torbay rigged. I despatched her under charge of two steady seamen, and a smart sailor lad, aged eighteen, named Charles Vivian. Shelley sent back the two sailors and only retained the boy; they told me on their return to Genoa, that they had been out in a rough night, that she was a ticklish boat to manage, but had sailed and worked well, and with two good seamen she would do very well; and that they had cautioned the gents accordingly.

Trelawney *Recollections* Chapter X

There is only one sketch of the yachts that Shelley and Byron had built that I know of, and that was found tucked into one of Shelley's leather notebooks. Shelley's small yacht is often described as a schooner, though Trelawney describes her as 'Torbay rigged', and in the sketch she looks like a gaff-rigged yawl of around 27 to 30 ft. Certainly, Brixham trawlers operating out of Torbay

3   Edward Trelawney *Recollections of the Last Days of Shelley and Byron* Ticknor & Fields, 1858

were gaff yawls, so it's likely Trelawney is correct here. That she carried a lot of canvas for her size is borne out by the sketch.

There has been a lot of speculation about the size of the *Don Juan* and Trelawney's accounts of her which vary over several editions of his book. There is also some doubt over whether the sketch by Shelley or Williams is of the two yachts at all. Given the scraps of information on the yachts in Trelawney's *Recollections*, the sketch is likely to be of the two yachts, especially as it was found tucked in Shelley's notebook – a keepsake of his yacht.[4]

Byron's yacht, *Bolivar*, is a different beast altogether. It is fully decked and looks a bit like a miniature frigate complete with gun-ports. That would have suited Byron's peacocky taste. It is probably 45- to 55 ft long, though it is hard to tell from the sketch, and is schooner rigged with squaresails.[5] Shelley's yacht was named the *Don Juan* in tribute to Byron's poem, though not without some strife over the naming. Shelley was originally going to call it the *Don Juan*, but later changed his mind and wanted to call it *Ariel*. Byron apparently got huffy about this and went out one night and painted the name *Don Juan* on it, much to Shelley's distress, though the *Don Juan* it remained.

Shelley was often out in the *Don Juan* sailing around the Bay of La Spezia with his friend Williams and young Charles Vivian. He professed himself most happy when out in the yacht, though Trelawney is derisory of Shelley's sailing abilities, and in his *Recollections* relates how he knew nothing of nautical ways, not even how to helm the boat. That sailing the yacht brought a certain calm and peace to the troubled Shelley is evident. In the Villa Magni he would have the most disturbing nightmares and by day he was inclined to much melancholy.

On July 1st Shelley set out to sail to Leghorn with Williams and young Vivian. It is just over thirty-five nautical miles from San Terenzo to Leghorn and with a fair wind Shelley, or more likely the more experienced Williams, could reckon on the voyage taking seven to eight hours. Trelawney was taking Byron's *Bolivar* down to Leghorn as well, though with a full crew of five seamen. Byron seems to have been somewhat indifferent to the goings-on and stayed in his villa on the Arno River. The boats stayed in Leghorn until July

4   See Donald B. Prell *The Sinking of the 'Don Juan' Revisited* Keats-Shelley Journal, Vol. 56 (2007).
5   A square topped schooner or brigantine rig.

8th when, despite the forecast of bad weather, Shelley or Williams decided to embark on the voyage back to La Spezia. They took with them the young sailor Charles Vivian and set off in the afternoon, despite entreaties from the local sailors not to go to sea. Trelawney was to accompany them in the *Bolivar*, but due to some mix up in the paperwork was detained in Leghorn by the authorities. So, it was that Trelawney watched Shelley, Williams and Vivian sail out of Leghorn bound for home. The Italian mate on the *Bolivar* pointed out to Trelawney a squall line out to sea.

…Look at those black lines and the dirty rags hanging on them out of the sky – they are a warning; look at the smoke on the water; the devil is brewing mischief.

Trelawney *Recollections* Chapter XI

The *Don Juan* disappeared into the black cloud that the Genoese mate on the *Bolivar* had seen. Not long after, the squall caused havoc in the port with strong winds and thunder and lightening. I have been caught in one of these squalls off the coast of Elba not far south of Leghorn.[6] In the 20 ft *Roulette*, we had the spinnaker up when the squall hit and knocked the boat on its side. Water was pouring into the cockpit, a non-self-draining cockpit, and somehow, I scrabbled up to the mast and got the sails down. We baled water out of *Roulette* for half an hour. Whenever another squall threatened, we doused all the sails. We were the slowest sailing boat around for weeks after.

It is likely that the *Don Juan* was swamped in the squall and those on board had little chance of survival. If they could not get the sails down in time she would have been pressed down into the sea and, as an open-decked boat, she would have filled with water. It is likely, but not certain, that the ballast would have taken her to the bottom and, though Edwards could swim, Shelley could not. Of the young Charles Vivian we have no knowledge, though it was not commonplace for sailors to learn to swim.

Trelawney rode to Byron's villa to report what had happened and when the weather had settled took the *Bolivar* along the coast to see if he could locate the *Don Juan*. He found a few objects, a water keg, the punt from the *Don Juan*, and a few bottles and other objects. The mutilated bodies of Shelley and Edwards washed ashore some ten days later. Trelawney describes them as near unrecognizable as the flesh had been eaten away from much of the

6   Heikell *The Accidental Sailor* Taniwha Press UK 2013

The Funeral of Shelley by Louis Édouard Fournier, 1889. The painting is not true to life. Mary, Shelley's wife, was not there, and there is some doubt as to whether Byron was.

bodies. Objects in the pockets of the remaining clothing and the clothing itself helped to identify the bodies. The young Charles Vivian was not found until some three weeks later and was buried in the sand above the high-water mark.

Shelley's remains were burnt in a pyre on the beach to satisfy the quarantine regulations and Trelawney would have it that he leapt into the flames and rescued Shelley's heart. It's unlikely he did anything of the sort. Shelley's ashes were interred in the Protestant cemetery in Rome not far from those of John Keats who had died a year earlier of tuberculosis. Trelawney later moved the grave to what he said was a better position near the edge of the cemetery where the last remains of the poet remain

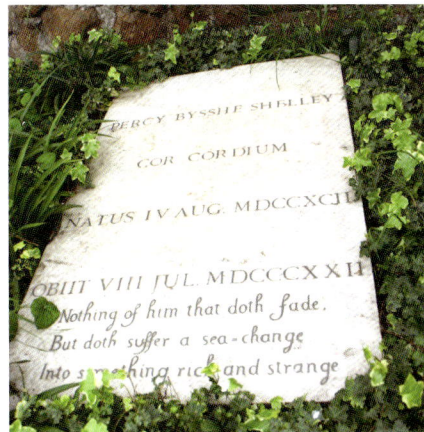

Gravestone of Shelley in the Protestant Cemetery in Rome. Giovanni Dall'Orto.

to this day. On his gravestone are a few lines from, perversely, Ariel's' song in Shakespeare's *The Tempest*:

Nothing of him that doth fade
But doth suffer a sea-change
Into something rich and strange.

That might have been the end of the story, except that the *Don Juan* was apparently salvaged by the same Captain Roberts who had supervised its construction. The yacht was reported to have sunk in 10 fathoms, around 18 metres. While it is possible that it was salvaged from the sea bottom, it maybe that the *Don Juan* was swamped and floating semi-submerged just under the surface. It was not to be the last heard of Shelley's yacht. The following letter was published in *The Spectator* on August 2nd, 1913.

To THE EDITOR OF THE SPECTATOR.1 do not remember to have read in any of the accounts of the drowning of Shelley anything about the subsequent history of the 'Don Juan' – renamed by Shelley the 'Ariel' – after she was recovered by Trelawny fifteen miles from shore, two months subsequent to the accident. It may be of interest to some of your readers, and worthy, perhaps, of record in the columns of The Spectator, to state what became of her. She was bought under the name of the 'Don Juan' at Zante in 1827 from the captain of a brig trading from England to that island, by five officers of the English 51st Regiment then quartered there. They each subscribed fifty dollars towards the purchase, the yacht, which was seven tons burden, thus costing them about £50. Shelley, it may be remembered, had paid £80 for her to Captain Roberts, who built her. The officers used her for going across to Tornese Castle on the coast of the Morea opposite, and one of them took a month's cruise in her to the island of Calamos. Probably, therefore, she was quite seaworthy. She was wrecked by breaking from her moorings one night in a gale of wind, when she was cast ashore and smashed to pieces, a mishap due to the negligence of the man in charge of her – a private in the regiment, formerly a sailor, who had gone ashore on that very British errand, a drinking bout. I give these facts on the authority of a signed statement which I have, and which was made many years ago, at my request, by my father, who was an ensign in the 51st at Zante in 1827, and one of the part owners of the boat. He added that he thought he remembered an interview with Trelawny in his country house at Zante, before they made the purchase, on the subject of the 'Don Juan', so it was doubt-less on his recommendation that they bought her. – I am, Sir, &c., ERNEST LAW. The Pavilion, Hampton Court Palace.

http://archive.spectator.co.uk/article/2nd-august-1913/15/shelleys-yacht-the-ariel-or-the-don-juan

Greece

The *Bolivar* was taken back up to Genoa, and in 1823 Captain Roberts wrote to Trelawney to say that Byron had sold it to a Lord Blessington for four hundred guineas.[7] As ever with Byron, it was rumoured that Lady Blessington was an intimate friend, at best just a confidante to his misgivings over his forthcoming Greek adventure.[8] Given Byron's history it is unlikely the relationship was purely platonic. Byron, by this time, had become involved with a British committee set up to help the Greeks fight for independence and had resolved to go to Greece with supplies and money to help the cause. On his early travels between 1809 and 1811, Byron visited Greece and the Levant. While in the eastern Mediterranean he and his entourage shipped on board HMS *Salsette* to Constantinople and later returned to England on HMS *Volage*. The voyages seem to have kindled a desire in Byron to lead some sort of military life. Before he embarked for Greece, he ordered a selection of uniforms and helmets for himself and the entourage, including Trelawney, though he apparently refused to wear the bizarre helmet Byron had ordered made for him.

He had not wholly confessed to anyone this somewhat school-boyish dream, but he gave it away by the accoutrements he ordered. There were magnificent green and gold and scarlet uniforms for himself, others of slightly less grandeur for his immediate staff, at least ten swords for different occasions, and a battery of firearms. And there were three gigantic helmets of his own design: for Pietro Gamba, who was eager to come with him, one that resembled a Prussian shako, of brass, green cloth and black leather, bearing on the front a semblance of Athene, and for himself and Trelawney plumed and brazen creations of the most menacing Homeric aspect…

David Howarth *The Greek Adventure* Collins, 1976 pp 129–130

Trelawney had advised Byron to buy a fast, armed yacht they could use as a scouting ship so they could find out what was going on in different parts of Greece.[9] Instead Byron chartered a coaster, the 120 ton *Hercules*, that sailed like a brick and was hardly suitable for out-running any craft that might pursue them. They set sail for the Ionian Islands in July 1823. On board, apart from Byron, were Trelawney, Doctor Gamba and half a dozen servants. The *Hercules* arrived in Argostoli in Cephalonia and Byron was immediately besieged by exiled Greeks who scented money in the whole enterprise. Envoys from various leaders in Greece arrived almost daily to entreat Byron and his war chest to come to one or other to help the cause.

7   Trelawney *Recollections* Chapter XV.
8   Maxine Feifer *Going Places* MacMillan, 1985 p 165
9   Trelawney *Recollections* Chapter XV

In Cephalonia Byron was at a loss as to how to proceed. He was constantly asked to join one or other leader and he seems to have half understood the constant entreaties for his presence were connected to the money that came with him. For months he did nothing; it seemed he was ready to settle down on Cephalonia, at the time under British rule and a safe haven from the fighting in other parts of Greece. Eventually he decided he must go to Missalonghi where a Greek leader called Alexandros Mavrocordato was fighting the Turks. Mavrocordato had written to Byron words that not only flattered but fomented some desire in him to achieve greatness in the Greek struggle.

You will be received here as a saviour… Be assured, My Lord, that it depends only on yourself to secure the destiny of Greece.

Quoted in Howarth *The Greek Adventure* p 144

I have sailed into Missalonghi numerous times, in good weather and bad, and it remains a solitary, almost forgotten part of Greece. On either side of the entrance to the dredged channel and canal that runs up to the town, the landscape is flat and featureless. It is all low marshland split by salt water lagoons and mudbanks.[10] Missalonghi appears to hover on the surface of the water on a low island in the patchwork of lagoons, a damp outpost that is an unlikely candidate for an important battle in the Greek struggle and hardly the sort of place Byron would imagine he would die in. It lacked grandeur and presence, but come to it Byron did, to be greeted by Mavrocordato and his band of guerrillas.

Not that the voyage across to Missalonghi was without incident. Byron hired two boats for the relatively short hop across to Missalonghi. As they approached the entrance to the Gulf of Patras a Turkish warship passed close by and the two boats scattered. The boat Byron was on headed north to a place called Dragomestre (now called Astakos), and there Byron waited until Mavrocordato sent several boats to escort him into Missalonghi. The other boat with Doctor Gamba on board was captured by the Turkish ship and taken to Patras. In the hold was Byron's money and his uniforms and other goods that would surely have given the game away if they had been discovered. As it turned out a remarkable coincidence saved them. The captain of Gamba's ship

10   Rod & Lucinda Heikell *Greek Waters Pilot* 13th ed. Imray, 2018

had sometime in the past saved the life of the Turkish captain who captured them and after a brief period they were allowed to continue on their way.[11]

Byron's voyage to Missalonghi was remarkable more for its comic action than for any real danger, as David Howarth records.

Byron himself liked boats, but had never learned much about them. And as they returned through the Oxia channel, the boat missed stays and ran aground in a squall. Two thirds of the crew climbed out on the bowsprit and jumped ashore, Byron told Loukas he would save him, and Dr Bruno stripped to his flannel waistcoat and running about like a rat (it was Byron's description) shouted 'Save him indeed! By God save me rather – I'll be the first if I can.' Thereupon, after striking twice, the boat blew off again.

Howarth *The Greek Adventure* p 149

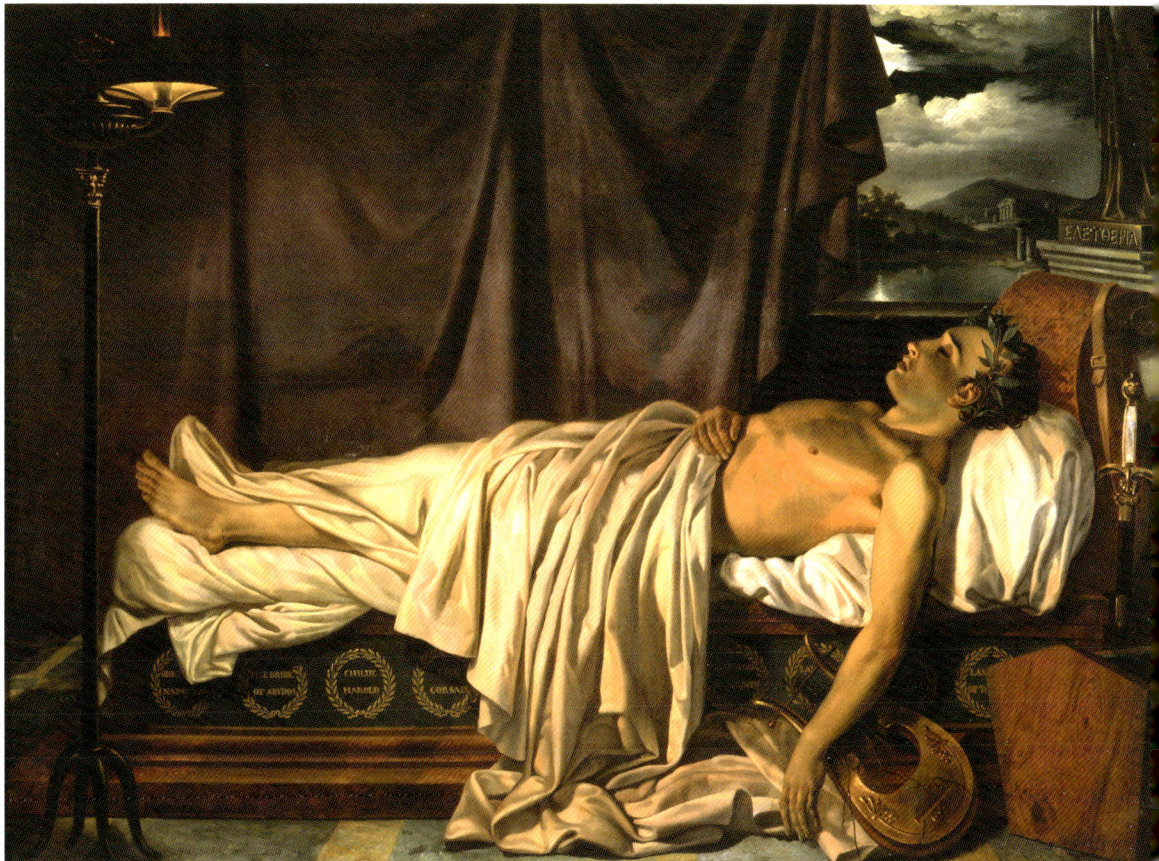

Lord Byron on his Death Bed. Painting by Joseph Denis Odevaere c.1826.

11   David Howarth *The Greek Adventure* Collins p150

When Byron finally arrived in Missalonghi in early January 1824 he was greeted with huzzahs and cheers by the Greeks. Mavrocordato and the Greeks may well have needed his money, but they also seemed genuinely pleased that he was on the battlefront. Mavrocordato appointed him Commander-in-Chief and Byron settled into a house in Missalonghi where he was daily visited by Greek leaders and their envois asking him for advice and, invariably, money. The events wore him down and Byron, never the healthiest specimen, contracted fever and died on April 19th, 1824.

Today in Missalonghi there are a few statues of Byron and a museum with a few paltry exhibits. Little remains to remind us of the poet's death in the salt lagoons of Missalonghi except perhaps the mosquitoes that are still there. The town remains curiously singular, almost un-Greek, though interesting both in its situation in the salt marsh and its historical significance in the Greek War of Independence. Trelawney had by now gone adventuring on his own but was to return to Zante, where he resided for a time before returning to England and writing his account of Shelley and Byron in the Mediterranean.

The canal leading through the lagoon to Missalonghi.

The Red Buoy (*La bouée rouge*) painted by Paul Signac in 1895.

6 WRITERS AND PAINTERS: THE FRENCH TAKE TO THE WATER

In the second half of the 19th century French writers and artists discovered the Mediterranean and its extraordinary light and lightness of spirit far from the dull cityscape of Paris and the grey beaches of northern France. For writers like Alexandre Dumas and Guy de Maupassant, the Mediterranean afforded a new life, an escape sufficiently distant from the intrigues and conspiracies of Paris, not to mention creditors, to reinvigorate the soul and fuel their writing. A part of this new life was to voyage on its waters in a yacht, and both Dumas and Maupassant had a passion for the sea and roamed far and wide on their own yachts.[1]

Their taste for the Mediterranean was much removed from the notions of the Grand Tour that Shelley and Byron initially came for, and they didn't have that Victorian sense of a checklist of things to do and see while sailing around the Mediterranean. For them there was the simpler pleasure of discovering the Mediterranean way of life and how to live it, the Mediterranean as a state of mind, a life on the water much removed from the rich and entitled visitors on stately yachts that oozed status and largesse rather than the simpler love of a sea and flapping canvas. There has always been a tension between the north and south of France, and it remains so to this day. The north is seen as venal

Maupassant's *Bel-Ami*.
Drawing by E Riou in *Afloat*.

1   Dumas on his *Emma* and Maupassant on his *Bel-Ami*

and conservative, while the south is more laissez-faire and inclined to the arts and radical thought.

Painters too, the Impressionists and neo-Impressionists, flocked to the south of France to try and capture the essence of the light that informs many of the paintings of Manet, Cezanne, Seurat, Signac and Matisse amongst others. These were painters who escaped from the studio and the stuffy conservatism of Paris and espoused the idea of working outside, en plein air, in a more intimate association with the landscape and the sea and people around it. Paul Signac was a devoted sailor and, on his *Olympia*, sailed much of the Mediterranean coast and islands, recording the sea and coast in his bright pointillist paintings. I have his *Sails and Pines*, a copy of course, on the wall. Others occasionally sailed with Signac and on other boats – any Impressionist and neo-Impressionist catalogue is replete with pictures of boats and the sea around the coast of the Mediterranean.

Alexandre Dumas and the *Emma*

Alexandre Dumas is known as a prolific author who wrote a whole series of novels that were popular in his day and still are. Some of these are well known: *The Count of Monte Cristo*, *The Three Musketeers*, *The Man in the Iron Mask*, *Twenty Years After*; while other novels and plays, of which there are an awful lot, are less well known today. As well as fiction, Dumas wrote non-fiction on his travels through Europe and one of these books concerns his yacht *Emma* and the voyage he made to Sicily, to aid his friend Garibaldi and the Red Shirts in their battle for a unified Italy.

The first few chapters of *On Board the Emma*[2] deal with a problem that many of us as yacht owners have had to deal with: what happens when you choose a yacht that is just so wrong you keep spending a small fortune to put it right. Throughout his life Dumas struggled with debt, not because he didn't earn a lot, but because of

Alexandre Dumas. Rajon.

2   Alexandre Dumas *On Board the Emma*, subtitled *Adventures with Garibaldi's 'Thousand' in Sicily* Fredonia Books, 2002

his spendthrift ways – not least on the alleged forty mistresses he had during his lifetime.[3] After a trip to Russia and the Black Sea, Dumas contrived to arrive on the little island of Syra (Siros) in the Greek Aegean. He had heard that you could have a yacht built here for half the cost of it being built in France and with the assistance of the Bavarian consul agreed a price with '… the best shipbuilder on the island – Paghaida'.[4] Although it might have seemed odd that Dumas went to the little island of Siros in Greece, in fact there were more boats built on Siros than in Provence in France or Liguria in Italy at this period. It was a hub of shipbuilding in the Mediterranean that only declined in the latter part of the 19th century.[5]

The cover of *On Board the Emma* showing a portrait of Garibaldi.

Things didn't go well. The *Monte Cristo*, as Dumas christened it, took much longer to build than estimated, the costs kept escalating, and when Paghaida eventually sailed it to Marseille and Dumas first saw his yacht, he quipped that 'She was reassuring as regards solidity, but disquieting as regards velocity'.[6] Dumas was not happy and frequently quotes the amounts he had to pay his captain and crew and for the work needed to finish the *Monte Cristo*. It was all going to cost more than the cost of building a yacht in France. The *Monte Cristo* was likely a typical gaff-rigged schooner common as trading coasters in the Aegean. They traded grain and other bulk cargoes all over the Mediterranean, and many of the islands had substantial fleets of these schooners, typically anywhere between 50 to 150 ft long, broad of beam, and usually without an engine until much later in the 19th century.

On a trip to Rome, by land as the *Monte Cristo* was still not fitted out, he heard of another yacht for sale in Marseille and hurried back to look at it.

I went thoroughly over her, searching into each corner like a Customs house officer. Everywhere she revealed the talent of the English builder, who had succeeded in every detail – comfort above all. She had everything necessary, as the bride has her trousseau – her plate,

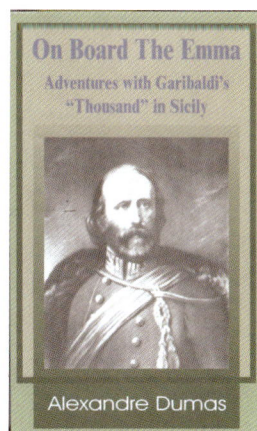

3   John Crace on Dumas' lost novel *Guardian* archives, May 2008.
4   Dumas *On Board the Emma* p 6
5   Delis Apostolos *Mediterranean wooden shipbuilding in the nineteenth century* Cahiers de Mediterranee 84, 2012
6   Dumas *On Board the Emma* p 8

her linen, her china, her lamps, her nautical instruments, and her carpets.

Dumas *On Board the Emma* p 34

She was named *Emma* after Dumas' mistress of the time, Emma Cordier. The *Monte Cristo* he sold at a considerable loss, though he still took the roguish Paghaida, the author of much of his misfortune, on as mate on the *Emma*. We know little about the *Emma* apart from a few throwaway facts that Dumas tells us, no doubt thinking that technical details would bore his readers.

… an entrancing little yacht – the very one you wanted, seventy-eight tons, built at Liverpool, made of mahogany and maple, copper bottomed – in short, a marvel.

Dumas *On Board the Emma* p 34

At this time, tonnage rules were changing and so it's difficult to know just how big the *Emma* was. I would guess she was around 70- to 80 ft long on deck and probably rigged as a gaff-rig schooner or possibly a gaff cutter. This is all guess work as the only picture of the *Emma* I can find is a newspaper illustration and may not be accurate. Unlike the *Emma*, Dumas himself loved to pose for portraits – in fact of the ten illustrations in *On Board the Emma*, five are portraits of Dumas. The one illustration we have of the wreck of the *Emma* in *Le Monde* in 1864 may not be of the *Emma* at all, though it shows a gaff-rigged schooner of around the right size.

On the 9th of May 1860 Dumas sailed for Genoa on the *Emma*. On board he had a band of eleven like-minded souls, a Captain Beaugrand and Paghaida as mate, and eight crew. Dumas was something of a bon vivant, fond of his food and wine,[7] and the *Emma* was victualled with ample provisions and more than ample supplies of wine and champagne. He also had on board a 'midshipman', a young lady dressed in midshipman's clothes as it turned out, and although no mention is made of her name, we can assume it was his mistress Emma Cordier.

It took some time to sail to Genoa, as Dumas recounts.

… the delay is caused simply by two difficulties that we have met with more than once – head winds and calms.

These are the drawbacks of the sailing vessel – but must it not be so? As an admirer of

---

7   Dumas had a lifelong affair with food and frequently mentions good meals and bad in his travel writing. He worked on his *Grand dictionnaire de cuisine* (Great Dictionary of Cuisine) for much of his life, but it was only published posthumously in 1873.

Fenimore Cooper, my preference must be forgiven – I prefer a sailing vessel, with all its disadvantages, to a steam-boat with all its advantages.

Dumas *On Board the Emma* p 99

In Genoa, Dumas found a letter from Garibaldi waiting for him. It urged him to 'rally where you hear my guns' and Dumas, ever the adventurer, decided to sail the *Emma* to Sicily forthwith.

Without an engine it took the *Emma* over three weeks to get to Palermo on Sicily. Captain Beaugrand took the boat down the west side of Corsica and then down the east side of Sardinia to avoid going anywhere near the Kingdom of Naples who were fighting Garibaldi and the insurrection in Sicily. Even with his sincere desire to join Garibaldi, Dumas couldn't but help indulging in a leisurely tour of Corsica and Sardinia. Eventually on the 11th of June he arrived in Palermo to find Garibaldi had taken the city, though the Neapolitans still controlled parts of it. With a bravura performance the *Emma* sailed into the harbour.

As far as one is able to judge, the harbour is full of warships, but they are too numerous for all to be Neapolitan. The Captain believes that he can recognise British and French vessels among them.

If there are English and French vessels in Palermo harbour, there is no reason whatever why we should not be there also; so the Captain gives the order to get the breeze behind us, and we advance towards Palermo at the rate of three miles an hour…

… so we are going to anchor between the fort of Castellucio-del-Molo and a Neapolitan frigate. We thus have the guns of the fort on our starboard side, and the sixty fiery mouths of the frigate to larboard.

Dumas *On Board the Emma* pp 218–219

Dumas went inland from Palermo to look at the battlefields where Garibaldi had taken on the Neapolitans and to re-acquaint himself with sites in Sicily he had visited long before in the 1830's. Ever the writer, it is no surprise that he was putting together various articles on Garibaldi and the 'Thousand' as well as helping to write Garibaldi's memoirs. In Agrigento on the south side of Sicily he re-joined the *Emma* and sailed for Malta. He was not there long before he sailed to Calabria to pick up arms for Garibaldi and ferry them over to Milazzo on Sicily.

A writer Dumas most certainly was, but one far removed from armchair theorising. In Milazzo he assisted Garibaldi as best he could and then left for

Palermo again. At dusk that night a Neapolitan steamer spotted the *Emma* and, recognising her as one of the vessels that had been assisting Garibaldi in Milazzo, attempted to ram the yacht.

'The steamer! The steamer!' cried the sailor on the watch.

'Luff! Luff!' shouted the mate.

This manoeuvre was put into execution at once, but before it could be completed, the steamer was upon us…

…The yacht was lifted up like a feather, and a sharp noise of cracking was heard. I was lying on the deck and was covered with water. The steersman was thrown down, and the mate tossed five or six feet into the air. Our cross-jacksail yard was broken, our spanker boom bent like a reed, and our mainsail rent. The stern of the yacht plunged into the water and emerged dripping wet.

Dumas *On Board the Emma* pp 430–431

Dumas made it to Palermo and had the *Emma* repaired. He subsequently sailed up to Salerno, which sits just under the southeast corner of the Sorrento Peninsula adjacent to Naples and, when Garibaldi triumphantly entered

Illustration from *Le Monde* December 1864 of the plight of the *Emma*.

Naples in September, Dumas joined him there, Garibaldi installed him in a villa in Naples and he lived there until 1864. We have to assume that the *Emma* was kept at Naples and possibly sailed back to Marseille when Dumas returned to France in 1864, but there are no records of this.

In 1864 Dumas lent the *Emma* to a friend of his, a Captain Magnan, for an expedition up the Niger River. Dumas himself was not part of the expedition.

Alexandre Dumas père, prolific writer, bon vivant, adventurer and generous owner of the *Emma*.

The writer, regretting that he could not join the expedition, put at his disposal his most luxurious maritime property: the schooner Emma. He also promises to promote this trip through the press and adds, 'I will not neglect anything to create dedicated allies in all clans of journalists.'

Report in *Le Monde,* December1864

The *Emma* left Marseille on December 12th, 1864 and encountered a ferocious storm at sea. Captain Magnan decided to run for shelter in Saint Gervais in the Gulf of Fos and here he put two anchors down. Still the storm battered the boat and some of the crew decided to swim for the shore. Eventually the *Emma* was left to her own devices and we know nothing more of her fate.[8]

Alexandre Dumas, novelist, traveller and bon vivant, died in 1870 at his son's house just outside Paris.

Guy de Maupassant and the *Bel-Ami*

In many ways Guy de Maupassant was the polar opposite of Alexandre Dumas. While Dumas was an extrovert who loved to meet up and party with friends on his *Emma*, Maupassant went sailing to get away from the crowds and find solace in the quietude of the sea. This was not always so. In Paris he lived life to the full in the company of literary greats like Flaubert, Balzac, Zola and Turgenev and was well known, especially to ladies of a dubious reputation, in the soirées and parties of fin-de-siècle Paris.

8   *Le Monde* December, 1864 www.centrefernandleger.com/47.html.

Employed in the civil service, he wrote by night and with the help of his literary friends soon became famous. His excelled at the short story form and has often been fêted as France's best short story writer. This period in his life was all to change and we know now that the later mercurial nature of Maupassant's character, his abrupt mood swings and his capacity to be charming and excessively rude at the same time, was likely due to the syphilis he contracted in his early liaisons with the ladies of the night.[9]

Guy de Maupassant. Photograph by Felix Nadar 1888.

If there was one thing that was a constant in Maupassant's life it was his love of the sea and sailing.[10] He showed an early interest in boats and even as an eight-year-old used the terms port and starboard when most children were still struggling to distinguish their right shoe from their left.[11] As he grew up his passion for boats was undiminished and while he lived in Paris he had a rowing boat he used on the Seine. As he became more successful as a writer, he discovered the Mediterranean and took to sailing along the coast of France.

His first boat was the *Louisette* of which we have little information except that it was an old whaling boat, presumably an open-decked boat of some sort.[12] His second was the *Flamberge* which he re-named the *Bel-Ami* after his second and most famous novel, *Bel-Ami* (published 1885). Maupassant bought the boat in Antibes and based it there for most of the time he spent on the south coast. It was an 11-metre (36 ft) gaff cutter built by Texier near Argenteuil on the Seine[13] and, from the illustrations by Edouard Riou in *Afloat*, was a straight-stemmed boat with a wide counter not dissimilar to fishing boats of the time, except instead of a rudimentary shelter and a hold for the fish, it had a proper

9   *Remembering Maupassant* BBC World Service www.bbc.co.uk/worldservice/arts/highlights/000808_maupassant.shtmll
10   Much of this information comes from Maupassant's book, *Afloat: A Journal of His Days at Sea*. Introduction by Marlo Johnston. Peter Owen, 1995.
11   In the Introduction by Marlo Johnston to Maupassant's *Afloat*.
12   Maupassant *Afloat* p 140
13   In the Introduction by Marlo Johnston to Maupassant's *Afloat*.

cabin and comfortable accommodation below. In one illustration Riou shows Maupassant reclining on one of the berths in the saloon which looks cosy and comfortable.

Maupassant hired two crew to run the *Bel-Ami* and writes affectionately about them.

Bernard, the skipper, is thin, easy-going, remarkably neat, careful and prudent; with a full beard, he has a straightforward look, an agreeable voice and he is loyal and sincere. Yet when he is at sea everything worries him: meeting a sudden swell forecasting wind at sea; a cloud stretched out over the Esterel which shows that the mistral is in the west; and even a rising barometer, since it could be due to a sudden squall in the east…

… Raymond, his brother-in-law, is a strong fellow, dark, with a moustache, bold and untiring, as loyal and sincere as the other, but less highly strung and changeable, calmer, more resigned to the treacheries and surprises of the sea.

Maupassant *Afloat* p 23

Maupassant's crew on the *Bel-Ami*. Drawing by E. Riou in *Afloat*.

The *Bel-Ami* at anchor. Drawing by E. Riou in *Afloat*.

Here and in numerous other passages in *Afloat*, Maupassant is evidently not just a passenger on board the *Bel-Ami*, but understands the wind and sea and the signs that hint at changes in the weather. He feels a bond to the sea that in some way helps him understand the madness that his syphilis, spreading to his spinal cord and up to his brain, has brought to his being and the way he sees the world. Sailing the *Bel-Ami* helps sooth the hallucinations and violent headaches that constantly beset him and which must have sired much of the grisliness to be found in some of his later short stories.

In *Afloat* Maupassant doesn't describe any long passages. He is pottering along the coast stopping overnight at St Tropez, St Raphael, Agay, Cannes and Antibes. His language can occasionally be a bit flowery for my taste, and at times he can be overly harsh about places and people, though more often his language captures the taste of the sea and the motion of

Maupassant in the cabin of the *Bel-Ami*. Drawing by E. Riou in *Afloat*.

the *Bel-Ami* in ways that other writers cannot. On departing St Raphael, he describes the sea and the wind in an almost hypnotic way.

The sea, without waves in the bay, was white with foam, white like a sheet of soapsuds, for the wind, the terrible Frejus wind that blows almost every morning, seemed to fall upon it to tear off the skin, which it lifted and rolled into little billows of froth, scattered, then at once formed again.

Maupassant *Afloat* p 82

After *Afloat* was published Maupassant sold the *Bel-Ami* that features in the book and bought a bigger yacht which he also called the *Bel-Ami*. The second *Bel-Ami* was originally called *Zingara*, in Italian the 'gypsy girl', and at 14.6 metres (48 ft) and 20 tons, was a more comfortable and sea-kindly yacht than the first *Bel-Ami*. She was a gaff yawl with a hefty spread of sail and was said to have been built in Lymington in 1879.[14] We know about the second *Bel-Ami* from the photograph and details about the yacht from her sale after Maupassant died.

In his short life Maupassant was incredibly productive. He wrote over 300 short stories, six novels, and three travel books, including *Afloat*. His syphilis

14   Stated in the introduction by Marlo Johnston to Maupassant's *Afloat* and from the advertisement for the sale of the *Bel-Ami*.

eventually overtook him and in 1892 he tried unsuccessfully to commit suicide. He was committed to an insane asylum and died a few months later, just short of his forty-third birthday. Following his death his beloved *Bel-Ami* was put up for sale.

Paul Signac and the *Olympia*

The new school of painters who flocked to the Mediterranean coast in the second half of the 19th century, and there were a lot of them, wanted to escape the formalism and innate conservatism of the north. Many were radical thinkers, socialists and anarchists who decried the evident corruption of Paris and sought some sort of freedom in the bright light of the Mediterranean. That this light that bathed the sea and the land influenced their work is evident in the bright dots of paint that have an elemental impact on the eyes; you can almost feel the summer heat shimmering off the canvas.

The line-up of avant-garde artists who journeyed down to the Mediterranean coast of France reads like a *Who's Who* of famous Impressionist and neo-Impressionist painters: Manet, Cezanne, Seurat, Signac, Caillebotte, Bonnard, Matisse and many others, not to mention their friends and hangers-on who formed friendships and a loose alliance of the neo-Impressionist school which linked together the various towns they settled in along the coast.

While everyone was painting the sea and coast, and while the seascapes of these painters are often dotted with the sails of boats out fishing or sailing for pleasure, of this group of painters it is Paul Signac who stands out as the one for whom sailing and the sea were integral to his work. In many ways sailing shaped his art.

Signac had a lifelong passion for boats and, like Maupassant, started off with a boat on the

Paul Signac on the *Olympia* in a painting by Theo van Rysselberghe in 1896. WikiArt.

Seine. He claimed to have owned twenty-nine boats including a canoe called *Manet Zola Wagner* that he used on the Seine.[15] The boat he did most of his sailing in was the *Olympia*, named after Manet's painting of an enigmatic nude woman lying on a bed while a servant presents her with a bouquet of flowers. There were no paintings or sketches of the *Olympia* made by Signac where we can definitively say that it is this or that boat in a sketch. The only two paintings are one by Pierre Bonnard and another by Theo van Rysselberghe, which are both from a perspective of amidships looking aft, so we don't get an overall idea of what the yacht looked like.

Sails and Pines. Paul Signac 1896.

The *Olympia* was built at the Kerenfor yard in Roscoff in Brittany sometime in the late 1880's.[16] It was 11 metres (36 ft) long and, from the paintings by Bonnard and Rysselberghe, it is most likely a gaff-rigged yawl similar to the Breton fishing boats the yard built at the time, though fitted out as a yacht. Signac usually sailed with crew and also raced the boat in various regattas.[17] In 1892, bereft at the death of his mentor and friend Georges Seurat, he upped sticks and sailed the *Olympia* down to the Mediterranean. From Brittany he sailed down the Atlantic coast of France to Bordeaux where he cut through the waterways of the Canal Lateral à Garonne and the Canal du Midi to Sète. Like Maupassant and many painters of the time, he hoped to find some sort of freedom, personal and artistic, in the south of France.

Signac originally trained as an architect in Paris and it was only after some sort of Damascene moment, when he went to see an exhibition of Monet's paintings, that he decided to be a painter. He was soon attracted to the

15   After the three people, the artist, writer and composer, he was inspired by. Marina Ferretti-Bocquillon *Signac 1863–1935* The Metropolitan Museum of Art Yale University Press, 2001.
16   The few details we have are from a page to do with the restoration of another Kerenfor boat, the *Nethou*.
17   Ferretti-Bocquillon *Signac*

theories of Georges Seurat which rejected the realist techniques and used dots of colour to build up a picture that gave a sensation or a feeling of luminosity to a painting. It was christened the pointillist school; Signac became a disciple of Seurat and refined the pointillist method in his paintings.

Signac also worked in a different way to many of the other artists at the time. He had always been drawn to the water and on the *Olympia* would undertake long cruises around the Mediterranean equipped with just his sketchbook, a pencil or two, and a box of watercolours. He made quick sketches and a few watercolours of the places he visited and then brought them back to make his pointillist paintings on a bigger canvas in the studio. As far as he was concerned his travels provided the kernel of his work to which he added the creative touch.

Personally, except for a quick indication which memory or a camera would often supply just as well, any artist's work must be creative. And isn't the painter just as well able to create at his table or at his easel as under a bridge or on a road?

Quoted in Ferretti-Bocquillon *Signac*

Paul Signac in Antibes in 1923 when he was the 'Official Naval Painter'.
Wiki Commons.

Signac settled in St Tropez where he bought a house to which he added a large studio. St Tropez was a small fishing village at the time, and not much popular because it faced into the bitter winds of the mistral.[18] This suited Signac, who wanted something more real than the popular suburbs of Cannes or Nice which the English had colonised and turned into a home-away-from-home to avoid the wet, grey winters of England. He urged fellow artists to come and join him and was instrumental in promoting the activities of the neo-Impressionists away from what he called the 'intellectual crap of Paris'. It is difficult to know just how

18   Rod & Lucinda Heikell *Mediterranean France and Corsica* Imray, 2015 p 230

far he cruised in the *Olympia*. Certainly, he sailed around the south of France and some of the Italian coast. Some sources mention Constantinople, though it is difficult to know if this was by yacht or overland.

In 1915 he moved to Antibes where he was appointed the *Peintre Officiel de la Marine* (Official Naval Painter) and he began painting a whole series of watercolours of the harbours around the coast of Mediterranean France. He still had the *Olympia*, which he sailed regularly (the painting by Pierre Bonnard is dated 1926–1928). He died in Antibes in 1935. There is no record of the fate of the *Olympia*.

View of Collioure. Paul Signac 1896.

The Earl of Cavan's *Roseneath* in Paxos in Greece.
Photo in *With the Yacht, Camera and Cycle in the Mediterranean.*

7 THE VICTORIANS

For the Victorians, yachting in the Mediterranean was largely the domain of the rich and titled. There was no intimate association with the idea of cruising a small yacht in strange waters as Paul Signac or Guy de Maupassant did in their small yachts with just one or two crew and friends. Nor the romance of Percy Bysshe Shelley sailing his small boat along the Italian coast. For the Victorians, cruising was to be done in style in large yachts, often very large yachts, with crew enough to guarantee a life afloat not too far removed from the luxury and opulence of life ashore.

Numerous books were written in the era on cruises undertaken in the Mediterranean, some of them accounts written at the time and others retrospectively from the logs and letters of the cruise. Most of these cruises were in substantial yachts, the superyachts of the time, such as *With the Yacht, Camera, and Cycle in the Mediterranean*, by the Earl of Cavan, published in 1895.[1] Others, like the account of the cruise of the *Royalist* in 1837, were compiled many years later.[2]

For many Victorians yachting was associated with yacht racing as opposed to cruising somewhere for the pleasure of it. Yacht racing on the River Thames was taking place prior to the Victorian era under the Cumberland fleet, but it was soon eclipsed in the 1820's by the Royal Yacht Club[3] based in Cowes on the Isle of Wight, and the Solent became the hub of yacht racing in the British Isles.[4] Yachts large and small were raced under confusing rating rules that constantly changed. For Victorians contemplating a cruise to the Mediterranean, as opposed to racing in the large yacht series that took place around the Riviera in the latter half of the Victorian era, the sort of yacht for such an adventure was invariably large. In 1847 *Sporting Life* had the following advice for anyone contemplating a yachting cruise to the Mediterranean.

The *Sporting Magazine* in 1847 suggested that the smallest yacht in which a Mediterranean

1   Earl of Cavan *With the Yacht, Camera, and Cycle in the Mediterranean* Sampson Low, Marston & Co., 1895
2   Gertrude L. Jacob *The Raja of Sarawak: An Account of Sir James Brooke K.C.B. LLD. Given Chiefly Through Letters and Journals* MacMillan, 1876.
3   It became the Royal Yacht Squadron in 1833.
4   See Douglas Phillips-Birt *The History of Yachting* Stein & Day 1974 for a good account of the history of early yachting in the United Kingdom.

cruise was practicable was a vessel of sixty to ninety tons, the cost of which should be estimated at £15–16 per ton, and which should be crewed at the rate of one man to every ten tons. A similar yacht could be hired, manned, and provisioned for £60–90 per month, at a cost of £1 per ton.

Janet Cusack *Nineteenth-Century Cruising Yachtsmen in the Mediterranean* The Journal of Mediterranean Studies, 2000 p 57

The Sporting Magazine in 1847 suggested that the smallest yacht in which a Mediterranean cruise was practicable was a vessel of sixty to ninety tons.
Illustration in *An Autumn Cruise in the Aegean* 1887.

Although different ideas about what 'yachting' was about were around in embryonic form in Victorian Britain and the juxtaposition of racing as opposed to cruising was something of a grey area, it would take time for the idea of cruising to form and it was not until the second half of the 20th century that the idea to sail down to the Mediterranean purely for the pleasure of it really blossomed. In Britain if there was one soul who had contrary ideas to those sailing and racing in the large yachts of the rich and well connected, it was Richard Turrell McMullen. He espoused the idea of cruising offshore in small boats for the 'common man', for love of the sea and sailing on it, and wrote glowing accounts of his adventures in small yachts. As early as 1850 McMullen was cruising around parts of the British Isles in small boats (his *Leo* was a half-decker just 20 ft long) and his philosophy was recorded in *Down Channel* which became a must-have bible in the library of small boat sailors.[5] In the preface he tries to explain what it is that draws him to this sailing life; its importance is that his philosophy inspired generations of sailors to go cruising in relatively small yachts after its publication.

For years I have been accustomed to hear remarks implying that a yachtsman's time must be heavy on hand, and hard to kill. It may be so in yachting proper, which consists chiefly in promenading on quays, esplanades, and piers, in suitable attire, of course, and in passing to and fro in a steam launch or gig, with colours flying; a delight indulged in only by the extremely affluent, or by those who ought to be so.

Yacht sailing, however, is a very different affair from 'yachting', and when carried on with spirit, as it is sometimes in large yachts as well as small, is anything but an idle recreation. It is always healthful and exciting, though not always a source of unalloyed pleasure.

Richard Turrell McMullen *Down Channel* Horace Cox Printers, revised 1893 edition

There may well have been small yachts cruising the waters of the Mediterranean in the Victorian era after the manner of McMullen, but there are scant records and most of the accounts we have are of large yachts with large crews. While some of those on large, crewed yachts patently had a passion for sailing and navigating, evident in some of the writing of the time, for many of those who left records of Mediterranean yachting cruises it appears that the principal object was to have a luxurious platform to view some of the old ruins around the shores of the Mediterranean, shoot a few grouse in Albania, and if possible bag a lion in North Africa.

Early cruises in the Mediterranean

Byron's yacht *Bolivar* was sold by Captain Roberts, who had supervised the original construction in Genoa, to Lord Blessington in 1823. As I have already guesstimated from the only sketch we have of Byron and Shelley's

5   McMullen *Down Channel* Horace Cox Printers, revised 1893 edition

yachts, the *Bolivar* was a fully decked schooner rigged with squaresails and probably 45- to 55 ft long, though it is hard to tell the length from the sketch.[6] Lord Blessington was Lord Mountjoy, the Earl of Blessington, married to the remarkable Countess Blessington. She had begun life as the daughter of an impoverished drunkard Irish farmer, had been sold into marriage to a military man, Captain Maurice St Leger Farmer, who beat her continuously, after which she fled to England where she met the Earl who, captivated by her beauty, married her. By all accounts she was admired greatly for her beauty, though she was also renowned for her intellect and was to become one of the best-selling authors of the age. The Blessingtons, complete with entourage, toured the Continent in 1822 and ended up in Genoa in early 1823. Here the Countess and Byron struck up a friendship that provided the material for her popular *Conversations of Lord Byron* published in 1834.[7]

The Countess Blessington was typical of the aristocratic ragtag colony of English who had migrated to parts of the Mediterranean to escape from the conservative moral atmosphere of Britain. Byron and Shelley were among those who found society in pre-Victorian Britain too constricting for their taste. There were others.

Eloping heterosexual couples often ended up in Italy. The best known are Elizabeth Barrett and Robert Browning, who made their legendary flight from Wimpole Street in 1846 and settled first at Pisa and subsequently in Florence. Another was Lady Eleanor Butler, who as Lady Lismore had eloped with an officer of the Guards. When the painter Cato Lowes Dickenson met her at Sorrento in 1851 she was living the life of a wealthy divorcee in the sun, with a villa overlooking Naples and a handsome yacht riding at anchor in the bay.

John Pemble *The Mediterranean Passion* OUP, 1988 p 102

There is little to go on when trying to find out what sort of yachts were around in these early years. Later in the 19th century it became fashionable to write about voyages to the Mediterranean and, when photography became popular at the very end of the Victorian period, there are photographs too. Dixon Kemp wrote extensively on yacht construction and the whys and wherefores of running a yacht in the late 19th century.[8] We know little about Byron's *Bolivar* and its subsequent history under the Blessingtons, nor about the yacht at anchor off Lady Butler's villa in Sorrento. What we do know has to

6   She may well have been longer, possibly 60 ft or so.
7   M. Sadlier *The Strange Life of Lady Blessington*
http://extra.shu.ac.uk/corvey/database/authors/datab/blessington/aabless/aablessbio.htm#10
8   Dixon Kemp *A Manual of Yacht and Boat Sailing* H. Cox 1895

be gleaned from accounts that mostly dwell on the life of the rich and often eccentric characters of the time and make some mention of the yachts they sailed to and around the Mediterranean.

Sir James Brooke and the *Royalist*

One of the earliest Victorian yachts to cruise the Mediterranean that we know something about was the *Royalist*, and she was doing a Mediterranean circuit as a training run for an expedition to the East Indies. The *Royalist* was built as a gentleman's yacht in 1834 in Cowes. She was around 80 ft long, 142 tons, and rigged as a topsail schooner.[9] *Royalist* was bought in 1836 by Sir James Brooke with an inheritance of £30,000, something over £3,000,000 today, left by his father. In 1837 he cruised the Mediterranean in preparation for a circumnavigation and exploration of the East Indies in hope of trade, probably with a little privateering on the side. We know only a little about the Mediterranean cruise and it is only briefly mentioned, much as an afterthought, in his letters and journals.[10]

Royalist project design by Michael Kasten.

The *Royalist* went first to Gibraltar and then hopped across to Malta where he based the boat for a cruise around the eastern Mediterranean. After doing a circuit of the eastern Mediterranean Brooke then sailed back to Spain. A book put together by a descendant much later in the 19th century is a collection of the journals and log and letters he subsequently wrote in England after the cruise, so it is a bit of a jumble to sort out what happened when and where. Once back in Spain his journal describes a journey on horseback to Grenada

9   Much of the history and information on the *Royalist* can be found on Michael Kasten's *Yacht Design* site where a project to build a replica of the *Royalist* was proposed to him. There are a lot of other interesting projects unrelated to this book on the site as well. www.kastenmarine. com/25m_schooner_royalist.htm

10   Gertrude R Jacob *The Raja of Sarawak* MacMillan 1876 p 61

to visit the Alhambra, but little else about the voyage apart from a gale in Biscay that whisked them back to England. Once in England he makes a mention of Asia Minor in a letter to a Mr Cruickshank.

A description of the wandering was sent by Brooke to Mr. Cruickshank on July 6th. 'Have you heard or can you guess where I have been? Spain, Greece, Turkey, Europe, Asia and Africa, all of which are combined in a very limited space in the Mediterranean. I have visited the most interesting places in the world, and made a cruise of a novel and classic nature on the coast of Asia Minor. We sailed in the winter to visit all the remains of the cities of the Ionian and Carian Leagues, amongst them Ephesus, Cnidus, Halicarnassus, and Rhodes. We found statues, carried away inscriptions, broke open tombs, traced

Sir James Brooke.
Painting by Francis Grant.

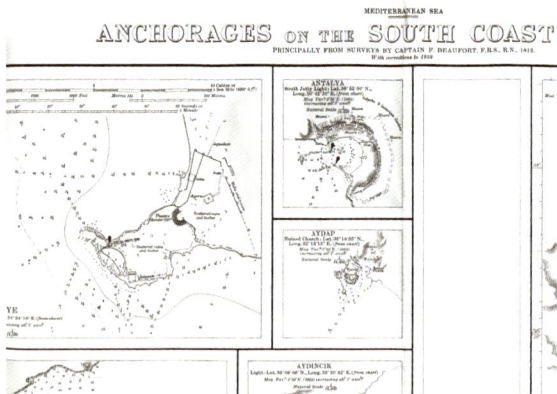

temples, etc., etc., all in a country as wild as even I could desire. It is impossible to write all these things in a letter, but you shall, if you care, and if you will take the trouble, read my bookie upon these matters. Even in that land, so close to civilized Europe, we penetrated into places quite unknown to modern times and modern charts.'

Jacob *The Raja of Sarawak* p 64

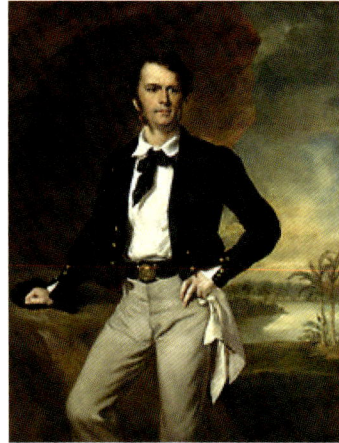

Portion of the chart surveyed by Francis Beaufort in 1812 and still issued by the Admiralty in the late 20th century..

Charts for Asia Minor are still not the most accurate to this day and he was possibly using some of the Admiralty charts surveyed by Francis Beaufort when he was there in 1811–1812. The charts for Kekova and nearby anchorages on the southeastern coast of Turkey that were still issued by the Admiralty with the original 1812 date on them up to a few years ago are possibly the

charts he used.[11] I have used the same charts to navigate around the area and, while they are a wonderful cartographic feat of the time, there are still errors that can confound the yachtsman cruising there to this day.

11   Rod & Lucinda Heikell *Turkish Waters and Cyprus Pilot* 10th ed. Imray, 2018

What we do know of the *Royalist* is that she was fairly typical of her era. Even though she was built as a yacht, she was also armed and not untypical of small naval vessels of the time. In Brookes' journals and letters, he proudly describes his vessel like this:

The Royalist, as already noticed, belonged to the Royal Yacht Squadron, which in foreign ports admits her to the same privileges as a man-of-war, and enables her to carry a white ensign. She sails fast, is conveniently fitted up, is armed with six six-pounders, a number of swivels, and small arms of all sorts, carries four boats, and provisions for four months... She is withal a good sea-boat, and as well calculated for the service as could be desired.

Jacob *The Raja of Sarawak* p 90

Recently there was a project to build a replica of the *Royalist* and the marine architect, Michael Kasten, looked at other yachts of this period for his inspiration and has this to say about his project to build the replica:

To assist in this 'discovery' process, my first task was to research the tops'l schooners of the period which had been built as yachts, both in the United Kingdom and in the US. They were at that time very much the same on both sides of the Atlantic. Though many vessels of that period were built as 'yachts' many of them were also employed by the Royal Navy as messenger boats and quasi-privateers. In other words, in exchange for certain privileges, these vessels were at the service of the crown.

www.kastenmarine.com/25m_schooner_royalist.htm

Records indicate that many of the yachts racing in British waters at the time and later were topsail schooners; only later did gaff-rigged schooners arrive on the scene. Byron's yacht, the *Bolivar*, built in Genoa, was a topsail schooner built to a British design under the supervision of Captain Roberts. Later in the 19th century large gaff-rigged cutters became more common and the schooner rig less common, though there were still advocates of the schooner rig for a cruising yacht right up into the Edwardian period.

Sir Thomas Acland and the *Lady of St Kilda*

In many ways the *Lady of St Kilda* was similar to the *Royalist*. She was 136 tons, around 70 ft long (21.3 metres), and like the *Royalist* was rigged as a topsail schooner. She had originally been built to carry fruit back from the Azores to Britain and was built for speed along the lines of the tea clippers plying the route between China and Britain. She was bought by Sir Thomas Acland, a rich Devon landowner with substantial interests in shipping, who

was so smitten by her lines that he had
her converted to a yacht and made several
cruises to the Mediterranean.

There is no account of her cruises, but
records of expenditure and some notes
from the log remain.[12] The first cruise in
early summer 1835 was to visit his son in
Lisbon and the second, later in the year, to
spend the winter in the Mediterranean.

THE YACHT "LADY OF ST. KILDA."
From a pencil sketch in the possession of the Trustees of the Melbourne Public Library.

Pencil sketch of the *Lady of
St Kilda*.

Sir Thomas, a headlong enthusiast in any interest which he embraced, became vice-
commodore of the Royal Western Yacht Club 1834–1838, commodore 1838–1842, and a
member of the Royal Yacht Squadron from 1834. In 1834 he purchased Lady of St. Kilda,
named after his wife who, in 1810, had been the first titled lady to visit that island, and, with
his family, circumnavigated England and Scotland, re-visiting St. Kilda. In 1835 he made two
voyages. The first, in early summer to Lisbon, Cadiz, and Gibraltar, had the main objective
of a visit to his son, a naval officer stationed at Lisbon. Lady returned to England in early
August for a family wedding, and the family left again on 3 October 1835 to winter in the
Mediterranean, partly to enable a daughter in poor health to spend a Mediterranean winter,
returning in September 1836.

Cusack *Nineteenth-Century Cruising Yachtsmen* p 63

The party spent three months in Rome while the yacht went to Malta for
maintenance and repairs. This little episode is interesting because the boatyards
in England charged more for labour and materials than the yards overseas in
somewhere like Malta and consequently English boatyards were missing out
on repair work to yachts that cruised the Mediterranean. Complaints were
made to the government and the Royal Yacht Squadron issued an edict as
Janet Cusack describes:

Sir Thomas was one of the last Royal Yacht Squadron members to get cheap repair work
at Malta, as in May 1837, following complaints, made by the Government, of yachts being
taken to foreign ports 'for the purpose of undergoing extensive repairs, or being fitted with
foreign stores', the Royal Yacht Squadron Committee forbade the practice and resolved that
'any member so offending [is] to be removed from the list of members'.

Cusack *Nineteenth-Century Cruising Yachtsmen* pp 70–71

The *Lady of St Kilda* returned to Britain in 1836 and was sold in 1841 to a
Plymouth syndicate in which the main player was the prominent Melbourne-
based merchant, Jonathan Binns. She was sailed out to Australia and based

12   Cusack *Nineteenth-Century Cruising Yachtsmen* p 62

The Earl of Cavan and the *Roseneath*

In *With the Yacht, Camera, & Cycle in the Mediterranean*, the Earl of Cavan described a cruise he made in 1894 on the 200 ton schooner *Roseneath* with a steam-powered auxiliary engine. His book is typical of several of the period and reflects the ideas of the well-heeled aristocracy and what they considered to be the proper way to go cruising. In the appendix to his book he has this to say on a proper yacht suitable for cruising the Mediterranean:

Two or three strong, good masts, in proportion to the size of the vessel – masts, I mean, upon which leg of mutton sails of tanned or waterproof canvas could be set – will be necessary of course … These sails should give her a stability at sea, which the majority of our Mediterranean yachts sadly require. With so many interesting ports at easy distances the one from the other, the whole way between Gibraltar and Constantinople, there can be no reason for going at a speed exceeding ten knots, which speed could easily be obtained under steam and sail. The dislike to going afloat would thus be much lessened in the minds of those who may not be good sailors, their comfort also would be enormously increased, and providing that time is not of overwhelming importance, I am certain that owners at the end of their cruise, will feel more satisfied with yachts such as I have described, than they could be with any greyhound-built vessel, of which such numbers are now to be seen in the Mediterranean. …As to the size of the vessel, she should certainly not be less than 150 tons. As to how large she should be, must, of course, depend upon the means at the disposal of the owner, and the purposes for which he requires her.

Earl of Cavan *With the Yacht, Camera, and Cycle in the Mediterranean* Sampson Low, Marston & Co, 1895 p 82–83

The Earl spent two years cruising the Mediterranean and the book details his cruise on the *Roseneath*. His party consisted of four ladies, including his

The Earl of Cavan and ladies on the Roseneath. Photo in *With the Yacht, Camera and Cycle in the Mediterranean*.

daughter Ellen and a friend, Olive, who took the remarkably crisp photos in the book. All of them, it seems, had to be able to play a musical instrument and have more than a passing interest in opera. The *Roseneath* had a piano in the saloon and this was not uncommon on other large yachts, where it seems a piano was an essential piece of equipment for a cruising yacht. The party joined the yacht

The *Roseneath* in her winter quarters for shooting in Albania.
Photo in *With the Yacht, Camera and Cycle in the Mediterranean.*

in Gibraltar, arriving on a P&O steamer, the *Ormuz*, because the *Roseneath* was only 200 tons and not the sort of boat to cross the Bay of Biscay in: 'We are all agreed as to what we will not do' the Earl emphatically stated.

While the yacht had a main saloon with a piano, cabins for the owner and ladies and other passengers, a galley, a water closet and other home comforts, it was nowhere near as capacious as a modern yacht of this size. At 200 tons I'd guess the length of the *Roseneath* to be around 130 ft or so. The boilers and steam engine would have taken up a considerable amount of space, perhaps one quarter to one third of the volume of the hull if you include coal bunkers. Add to this the cabins and mess room needed

Visiting Sir William Scott's *Christine* in Pagania on the Greek – Albania border. Photo in *With the Yacht, Camera and Cycle in the Mediterranean.*

for a captain and mate, an engineer and mate, perhaps ten crew, a cook and assistant, and at least a couple of servants for the party, and you have taken up yet more volume. Stores need to be carried and spare sails and other spares stowed on board. This would likely leave around one third of the yacht for the fitting out of the accommodation for the owner and party.[21] On the 83 ton yacht, *Wave*, built in 1848, Janet Cusack has this to say on the owner's accommodation:

The use of the thirty feet of hull left for the main accommodation was planned with considerable ingenuity to include four cabins, a saloon, steward's pantry, and two water closets. Saloon furniture included fireplace and piano (both unlikely to be found in a modern yacht), and space was found for a desk, library, second bookcase, and sideboard, while sofa seats and extra bedplaces extended the passenger capacity. Smoking was obviously not acceptable in the main public area, and a smoking room is designated (rather surprisingly) in the sail store.

Cusack *Nineteenth-Century Cruising Yachtsmen* p 49

The Earl and his party cruised the Mediterranean from Gibraltar to Constantinople. They made frequent excursions ashore and the Earl recommends various hotels and contacts for anyone visiting these areas. En route they went grouse shooting in Albania, shot a wild boar weighing over 250 lbs/113 kg (there is a photo of the beast hanging off the side of the *Roseneath*), visited numerous archaeological sites in Sicily and around the Aegean, before returning to Gibraltar where they took a steamer back to Britain after

250 lb boar shot in Albania and hanging off the *Roseneath*. Photo in *With the Yacht, Camera and Cycle in the Mediterranean*.

a full two years of life on board. In his advice to others contemplating a cruise on a yacht in the Mediterranean he has this to say:

… first-class yacht-racing, gambling, and luxuries can only be found on the South Coast of France, and a winter can be enjoyed very luxuriously between the ports of Gibraltar and Genoa. Shooting can be obtained on the coasts of Asia Minor, some of the Greek or Ionian

21   See Cusack *Nineteenth-Century Cruising Yachtsmen* pp 49–51

Islands, and Albania. Lions cannot now be found within a day's rail of any yacht anchorage in North Africa… My readers may take my word for it, that if they anchor anywhere along the coast of North Africa, and then give up ten days to travel in pursuit of lions, they will be unusually lucky if they return with one good specimen.

Earl of Cavan p 43–44

Ptarmigan

In *Sketches of a Yachting Cruise*,[22] Major Gambier Parry describes a cruise in the Mediterranean in the late 1880's on board *Ptarmigan*, a 180 ton schooner. This year-long cruise was somewhat different to that of the *Roseneath*, as the *Ptarmigan* had no auxiliary power and consequently was entirely dependent on the wind to get about. This led to a few hairy moments, as the major describes, when the *Ptarmigan* came down the Evia Channel and through the narrow gap at Khalkis in Greece. The channel has been known for its fierce tidal currents since antiquity and tradition has it that Aristotle flung himself into the channel because he couldn't explain the phenomenon.[23] It has been spanned by a movable bridge since antiquity which opens at slack water, or as near to slack water as you get here, to let craft through the narrow gap.[24]

… the difficulty was to prevent the yacht getting broadside on to the stream, all the way she had on her being due to the force of the current. The launch steamed away vigorously, but with small effect, and, before we could stop her, the yacht twisted right round. A warp was at once got out and made fast to a vessel anchored below us, and

Major Gambier Parry and *Ptarmigan* outward bound to the Mediterranean.
Illustration in *Sketches of a Yachting Cruise*.

22   Major Gambier Parry *Sketches of a Yachting Cruise* W H Allen, 1889
23   Aristotle likely died of a stomach complaint just outside Athens.
24   Rod & Lucinda Heikell *West Aegean* Imray 2014 pp 235–237

for half an hour all hands had to work hard to prevent the yacht from going aground. As if to warn us of what we might expect, three vessels were lying hard and fast on the rocks not fifty yards off …

Major Gambier Parry *Sketches of a Yachting Cruise* W H Allen, 1889 p 201

I've been through the narrow channel at Khalkis numerous times with an engine and it's still a nail-biting exercise. The *Roseneath* could have steamed through, though from other descriptions it does appear that some steam-powered coasters had come to grief in the narrows. The major goes on to describe how they were often becalmed and there was nothing for it but to wait for wind while steamers in the distance ploughed on through the calm weather.

The *Roseneath* and the *Ptarmigan* were schooner rigged but with gaff-rigged sails on the masts. Square sails on the topmasts had been abandoned and a gaff topsail was hoisted above the gaff mainsail. One thing the *Ptarmigan* had over the *Roseneath* is more commodious accommodation, since it did not have bulky steam boilers installed nor bunkers for coal. You needed to be somewhat more of a purist to sail the *Ptarmigan* and to be thoroughly proficient in

Ptarmigan negotiating the narrows at Khalkis. Illustration in *Sketches of a Yachting Cruise.*

your seamanship and pilotage in strange waters. The major evidently had these qualities and right at the very beginning of his book tells us that 'There is a charm in yachting which, once experienced, never dies.'

One element that is starting to be defined here is the split between cruising yachts and racing yachts. Yacht racing had mushroomed in Britain, particularly in the Solent under the aegis of the Royal Yacht Squadron, and attitudes were diverging on what a 'proper' cruising yacht should be as opposed to the sort of yachts bound by rating rules in the racing fleets. The debate could be acrimonious at times and the various racing yachts that sailed down for the yacht racing in the south of France were often criticised as unseaworthy and uncomfortable for a long cruise in the Mediterranean. What was also apparent was the split between sailing yachts and steam yachts, as more and more of the latter cruised the Mediterranean to the distress of the sailing purists. The major on *Ptarmigan* looked on the whole affair with some sadness.

> … the quiet of a sailing vessel is now, to the traveller, almost a thing of the past, and the majority of yachts, even cruising in foreign waters, are steamers. It is the influence of the times. We are no longer satisfied with any element of uncertainty in our travels… and thus we annihilate distance and economise time, but the romance of travel becomes more and more a thing of the past.
>
> Parry *Sketches of a Yachting Cruise* p 16

It's a sentiment many echo today.

Bringing Cowes to the Mediterranean

Around the western Mediterranean, a number of yacht clubs were established in enclaves in the south of France and the Riviera much visited by the British, and in several British naval bases, notably Malta and Gibraltar. The object of these clubs was largely to foster racing, and numbers of yachts would sail down from Britain in the spring to the Mediterranean to take part in races in the summer before returning in the autumn to the Solent. Most of the racing on the south coast of England was in the Solent, and the Royal Yacht Squadron was the prime mover for racing here and instrumental in devising the rating rules. The establishment of a national formula for rating rules for yacht racing did not happen until the late 19th century. Prior to this different clubs in different regions devised their own rules and it was not until 1875 that the Yacht Racing Association was formed, and codified sailing rules and a handicap system were introduced.[25] Bit by bit these rules were adopted by the clubs in the Mediterranean so that racing along the coast in the south of France was governed by rules much like those for racing in the Solent.

Royal Gibraltar Yacht Club

The Royal Gibraltar Yacht Club is one of the oldest in the Mediterranean and can trace its origins back to 1829. It was formed by two officers of a regiment

---

25   Dixon Kemp, the journalist and author, was instrumental in devising the rules and handicap system. See Dixon Kemp *A Manual of Yacht and Boat Sailing* 1895/2018, Forgotten Books reprint.

stationed here who had arrived by yacht in the same year. The *Gibraltar Chronicle* for June 25th, 1829 reported that two yachts had arrived in the port.

Eng. Cutter (yacht) 'Arrow', Commander McKenzie, 5 days from Cadiz and 2 from Tangier, for Gibraltar. Passengers Lieuts. Clarke and Bayley and Asst. Surgeon Gillice.

Eng. Cutter (yacht) 'Rover', Commander Tryon, 4 days from Cadiz and 2 from Tangier, for Gibraltar. Passengers Lieuts. Bell and Talbot and Asst. Surgeon Brown.

RGYC site http://www.rgyc.gi/history.php

Commander McKenzie and the Assistant Surgeon Gillice lost no time in forming the Gibraltar Yacht Club a month later and invited other officers in the garrison to join. This makes the club one of the oldest in the world outside of Britain. Peter Johnson records that research by the commodore of the club in 1929 '… believed it was the eighth in the world after the Cork, Thames, Squadron, Dee, Loch Long, Northern and Western.'[26] In 1837 it was awarded a warrant by the Admiralty '… authorising the vessels belonging to the Club to wear a St George's or White Ensign and a cornet or burgee', though in 1842 the warrant was withdrawn and the club adopted a defaced blue ensign.[27]

Société des Regates Cannes

The British started to come to the south of France and the Italian Riviera in the late 18th and early 19th centuries to escape the hard winters of Britain and to soak up the life-giving sun in the south. Typical of these was Lord Brougham who settled in Cannes, building the Villa Eleonore Louise, named after his daughter, who sadly died before it was finished. Cannes soon became his second home, as Patrick Howarth describes.

He regularly spent his winters there, writing books on politics, philosophy and history, and analysing the habits of bees. He found that in Cannes there were only three days out of 111 on which he could not carry out certain experiments with light which interested him, whereas at Brougham Hall in Westmorland at the same time of year, there were only about three days out of 111 on which he could.

Patrick Howarth *When the Riviera Was Ours* Century, p 19

Lord Brougham persuaded several of his friends to move to Cannes and build villas there, so that by the time he died in 1868, the population had increased from 3,000 to 10,000. One of the important changes to Cannes for which Lord Brougham was responsible was the construction of the harbour. He

26   Peter Johnson *Yacht Clubs of the World* Waterline Books 1994 p 53
27   RGYC site http://www.rgyc.gi/history.php

was a good friend of King Louis-Philippe and in 1840 persuaded the king to provide funds for its construction. In 1859 a society for organising yachting regattas was formed, naturally enough with Lord Brougham as president, and in 1860 the first regatta was held. Cannes was given, rather patronisingly, the title of the 'Cowes of the Mediterranean' and became a popular port of call for yachts cruising the Mediterranean. However, the harbour was still not entirely safe. Guy de Maupassant, cruising in his beloved *Bel-Ami*, called Cannes '... a dangerous port, unsheltered ... where all vessels are in peril'. It was later modified and given better protection and Lord Cavan, after a lengthy Mediterranean cruise, gave it the thumbs up.

This harbour has been greatly improved during the last three or four years. Only four years ago, when I stayed there, it was not uncommon to find yachts moored with their sterns on the mole, laying side by side with one, or possibly two colliers discharging coal. All this has been greatly improved; yachts now have their separate berths, as the mole has been considerably extended.

Earl of Cavan *With the Yacht, Camera, & Cycle in the Mediterranean* p 59

A new mole was built in 1904 and named the Jetée Albert-Edouard in honour of the Prince of Wales, a regular visitor to Cannes, who brought his yacht down for the summer season of racing. Further along the coast at Monaco, Nice and Menton, there was also a summer season of Mediterranean racing and Prince Albert attended these in the last yacht he had designed and built, *Britannia*, launched in 1893. *Britannia* was a 220 ton gaff-rigged cutter, 120 ft (37 metres) long, designed by George Lennox Watson[28] and a near sister ship to the Watson designed *Valkyrie II* which challenged for the America's Cup in 1893. After winning twenty-four of the forty-three races she entered in home waters, Prince Albert decided to take *Britannia* to the Mediterranean for the summer racing season there.[29]

Britannia's second season began early with a passage across the Bay of Biscay, round the Rock of Gibraltar and into the Mediterranean to enter the increasingly popular series of races that were held along the French Riviera. In contrast to his attendance of UK events, The Prince of Wales did not rely on the support of the Royal Yacht Osborne during Britannia's tour of the Cote D'Azur. Instead, he lived onboard Britannia while competing in the regattas hosted by Cannes, Monaco, Mentone and Nice.

Paper by Richard Johnstone-Bryden *The Royal Sailing Yachts* p 3

28   He also designed the RNLI lifeboats that were popularly called the 'Watson lifeboats'.
29   Paper by Richard Johnstone-Bryden *The Royal Sailing Yachts* p 2

Britannia off Cowes. Wiki Commons.

Britannia was duly inherited by King George V who became so attached to the yacht he requested that it be sunk after his death. It was duly scuttled off St Katherine's Point on the Isle of Wight in 1936.

Along with Cannes, the Société des Régates of Monaco was another popular racing venue. The Société des Régates was established in 1888 by Prince Charles III and his son Prince Albert, although racing in the Bay of Monaco was recorded as early as 1862.[30] Later in the 20th century, Monaco became a magnet for the rich and famous, including Aristotle Onassis, and the inevitable entourage of followers and hangers-on who gravitated to a port crammed with superyachts.[31]

Regio Yacht Club Italiano

Established in Genoa in 1879 on the initiative of Augusto Vittorio Vecchi, its first president, and a group of sailing enthusiasts, the club was formed to

30   www.yacht-club-monaco
31   See Chapter 11, The Rich and the Super-rich, Part I: Greek Tragedy.

promote yachting and yacht racing. At the far end of the Italian Riviera and consequently not far from the clubs at Cannes and Nice, it was the first Italian club on the Mediterranean. Italy was a comparative latecomer to yachting and to the establishment of yacht clubs. The harbours on the Italian coast were largely for poor fishing communities, and royalty and the aristocracy were late into the yachting scene compared to Britain and France.[32]

The Italians had a champion in Augusto Vittorio Vecchi, who was not only the driving force behind the formation of the Regio Yacht Club Italiano, but also behind the formation of the Lega Navale Italiana in La Spezia in 1897, the forerunner of all the Lega Navales dotted around the Italian coast today. The club had august beginnings.

Its main purpose was to 'take positive actions to promote our military and merchant navy, propagate a seafaring spirit in Italy and the love for things related to the sea, and favour any measure that aims to promote the Italian marine industry.' To meet its goal the association established decentralized sections in Naples, Venice and Genoa, as well as in hinterland centres such as Milan and Turin, to promote seafaring culture through a nationwide presence.

Piccinno and Zanini *The Development of Pleasure Boating and Yacht Harbours in the Mediterranean* p 86

Despite the promulgations of the Lega Navale, it would be some time before yachting became popular in Italy. Not until after the Second World War would Italians embrace yachting with the fervour they do today.

Royal Malta Yacht Club

The Royal Malta Yacht Club has had its ups and downs over the years. According to the history of the club there may have been a cruising club here as early as 1835. In 1873 a royal warrant was issued to the club, which was then mainly composed of officers and others serving in the British naval base on Malta. By the early 1890's the club had virtually ceased to exist. In 1896 the Rhoda Sailing Club was formed. During World War I the club was once again in abeyance and not until 1921 did it re-form, finally becoming the Royal Malta Yacht Club again in 1928.[33]

---

32   Luisa Piccinno and Andrea Zanini *The Development of Pleasure Boating and Yacht Harbours in the Mediterranean Sea: The Case of the Riviera* Ligure International Journal of Maritime History June, 2010 pp 84–86.
33   www.rmyc.org/about-rmyc/history/

There can be little doubt that despite all the ups and downs of the club there was much cruising going on here and many of the accounts of cruising in the Mediterranean in the 19th century mention stopovers in Malta. In fact, the Rhoda Sailing Club was originally formed by a syndicate who cruised in a 30 ton cutter, the *Rhoda*. Only later did the club begin to organise yacht racing.[34] Today it organises the popular Middle Sea Race from Grand Harbour around Sicily, Stromboli and the Egadi Islands back to Malta.

Dockyard Creek and Kalkara Creek in Malta – a popular spot for yachts for two centuries and more. Photo Malta Tourism Authority.

34   www.rmyc.org/about-rmyc/history/

STEAM YACHT NAMOUNA.

The Property of James Gordon Bennett, Esq.

Gordon Bennett Jr's steam yacht '*Namouna*'. Painting by Charles Parsons.

8 THE AMERICANS ARE COMING

Sailing for pleasure quite possibly started in America in the late 17th century when the burghers of New Amsterdam, in the New World, began taking workboats out for picnics and short excursions around Long Island Sound. Although the evidence is scant, it is likely that some prosperous merchants fitted out local workboats with some home comforts and, though it may be difficult to call them yachts, still a tradition was growing such that a print by William Burgis from 1717 showed yachts sailing in New York Harbour with a description which mentions the yacht *Fancy* turning to windward. In the Memorial History of New York there appears the following description of the period.

Racing on the water was not much in fashion, though the gentry had their barges, and some their yachts or pleasure sail-boats… the most noted yacht was the Fancy belonging to Colonel Lewis Morris, whose Morrisania Manor, on the peaceful waters of the Sound, gave fine harbour and safe opportunity for sailing.

Quoted in Douglas Phillips-Birt *The History of Yachting* Stein & Day 1974 p 33

The American tradition of yachting evolved in tandem with that in Europe, though there are clear differences in the design and build of many American yachts. Most of them were still built along the lines of working boats used for fishing and transport, just as they were in Europe. However American design soon favoured a harder turn of the bilge and a finer entry than British yachts. Other innovations like the centreboard were pioneered in America in the early 1800's, where sailboats had to negotiate and anchor in shallow water. In 1851 when the schooner *America* visited the Solent to race against the cream of the English big boat fleet and won the race around the Isle of Wight, it was well and truly drubbed into the British that the American design of the hull, rigging and sails on the *America* were well advanced, producing a boat that was fast, handy and seaworthy –

The schooner *America* off the New York Yacht Club. Oswald W. Brierly.

it had, after all, sailed across the Atlantic. After the *America* won the race, the cup awarded became known as the America's Cup. It remains the oldest international sporting trophy in the world still competed for; it would remain in America for the next 132 years until Australia finally wrested the cup from the New York Yacht Club in 1983.[1]

The Americans, always keen to visit decadent and ailing Europe, sailed a number of large yachts across to the Mediterranean, sometimes with odd notions about the object of the cruise. The first American yacht, arguably the first private yacht to cross the Atlantic and cruise the Mediterranean, was *Cleopatra's Barge* in 1816. Others followed later in the century, but it is George Crowninshield's *Cleopatra's Barge* and Gordon Bennett's *Lysistrata* I'll look at here. Both yachts were owned by eccentric owners who indulged their whims and tastes in odd ways; two different owners with eccentric notions, yet in many ways so similar.

There is one coda here of a yachtsman of an entirely different ilk who nearly cruised his yacht in the Mediterranean. Joshua Slocum in his beloved 36 ft (11 metre) sloop *Spray* dropped anchor in Gibraltar on August 4th, 1895, after a fast passage from Boston via the Azores. His intention was to sail through the Mediterranean, but he was warned not to do this.

MONDAY, August 25, the Spray sailed from Gibraltar, well repaid for whatever deviation she had made from a direct course to reach the place. A tug belonging to her Majesty towed the sloop into the steady breeze clear of the mount, where her sails caught a violent wind, which carried her once more to the Atlantic, where it rose rapidly to a furious gale. My plan was, in going down this coast, to haul offshore, well clear of the land, which hereabouts is the home of pirates; but I had hardly accomplished this when I perceived a felucca making out of the nearest port, and finally following in the wake of the Spray. Now, my course to Gibraltar had been taken with a view to proceed up the Mediterranean Sea, through the Suez Canal, down the Red Sea, and east about, instead of a western route, which I finally adopted. By officers of vast experience in navigating these seas, I was influenced to make the change. Longshore pirates on both coasts being numerous, I could not afford to make light of the advice.

Joshua Slocum *Sailing Alone Around the World* Epub Gutenberg Foundation. First published 1900 p 34

Far be it from me to comment on the great Slocum's decisions, but numbers of yachts were cruising the Barbary Coast at this time, stopping in Morocco, Algeria, Tunisia, Libya and Egypt. Mind you, none of the accounts are

---

1   The America's Cup was originally called the Hundred Guinea Cup and was renamed after the *America* won it in a race around the Isle of Wight.

from a singlehanded sailor on a 36 ft yacht without auxiliary power and I guess the perception of where to sail to is radically different when viewed from the deck of a small boat compared to the view from the deck of a fully crewed little ship. Joshua Slocum went on to make the first singlehanded circumnavigation of the globe and his book, *Sailing Alone Around the World*, became an international best seller.

George Crowninshield, Jr and *Cleopatra's Barge*

Cleopatra's Barge[2] is often cited as the first American yacht and, while it is clear she was not the first yacht in America (think of *Fancy* in the print by Burgis from 1717) the boat that George Crowninshield, Jr had built in Salem, Massachusetts was the first luxury yacht built solely as a yacht. Although the hull is typical of trading boats of the time, a bluff-bowed square-topped schooner rig,[3] her interior was anything but work-a-day. *Cleopatra's Barge* was 100 ft (30 metres) overall and weighed in at around 190 tons.[4]

Down below no expense was spared on fitting her out: the cabins were spacious with ornate inlaid panelled walls and ceilings; sofas were ornately carved with lyres on the back and covered in fine velvet and gold braid; the finest chinaware, glassware and silver service was produced specially for the yacht; velvet grab-lines were strung throughout the cabins and each cabin had an ornate fireplace; overall the fitting out of the yacht was of over-the-top sumptuous furniture in the Napoleonic style

Cleopatra's Barge. Painting by George Ropes 1818. Wiki Commons.

and it was no secret that the owner greatly admired Bonaparte.[5] The outside was just as eccentric, with stripes along one side of the hull and a herringbone pattern on the other. Twelve cannons were carried on deck, though given the deck layout it is unlikely they would all have been of use as they were

---

2   It was originally named *Car of Concordia* but was changed to *Cleopatra's Barge* before it was launched.

3   A square-topped schooner commonly called a Hermaphrodite rig. From pictures of her she carried squaresails on the foremast and a gaff rig on the main mast.

4   Phillips-Birt *The History of Yachting* p 33.

5   There is a mock-up of the interior of *Cleopatra's Barge* at the Peabody Essex Museum in the USA.

obstructed by various fittings including a wooden statue of an Indian chief set on deck to supervise.

The owner of this unusual yacht was George Crowninshield, Jr, the flamboyant son of a prosperous merchant and mariner in Salem, Massachusetts. The cost of construction was reputed to be $50,000 and the opulent fitting out of the yacht another $50,000, something over three million dollars today. Just why George built the Cleopatra's Barge is not really known, though he was considered to be something of a dandy and did describe the object of his cruise to be 'a voyage of amusement and travel in the Mediterranean'.6 He appointed his cousin Benjamin Crowninshield as captain and brought along his son, also called Benjamin, to record the voyage and paint watercolours along the way.

The cruise across the Atlantic got underway once the ice had melted in Salem harbour and *Cleopatra's Barge* reached Horta on Faial Island in the Azores on April 24th, 1817. He carried on to Madeira, Gibraltar, Barcelona and Marseille, where the ship was repainted and repairs were carried out. He then cruised along the French and Italian Rivieras to Italy and down to the Tuscan Islands, Civitavecchia, and to Rome and Naples. In many ways *Cleopatra's Barge* was a forerunner of today's superyachts touring the French and Italian Rivieras where gawping crowds would flock to see this opulent arrival in port. Unlike today's superyacht owners who want nothing to do with the hoi-polloi, George welcomed the public on board, and it is reported that in Barcelona some 8000 people were given a tour of the yacht during her stay.7

There was an undercurrent to George Crowninshield's voyage to the Mediterranean that I touched on earlier: his admiration of Napoleon Bonaparte. Napoleon had escaped from Elba in 1815 and, landing in France, began the Hundred Days rule culminating in the Battle of Waterloo where he was finally defeated by Wellington and the British and Prussian forces. Fleeing to Paris and then to the south of France, it was known Napoleon wanted to seek refuge in America. The British navy blockaded the south of France and Napoleon eventually surrendered to the British and was taken to

6   *The Story of George Crowninshield's Yacht Cleopatra's Barge. On a Voyage of Pleasure to the Western Islands and the Mediterranean 1816–1817 Compiled from Journals, Letters and Logbooks by Francis B. Crowninshield.* Boston: Hathi Foundation, 1913 p 16
7   Phillips-Birt *The History of Yachting* p 34

England before being exiled to the island of St Helena in the South Atlantic. Did George Crowninshield believe he could help Napoleon and rescue him from St Helena? One story told is that he wished to rescue Napoleon's wife, the Empress Marie Louise who was ensconced in Rome, and take her to the erstwhile Emperor exiled on St Helena in the middle of the Atlantic. As it turned out, Marie Louise was quite happy in Rome with a large part of the fortune amassed by Napoleon and a lover to help her spend it – she declined the offer. It is known that he visited some of Napoleon's supporters on Elba and met Napoleon's mother who had moved from Corsica to Rome. They were also visited by the captain of the French brig *Inconstant*, along with Napoleon's doctor, who had spirited Napoleon from Elba in 1815.[8]

George Crowninshield returned to Salem in *Cleopatra's Barge* and died unexpectedly just six weeks after arriving. The yacht was then sold to another Crowninshield and stripped of her finery which was sold at auction.[9] She was then used to carry cargo around the eastern seaboard of America until, in 1821, she was sold again and made a voyage to Hawaii. In a bizarre twist, she was bought by the King of Hawaii, King Kamehameha II, who renamed her *Ha'aheo o Hawaii* (*Pride of Hawaii*) and used her as the royal flagship of the islands. It is not known whether she was again refitted as a yacht. Sadly, she was lost, allegedly by her drunken mate, on a reef in April 1824.[10]

Reconstruction of the saloon in *Cleopatra's Barge* in the Peabody Museum, Salem Massachusetts.

8   www.wavetrain.net/boats-a-gear/484-cruising-sailboat-evolution-cleopatras-barge
9   The amounts realised from the sale were a fraction of the original cost. See the introduction to *The Story of George Crowninshield's Yacht Cleopatra's Barge*.
10   Prof. W. D. Alexander ,*The Story of Cleopatra's Barge* Papers of the Hawaiian Historical Society No. 13, 1906.

Gordon Bennett, Jr

Wandering around the harbour town of Beaulieu on the French Riviera you will come across a street named in honour of the proprietor of the *New York Herald*, James Gordon Bennett. Bennett spent much of his life in Europe between Paris and Beaulieu where he lived in the Villa Namouna – that is, when he was not on his yacht, also called *Namouna*, and later on his subsequent yacht *Lysistrata*. It's no surprise that the phrase 'Gordon Bennett' was adopted into the English language as an exclamation for anything outrageous. Gordon Bennett, Jr was as eccentric as they come and fabulously rich to boot.

His father, James Gordon Bennett, Sr, arrived in the USA penniless from Scotland and founded the *New York Herald* in 1835. He soon built the paper into something along the lines of today's tabloids with juicy and sensational news at a cheap cover price. It's said that he once told a young reporter that 'the object of the modern newspaper is not to instruct, but to startle and amuse'.[11] Not surprisingly, Bennett, Sr had quite a few detractors, especially in high society America where he delighted in exposing lurid tales of the rich and famous. Worried about the disapproval that might come down on his son from the reporting in his paper he sent him off to Paris to be safe from retaliation and to acquire an education if he could. Bennett, Jr arrived back in the USA in a 77 ton yacht his father had given him, the *Rebecca*, and as a teenager started to make a splash on the New York scene. He was elected to the New York Yacht Club at age sixteen, the youngest member ever elected, and made something of a name for himself racing yachts around Long Island.

Bennett, Jr put most of today's generation of 'frat' kids to shame with his exploits in New York. Not for nothing was he known as 'The Mad Commodore': he liked to drive a coach and horses around the streets naked; was reputed to have urinated in his prospective father-in-law's fireplace in front of everyone while at dinner; and indulged in rabble-rousing drinking bouts with his friends which were the talk of the town. It was at one of these sessions that he made a bet with two of his drinking companions that his yacht, the *Henrietta*, was faster than the yachts of his two friends, the *Fleetwing* and the *Vesta*. *Henrietta* was a schooner-rigged yacht of around 205 tons while

11   Jenna Scherer *The Fabulously Eccentric Life of James Gordon Bennett, Jr.*
mentalfloss.com/article/64130/fabulously-eccentric-life-james-gordon-bennett-jr

the *Fleetwing* and Vesta were slightly larger. The bet was $30,000 each, winner take all, so $90,000: around three million dollars in today's money. The race was to be from New York across the Atlantic to the Needles off the Isle of Wight. For some reason they decided the yachts should race straight away even though it was winter, and the certainty was they would hit bad weather on the way. Bennett, Jr was the only owner to accompany his yacht, though he hired a captain for the race, one Samuel Samuels, with a reputation for driving a boat hard. The *Henrietta* won by a whisker and Bennett, Jr returned to continue his profligate ways in New York.[12] Winning the race convinced Bennett, Sr that his son had proved himself worthy of running the *New York Herald* and duly handed the helm over to his son.

Bennett, Jr also had a strange predilection for owls. In 1861 he had enlisted with the US Navy and took his yacht to patrol the waters of the eastern seaboard. The story goes that one night the hoot of an owl woke him and he went up on deck just in time to prevent the yacht running aground. Thereafter Bennett, Jr surrounded himself with owls: he ran newspaper articles on the preservation of owls; collected statuary and live owls; on his yacht *Lysistrata* an owl served as the figurehead; and he had bronze owls with glowing eyes arraigned along the top of the new headquarters for the *New York Herald* he had built in 1890.[13]

The incident with his prospective father-in-law, variously described as dinner with the family or at a fête they were attending, was the occasion for Bennett, Jr to leave New York and spend much of the rest of his life in Europe. Frederick May, the son of his prospective father-in-law, challenged him to a duel because of his unseemly behaviour and though pistols, and for that matter duels, were outlawed in many states and considered ungentlemanly in the others, nonetheless the duel took place. Fortunately, neither of them was hurt but a mortified Bennett, Jr decided to leave town.

He moved to Paris and then to the south of France. His first steam yacht, *Namouna*, 616 gross tons, was built at Newburgh, New York in 1882, though it spent much of its time in the Mediterranean. She is possibly named after the ballet *Namouna* by Edouard Lalo, premiered in 1882. At a guess from the

12   Phillips-Birt *The History of Yachting* p 199
13   Ross MacTaggart *The Golden Century: Classic Motor Yachts 1830–1930* W. W. Norton, 2001 pp 56–58

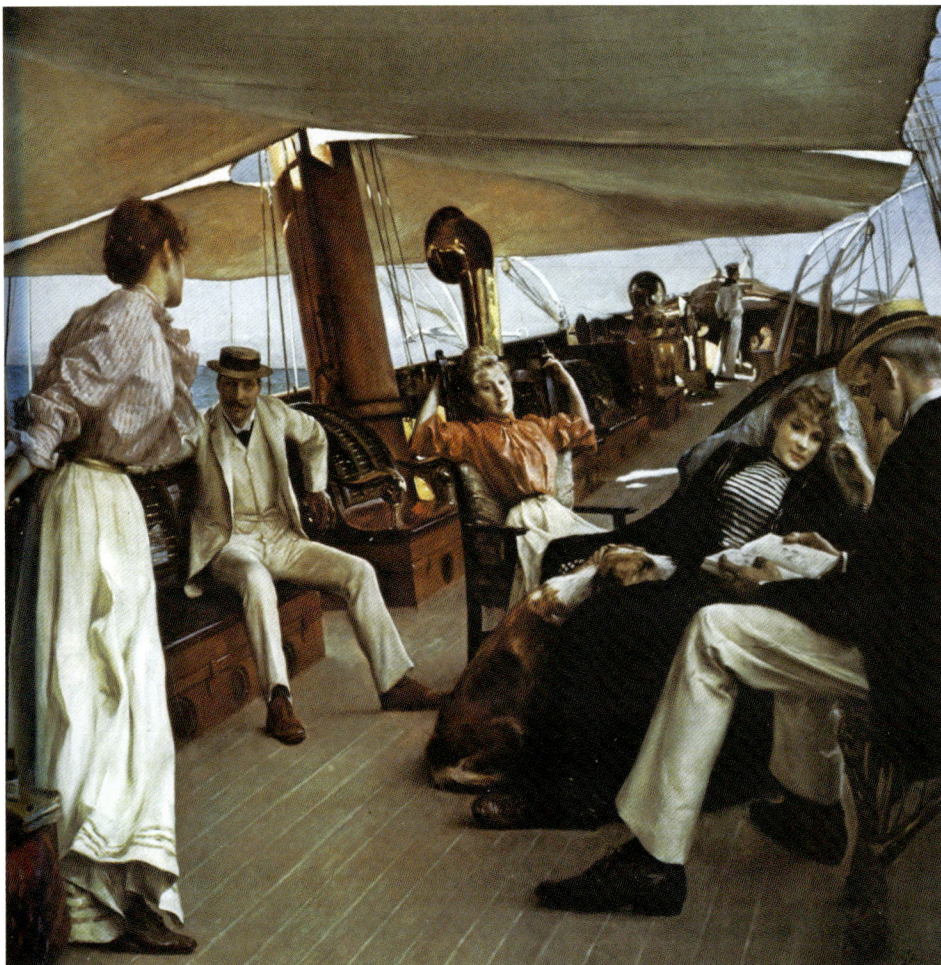

On the Yacht 'Namouna', Venice, by Julius LeBlanc Stewart 1890. Bennett is on the left of the picture in the white suit.

paintings, I'd say she is in the region of 200 ft long with a clipper bow and an elegant counter stern. She had three vestigial masts and the painting by Charles Parsons made at her launch shows sails furled on the booms of the masts. There is a painting by Julius L. Stewart showing guests on the aft deck of the *Namouna*, including quite possibly Gordon Bennett, Jr himself in a white suit and straw boater, sailing in the Adriatic.[14] You can't help but think that the boat is rolling somewhat, so that everyone is holding on or braced for

14   Phillips-Birt *The History of Yachting* p 153

the roll and heave of the boat. From this painting the beam of the *Namouna* appears to be quite narrow for a steam yacht of this length.

Bennett, Jr spent a lot of time on the yacht entertaining artists, painters including Julius L. Stewart, exiles and general hangers-on including, it is said, a young Winston Churchill. A bon vivant Bennett, Jr may have been, but he still ran the *Herald* in New York from his boat, working on stories and cables early in the morning in time to cable instructions back to New York. He also started the *Paris Herald*, which duly became the *International Herald Tribune*.

He took after his father in his search for spectacular stories, and one of his newspaper coups was to fund the expedition of Henry Morgan Stanley to look for the missing missionary Dr Livingstone in Africa. Stanley was a regular reporter for the *Herald* and Bennett, Jr packed him off in style with an armed guard and a small army of porters. It may be apocryphal, but the expedition was said to have been led by a flag-bearer with the flag of the New York Yacht Club flying proudly in the deepest jungle of Tanzania.[15]

In 1900 Bennett, Jr ordered a new yacht from the designer G. L. Watson. This was to be a monster, some 314 ft long (95.7 metres) and weighing in at 2800 tons. The twin-screw steam-powered yacht has been described as looking like a naval vessel with a plumb bow and turtledeck cover over the foredeck. A mast abaft the funnel was purely for signal flags and for flying courtesy flags and club burgees, though it did have a yard arm on it. The yacht cost something in the order of $650,000 to build, around $200 million in today's money. The *New York Times* had this to say on the new superyacht.

LONDON, March 16. – James Gordon Bennett's new steam yacht Lysistrata, designed by George L. Watson and built by W. Denny & Brothers, has just completed her trials, and is said to have given the greatest satisfaction to her owner, designer and builders. Over an eighty-five-knots course the Lysistrata showed a mean speed of 19½ knots, and without forced draught 16½ knots. The yacht handles admirably, has twin screws, and 6,500 horse power. During her high-speed trial the machinery acted faultlessly. There was no heating or complications of any kind, and so cool were the bearings at the end of the trial that the Chief Engineer said he was prepared to drive her another 300 miles without fear of the results.

The Lysistrata is destined to excite much comment when she appears completed in May. She is of 2800 tons, has a perfectly straight stem, has a storm deck fore and aft, a single huge funnel, with one mast abaft it, and one square yard for signalling purposes. The interior arrangements are quite unique, and generally speaking, she is unlike any yacht ever built. She

15   Scherer *The Fabulously Eccentric Life of James Gordon Bennett, Jr*

has no bowsprit, but a feature at the stern and bow are large owls with electric eyes, amid a scrollwork of mistletoe. More striking than all else in the yacht are the anchors, which are stockless, like those used on board warships, the shaft being drawn into the side of the ship. The hull has the appearance of being made out of a solid piece of metal, so highly is it polished and beautifully finished.

New York Times March 17, 1901

Lysistrata. Wiki Commons.

The *Lysistrata* was named after Aristophanes' bawdy play in which the women of Athens and Sparta conspire to refuse to have sex with their husbands until they stop fighting in the Peloponnesian War. Just why Bennett Jr named it thus is something of a mystery, but then the man himself was something of an enigma. The *Lysistrata* had all sorts of luxuries and amenities tailored to Bennett, Jr's tastes. She had opulently fitted saloons and cabins, a Turkish bath, several theatres, and a stall in the stern for a couple of Alderney cows to provide fresh milk. Owls, of course, dominated the décor, including an owl with flashing electric eyes on the bow and one at the stern. Bennett, Jr also had a steam launch built to accompany the *Lysistrata*.

The large steam launch *Sereda*, built to his order by Simpson Strickland at Dartmouth, 1890, in addition to a custom-built engine had 'fittings of a most luxurious description, she has plate glass all round. Special upholsterers from Paris are engaged on her interior decoration.'

Cusack *Nineteenth-Century Cruising Yachtsmen* p 51

Bennett's owl with glowing eyes on *Lysistrata*.
Photo Wiki Commons.

It was Gordon Bennett, Jr's eccentric habits that propelled his name into the English language as an exclamation of surprise or shock. Bennett, Jr's eccentricities became a byword in his own time. He abhorred playing cards and would have his crew and passengers' baggage searched for any offending pack. If he found a pack of cards, he extracted a sly revenge by taking out the four aces and throwing them away before returning the pack to the bag. He didn't like beards and no-one on board was allowed to have one. One of his newspaper editors who stubbornly refused to shave his beard off followed the boat from port to port until he finally resigned from the paper in disgust.

In one port, reputedly on the south coast of France, when a troupe of actors came aboard to perform a play, he was so delighted with their performance that he sailed off with them and would not return until they had performed their entire repertoire.

The dining room on *Lysistrata.*

On the back of *Lysistrata* he carried a car, reportedly a De Dion-Bouton, that would be craned ashore so he could drive around. Bennett, Jr organised one of the first car races, the Gordon Bennett Cup Race, a forerunner to Grand Prix racing, with four closed-circuit races in France and one each in Ireland

Namouna by Julius Le Blanc Stewart 1886. Bennett is seated on the lower deck.

and Germany. He also organised hot air balloon races and introduced polo to the USA.

When he was not on the *Lysistrata*, Bennett, Jr resided at the Villa Namouna in Beaulieu-sur-Mer. His behaviour ashore was as eccentric as when he was afloat. In Monte Carlo he couldn't get a seat on the outside terrace of his favourite restaurant so, with typical panache, he bought the restaurant and gave it to the Egyptian waiter, Ciro, who normally served him on the terrace.[16] Bennett, Jr was finally married, at age 73, to Maud Potter, the widow of George de Reuter (of Reuters news agency), enjoying five years of married life before he died at the Villa Namouna in 1918. The *New York Herald* was sold in 1920.

James Gordon Bennett, Jr.

According to the Registry of Scottish Ships, the *Lysistrata* was sold to the Imperial Russian Navy in 1914 and renamed the *Yaroslavna* and was used on patrol in the Arctic. In 1918 she was seized by the Royal Navy though soon handed back to the Russian Navy. She was used as a fisheries patrol vessel before being broken up in 1966.[17] G. L. Watson's original military styling and speed obviously impressed the Russians, though you must wonder about the stall for the cows and the Turkish bath. Certainly, the *Lysistrata* was a forerunner of many of today's megayachts, though sadly today's owners have few of the eccentric interests of Gordon Bennett Jr.

16   www.francetoday.com/archives/inventing-the-riviera/
17   www.clydeships.co.uk/view.php?ref=15179

Driac II under squaresail. Photo in *MacPherson's Voyages.*

9 TWO WORLD WARS AND THE GREAT DEPRESSION: EARLY 20TH CENTURY TO WWII

The first half of the 20th century encompassed cataclysmic events that dramatically affected the countries around the Mediterranean: two world wars; civil wars; the rise of totalitarian regimes; the Great Depression; the creeping industrialisation of countries that had been largely agrarian; and cultural shifts that turned societies upside down. All of these impacted on the yachting scene in the Mediterranean in various and different ways.

Up to the first world war yachts still cruised to and around the Mediterranean, but many of the accounts we have are from yachts more like little ships with wealthy owners. Cruising in small yachts was in its infancy, although becoming more popular in home waters and, importantly, more egalitarian. McMullen had shown the way for the amateur yachtsman in the latter half of the 19th century with the publication of his classic *Down Channel*.[1] In 1880 the Cruising Club was formed in England by a small group of yachtsmen who cruised rather than raced their yachts. There was a clear schism between those who raced and those who cruised, the

Hilaire Belloc.

latter believing that yacht racing and the razzmatazz of yacht clubs promoting the racing was an abomination that had little to do with the quiet exhilaration of guiding a small boat into harbour in good weather and bad. Hilaire Belloc, the poet, author and passionate sailor, who wrote extensively on cruises in his yacht *Nona*, had this acid comment to make about cruising and racing:

For no one can doubt that the practice of sailing, which renews in us all the past of our blood, has been abominably corrupted by racing … Remember and write it down: "Cruising is not racing." If your boat is a home and a companion, and at the same time a genius that takes you from place to place … a good angel, revealing unexpected things, and a comforter and an introducer to the Infinite Verities – and my boat is all these things – then you must put away from yourself altogether the idea of racing.

Hilaire Belloc quoted in Phillips-Birt *The History of Yachting* p 140

1 McMullen *Down Channel* Horace Cox 1891 (revised edition)

The beginning of the century saw not just feisty individuals like Hilaire Belloc and others make the case for 'just cruising' as opposed to racing, but also saw an increase in the numbers of clubs and associations that unashamedly espoused cruising. The Cruising Club was given a royal warrant in 1902 and became the Royal Cruising Club. From the 1880's it published charts and an annual account of cruises and pilotage notes made by members in its *Roving Commissions*.[2] In 1908 the Cruising Association was formed, an altogether more egalitarian organisation for cruising yachts that included Arthur Ransome, the author of the *Swallows and Amazons* series, amongst its founding members.[3] In the USA the Cruising Club of America was formed in 1921, though some members believed it lost its way when it began to organise ocean races.[4] In London the Little Ship Club was formed in 1926 so sailors in London and nearby counties could 'get together and swap yarns'.[5]

While much was being written about cruising, and as cruising organisations came into being, there appeared to be little interest in cruising the Mediterranean. Most accounts of those that did cruise there were not of the simple amateur in a modest craft, but rich owners in what we now call superyachts. Janet Cusack has suggested that the divisions between rich owners indulging in conspicuous consumption and lesser mortals cruising in modest craft they fitted out themselves and crewed alone or with friends related largely to demonstrating ones' social position in a society.

David Cannadine suggested that display, and a claim to membership of a ruling leisure class in the Victorian era was strongly linked to the number of domestic and other servants employed. Yachting provided an ideal opportunity for conspicuous consumption of this type, involving large numbers of male servants, some highly skilled and well paid professionals, such as the master, engineers, and doctors. Some carried an even more expensive French chef, whose presence reinforced lavish maritime entertainment.

Cusack *Nineteenth-Century Cruising Yachtsmen in the Mediterranean* p 53

Of yachting organisations and cruises made by the nationals in the countries around the Mediterranean, there are few records, or at least few records I can track down. There were certainly large yachts owned by royals and the rich and famous cruising the Mediterranean where there is often an account,

2   In 1976 the Royal Cruising Club Pilotage Foundation was formed with a remit to publish pilotage guides. rccpf.org.uk/Default
3   www.theca.org.uk/home
4   It still organises the Newport to Bermuda Race.
5   littleshipclub.co.uk/little-ship-club-history

even a book, describing the cruise. Other records that survive are of unusual or sensational histories, like that of Mussolini's yacht. Of small boat cruising in the Mediterranean there is little, though like the voyages of A. G. H. MacPherson chronicled by the Royal Cruising Club, there must have been other, more modest cruises going on that were not recorded or where the records have been lost.

Megayachts in the early 20th century

As in the Victorian era, large yachts continued to cruise the Mediterranean in the years leading up to the Second World War. The early 1930's seemed to be good years, with two books published on big boat cruises in the Mediterranean: one English and the other American. *Sunbeam Ahoy* by Mary Richardson describes a cruise in the 659 ton *Sunbeam II* owned by her uncle Sir Walter Runciman.[6] *A Yacht in Mediterranean Seas* by Isabel Anderson describes a cruise in *Sayonara*, an 854 ton steam yacht owned by American millionaire Anthony Drexel, Jr. and chartered by Isabel Anderson's husband.[7] It seems that the owners of megayachts often brought along someone, frequently a woman, to write up the cruise and provide sketches of sights along the way or to take photographs of the sights. On *Sunbeam II* Mary Richardson was invited by her uncle Lord Runciman to chronicle the cruise, and earlier, on the *Roseneath*, the Earl of Cavan cited one of his female guests, Olive, as the photographer for his book.[8]

Sunbeam II

In many ways *Sunbeam II* was not dissimilar to yachts that had cruised the Mediterranean in Victorian times. The photo in the frontispiece of Mary Richardson's book is of a large, three-masted gaff-topsail schooner that we are told is 659 tons, designed by G. L. Watson and built by Denny Brothers in Dumbarton. Records from the Royal Northumberland give her build date as 1929 and put her length at 195 ft (59 metres). She was modelled on a former yacht, a schooner built in 1874, the *Sunbeam*, that the Runciman family had bought in 1922, so it not surprising it is similar to other large yachts cruising in

---

6   Mary Richardson *Sunbeam Ahoy* Andrew Reid & Co, 1932
7   Isabel Anderson *A Yacht in Mediterranean Seas* Marshall Jones Co, 1930
8   All four guests of the Earl on the *Roseneath* were women.

Victorian times.[9] Her one concession to modernity was that she was powered by a diesel engine, built by the Atlas Diesel Company, which would have been significantly more compact than the steam engine and coal bunker that took up so much space on a yacht like the *Roseneath*.[10]

Sunbeam II. Photo in *Sunbeam Ahoy.*

Mary boarded the *Sunbeam II* at Southampton and they immediately set off across the Bay of Biscay. It was not a smooth passage, even on a yacht of this size, and unlike so many others who opted to get the train or a steamer down

9   rnyc.org.uk/historic-yachts/2013/06/sunbeam-ii/
10   See Chapter 7, The Victorians

to the Mediterranean to board a yacht, Mary and the other guests suffered a rough voyage to get there.

We had a truly lively night, being pitched out of our bunks like so many parcels and not always landing this side up with care. Everything that could move was jerked out of place and sent flying through space like cocoanuts at a fair. Nobody slept. Mrs Anderson was thrown right across her cabin, where she ricocheted from the wall to her bed, getting a black eye in the process.

Richardson *Sunbeam Ahoy* p 7

Once into the Mediterranean they cruised to Spain, down to the North African coast and then up to Malta, up the Adriatic to Venice and then back down again to Greece and then westwards back to Gibraltar and so to Southampton. In many ways this early 20th century cruise had all the hallmarks

Sir Walter Runciman on *Sunbeam II*. Photo in *Sunbeam Ahoy*.

of the Victorian era: the guests entertained themselves with music and a play they had written, the *Sunbeam*; rounds of bridge were played; they visited ancient sites and museums; they had dignitaries on board in some of the ports and attended dinners ashore in others. The book has some charming ribald humour in places such as in Naples, where the washerwomen rowed out to *Sunbeam II* and importuned her uncle.

The saloon on *Sunbeam II*. Photo in *Sunbeam Ahoy*.

Uncle alone seemed to attract them. As soon as ever they spotted him, immaculate as usual, and looking very splendid, they had eyes for no one else. "Him nice gentleman, me wash you, very cheap, goodbye" were some of their choice greetings. An extremely plump woman with a very pretty smile quite lost her head in her admiration of Uncle. She jumped about in her boat like a jack-in-the-box, calling out joyously, "Me like you, good night, sporty boy."

Richardson p 101

In other passages Mary joshes with the crew, though you are always aware she is doing so from a distance. The 1930's was to some extent at the end of Empire and, not surprisingly, the sentiments expressed by the guests on board were those of the aristocracy and entitled families that were current at the time. While all around them the effects of the Great Depression are being felt and where large numbers of people from the countries around the Mediterranean, from Greece, former Yugoslavia, and Italy, were emigrating to America, Australia and New Zealand to find work and a better life, there is little mention of the hardships of the local populations or of the privations of the crew on *Sunbeam II*. There is virtually no mention of the Great War or the devastating effects of the war on the landscape on countries bordering the sea, nor of the rise of Fascism under Benito Mussolini in Italy. In the end these sorts of observations were not the purpose of this sort of book and it would probably have been deemed unseemly to make them when the object was to display status and wealth, as Janet Cusack notes.

Display could be brought to a wider audience by the keeping and publication of journals of voyages undertaken. This was often a task performed by the ladies of the party, as with Mrs. Brassey of Sunbeam, and Mrs. Harvey of Claymore; it could be delegated to the doctor, as on Crusader, but some owners used well-known writers to record their travels, as when Mr. John Burns steamed Mastiff to Iceland in 1878, taking Anthony Trollope as 'Chronicler'.

Janet Cusack *Nineteenth-Century Cruising Yachtsmen* p 53

Sayonara

The voyage on the steam yacht *Sayonara* was different in many respects to that of the *Sunbeam II*. Isabel Anderson's husband, Larz Anderson, who was in the diplomatic service, had chartered the yacht for her. Isabel could have chartered the yacht herself as she was a Boston heiress who had inherited 16 million dollars from her mother at the age of five in 1881. Despite her wealth she had a doctorate in literature and was a well published travel author: in the frontispiece of *A Yacht in Mediterranean Seas*

The party from *Sayonara* exploring Meteori in Greece.
Photo in *A Yacht in the Mediterranean.*

there are fourteen travel books and nine children's books listed as published by the author. It seems that the object of the cruise was to gather the material for her next travel book, although she jauntily refers to the purpose as being purely for the joy of travel.

The *Sayonara* was originally built as *ULII* in 1911 as a luxury yacht for the Austrian Archduke Charles Stephen, a member of the Habsburg dynasty and a Grand Admiral of the Austro-Hungarian Navy. Some accounts mention that she was built for Archduke Ferdinand, whose assassination in Sarajevo triggered the events leading to the Great War, but this seems unlikely given the records we have, although he likely accompanied Archduke Charles Stephen on board at some time. She was built by Ramage and

Sayonara.
Photo in *A Yacht in the Mediterranean.*

Ferguson Ltd. of Leith, with a gross tonnage of 854.43, and length 185 ft (56 metres).[11] After the Great War she was sold in 1927 and renamed *Vanduara* before being bought by Anthony Drexel, Jr. in 1930. Drexel, Jr. was the son of Drexel, Sr. who had made his money in banking, including being a co-founder of Morgan Stanley. Drexel, Jr., much like Gordon Bennett, Jr., was something of a playboy who, after his father's death in 1893, decided to live in Europe. It's not known how the Great Depression affected the fortunes of Drexel, Jr. and he died in 1934, just four years after acquiring *Sayonara*.[12]

Isabel Anderson's account of cruising around the Mediterranean, through the Adriatic, the Aegean and then back up the western coast of Italy to Leghorn (Livorno), tells us more about the history of the places than it does of everyday life around the shores of the Mediterranean. She is evidently well versed in the ancient history of places along the way, but less so in recent events. In

11   Lloyds Register of Yachts 1911
12   en.wikipedia.org/wiki/Anthony Joseph_Drexel_Jr.

Sarajevo she views the place where the Archduke Ferdinand was assassinated, and then skips on to the delights of a cup of coffee on the balcony where they are staying. This is almost like a virtual tour and, in this respect, not so very different from the account by Mary Richardson of the cruise in *Sunbeam Ahoy*. Cruising in this way seems as much about short passages along the coast interspersed with sightseeing ashore, shopping and dinners with the expatriate community or local dignitaries, as it does with some deeper association with the Mediterranean.

This was a time of transition between the decline of the British Empire, the Great Depression and the rise of totalitarian regimes in Europe. In most ways the owners and guests of the *Sunbeam II* and *Sayonara* were insulated from these events, or chose to insulate themselves. Not until the voyages of A. G. H. MacPherson in the 1930's do we get close to a sailor and a yacht of more modest means, echoing the small boat cruising that had begun in northern climes with the likes of McMullen, Claud Worth and Arthur Ransome.[13] MacPherson's two voyages to and around the Mediterranean were a precursor to the small boat voyages that would become more commonplace after the Second World War.

MacPherson and *Driac* and *Driac II*

Arthur George Holdsworth MacPherson came to sailing late in life. He spent most of his life in business in India and after returning to England in the 1920's decided to go cruising. He was by now well into his fifties with little or no sailing experience, but a big desire to indulge in some long-distance cruising. Only one thing stood in the way. In India and later, when back in England, he had accumulated a large collection of paintings, prints and other memorabilia related to seafaring. This collection of some 12,000 items had pretty much bankrupted him, or at least threatened to. He appealed for some national body or private individual to preserve the collection for the nation. Finally someone did.

Like the hooked flounder, in fact, I was giving my last flop at the bottom of the boat when Sir James Caird – who had already saved the Victory from extinction – stepped into the breach (July '28) and performed a similar office for the Collection and myself. The Collection laid

---

13   R. T. McMullen *Down Channel*; Claud Worth *Yacht Cruising*; Arthur Ransome *Racundra's First Cruise*.

the foundations of the National Maritime Museum at Greenwich.

A. G. H. MacPherson *MacPherson's Voyages* Ed. John Scott Hughes Methuen & Co 1946 p x

His first boat was a 40 ft Bermudan cutter that he named *Driac* – his benefactor, (Lord) Caird, spelt backwards – and he learnt to sail her on a voyage to the Mediterranean and back. Two years later he had a smaller boat built, and it was in the 32 ft *Driac II* that he made his most ambitious voyages. Between 1932 and 1938 MacPherson sailed her around the Baltic Sea and to Iceland before setting out on his most ambitious voyage to the Mediterranean and then down the Red Sea and across to southeast Asia. On the return trip to South Africa he became ill with the phlebitis that had troubled him for some time and he turned the boat over to his trusty first mate, Bill Leng. MacPherson died in 1942.

MacPherson wrote logs of his voyages which were published by the Royal Cruising Club. After the Second World War these were edited and collected together into a small volume called simply *MacPherson's Voyages*. It is printed on that crumbly post war paper that has yellowed with time and comes complete with a stamp proclaiming:

BOOK PRODUCTION WAR ECONOMY STANDARD

THIS BOOK IS PRODUCED IN COMPLETE CONFORMITY WITH THE AUTHORISED ECONOMY STANDARDS.

MacPherson writes in a spare and astringent manner that often concealed some real hardship on passages. Hardly ever does any real irritation with the boat or his crew come to the surface except in a few sardonic asides. In *MacPherson's Voyages* there is a photo of him on the deck of *Driac II*. He is a tall lanky man, skinny almost, with a buttoned pea jacket and wellingtons turned down at the top. He has a straight-stemmed pipe in his mouth and a black peaked sailors cap on his head. In this and other pictures he looks at ease, but in one photo of him at the helm there is a hint of vulnerability, as if caught off guard and out of step with Empire.

The first *Driac*, the 40 ft Bermudan cutter, was built by Camper and Nicholson at Gosport and launched in 1930. In most ways the design of the yacht was typical of yachts of this type built around the United Kingdom and wouldn't have been out of place on the Solent or in the Channel except for two things.

She had a small auxiliary Kelvin petrol engine to get in and out of harbours or to power through calm patches. And she was Bermudan rigged, with roller reefing on the mainsail when many yachts were still gaff rigged. With his usual wit MacPherson remarked that she was 'launched on a Friday and started business on a 13th; so all the traditional customs were observed'.[14]

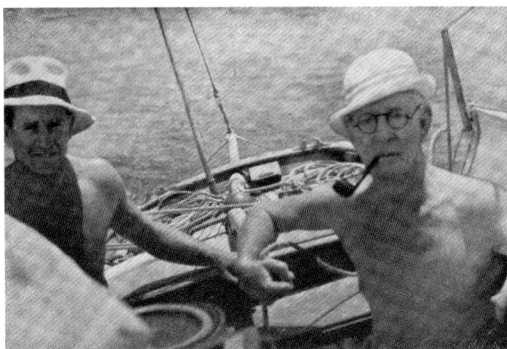

Bill Leng and MacPherson on *Driac*.
Photo in *MacPherson's Voyages*.

MacPherson set off promptly for the Mediterranean, with one crew and a boy, to beat his way down the Atlantic coast, encountering head winds for most of the passage. Once into the Mediterranean he cruised the Spanish coast before crossing to Tunisia and then on to Malta where he arrived in early December. After a brief respite, MacPherson set off again in early February. Anyone who has sailed in the Mediterranean in the winter will know that the weather can be violent, with depressions sallying through from the Atlantic with some fury.[15] This was to be the case for MacPherson's voyages up the Italian coast where he often had to stay in harbour for days waiting for stormy weather to pass through.

On his travels MacPherson pops in and out of harbours and anchorages on his route as much for convenience and shelter as to see the sites – though he does do some of that as well. He experiences all the highs and lows of sailing a small yacht out of season and comments freely on other yachtsmen he comes across, though there are not that many of those until he gets to the Riviera and Côte d'Azur.

This was my first visit to the Riviera, and I found it quite amusing and instructive. As the seafaring consists of popping from one hole to another, I will condense matters by saying that we arrived at Marseille from Toulon 10th April, having bestowed our patronage on Monaco, Nice and Cannes. The weather was perfect but almost airless, and it was generally up to Mr Kelvin. The yachts and cars were gorgeous, their owners and lady friends splendiferous; and I saw Charlie Chaplin – and assisted to judge a dancing competition.

MacPherson pp 9–10

14   MacPherson *MacPherson's Voyages* p1
15   Rod Heikell *Mediterranean Cruising Handbook* Imray 2012 p160

The voyage back to England was as eventful as it could be only under MacPherson, but *Driac* successfully arrived back through thick and thin in 1931. In the spring of 1932 he took delivery of *Driac II*. Surprisingly, *Driac II* was a smaller version of the original *Driac* at just 32 ft LOA and was designed by Sidney Graham and built by Harry Feltham in Portsmouth.[16] The reason it is surprising is that MacPherson planned to sail down to the Mediterranean again and then continue on down the Red Sea and across the Indian Ocean to southeast Asia.[17] MacPherson warmed up for his big adventure by straightaway sailing *Driac II* to the Azores and back to Portsmouth via northern Spain. In 1933 he sailed to Iceland and back and then in the autumn of the same year sailed to the Baltic and to Leningrad (St Petersburg). In 1934–35 MacPherson sailed to the Caribbean and back eastwards across the

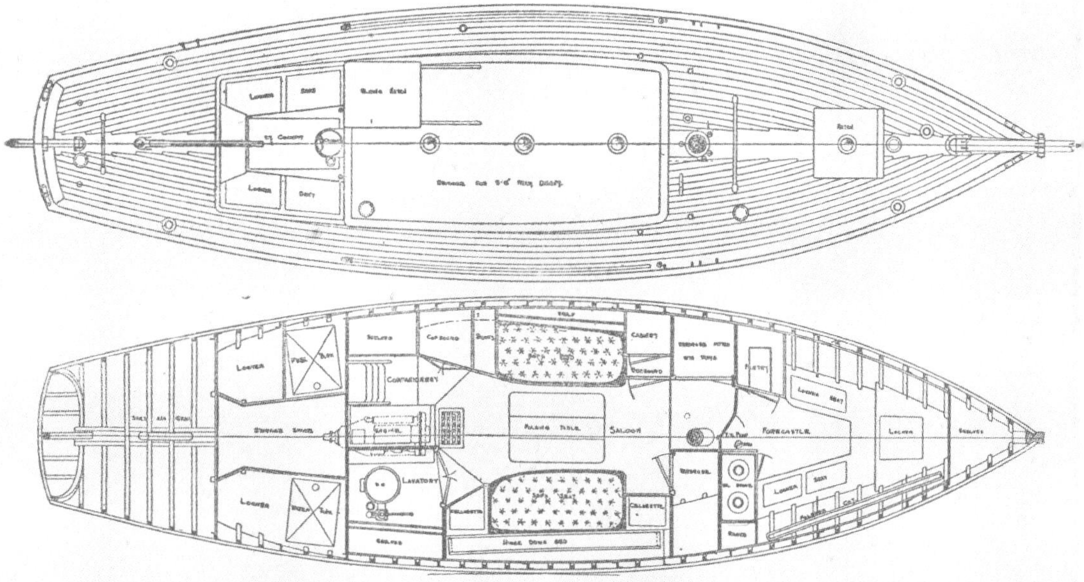

FIG 2 *(continued)*. DECK AND ACCOMMODATION

Driac II deck plan and interior layout. Diagram in *MacPherson's Voyages.*

16   Appendix II in *MacPherson's Voyages* has all the details and line drawings of *Driac II*.
17   A voyage I have made in a boat very similar to *Driac II* as recounted in *Sailing Ancient Seas*.

Atlantic to Gibraltar – he was now in his early sixties and evidently wanted to get a whole lot of cruising done before his demise.

MacPherson's cruise through the Mediterranean to Haifa in Israel involved his usual practice of hopping from port to port as well as some longer trips, as when it took him a full week to sail from the Strait of Messina to Cephalonia in the Greek Ionian Islands. Here he sailed to the Corinth Canal and then down through the Greek islands in the Aegean to Turkey and on to Cyprus and finally to Haifa. His aim was to get to Haifa, where his brother was stationed, and then ship *Driac II* back to England on a steamer. He laid the boat up at Haifa and Bill Leng, his faithful sailing companion, returned to England for a holiday. MacPherson took a year off, travelling around the world on steamers and contemplating his future plans, and somewhere along the way he ditched the idea of shipping his yacht back to England and planned a cruise around the Greek islands. Like so many of us he had been entranced with the place, although this rarely shows in his dry prose.

Bill Leng returned early to Haifa and, when MacPherson arrived in May 1936, *Driac II* was very nearly ready for sea. Together they sailed around the Aegean and up into the Black Sea to Romania before returning to the Aegean. There was obviously a stirring of sea fever afoot in other countries and MacPherson mentions a Turkish yacht he encountered.

Driac II hauled out in Haifa. Photo in *MacPherson's Voyages.*

Met a delightful retired Turkish naval captain, who was in a ketch which he said he had built in his back yard. Gave us a lot of information, and though he depresses us as regards the habits of Turkish port officials, cheered us up by saying we ought to have a soldier's wind in the Black Sea.

MacPherson p 102

MacPherson was still not satisfied with his Mediterranean cruise, so he decided to make a quick dash to the Adriatic where he explored the Albanian and Dalmatian coasts and islands before an about turn and the voyage back through the Ionian to Alexandria in Egypt. It makes you quite breathless reading the logs of such extensive cruises in a 32 ft yacht with a diminutive auxiliary engine.

When MacPherson decided he was still not done with cruising is not logged. If it was it would have been mentioned with a typical pithy aside. In October 1936 MacPherson and Bill Leng sailed for Port Said to transit the Suez Canal. At the wrong time of year, he ventured into the Red Sea and bit by bit sailed to India and then onto southeast Asia. In 1937 he cruised the Spice Islands and then in 1938 made the passage to Durban in South Africa. He was in his 70th year and had suffered with ill-health for a while. He gifted *Driac II* to Bill Leng and returned to England.

There is a sea change that has gone on in these years. To some extent it was around in the 19th century with Maupassant and Dumas in their yachting adventures, where crew were friends and, even when paid hands were employed, they were regarded as sailing companions and not boat servants. With MacPherson there is a different attitude to crew and those who go to sea on small boats when compared to the attitudes towards the crews employed on large luxury yachts like *Sunbeam II* and *Sayonara*. The crew on large sailing yachts owned by rich owners and the aristocracy were just crew, paid crew not far removed from servants. Even the officers on board were not always regarded as of the same status. The relationship between crew on *Driac II* was a different matter. Bill Leng penned this tribute to MacPherson in a foreword to the book.

What a disastrous year 1931 was for millions who were caught in a world slump which did not seem to make sense, but which unfortunately was only too real.

I lost my job as a cabinet-maker, and the future had for me a dismal outlook. But if I had only known, sunshine in the shape of Driac II was just around the corner…

And so early in 1932 began a sailing partnership that was to last for seven years, until Mac was practically forced by ill-health to say goodbye to Driac II in South Africa and give me the proud privilege of bringing her home on her last journey from Durban.

You will notice that I take the liberty of describing our voyages together as a 'sailing partnership', because that was exactly what it was. Right from the start, when we went over to the Channel Isles and St. Malo, I was treated not as a paid hand, but as a sailing companion.

Bill Leng in *MacPherson's Voyages* pp xiii–xiv

The democratisation of cruising yachts for pleasure that had been happening around the shores of northern Europe and must have been happening around the Mediterranean as well was about to be shattered by the events of World War II. It's indicative of MacPherson's spirit that, though in his seventies, on the outbreak of war he immediately volunteered for naval duty by the simple expedient of subtracting ten years from his age. He was also involved at Dunkirk and in his account to Bill Leng described the evacuation off the beach in typically droll fashion.

I never really was quite clear how he eventually got on board, but he did it somehow or other further east along the coast, and what with cases of sea-sickness and other trifling details he found himself heading for Dunkirk as navigator.

Once over there in the infernal din it was only natural that he should rush in with the small boats to pick up that seemingly never-ending trail of British soldiers and then not able to find his ship again. As he says, however, he simply rushed his human cargo to the nearest one he saw, and when it was time to get going himself he just followed suit.

Bill Leng p xv

Mussolini's yacht

While *Sunbeam II* and *Sayonara* were cruising the Italian coast, and while MacPherson untypically makes no mention of it in his logs, Benito Mussolini, Il Duce, had by 1925 turned Italy into a police state with his Fascist party in sole command. We would know little about Mussolini's yacht were it not for its relatively recent seizure as part of the assets of Salvatore Squillace, who had links to convicted mafia bosses and owed an estimated €28 million for tax evasion. The yacht, named *Fiamma Nera* (*Black Fire*), was seized by the tax authorities in 2016 along with farms, a castle, apartments, luxury cars, offices and stores in Rome, as well as two other boats.

Fiamma Nera under sail after her arrest by Italian customs. Photo *La Stampa*.

The yacht was gifted to Mussolini by his Fascist friend Alessandro Parisi in 1935. It was originally named *Konigin II* and was built to a Dutch design by the

German boatyard Abeking and Rasmussen in 1912.[18] The yacht, a Bermudan rigged yawl, was 78 ft (23.7 metres) and 40 tons, possessed of stunning grace and with enough accommodation for a tryst in luxury.[19] Mussolini apparently used it for love trysts with his mistress Clara Petacci; it is uncertain just how much sailing he did in the yacht. With the collapse of the Fascist regime in 1943 Mussolini had the boat scuppered so it wouldn't fall into German hands. It was recovered after the war and restored with the name *Serenella*. After a series of owners, it was eventually bought by one of the shell companies Squillace had set up.

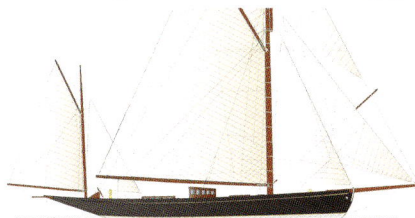

Konigin II from the Duck Design Studio in Rome.

Squillace had attempted to hide the yacht from the notice of the authorities by getting his captain to take it to Valencia where a refit changed the colour of the hull to white and some of the brightwork on deck was painted white to change the yacht's appearance. Frankly, it would be difficult to really change the appearance of a classic yacht like this one, and not surprisingly the yacht was tracked down by the Italian customs force. It may be that the Duck Design Studio in Rome was also commissioned to do a refit of the yacht as it appears on their website with a line drawing under the name *Konigin II*.[20]

As well as Mussolini's yacht there must have been numerous other yachts around Italy, and indeed around Spain and France, but little is recorded of them. No doubt many were destroyed in Axis and Allied bombing raids on the harbours and harbour installations around the coasts of the Mediterranean and many more were seized as war prizes in 1945. And sadly, many were just left to rot in the aftermath of a war that destroyed livelihoods and for a while left a seascape bereft of the idea of sailing for pleasure.

---

18   Reuters report www.rt.com/search?q=mussolinis+yacht.
19   www.yachtevela.com/konigin-ii-1516.html
20   www.duckdesign.it/en/koniginii-2.html

Crab at anchor. Photo Robin Minney.

10 POST WORLD WAR II TO THE 1960's

The Second World War left the shores of the countries around the Mediterranean devastated. Whether friend or foe, populations were displaced, cities and towns reduced to rubble, and national pride was trampled into the ruins of the war. Not surprisingly, sailing for pleasure was far from the minds of European citizenry, and the very idea of cruising a yacht around the broken shores of the Mediterranean would have seemed somehow ill-advised. And yet the desolation of war can give rise to strange yearnings and inexplicable cravings for a different life away from the humdrum and grey horizons of home. Just a few years after the end of the Second World War George Millar decided to sail from England down to Greece.[1]

It so happened that we considered making a voyage to Greece in a small boat at a time when the British people, fatigued by the war, the grimness of continuing rationing and emergency laws, and the exhausting process of Britain's inevitable political earthquake speeded and intensified by the war, were suffering from lethargy…

Isabel reacted with energy inversely proportional to this lethargy. "I know that one can get anything in England if one takes the trouble to look for it. Is it illegal to buy a yacht? No. Well we are going to buy one."

George Millar *Isabel and the Sea* Century 1948/1983 p 15

He wasn't alone in his ambition to set off on a voyage down to the Mediterranean. Others in the 1950's would follow. In 1955 two second-year students at Oxford, Penny Minney and Sally Humphreys, with other assorted crew along the way, set off from Malta to sail around the eastern Mediterranean in a 17 ft open lifeboat named *Crab*. They eventually made it to Istanbul and then sailed the cockleshell craft back to Rhodes and set off across the Aegean to the Saronic Gulf. It was a voyage of youthful hope and exceptional fortitude along the shores of countries still recovering from the effects of the war.[2]

In 1951 Ernle Bradford and his wife Janet set off down the French canals bound for the Mediterranean. They were to end up spending three years there and Ernle Bradford wrote a number of books describing his cruises around parts of the Mediterranean and of the history of the place. It all started in Alexandria in the war where he found a copy of Chekhov and read a line

1   George Millar *Isabel and the Sea* Century 1948/1983
2   Penny Minney *Crab's Odyssey* Taniwha Press 2016

in it that was to provide the impetus to sail the Mediterranean: 'Life does not come again; if you have not lived during the days that were given to you, once only, then write it down as lost…'[3]

The decision was quickly made. We would get rid of our flat, sell our furniture, cut our links with England, buy a boat – and go…

I had acquired a taste for the free life during the war, but there are some who are born with the knowledge of it in their veins. For them the conventional life is a kind of torture. They hate it more than the domesticated animal would hate freedom.

Ernle Bradford *The Journeying Moon* Grafton Books 1958/1987 p 31

Ernle Bradford was one of those who upped sticks and sailed to the Mediterranean soon after WWII. Photo from the flyleaf of *Mediterranean Portrait of a Sea.*

Much of the impetus to get away in a small boat and sail the Mediterranean had its origins in the chaos of war. Some who had been away fighting in foreign countries got a taste for travelling, not by any conventional means or in great luxury, but through their own endeavours on a small ship. Voyages across the oceans after the war in comparatively small boats showed that, with fortitude and some luck, a small yacht could be sailed almost anywhere, and a voyage to the Mediterranean, to the sights and smells and flavours of the countries around its shores, was an enticing prospect compared to the dreary nine-to-five of a job in Britain. The Royal Cruising Club and the Cruising Association had numbers of members who cruised locally and abroad in small yachts. Voyages across the Atlantic by sailors like Humphrey Barton in the 25 ft *Vertue XXXI*, the Smith brothers in the 20 ft *Nova Espero*, Patrick Ellam in the 20 ft *Sopranino*, Adlard Coles in *Cohoe*, and Anne Davidson in the 23 ft *Felicity Anne*, these pioneers and others showed that small boats could safely make long passages and survive gales at sea. Some of these Atlantic adventurers went on to cruise in the Mediterranean, notably *Sopranino* under the guidance of Charles Violet, and Humphrey Barton on the 38 ft *Rose Rambler*.

Apart from the Royal Cruising Club and the Cruising Association, other cruising associations came into being and encouraged small boat cruising.

3   Ernle Bradford *The Journeying Moon* Grafton Books 1958/1987 p 23

The Ocean Cruising Club was founded in 1953 by Humphrey Barton with the only prerequisite for membership that a person had to have completed a passage of 1000 miles.[4] The American Seven Seas Cruising Association was formed in 1952 as '…a disorganization of sailboat live-aboarders' and every member of the association is made a commodore: '… a tongue in cheek gesture toward overdone club officialdom which at times so alters yacht clubs that the yacht is no longer important and only the club remains.' It still has one of the best cruising association maxims: 'Leave a clean wake.'[5]

Towards the end of the 1950's some of the bigger yachts began to return to the Mediterranean, though in those days something like a 60-footer was regarded as a big yacht. Most cruised in the western Mediterranean; few ventured into the Adriatic and the eastern Mediterranean. Right up until the sixties a voyage to the Mediterranean was an adventure equal to a voyage to the South Seas or the Caribbean, not in distance and days at sea, but in the sense of an adventure that offered excitement and the unknown. The western Mediterranean was barely known and the eastern Mediterranean little visited at all.

George Millar and *Truant*

George Millar bought his yacht, a Cornish fishing boat hull fitted out as a yacht, in Moody's Boatyard on the Hamble in 1946, just a year after the end of the war. She was a beast of a boat, nearly 50 ft long, ketch rigged, with two Commodore petrol engines, and had been sitting in the boatyard throughout the war. George had a little sailing experience but had never been on a voyage like the one he contemplated in *Truant*, through the French canals to the Mediterranean and on to Greece. What he did have was an obstinate conviction that he needed to escape from the grey, homogenous shores of England to adventure again abroad.

George Millar had been the Paris correspondent for the *Daily Express* in 1939 when the war began and lost no time in signing up for the London Scottish Regiment. He was soon sent to North Africa where he was captured by the Africa Korps and sent to a POW camp in Taranto at the bottom of Italy. When the Italians surrendered in 1943, he was put on a train to Germany

4   OCC paper researched and written by Tony Vasey, *The Ocean Cruising Club: The First 50 Years* 2003
5   ssca.org/#/history/

but managed to jump off near Strasbourg. With the help of the French Resistance he travelled over the Pyrenees to Spain where he managed to get back to Britain. He joined the Special Operations Executive (SOE) and was parachuted back into France to work with the French Resistance. He wrote a book about his escape from the POW camp, *Horned Pigeon*, published in 1945; and a book about his time in the SOE and France, *Maquis*, published in 1946.[6] The latter book, reckoned to be one of the best books written about the SOE, came out just as he was getting ready to leave in *Truant*.

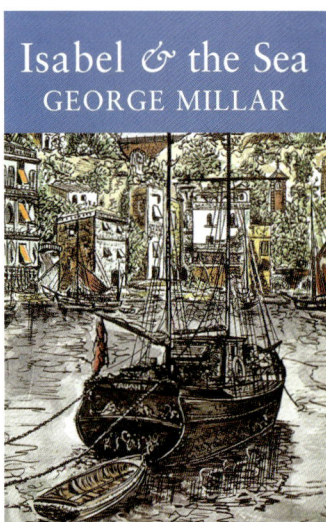

Cover of *Isabel and the Sea*.

Millar had a bad homecoming in Britain at the end of the war. After his internment in the POW camp, several close calls where informers nearly betrayed him to the Germans, and his remarkable exploits in France for the SOE, the much-decorated hero[7] arrived back to find his wife of nine years, Annette (Stockwell), was now in love with someone else and wanted a divorce. Millar married a friend of Annette's, Isabel Paske-Smith, the half-Spanish daughter of a diplomat. In many ways the voyage down to Greece described in *Isabel and the Sea* was a paeon to Isabel and resurrection for him.

George and Isabel made their way across the English Channel to Le Havre and entered the French canal system there. They learnt how to handle *Truant* and get on with living on board as they went along. In Le Havre George looked around the ruins of a once great city to find only rubble and dust. A fisherman who had helped him moor up pleaded with him to take him and his family to Marseille where at least there was a 'soft climate', even if there was still little to eat. All the way through the canal system George describes the ruin and desolation brought about by the war. Life on board also affected George in a different way and he had recurrent nightmares about his abilities to look after *Truant*.

Shouts and screams woke Isabel at midnight. "The controls are gone! We are drifting!" …I

6   Obituary to George Millar published in *The Independent* Saturday 26 March 2005.
7   He had the Military Cross, Distinguished Service Order, and from the French, the Legion d'Honneur and the Croix de Guerre avec Palmes.

George and Isabel Millar.

was crawling on the cabin floor. This was not the first nightmare I had suffered since we left England in *Truant*, and we came to believe that, while most men are quick to state that they leave all their cares behind them on taking to the water, with me the usual hearty process was reversed, and my first reaction was to become nervous and harassed.

Millar *Isabel and the Sea* p 63

In Marseilles George had *Truant* re-rigged and continued on along the French Mediterranean coast to Monte Carlo where he came across an assorted gaggle of yachts both big and small. The owners were of various nationalities: British, French, Swiss and Italian – so evidently there were other yachts cruising the French Mediterranean coast. Some of the yachts had made their way down to the Mediterranean, but most had been there before the war and either their original owners or new owners had resumed sailing afterwards. George comments on the differences between the poor and dispossessed and the still evidently rich who had somehow retained their wealth since the end of the war.

As I walked along the quay studying the different boats, and looking for practical hints in their rigging, I realised that I would not change old *Truant* for any of them, and that I found in *Elpis*, *Truant*, and the Breton yawl, qualities of strength and character absent from the opulent harbour crawlers. I decided I was beginning to learn something about boats.

Millar *Isabel and the Sea* p 184

All through their travels around the coasts of France and Italy they came across the destruction and detritus of the war. Dust blowing off the ruins of bombed cities and towns is frequently mentioned. Cunning urchins lurked around the streets and the harbour looking for a way to survive.

Truant being launched. Photo National Historic Ships archive.

Sunken ships obstructed harbours and the entrances to harbours. The Germans had frequently blown up harbour installations so they would be useless for the advancing Allied troops, and mines still littered the sea. And yet, despite the carnage around them, the Millars found markets filled with fresh fruit and vegetables, restaurants serving good wine and good food made with whatever the owners could find in the markets, and a sense of *joie de vivre* that the war was over and life could begin again. Even if life was difficult, as the proprietress of one shop related to them… 'First it was the bombers, then the Germans, then the Partisans, then the Allied soldiers, and now our own thieves.'

Truant arrived in Zante in the Greek Ionian to find the town more or less intact after the war. The shops had

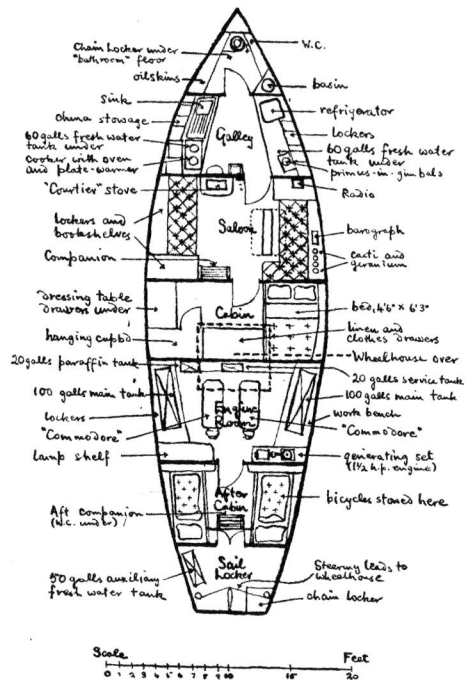

Truant's layout. From *Isabel and the Sea.*

lots of fresh fruit and vegetables and there was even a good restaurant or two. The Italianate architecture charmed them, and the only bad news was that the Corinth Canal was still closed from war damage, so they would have to sail around the Peloponnese to get to Piraeus. This proved to be a stormy trip and the two capes at the bottom, Tainaron (Matapan) and Malea, stood in their way before they could head for the Saronic Gulf and the home islands around Athens.[8]

Off Cape Malea – those capes! – we were caught flying far too much canvas, in rain-squalls with a sudden alarming weight of wind. We were obliged to jump about and "let everything go". We saved the sails, and nothing carried away except, strangely enough, the boom lacing of the mizzen. Once around the cape we had completed the worst part of our journey and

8   See Rod & Lucinda Heikell *Greek Waters Pilot* 13th ed Imray, 2018 Chapter 2

could turn north-east to Aegean waters that are generally supposed to be kindly.

Millar *Isabel and the Sea* p 323

Once into the Saronic, the Millars spent much time around Poros. They even named their favourite cove on the island where they kept *Truant* most of the time: Truant Cove.[9] They had taken *Truant* up to Piraeus but didn't much care for it compared to Poros which they considered the most beautiful island in the Saronic. The boat was permanently moored in Truant Cove and here they were visited by all sorts of people including the painters Lucian Freud and John Craxton, who were living on Poros at the time. Various other exiles, artists, poets, writers, and some who were just well connected, peopled the horizon of the Millar's time in Poros. Eventually George and Isabel decided it was time to return to England and they sold *Truant* in Greece to an English general stationed in Athens.

So, as we negotiated the rough ground between the slipways I sat looking backwards as though out of the opening of a tent during an earthquake. That was the last I saw of *Truant*.

Millar *Isabel and the Sea* p 408

It was not to be his last sailing trip to the Mediterranean. In *A White Boat from England*[10], George Millar describes their second trip to the Mediterranean in the 45 ft Buchanan sloop, *Serica*. In his typically self-deprecating way George describes the object of his book like this:

If I dare now to give an account of a journey by sea in a small boat from England to the Mediterranean it is because I enjoyed it and suffered it and wanted to share those feelings. What I must make clear is that I am not pretending to teach in describing so ordinary a journey. As a novice, my envy for those navigators who know or seem to know exactly what they are about is occasionally tempered by a suspicion that I get at least as much enjoyment out of our little promenades as they do out of their great ones.

George Millar *A White Boat from England* Heinemann, 1951 p vii

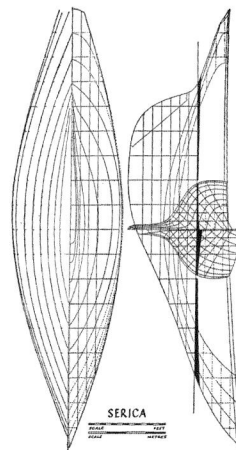

Line drawing of *Serica*. From *A White Boat from England*.

This time, instead of getting to the Mediterranean by the French canals, George decided to cruise around the Atlantic coasts of France, Spain and

9   See Rod & Lucinda Heikell *West Aegean* 3rd ed. Imray, 2014 p 95
10   George Millar *A White Boat From England* Heinemann 1951

Portugal before entering the Mediterranean through the Strait of Gibraltar. They cruised around the coast of Spain up to the south of France where, after numerous adventures and encounters with all sorts of characters, they left *Serica* at St Jean Cap Ferrat.

The book is a great read, though for me it has less dramatic appeal than their first adventures in *Truant* and less about a Europe still recovering from the war. In the short time between the cruises in *Truant* and *Serica*, the populations in Europe had been busy putting their lives back together, and between the national governments and the Marshall plan, which gave over $13 billion (around $115 billion in today's money) in aid to help rebuild the economies of western Europe, much of the infrastructure around the coast had been rebuilt.

Ernle Bradford and *Mother Goose*

Ernle Bradford and his wife Janet set off for the Mediterranean in a forty-year-old 10 ton Dutch *botter* that most of their sailing friends said shouldn't go to sea. Ernle was the sort of man for whom the word 'shouldn't' just goaded him on to do it. His wife, Janet, had considerably more sailing experience than Ernle, so that between the tales he spun of the 'smell of thyme on the wind' and the 'Aegean islands raising their opal heads out of a May morning',[11] they made a formidable combination to sail down to the Mediterranean. Ernle kept quiet about his plans and only mentioned that they might take her across the Channel if the weather was calm.

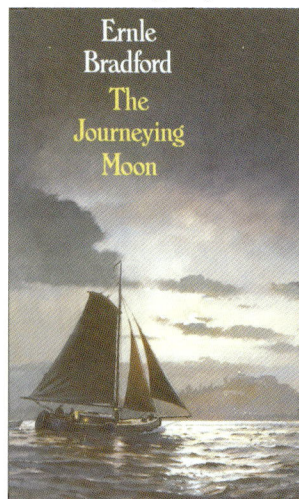

Cover of Ernle Bradford's *The Journeying Moon.*

They made it across the Channel to Le Havre and once there could release the genie, the truth of their endeavour, that had occupied them in England.

The first leg of our voyage was over. Now we could confess to each other what we had never confessed to inquisitive long-shoremen or even to friends: that this was not just a casual trip to France 'only if the weather's fine'. This was the end of

---

11   Janet was the first woman to win the Little Ship Club Trophy for seamanship and navigation. Bradford *The Journeying Moon* p 31

one life and the beginning of another… Our course lay eastward to the dolphin-haunted waters; to the islands of thyme and silver rock, and the high noon that leaves no shadows.

Ernle Bradford *The Journeying Moon* 1958/1985, Grafton p 31.

Their trip down through the French canals was a delight and the two of them fell into the rhythm of French life and the camaraderie of the *marinières* on the barges that plied these waterways. It soon becomes apparent in his book that Ernle has little time for the norms and attitudes of many who go sailing: he preferred to call *Mother Goose* a 'boat', as opposed to a 'yacht', since the latter had connotations of blazers and aloof attitudes; he

Ernle Bradford on *Mother Goose.* From *The Journeying Moon.*

despised the yachtsmen who decried those they met in different countries as 'Johnny Foreigners' who 'should readily respond to a shout of "Hey! You there!"'; he loved the company of rough *matelots* and the smell and taste of the food in the countries he visited; he described himself as a 'sailor' rather than a 'yachtsman' because 'the latter suggests a wealth which I did not possess and an outlook towards sailing which was very different from mine'.[12]

Ernle and Janet sailed *Mother Goose* around the French and Italian coasts and then across to Greece. The devastation of the war that George Millar had described was still apparent: many of the harbours and the shoreside buildings were still in ruins and sunken obstructions littered the approaches to harbours and anchorages. There were few other yachts around although some were attempting to trade along the coast.

Few British yachts were cruising the Med in 1951. There were, however, yachts from other European countries, some of whose owners were free spirits hoping to augment their funds by trading along the Riviera. We met two young Dutchmen in a very small 16-foot boat hoping to interest commercial enterprises in Dutch products; and later a British-registered *lemsteraak* belonging to a retired London art gallery owner loaded with a cargo of rice to sell in the markets of coastal towns.

Janet Verasanso *The Med in the Fifties* Marine Quarterly Winter, 2017 p 44

12   Ernle Bradford *The Journeying Moon* p 167

The little Dutch *botter* was a stout sea boat and, despite the qualms of many of his yachting friends, it performed well, even if it was no greyhound of the seas. After several years of sailing around the Mediterranean they took the boat back to Malta where they sold her. Selling a boat that has safely taken you on long voyages is never a joyous occasion and they soon had their eyes on another boat in Malta.

Here we discovered the pilot cutter *Mischief* lying disconsolate and unloved, moored between two buoys in Kalkara Creek off Valetta Harbour… Who had sailed her to Malta remains a mystery to me; the Mediterranean was certainly an unlikely choice of cruising grounds for a vessel designed for the western approaches to the Bristol Channel. She belonged to a local ship chandler who had taken a liking to our ship Mother Goose. After some hard bargaining we became *Mischief*'s new owners.

Janet Verasanso *Grace Darling*, afterward to H. W. Tilman *Mischief Goes South: Every Herring Should Hang by its Own Tail*. New Edition 1966/2016

They managed to get her seaworthy enough to sail to the Balearics and there they hauled her out in Puerto Andratx before returning to England to earn some money. Eventually they were contacted by a friend suggesting he knew someone who would be interested in buying *Mischief*. That someone was H. W. (Bill) Tilman and the boat was subsequently sold. Part of the deal was that Ernle and Janet would help sail her down to Gibraltar and after a disagreeable passage, disagreeable because Tilman considered a woman on board as tantamount to the source of all evil, and because his neo-Victorian manner was rude and coarse, not surprisingly, Ernle and Janet and the other crew all jumped ship in Gibraltar. Janet maintains she was the only woman ever to sail with Tilman, albeit briefly.[13]

At this stage the couple had fallen in love with different parts of the Mediterranean. Janet had found her spiritual home in the Greek islands while Ernle was attached to Sicily and Malta. Janet went on to sail her own boats in the Pacific and the Caribbean before returning to Greece where she sailed a Vertue and then a Corribee right up to 1995.

Ernle Bradford was a prolific writer and eventually settled in Kalkara in Malta. His *The Wind off the Island* is a paeon to his love for Sicily and describes in some depth sailing around there in *Mother Goose*.[14] His book on tracking

13   Verasanso *Grace Darling*, afterward to Tilman's *Mischief Goes South: Every Herring Should Hang by its Own Tail*.
14   Ernle Bradford *The Wind Off the Island* Hutchinson, 1960

the possible route of Odysseus around the Mediterranean, *Ulysses Found*, is a readable classic that is as good or better than most of the books retracing the track of Odysseus.[15] Many of his other books are on the history of events in the Mediterranean and the history of seafaring. He died in 1986.

Charles Violet and *Nova Espero*

In 1952–53 Charles Violet sailed the diminutive *Nova Espero* down through the French canals to the Mediterranean and onto to North Africa and Malta.[16] He had already crossed the Atlantic in *Nova Espero* with Stanley Smith and had a hankering to go sailing on his own.

I was not puzzled about where to go. As a schoolboy I had learnt, often painfully, some of the history and geography of the Mediterranean countries, and I had always wanted to visit them. To sail alone has always had great appeal to me. Lurking in the dark corridors of my mind has been the idea that out alone on the wide expanses of the sea it might be possible to lift a corner of the veil that keeps life a mystery to most of us.

Charles Violet *Solitary Journey* Mariners Library 1954/1962 p 16

Nova Espero was a 20 ft clinker-built sloop, later converted to a yawl.[17] She had barely sitting room inside the cabin, which was anyway a later addition – on her first voyage across the Atlantic she had only an upturned dinghy over the cockpit for shelter.[18] He had a 4hp Seagull outboard to get through the canals and for calms, though he had so little money for petrol he always sailed when he could. He had only a few small-scale charts with him as he couldn't afford to buy an adequate set of Admiralty charts – something those of us who followed in later years on tiny budgets were familiar with. His trip, some 5000 miles in all, was accomplished on a shoestring budget. In the Appendix on food in *Solitary Journey*, Charles relates '… spent only £60 in cash, and felt very fit at the end of it all'.

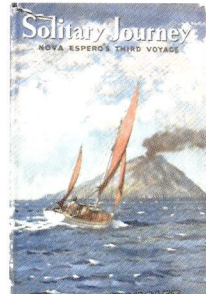

Cover of *Solitary Journey*.

15   Ernle Bradford *Ulysses Found* Sphere Books, 1963
16   I'm assuming it was 1952–53, as Stanley Smith and Charles Violet sailed *Nova Espero* across the Atlantic in 1951 and Charles Violet's *Solitary Journey* was published in 1954.
17   *Nova Espero*: 20 ft LOA. 15 ft 11 in., LWL. 6 ft 3 in. beam. 2 ft 10 in. draught
18   voicesonthewight.com/tag/colin-smith/

Following in the footsteps of George Millar, he crossed the Channel and went down through the French canals to Port St-Louis du Rhone in the Mediterranean before cruising to Corsica, down the coast of Sardinia and across to Tunisia before reaching Malta. He attempted to sail from Malta to Greece, indeed his ambition was to sail up to the Black Sea, but constant headwinds eventually defeated him, and he turned back to Malta before reaching Greece. He then re-traced his steps back to the Riviera and into the Canal du Midi and Canal Lateral à Garonne to reach the Bay of Biscay. He hopped around the Brittany coast and finally crossed the Channel to return home to the Isle of Wight.

In *Solitary Voyage* you get the impression that, though he liked his own company well enough, still he was glad of company he met along the way. He mentions the unfailing generosity of the locals he met in the countries he passed through and enjoyed the company of 'rough and regular' folk as opposed to the 'Yacht Club' types on large crewed yachts around the Riviera. There is a certain wistfulness to some of Charles's narrative that is not wholly explained in the book, though it is of an era where certain views were held of the world, of women, of the norms and mores of a society still recovering from the war. The swinging sixties and the transformation of a drab post-war Europe into a more prosperous and hopeful era was still some time away.

Crab's Odyssey

Crab's voyage almost didn't happen. When Penny and Sally and two friends were travelling out to Malta for the first time to sail *Crab*, the ferry they were on from Sicily to Malta hit a reef off the coast of Malta in fog and they had to abandon ship. Fortunately, they were not far from the island and reached shore safely to start their own voyages in the 17 ft open lifeboat *Crab*.[19]

The impetus to take on such a venture in 1955, well before the advent of women's liberation in the sixties, was both bold and brave. Women were still regarded with some suspicion in the 'Royal' yacht clubs where the membership was predominantly male. Both girls were studying classics at Oxford and both were avid dinghy sailors. They wanted adventure and to explore the shores of the eastern Mediterranean. That their respective families agreed to

19   Penny Minney *Crab's Odyssey*, Chapter 1

the venture is remarkable, and so Penny and Sally found themselves the proud owners of a ship's lifeboat that had been lying in the forecourt of a petrol station in Malta.

Sally was honest when she wrote in 1955 to her parents that she only intended to sail *Crab* from Malta to Sicily and back, but my sights were already set for further horizons and our increasing confidence in the summers that followed gradually made my dreams come true. We dressed up our adventures as serious research into merchant shipping and got to know intimately the sea approaches, harbours, markets, mountains and pathways of many of the places that we read about in university textbooks.

Wreck of the *Star of Malta*.
Photo *Crab's Odyssey*.

Penny Minney *Crab's Odyssey*
Taniwha Press p 13

Crab was a clinker-built lifeboat just 17 ft long with a mast and sails but no engine. They found a berth for *Crab* in Kalkara in Valletta Harbour and carried out sea trials that identified some modifications that were needed,

Penny steering *Crab*. Photo Robin Minney.

including a longer mast and more sail area and an additional six inches of oak keel to stop the boat making so much leeway. *Crab* was rigged with a lugsail main and a small jib and had no cabin, though it did have buoyancy tanks. A Seagull outboard on loan from Penny's father provided motive power in calms. Room on the boat was limited, so with four on board personal belongings were limited to 'one pair of long trousers, one of shorts, one shore going outfit and only one pair of footwear'.

The first voyage to Syracusa on Sicily went well for the passage across. The trip back was not so straightforward and, caught in a violent storm, they were set back to the Sicilian shore and helped to beach *Crab* by fishermen in the town of

Pozzallo. Throughout the book there are passages describing the wonderful hospitality of poor villages where they are taken in and treated as honoured guests in the age-old manner that travellers have always been treated in the Mediterranean. Eventually the storm abated, and they sailed *Crab* back to Malta. It had been a steep learning curve and Penny does mention there was at times a certain tension on the boat – not surprising when

Life on board was crowded: 'one pair of long trousers, one of shorts, one shore going outfit and only one pair of footwear'. Photo Robin Minney.

you cram four people and supplies and belongings into a 17 ft boat with just 6 ft beam.

The next year, in 1956, they sailed *Crab* from Malta to Corfu. After the previous summer and *Crab*'s successful voyage to and from Sicily there was no shortage of volunteers for crew. Sally, the skipper, wrote them all a letter describing what they might expect.

She warned them about the rigours of being out at sea in an open boat, fried from dawn till dusk by sun and wind, while proceeding towards our destination at half a knot for hours on end and being constantly doused with spray, but it did not deter them.

Penny Minney *Crab's Odyssey* p 57

One of the volunteers was Penny's father, the novelist Richard Hughes affectionately known as Diccon, who would crew on the first part of the trip from Malta to Sicily.[20] With various changes of crew, *Crab* crossed to the toe of Italy and cruised around the coast until the heel where they crossed to the little Greek island of Othoni and on to Corfu. There were adventures ashore as well. In Calabria Sally had taken a bus to intercept a new crew member as *Crab* would not be at the place agreed beforehand. While waiting she took her book to read in a secluded spot where a local came by with clear intentions of carnal relations.

A man came by with a frisky young mule and showed clear signs of wanting to rape me.

20   Richard Hughes authored *A High Wind in Jamaica* and *In Hazard*, amongst others.

What happened?

Nothing clever on my part. He found he couldn't catch hold of me, and at the same time keep hold of his mule, and in the end decided he'd better keep hold of the mule.

Penny Minney *Crab's Odyssey* p 79

In 1957 *Crab* was sailed to Piraeus via the Corinth Canal and up to the northern Sporades and back again. In 1958 the most ambitious cruise for *Crab* was planned, from Piraeus across the Aegean and up to Istanbul. By now Sally and Penny had completed their degrees at Oxford and had hatched a plan to use *Crab* to test the theory that ancient merchant ships could not sail through the Dardanelles and into the Black Sea against the prevailing wind and current.

Our planned route to Istanbul from Piraeus, after rounding Sounion, ran northwards again inside Evia, then northeast across open water to Lemnos, then through the Dardanelles and the Sea of Marmora. Returning, when we emerged from the Dardanelles, we would sail down the east side of the Aegean to Rhodes, then westwards across the Aegean, following the traditional routes for merchantmen.

Penny Minney *Crab's Odyssey* p 194

Penny's father Richard Hughes, Diccon, joined the crew of *Crab* for the passage to the Dardanelles and was much teased for being such an old man on such a frail craft. Not that Diccon was worried; he professed to love the simple life on the boat, so much so that when crew could not join them in Cannakale in the Dardanelles, he promptly offered to crew up to Istanbul. Life was simple, even primitive, on board *Crab*, but the girls and crew who arrived in different places to help get *Crab* on her way rubbed along together and celebrated any hardship with humour and fortitude.

The trip was hardly a rest-cure. A typical day on board would begin at 2.00 am, when there would be a sudden clatter and shouting as the fishing boats moored round us in the harbour loaded up, lit the great Tilley lamps that hung over the stern to attract the fish, and set off. This would be followed at 4am by the coastal caiques starting up their diesel engines and departing. We ourselves would usually rise and be under way by 5.30 am, to make the most of the cool of the early morning. There were no sleeping bags to put away, for there was no room for such

Crab at anchor. Photo Robin Minney.

luxuries on board; we simply put sweaters and jeans on to sleep. Breakfast consisted of tea without milk, and bread – the delicious, tough Greek bread spread with jam or honey – but no butter, as we had no refrigerator. Breakfast was eaten underway. At midday we would find a deserted cove where we could swim and eat, wash clothes and spread them on the shore to dry, and spread our limbs in comfort to sleep in the shade of a tree till the shadows began to lengthen again.

Penny Minney *Crab's Odyssey* pp 201–202

Crab motored up the Dardanelles using the ailing Seagull outboard, keeping closer in towards the shore out of the main current and taking advantage of back-eddies on the edge of the narrow strait. Southerlies blowing up the Dardanelles are not as frequent as the normal meltemi that barrels down from the north, but is also not so unusual if you strike it lucky or have the patience to wait until southerlies blow.[21] *Crab* eventually reached Istanbul and made her way up the Bosphorus with a light following wind, under sail, oars and outboard, battling against a current of up to seven knots round one of the headlands. By means of a tow rope ashore they managed to get around the headland out of the worst of the current, so proving that a small boat that was not at all handy going to windward could make the passage.[22] Once in Istanbul they explored the city until it was time to turn *Crab's* prow back towards the Aegean and Rhodes.

The story had a happy ending for Penny in Rhodes when Robin Minney, one of the co-owners of the boat, popped the question to her and she answered in the affirmative. *Crab* was sailed back through the Aegean as far as Naxos where the meltemi howled and it seemed they would never get back to Piraeus. Eventually *Crab* was taken as deck cargo to Piraeus and put back in the water for her last days under sail in the command of Sally and Penny.

Hammond Innes meets Tito in the 1960's. Photo in *Sea and Islands.*

21   Rod & Lucinda Heikell *Turkish Waters and Cyprus Pilot* Imray 2013 pp 50–53
22   Tim Severin also took advantage of southerlies in the Dardanelles when he sailed his replica Homeric scouting ship up to the Black Sea. Tim Severin *The Jason Voyage* Hutchinson, 1985

Hammond Innes and the *Mary Deare*

Hammond Innes was a prolific writer who wrote over thirty novels, children's books and some non-fiction describing his travels. Many of Hammond Innes' novels reflect his love of the sea, so it is not surprising that he was an avid yachtsman and, in true Innes style, he researched many of the locations in his novels under sail. The novel that catapulted him into the best-seller list in 1956 was *The Wreck of the Mary Deare*, a story of high seas salvage and intrigue on an old tramp steamer, *Mary Deare*. It was later made into a film, *The Wreck of the Mary Deare*. Innes's second yacht, bought largely from the proceeds of his book and the film, was, not surprisingly, called *Mary Deare*. Innes made numerous long passages in her including sailing down to the Mediterranean in 1963, described in his collection of travel essays *Sea and Islands*.[23]

Mary Deare was a 42 ft Robert Clark design, built in Holland of steel and fitted out in Suffolk. Innes succinctly stated his requirements to the designer like this: '… she should be able to race without ignominy and at the same time sail anywhere in the world.' The line drawings of the *Mary Deare* show a long, scooped spoon bow and an elegant counter stern. She had berths to sleep six and '32 lockers and drawers for stowage'.

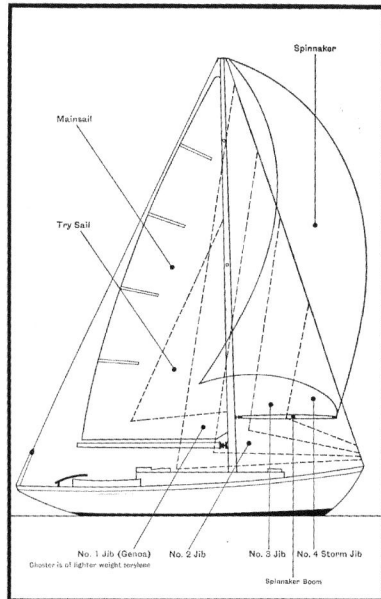

Mary Deare line drawing. Diagram in *Sea and Islands.*

Before heading off to the Mediterranean, Innes first cruised around Scandinavia, shaping a course across the Bay of Biscay in early May 1963. They nearly didn't make it to the Mediterranean when rigging problems caused Innes to divert to La Rochelle for repairs. Once these had been made, they did long legs to Gibraltar and then onto the Balearics and across to St Tropez to meet his French publishers. From here he cruised across to Corsica and Sardinia before heading down to Malta where Innes planned

23   Hammond Innes *Sea and Islands* Collins 1967

to leave the *Mary Deare* until the next year. The idea for a cruise down to the Mediterranean had been the idea of his wife, Dorothy, but he was soon enchanted by the place.

Other sailors have described Ibiza, but coming straight from Atlantic waters the first sight of it remains a unique experience touched as it is with the magic of the Mediterranean. The dark interiors of its small shops yield embroidery, gaily-painted pottery, wrought iron, straw-work – there is even a herbalist – and over all hangs that warm southern scent that is composed of charcoal fires, olive oil and herbs.

Hammond Innes *Sea and Islands* p 59

In 1964 Innes flew back out to Malta to re-join *Mary Deare*. The boat had been damaged in a winter gale and Innes had his doubts about whether it would be ready to go sailing. In the event, an immaculately clean boat with a repair that '… only the closest examination showed the area of bulwark where repairs had been carried out' lay bobbing to her mooring off Manoel Island. Although there were still few yachts sailing in the Mediterranean, facilities for the care and repair of yachts were springing up in places like Malta, where yachts could be safely left for the winter.

With crew enough for the trip, he set off for Pylos on the Peloponnese and, despite engine problems, was quickly around into the Aegean. The meltemi, the prevailing wind in the Aegean , forced him to wait for better weather in some of the islands scattered across the Aegean, but in the end he described a complete island-hopping loop around the Aegean and returned to Malta with the *Mary Deare*.

Innes is sailing around the eastern Mediterranean in the early 1960's and it is remarkable how few other yachts he comes across on his travels. He remarks that they only 'saw one yacht under sail the whole time we were in Greek waters', though they saw numbers of

Mary Deare at anchor. Photo in *Sea and Islands*.

Hammond Innes at Sounion in Greece.
Photo in *Sea and Islands.*

big sailing yachts and local schooners which 'keep their sails stowed'.[24] Innes resolved to return to the eastern Mediterranean the next year and cruise the Ionian – Odysseus' sea.

For most of his writing life Hammond Innes spent six months researching his next novel and six months in the winter writing it. He was a prolific writer. In 1965 he cruised around the Ionian islands and at some time, cruising down the Meganisi Channel between Levkas Island and the Rorschach blob of Meganisi Island opposite, he would have come across the caves in the cliffs on the southeast corner of Levkas. This must have given him the germ of the idea for his *Levkas Man*,[25] a novel about a famous anthropologist investigating the early ascent of man in this part of the world.

The next year, 1966, Innes sailed to Istanbul and, in the Corinthian spirit, he really did sail as his engine was again out of commission. They worked up the Turkish coast from Bodrum until Kusadasi where the engine was fixed, and they could then proceed to the Dardanelles. Innes was happy he now had an engine again but you can see he revels in the joys of being under sail.

It was very beautiful that night and, as always when we are driving through a kindly sea, Dorothy sat alone in the bows for a while before turning in. From where I stood at the helm I could just see her head, very still, in silhouette against the stretched Terylene of the genoa.

Hammond Innes *Sea and Islands* p 153

They successfully got to Istanbul before turning back for the long haul to Malta. Innes had almost come to think of Malta as home and, though he eventually took *Mary Deare* back to England; for a while, this was his home. *Levkas Man*, the novel he wrote set in Greece, has an underlying theme to it of the descent of man into a world where we have forgotten our place and are ruining the habitat that nourished us. He once said that, 'As we have become more technological, we have lost a lot… There were things those early people

24   Hammond Innes *Sea and Islands* p 101
25   Hammond Innes *Levkas Man* Collins, 1971

understood that we don't.'[26] He gave up sailing in his late sixties and devoted himself to planting trees on his estate. Characteristically, he wrote a novel about his tree planting passion: *High Stand*, published in 1985.

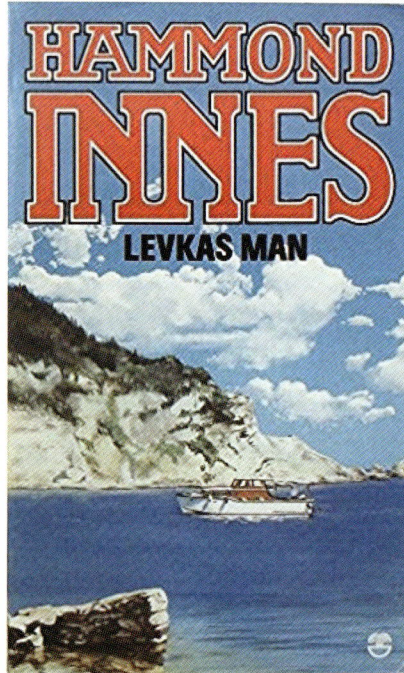

26   Quoted in the Obituary to Hammond Innes in the *Independent*, Saturday 13 June, 1998.

Creole. Photo Liliane Paingaud. Wiki Commons.

11 THE RICH AND THE SUPER RICH: PART I. GREEK TRAGEDY

At the beginning of the Second World War the merchant shipping fleet had been decimated. It had either been co-opted into the war effort or sunk by one side or other in the war. The Americans realised the scale of the losses and embarked on a ship-building programme using assembly line automation to build the ships at a much faster rate than pre-war techniques. One of the major innovations was to weld the ships' hulls rather than riveting them. At the end of the war the American government had a considerable surplus of these 'Liberty' ships and offered to sell them at a knock-down rate to European governments. The Greek government stumped up a sizeable bond for Greek shipowners to replace their fleets, and not surprisingly many shipowners jumped at the chance.[1]

The purchase of these 'Liberty' ships massively increased the tonnage under Greek shipowners to the largest in the world, a position they still hold today by some margin.[2] While some of these shipowners remain hardly known to the general population (people like the Livanos family and Kostas Lemos) others were only too happy to be in the limelight, and names like Aristotle Onassis and Stavros Niarchos became well known. Part of the allure to the public and the ever-present paparazzi revolved around their yachts, and the rivalry between the two men over who had the biggest and best in Monaco harbour is well recorded. When Niarchos was buying *Creole*, the three-masted schooner, it is said that the only question he asked was 'whether anyone else had a yacht like it'.[3]

Onassis and *Christina O*

Aristotle Onassis started building a shipping fleet when he realised that the owners of the ships transporting the cigarettes from his factory in Argentina were making more money than the cigarette factory. Ari, as he was commonly known, was born in Smyrna, present day Izmir, on the Turkish Mediterranean

1 Article by Gelina Harlaftis, *Cornerstone of Greek Shipping: 100 Liberties* Ekathimerini 19 July, 2012
2 Safety4Sea 25/05/18 safety4sea.com/greece-the-leader-in-global-merchant-fleet/
3 Anecdotal from a conversation with the author on *Creole* in Zea Marina.

coast, and was taken to Argentina as a child when the Greeks were ejected from Turkey in 1922. He moved into shipping during the Second World War and after the war built up his fleet with the purchase of 'Liberty' ships from the USA. By the early 1950's he was a wealthy man.

His first yacht was called *Olympic Winner*, though we know little about her except that he first visited Monaco in this yacht. His second yacht, *Christina O*, was his 'baby', and he lavished attention and money on her throughout the rest of his life.[4] *Christina O* was originally called HMCS *Stormont*, a surplus Canadian anti-submarine frigate that he bought for its scrap value of $34,000 in 1954. The boat was taken to Germany and Onassis spent a reputed $4–5 million dollars on fitting her out to be one of the most opulent yachts afloat. Even today at 99 metres long (325 ft) she is one of the bigger superyachts in a world of very big yachts.[5]

Right from the beginning Onassis wanted *Christina O* to impress and, while some of the interior furnishings were showy and some downright bizarre, the overall feeling was of light and soft pastel colours throughout the yacht. He had the stools in the bar covered with a soft ivory-coloured leather-like

Onassis' *Christina O*. Photo Shutterstock.

---

4   Properly *Christina O*, named after his daughter, though the 'O' was often left off the name in conversation.
5   Roger Lean-Vercoe and Peter Boulton *Iconic Yachts: Christina O* Boat International 14 January, 2015

material that Onassis liked to inform his guests was made from the foreskins of whale penises. His rival, Stavros Niarchos, was reputed to have had his own bar stools covered with the same material when he learnt of *Christina O's* quirky fittings. The round swimming pool had a floor that could be raised to convert it into a dance floor. Everywhere on the yacht was decorated with Greek motifs: the swimming pool floor had a mosaic depicting the Minotaur; the guest cabins were all named after Greek islands; the master bathroom featured motifs from Minoan Knossos on Crete; engraved orca's teeth surrounded the bar along with the bizarre bar-stool covers; and down below was a concert room where his favourite bouzouki bands (which he frequently flew in) played for him.[6]

In 1946 Onassis met the daughter of the richest shipping magnate in the world, Athina (Tina) Livanos. She was almost half his age, but he courted her, and they married. The couple had two children: a son, Alexander, and a daughter, Christina, after whom Onassis named his yacht. In a bizarre twist Tina would later remarry, to Stavros Niarchos, Onassis' great rival. By the time he had *Christina O* refitted Onassis was a shaker and mover, and nowhere more so than in Monaco.

In the 1950's Monaco was on its uppers. Income from the casino had declined dramatically after the war amid competition from other cities along the Riviera and the once great hotels and other waterfront buildings were looking shabby and facing the possibility of going bankrupt. Even so, it was Onassis' favourite port of call on the Riviera and he often moored his first yacht, *Olympic Winner,* and later *Christina O,* there – the latter the biggest yacht in the harbour at the time. Onassis was canny enough to know that the rich and famous and their business associates would be attracted to parties on a yacht like *Christina O,* and his guest list of those who attended over the years was extraordinary: Winston Churchill first met John F. Kennedy and Jackie on board; Marilyn Monroe graced the decks; Frank Sinatra crooned on the after deck while Rudolf Nureyev preened ; Liz Taylor and Richard Burton argued and made up; and famously Maria Callas, often said to be the greatest soprano in living memory, was a perennial visitor and, in due course, became Onassis' mistress. It is said that Tina eventually divorced her husband because his affair with Maria Callas was so public that she felt constantly humiliated.

6   Nancy Holmes *The Dream Boats* Prentice-Hall, 1976, Chapter 5

With a little research and, no doubt, some advice from the rich and well connected who attended his parties, Onassis started investing in the Société des Bains de Mer (SBM), a real estate corporation which ran the casino, and by 1951 had a controlling share in it. His vision for Monaco was of something along the lines of a Vegas-sur-Mer, where the rich and famous would come to gamble, party and just generally hang out. Soon Onassis was popularly known as 'the uncrowned king of Monaco', a title which understandably rankled with Prince Rainier, the ruler of the principality. There was little Rainier could do about the major shareholder in the casino that kept his miniature kingdom fiscally afloat, so for a while he rubbed along with Onassis, though personally he had a different vision for Monaco from the shipping magnate. It is even said that the fairy-tale marriage of Prince Rainier to the Hollywood starlet Grace Kelly in 1956 was masterminded by Onassis.

Onassis' love of Monaco began to wain in the 1960's. The cunning Prince Rainier had secretly issued more shares in the SBM, bought them up himself, and so wrested the controlling interest in the company away from Onassis and back under the control of the royal family. In 1962 Onassis bought the island of Skorpios and the adjacent islet of Skorpidhi in the Greek Ionian for a paltry $10,000. One

Onassis's private island, Skorpios, in the Ionian.

of the first things he did was to lay a huge mooring in the channel between Skorpios and Skorpidhi for *Christina O* and construct a small harbour for the tender from *Christina O* to land guests on the island. The island itself was landscaped and turned from a barren rock into something close to a park. It even had a small farm to provide fresh milk and eggs – probably the most pampered cows in the world.

In 1968 Onassis married Jackie Kennedy on Skorpios, some six years after the assassination of her husband, President John F. Kennedy. The marriage of the beautiful Jackie to a now somewhat older and quite rumpled Greek tycoon led to much gossip by the press. Onassis finished his long-standing, fiery affair

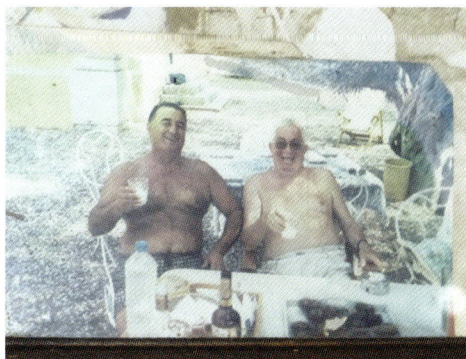

Nic the Greek and Onassis, photo in Nic's taverna in Nidri.

with Maria Callas to marry Jackie and so earned the enmity, not just of Maria Callas, but also his daughter Christina. The elegant Miro-like beach house on the south side of Skorpios was built for Jackie – at some expense for such a simple structure. After Onassis' death in 1975 Jackie hardly visited the island.

I visited the island in 1979 with one of the then caretakers and a local taverna owner, Nic the Greek, from Nidri on Levkas Island. Nic was a friend of the Onassis' and he still has photos up on the wall of the taverna of Ari and Jackie eating and drinking with him when they still came to Skorpios. The island is a stunning spot, more like a landscaped park than a wild place, with a simple graveyard and chapel on a stubby headland where the Onassis clan is buried. There is accommodation for guests ashore, should they want it, and accommodation and service quarters for staff. Normally around 40 staff were on the island, although more could be drafted in if needed. Ari always stayed on board his *Christina O* rather than ashore. From 1977, when I first saw *Christina O* moored off Skorpios, to 1978 when Onassis' daughter Christina, who inherited the yacht, donated it to the Greek government, it sat sadly off the headland where Ari was buried. He had died in 1975 in France and was buried in the simple graveyard on Skorpios with his son Alexander, who had died in a plane crash two years before. Onassis always maintained that the death of his son was a CIA plot against him and his family.

Nic the Greek today.

The Greek government seemed somewhat embarrassed by Christina's donation of the yacht and for years it sat rotting in Piraeus. Eventually *Christina O* was rescued by an old Onassis family friend, another wealthy shipowner, John Paul Papanicolaou, who spent an estimated $50 million restoring her to her former glory. She now charters in the Mediterranean.[7] The island of Skorpios was recently sold to the daughter of a Russian oligarch, Ekaterina Rybolovleva, by the last heir of the Onassis fortune, Athena, Christina's daughter, who has rarely visited the island and seems to have little interest in things

Nic the Greeks' taverna still in the same location in Nidri.

Greek – unlike her grandfather who, after making his millions, gravitated back to the land of his forebears.[8] In a sad way the Onassis dynasty has come full circle, with all three Onassis's – Christina died of a drug overdose in 1988 and is buried on the island alongside Aristotle and Alexander – in a peaceful place overlooking the sea that is the last connection the Onassis dynasty has to Greece.

Stavros Niarchos and *Creole*

Niarchos found *Creole* rotting on the south coast of England in 1947. If he did in fact ask the question of 'whether anyone else had a yacht like it', he would have, or should have, been told that *Creole* is the largest wooden sailing yacht ever to have been built and remains so today.[9] He bought and transported her to the INS shipyard in Germany where he spent millions of dollars restoring her to her former glory.

The yacht, then named *Vira*, was commissioned in 1926 by the American millionaire Alexander Smith Cochran, who inherited an estimated $40 million in the shape of the Alexander Smith Carpet Company, founded by his father.

7   Lean-Vercoe and Boulton *Iconic Yachts*
8   Helena Smith *Aristotle Onassis heir sells private island to Russian oligarch's daughter* Guardian 16 April, 2013
9   At 214.20 ft/65.30 metres *Creole* remains the largest wooden yacht still sailing in the world. At present a longer wooden sailing yacht, the four masted schooner, *Dream Symphony*, at 482 ft/147 metres, is being built in Mugla in Turkey.

Often called the most eligible bachelor in America, he spent much of his time and a fair proportion of his inheritance sailing. When he commissioned *Vira* his brief was for Charles Nicholson to design the most beautiful sailing yacht in the world. Things didn't go well right from the beginning. It took three attempts to break the champagne bottle on the bows at the launch of the yacht in Gosport. When Cochran first saw *Vira* he immediately ordered the designer, Charles Nicholson, to shorten the masts by 10 ft (3 metres) because he considered the rig too lofty for the crew to handle. Still not satisfied when that was done, he ordered the masts to be reduced in height still further before he sailed off in her. With the shortened masts her performance was sluggish, so he had some of the ballast removed to improve her speed. The end result was that she became too tender under sail.[10]

It was all to end badly for Cochran. When he commissioned *Vira* he was already suffering from tuberculosis and finally succumbed to the disease in 1929. The boat was sold to a Maurice Pope who returned the yacht to the Camper and Nicholson yard to have the masts lengthened. It was he who christened her *Creole*, apparently from a delicious dessert his chef made.[11] He

Creole under sail.
Wiki Commons.

used the yacht around the Solent until it was bought by Sir Connop Guthrie who again returned the yacht to the Camper and Nicholson yard for her to be restored to the original design specifications of Charles Nicholson. He raced her successfully in regattas around England until the outbreak of the Second World War when she was loaned to the Admiralty. Her masts were removed, and she took up mine-hunting duty off Scotland under the name *Magic Circle*.[12]

Guthrie died at the end of the war and *Creole* was left, unloved and looking nothing like her former self after her stint as a mine-hunter, until 1947 when Stavros Niarchos spotted her and bought *Creole*. He took *Creole* to the INS yard in Germany to be restored where he spent hundreds of thousands of

10   Gucci's *Creole* //theislander.net/gucci-s-creole/
11   Keith Dovkants *The Curse of Classic 63m Yacht Creole* Boat International 1 December, 2015
12   Dovkants *The Curse of Classic 63m Yacht Creole*

dollars bringing her back
to life. Her sleek black hull
was repainted and her spars
repaired and stepped. He
added the raised varnished
deckhouse she still has and
had the interior restyled,
including hanging some of
the valuable works of art he
owned in the saloon and
cabins. It is clear Niarchos
had fallen in love with the
three-masted schooner and
she was soon down in the

Creole in Nice. Photo by Trayex. Wiki Commons.

Mediterranean in the old haunts of Monaco and moored off Niarchos' private
island, Spetsopoula, located a short distance off the southeast corner of the
larger island of Spetsai in the Saronic Gulf.[13]

While Niarchos had other yachts, notably the 102 ft gas turbine powered
Mercury that could do 50 knots, and later his *Atlantis*, at 380 ft (116 metres),
a yacht built to out-do Onassis' *Christina O,* it was *Creole* that he used most
often.[14] Niarchos lavished attention on her and supervised the running of the
boat himself. He sailed her often and is said to have called the yacht 'home'. In
1956 and 1958 he loaned *Creole* to the newly formed Sail Training Association
in Britain, a charitable organisation formed to foster sailing skills for young
people, and even sailed on her for a number of voyages with the Association.[15]

Around the time that Niarchos rescued *Creole* from rotting away in England,
he courted and married Eugenia Livanos, the sister of Onassis' wife, Tina
Livanos. In 1970 they were on holiday on *Creole*: Stavros Niarchos, Eugenia his
wife, and Tina, now divorced from Onassis. On the 3rd of May, Eugenia was
found dead in her cabin from what the coroner determined was an overdose
of barbiturates. The story has a shady history to it, although nothing was ever

13   Rod & Lucinda Heikell *West Aegean* Imray 2014, p 129
14   Holmes *The Dream Boats* pp 64–66
15   The Sail Training Association was formed in 1956 and became the Tall Ships Youth Trust.
Stavros Niarchos went on to fund the building of a three-masted schooner for the Trust, the
Stavros S Niarchos.

proved. The coroner reported bruises on Eugenia's neck and arms and the story from one witness was that Stavros Niarchos had tried to force himself on Tina and Eugenia, on intervening, had died in the ensuing ruckus. Niarchos was never charged and there were rumours that his connections to the military junta then running the country may have helped his acquittal. The official verdict of the coroner, of a drug overdose, stood.[16]

In 1971 Niarchos married Tina, Eugenia's sister and Onassis' ex-wife, and all seemed well until she too died of a suspected drug overdose in Paris in 1974. After the death of Eugenia on board *Creole* Niarchos seemed to lose interest in the yacht and it sat forlornly in Zea Marina in Piraeus, going nowhere. I remember seeing it there with a skeleton crew and bizarrely, though it had no guests on board, it did have an elaborate fresh flower arrangement on the cockpit table.

In 1977 *Creole* was sold to a Danish sailing school that took ex-gang members, young people recovering from drug and alcohol addiction, and youth offenders who had generally been on the wrong side of the law, on extended voyages on sailing yachts to instil confidence in them and to teach them to work as a team. I had met one of the rough 40-footers belonging to the school previously and had a look at the spartan interior where up to six crew could sleep and talked to one of the ex-gang members crewing it. No alcohol or drugs were allowed on board and the crew all had to cook, clean and sail the boat under the aegis of the teacher in charge. I was impressed with the project, though on reflection it seemed to me to be a little overly disciplinarian and the young crew somewhat cowed under the teacher in charge.

It turns out that the organisation which bought *Creole*, an organisation operating under various names and usually shortened to Tvind, the town where it began life in the 1970's, is a somewhat murky entity where the panel controlling the various 'charitable' NGOs and known as the 'Teachers Group', have diverted large amounts of money to their own purposes and to the lifestyle of the founder, Mogens Amdi Petersen. It has been described as a non-religious cult rather than a charity. The core group of the 'Teachers Group' were convicted in absentia in Denmark of tax evasion and money

16   Dovkants *The Curse of Classic 63m Yacht Creole*

laundering and are now believed to be living in Mexico, which does not have an extradition treaty with Denmark.[17]

Creole was taken to Nyborg in Denmark where Tvind based other boats it had, though she was little used except for what the sailing school called 'pleasure trips'.[18] Eventually the upkeep of the yacht and problems of certification for the professional crew on board and of the safety equipment required for a 'school ship' proved to be too much for the Tvind organisation and *Creole* was sold to Maurizio Gucci of couturier fame.[19] *Creole* was again taken to a shipyard to be refitted, this time the venerable Cantiere Navale dell'Argentario in Santo Stefano on the Tuscany coast.

It took six years and vast amounts of money to restore *Creole* to her former self. Once the black hulled beauty was ready, Maurizio toured the Mediterranean and raced her in the Classics Races in places like Barcelona, Palma and St Tropez. I remember seeing her at anchor in Minorca, complete with a replica launch of the period when she was built that was used to ferry guests ashore and back. Needless to say, the crew were turned out immaculately, looking something like French *matelots* of a bygone age.

Maurizio Gucci, heir apparent to the Gucci fortune, was something of a man about town. He married Patrizia Reggiano, who had an eye for the good life as well. Of her life she once said 'I'd rather weep in a Rolls-Royce than laugh on a bicycle'.[20] Though Patrizia was a hard-headed sort of person, she also had a superstitious side and wanted Maurizio to hire a psychic to cleanse *Creole* of evil spirits. He duly hired a psychic called Frida to take on the job.

17   Much of the source material is in Danish, but there have been a few reports in English of the Tvind group. For additional material you need to go to Danish sources.
Michael Durham *Enigma of the Leader* Guardian 9th June, 2003
www.tvindalert.com/ A website exposing the Tvind organisation.
Paul Henley BBC *Crossing Continents/Denmark's Tvind* 21st March, 2002
18   www.fyens.dk/nyborg/Farvel-til-Tvind-skibene/artikel/974725
19   The Tvind organisation had a three-masted schooner built in the Faenoe Shipyard near Kolding in the late 1980's after the sale of *Creole*. It was principally for the use of the Tvind founder Mogens Amdi Petersen and was for a time berthed in Miami. The *Butterfly McQueen*, named after the black American actress who played the maid in *Gone with the Wind*, was later delivered to Australia where it sat on the mud for years. Eventually it was sold, refitted and re-named *Southern Cloud*.
PDF of unpublished MA thesis by Steen Thomsen entitled *Concerning Tvind*.
www.superyachttimes.com/yacht-news/the-resurrection-of-superyacht-southern-cloud
20   Quoted in Dovkants *The Curse of Classic 63m Yacht Creole*

The episode is detailed in Sara Gay Forden's acclaimed book, *The House of Gucci*. Forden wrote that Frida "went into a trance" and walked through *Creole* mumbling incomprehensibly. "Open the door, open the door," Frida cried out suddenly as Maurizio and Patrizia looked at each other, puzzled. They were standing in an open corridor; there was no door. But the Sicilian crew member turned ashen. Before the restoration of Creole, there had been a door in that very spot, he said.

Forden goes on to say that Frida pointed to a place where, the psychic said, Eugenia Niarchos's body had been found. Then she snapped out of her trance, said, "It's all over" and declared Creole "free of evil spirits".

Quoted in Dovkants *The Curse of Classic 63m Yacht Creole*.

While *Creole* may have been cleansed of bad spirits, there was still a fiscal storm ahead for Maurizio. In 1987 he was accused of buying *Creole* with funds he had diverted to a Panamanian company. He directed his captain and crew to take the yacht to Spain and then escaped over the border to Switzerland. A year later he was acquitted, and he re-joined his beloved *Creole*. By now he had split up with Patrizia and moved in with his lover Paolo Franchi. Then, in 1995, when Maurizio was arriving at his office in Milan, a gunman stepped up, fired three bullets into his back and, when he had slumped to the floor, another into his temple. Two years later his ex-wife Patrizia was arrested and accused of hiring a hitman to kill Maurizio. She was sentenced to twenty-six years in prison and served sixteen before being paroled in 2014. Maurizio had been spending vast amounts of money on *Creole* and living with his lover on board. He had announced his intention to marry Paolo and that, it seems, was a step too far for Patrizia.[21]

Creole, along with Maurizio's considerable fortune, was inherited by his daughters, Allegra and Alessandra. They keep the yacht in immaculate shape, in memory of their father they say, and it is seen all around the Mediterranean.[22]

Creole in Italy.
Photo Robert McCabe.

21   Abigail Haworth *The Gucci wife and the hitman: Fashions darkest tale* The Observer 24 July, 2016
22   Quoted in Dovkants *The Curse of Classic 63m Yacht Creole*

Was *Creole* a 'cursed yacht'? It certainly seems that the history of her owners has been a troubled one. As some have said, even her recent history is reminiscent of a Greek tragedy.

John Carras and *Argonaftis*

In October 1980 I was in Porto Carras on the Khalkidhiki researching my yachtsman's pilot for Greece. The weather was turning, and I was stuck in the marina for days waiting for the gale force winds and driving rain to die down. There were few yachts in there at the time and the marina was dominated by the 187 ft (57 metres) hull of *Argonaftis*. The three-masted schooner took up most of the north side of Porto Carras and I soon struck up a conversation with some of the Greek crew looking after her. She had been built to a design by Robert Clark in the De Vries Lentsch shipyard in Holland in 1960 and sailed down to northern Greece where she had sat for most of the last twenty years. She was built for John Carras, the shipping magnate, and was originally called *Carina* after his wife. He later renamed her *Argonaftis*: sailors of the Argo, Jason's ship used in the quest for the golden fleece. Apart from his shipping business, in 1963 John Carras started to develop Porto Carras marina and the large estate around it, a strange and improbable place, along the lines of the French developments around the coast of Languedoc-Roussillon.[23]

Argonaftis was a pretty three-masted schooner, though the deckhouse was unusual. All the windows and portlights had heavy metal shutters that locked down. The rest of the yacht also appeared to be locked down, though all her sails were fitted, and she looked spruce and ready for sea. One evening over a beer with the first mate on the yacht I mentioned her strange locked-down appearance. The story he gave me may be apocryphal as there is nothing written on the subject, but it is nonetheless interesting.[24]

Argonaftis was conceived as an escape vehicle in the event of a nuclear war. She was kept ready to go to sea at a moment's notice, with the crew briefed that within twenty-four hours she should be ready to leave harbour and make for a safe destination – wherever that might be.

---

23 Rod & Lucinda Heikell *Greek Waters Pilot* 12th ed. pp 373–374
24 I made a few scribbled notes at the time, now lost, but do remember the conversation vividly.

The boat was kept fully provisioned, had full water and fuel tanks, and could be locked down, (hence the heavy metal shutters), to stay at sea for a year. She carried 32,000 litres of fuel which gave her a range of 3000 miles at twelve knots. She carried 21,830 litres of water.[25] And she was rigged as a staysail schooner, so a small crew could handle her under sail.

John Carras died in 1989 and the boat was sold to a Dutchman, John Deuss. He renamed her *Fleurtje* and kept her in Bermuda where he lived for much of the time, although she was also down in the Caribbean islands and over in the Mediterranean in the northern summer. The name John Deuss may be familiar to some as an oil trader who by various means, most of them illegal, broke the oil sanction on apartheid South Africa in the 1980's. *Fleurtje* is the name of one of the oil tankers he used to do so. He is estimated to have made nearly half a billion dollars. He also established a bank in Curaçao that effectively laundered money, his own and others. In 2006 he was arrested for fraud, money laundering and tax evasion. In 2012 he was given a six-month suspended sentence and ordered to pay forty-seven million dollars to the Dutch government, around half of what he was being prosecuted for. In the meantime, *Fleurtje* was put up for sale, though it is uncertain if she has been sold yet and whether John Deuss remains the owner. Maybe she is kept ready in the event of a major catastrophe.

Fleurtje, previously *Argonaftis*. Photo Alamy.
25   Frances & Michael Howarth *Fleurtje* Boat International February 2018

The Ionian: the perfect flotilla area. Here, in Nidri in the Inland Sea.

12 THE FLOTILLA STORY

The genesis of flotilla sailing is tied into the era of the 1960's and 70's when the democratisation of sailing, of the idea of going on holiday in the Mediterranean, was beginning to take root not as the prerogative of the rich or an adventure for the tough, but as something the man in street could aspire to. The very idea of sailing in turquoise waters under a blue sky with the heat of the sun on your back was to tempt many who would otherwise have turned down a sail in the muddy swatchways of Essex or the shouting and testosterone enveloping racing in the Solent. I should disclose at this point that part of this history takes a personal twist since I was involved in the early days of flotilla sailing, though I have tried to be as objective as you can with a personal history.

Flotilla sailing started in Greece in the 1970's and has proved enduringly popular ever since. Eric Richardson started the first flotilla, the Yacht Cruising Association (YCA), in 1974. The origins of the idea are somewhat lost in time, but somehow Eric developed the idea of a little fleet of identical boats shepherded by a lead boat with a skipper, engineer and hostess on board, accompanying them on a more or less set route around the Greek islands.

The humble 24 ft Snapdragon that started it all off in 1974. Photo Mike Cox.

Up until this point it was difficult to find a yacht to sail around the Mediterranean unless you sailed your own little craft down or you had the money to charter one of the large charter yachts dotted around various places – mostly in the western Mediterranean and a few spots around parts of Italy and Greece. In many ways the concept of flotilla sailing was to do with the democratisation of yachting and making it affordable for more people to charter a yacht around the Greek islands. The concept of flotilla sailing emerged on the back of all-inclusive package holidays which had become popular by the 1970's.[1] Horizon Holidays and later Clarksons were the pioneers who operated all-inclusive holidays to Corsica, Italy and Spain in the 1950's and 1960's that enabled the less well off to go on holiday to foreign places.

Eric Richardson had worked in the budget flight business for a number of years, so was well acquainted with the concept of the package holiday. Still the idea of an all-inclusive sailing holiday in Greece was considered at best adventurous and at worst a foolhardy idea that would end in disaster.

The sailing press in general was very cool. One editor said he thought the idea impractical and YCA would be on the rocks in a few weeks. Others intimated that the tone of the sport was being lowered, and flotillas would 'encourage the wrong sort'.

Mike Jakeways *From the Deck of Your Own Yacht* FloMo Publishing, 2009 p 20

To an extent this snooty attitude has endured to this day, although it now encompasses criticism of bareboat charter as well as the flotillas. And it's not confined to pompous yacht club members and the 'better class' of people who go sailing in the Mediterranean. A lot of nonsense and a sort of snobbery revolves around the idea of flotilla sailing. Comments like: 'it is just like ducklings following the mother duck'; 'I want to get away from it all and not sail together with other boats'; and 'it's just a package holiday afloat', are all too often attached to the idea of flotilla sailing by private yacht owners, a few chartering bare boat yachts and even by some would-be charterers of flotilla holidays. In practice, none of it is like this and those who go on flotilla holidays often return again and again. Sailing Holidays probably holds the record with one customer who has been on a flotilla sailing holiday 90 times throughout the history of the company.[2] Nor is it solely a matter of sailing experience. Often experienced sailors who own a yacht at home choose to take the flotilla option for the social side with a bit of one-design racing on the side.

Since those early days, flotilla sailing has expanded to other Mediterranean countries and further abroad to Thailand and the Caribbean. Thirty years on a lot has changed. In the first few years it may come as a surprise to some that

1   This despite the collapse of Court Line in 1974 which by then owned Horizon and Clarksons. Some 50,000 were left stranded at airports, mostly around Europe, and around 100,000 lost deposits on holidays.
2   Conversation with Barrie Neilson, the owner of Sailing Holidays Ltd.

only the lead boat had a VHF radio. Otherwise communication was by flag from the lead boat to the other flotilla boats and if anyone went missing you had to chase after them, desperately trying to attract their attention, and then shepherd them back to where they were supposed to be going. In 1978 in the Saronic I lost half the flotilla during a thunderstorm when rain reduced the visibility to 100 metres or so for an hour. It took all afternoon to find the lost boats which had been scattered all over the Argolic Gulf.

Flotilla sailing is a good option for families... well for anyone really.
Photo Sailing Holidays Ltd.

Getting spares and equipment out to the boats today is a streamlined operation and companies keep large stocks of spares for their fleets. In the early days we asked customers coming out to bring spares through with their luggage. Newcomers would wander through the airport with hatches, engine spares, sails, even an anchor on one occasion, and pile them up in front of the rep who was organising the bus transfer to the flotilla base. We, in turn, would provide them with bad wine and as much local brandy as they could drink for all their trouble.

While today things are very different to those early days – the yachts are bigger and better equipped, the shore bases are more sophisticated and carry large stocks of spares, new airports have opened for international flights making transfers to sailing areas easier – still, the essence of flotilla sailing that began forty-five years ago has remained the same since Eric Richardson's moment of inspiration.[3]

In the beginning: The Yacht Cruising Association

In 1956 Eric Richardson, who had been serving in the army during the Suez crisis, went on R & R to Athens. He managed to find a dinghy and went sailing out of Athens. Still, he wanted to sail further, but found it difficult to hire a yacht to sail around the Greek islands. In 1973 when he was working out the bare bones of what became the Yacht Cruising Association, he must have remembered his time there and again travelled to Greece. What if, he mused, you could hire a small yacht and cruise around the coast and islands of Greece. He was only a few steps away from the concept of flotilla sailing, where several yachts sailed together with a lead boat which had a skipper to brief them on the sailing and destinations, an engineer to keep the boats together, and a hostess who would look after the social side of things.

Eric Richardson.
Photo Sailing
Holidays Ltd.

In September 1973 he ordered eleven 24 ft Snapdragons from Thames Marine with the possibility of ordering more if YCA proved successful. The initial boats were all bilge keelers so that if the company didn't get off the ground, the boats could be re-sold in Britain.[4] Eric wanted to exhibit at the London Boatshow in January 1974 but couldn't get a stand. Instead he hit on the idea of putting one of the Snapdragons outside Waterloo Station advertising sailing holidays in Greece on this very yacht. It was marketing genius and by the end of January the

3   Much of this recent history comes from my scribbled notes from conversations with old friends Barrie and Heidi Neilson, the owners of Sailing Holidays Ltd and a part of flotilla sailing since 1979; with Chris and Shan Blunt who worked for various flotilla companies in Greece and Turkey from 1979; with Mike Cox, a founder member of YCA and later of Sunsail; Nigel Wadlow who was involved with FSC and Yacht Tours; and my own experience from 1977 and on. See also Mike Jakeways *From the Deck of Your Own Boat* and Barrie Neilson *Sailing Holidays: A Pictorial History of a Unique Company* Sailing Holidays, 2014.
4   Eric Richardson's letter to Thames Marine is reproduced in Mike Jakeways *From the Deck of Your Own Yacht* p 15.

flotilla season was fully booked. Now all that was needed was to equip the yachts and get them down to Greece. And to find a skipper, engineer and hostess.

The first skipper was Janet Green with David Archer as engineer and Eric's children's au pair, Megan Duncan, as hostess. The Snapdragons were sailed from Ramsgate across the Channel to Calais where they were loaded, two at a time, onto a trailer and

YCA yachts being trucked down to Brindisi. Photo Mike Cox.

trucked down to Brindisi on the heel of Italy. Here the yachts were rigged again and sailed down to the Ionian islands and through the Corinth Canal into the Saronic where, it was planned, the yachts would be based.

For the first brochure for the 1974 season Eric had devised a route starting in Vouliagmeni near Athens and pottering down around the 'home' islands of Aegina, Poros, Hydra and Spetsai. The brochure had pictures of some of the places they were going to, but none of a Snapdragon in any of the locations for the simple reason that none were down there yet. Ever resourceful, Eric took two of the Snapdragons out into the Thames Estuary and snapped pictures of it sailing with some scantily clad people enjoying life in the winter sun off Canvey Island. Even the photo on the front of the brochure was a stock photo of a yacht anchored in the turquoise water of a bay in Mallorca.[5] A two-week holiday cost £78 a person, with four sharing a yacht, and included flights on British Airways to Athens.[6]

Once the boats were out in the Saronic it soon became apparent that instead of Vouliagmeni, the island of Aegina would make a much better base to start from. Despite the warnings from yacht clubs and the yachting press about how it would all end in tears, the first flotillas were a roaring success and bookings were quickly filled up for 1975. The only storm cloud on the horizon was the rule of the colonels who had seized power in a coup in 1968

5   Mike Jakeways *From the Deck of Your Own Yacht* p 18–19
6   From the 1973 advert for YCA in Mike Jakeways *From the Deck of Your Own Yacht* p. 21.

YCA fleet laid up for the winter in Sivota in the Greek Ionian. Photo Sailing Holidays Ltd.

and whose totalitarian rule was becoming increasingly unpopular.[7] In July 1974 the colonels backed a coup in Cyprus and on July 20th Turkey invaded Cyprus in retaliation. During the crisis Athens airport was closed for ten days before the flotilla charterers could get a flight home. After that the flotilla crew could handle just about anything.

For the 1975 season Eric ordered another eleven Snapdragons, though this time he specified the fin keel version as he was confident he could fill the two flotillas operating around the Saronic. Because the fin-keelers were higher than the original bilge keel boats, they couldn't be loaded on a trailer in the same way to transport them down to Brindisi. Instead, the keels were removed and the yachts transported without them. In Brindisi the keels were re-attached and the boats launched. In 1975 Mike Cox, a former sailing instructor with the army who had raced on *British Soldier* in the Southern Ocean on the Whitbread Round the World Race, joined YCA as skipper for the second fleet

7   For a modern fictional take see J. C. Graeme *To Ithaca* Taniwha Press 2016.

Improvised scaffold hoist to service the yachts in the early days. Photo Mike Cox.

in the Saronic. It was decided to base the fleets at Epidavros on the Peloponnese and, for the two-week cruise to go west again to Spetsai, and then allow independent sailing up around the Argolic Gulf.[8]

The concept of flotilla sailing was evolving over this second year, with some flotilla skippers keeping a tight rein on their charges while a skipper like Mike Cox had a more relaxed attitude. In the second week of the flotilla there was more independent sailing allowed when the new charterers had got used to their charges. YCA were still the only players in the game and had the concept of flotilla sailing holidays to themselves. This was to change in 1976 when new players arrived on the scene. Eric must have sensed what was going to happen and for the next year decided on a bigger yacht, the Mirage 28, and on a new area in the northern Sporades, keeping the two Snapdragon fleets in the Saronic.

By 1977 Mike Cox was in the office with Eric organising the new fleets and scouting out new areas. At this time YCA had two fleets in the Saronic, two in the northern Sporades and two in the Ionian. A change in Greek law required the boats to be registered under the Greek flag with a Greek company owning 51% of the operation. Previously the law had required a Greek skipper on every boat except if the yachts belonged to a club or an association – hence the name Yacht Cruising Association. Likewise, Flotilla Sailing Club that started in 1976 was called a 'club'.[9] All the flotillas had an agent to sort out problems in Greece and the lead crew also formed close relationships with taverna owners, boatyard owners and locals in the villages and hamlets they visited. A flotilla of twelve boats turning up with between forty and fifty people wanting to eat out, often in places off the beaten track, was a windfall for a taverna owner. It never ceases to amaze me that when you turn up years

8   For these early locations see Rod & Lucinda Heikell *West Aegean* Imray 2014.
9   Mike Jakeways *From the Deck of Your Own Yacht* p 13

later at a taverna that you frequented with a flotilla, the owner, or likely his son or daughter, will greet you like an old friend and usher you in to meet the family again.

In 1979 YCA started to build its own 29 ft charter boat for the flotillas. The Julian Everitt designed YCA 29 was built by YCA in a factory at Eastbourne. The first fleet of YCA 29s went to the Dodecanese. Charterers flew into Rhodes and then the flotilla popped over to Turkey to cruise the Lycian coast. The Greek authorities were not very happy about this, so it was fortuitous that Dalaman Airport, formerly a military airport, opened in 1982. Mike Cox relates how Eric Richardson wrote to the Turkish authorities explaining that opening the airport would bring in large numbers of tourists including his own charterers. The first flight to arrive at the airport, carrying YCA's charterers, had the pilot pull out of the landing when he saw soldiers lining each side of the runway; only after he had been reassured that they were there to welcome this first commercial flight into the airport did he relent and land.

YCA Mirage fleet in boisterous conditions in the Ionian. Photo Mike Cox.

An expanding travel industry meant new areas were opened up to tourism and to some extent flotilla sailing piggy-backed on this expansion. Flotillas need some basics to thrive. An airport with commercial flights that is ideally not more than six hours' transfer time away (three hours these days). A sailing area that offered enough variation for charterers to have the choice of a restaurant in a town or village or to anchor away from it all. And, of course, the lead boat team who, depending on their abilities and affability, could make or break a flotilla holiday.

In the 1980's, as new mass tourism areas in the Mediterranean were explored and as the governments of the countries around the Mediterranean saw the economic benefits of this tourism, so flotilla sailing spread to other countries and sailing areas. In 1981 YCA was operating a flotilla of Sigma 33s out of

Split in Yugoslavia – the war was yet to come. By 1983 there was a flotilla operating between Corsica and Sardinia, and in Turkey new bases were set up around the coast near new sailing areas. YCA even set up a flotilla in the Greek Cyclades, a notoriously windy area, though the flotilla only operated in the early and late season when the meltemi was not at its strongest.[10] An attempt was also made to run a flotilla around the Peloponnese, though this route was ultimately abandoned as the area is notorious for changeable weather and some of the legs on the flotilla itinerary were quite long.

In 1983 YCA hit a bump in the road in what had been, give or take a few complications, a steady rise in the operation and expansion to new sailing areas. A number of competitors came and went, and some companies merged to consolidate their position, but YCA remained at the top of the tree. In the spring of 1983 a fleet of eight YCA 29s on delivery from Brindisi were arrested in Corfu. The delivery crews spent a week in prison before Eric could get them out and the boats and the spares for the flotilla that the boats were carrying were impounded. The boats sat neglected in Corfu and deteriorated as time went on.

The reasons for the mass arrest of the boats was subject to much rumour. I heard that the boats were arrested for not declaring the spares they carried. Other rumours circulated, including that the boats were destined for Turkey and the Greeks were unhappy with that; that the delivery crews didn't have work permits or proper qualifications to be on the boats; and that there was some envy over a foreign company sailing in Greek waters and turning a profit.[11] Whatever the truth, it took a while for YCA to re-group and for Eric to settle back into the groove of running a large charter company.

By the late 1980's Eric Richardson had decided he wanted to sell the company. It had fleets all around Greece and Turkey and around the coast of the former Yugoslavia. Various other companies were around, but it was Chris Gordon of what was to become Sunsail who brokered a deal to merge and buy YCA. In 1988 the company added the YCA fleets to its portfolio and, despite some rocky times ahead, emerged as the biggest yacht charter operation in the world. Most of its yachts were based in the Mediterranean, but its sailing

10   The meltemi normally blows hardest through July to August. See Rod & Lucinda Heikell *Greek Waters Pilot* Imray 2018 pp 29–31.
11   Conversations with those on the ground at the time and Mike Cox.

areas would soon encompass the Caribbean, Thailand, the Seychelles, French Polynesia, the Solent, even New Zealand and Tonga, with varying degrees of success, to dominate the yacht charter market.

Flotilla Sailing Club becomes Sailing Holidays

Flotilla Sailing Club started up in 1976, hard on the heels of YCA. It was the brainwave of Tom Keen, and the story goes that he had tried to book a sailing holiday with YCA in the previous year, was told that they were full, but he could put his name down for the next year. For various reasons Tom decided that this new concept would be a good investment and in addition would give his somewhat idle sons, who were living the good life in Corfu, a job to do running the company.[12]

Tom Keen was the son of a chicken farmer from Reading. In the Second World War he joined the RAF as an aircraft fitter and was based in Singapore. When the Japanese arrived he decided on a remarkable escape plan.

Tom Keen.
Photo Sailing Holidays Ltd.

According to legend, Tom and his friend temporarily 'borrowed' a light aircraft and flew south until they were almost out of fuel over an Indonesian island, where they landed on a beach. They came to an arrangement with a local man to trade the aircraft for a boat and they set off on a perilous voyage to Australia. They made it however and were immediately pressed into service keeping the Australian Air Force in the air.

Neilson *Sailing Holidays* p 12

Once back in Britain Keen returned to chicken farming and bought up other chicken farms. He then expanded into buying redundant mills and factories in the Midlands that he divided up and let as small industrial units.

Maybe Tom got the inspiration to set up a flotilla company from his boat trip to Australia. He certainly had an interest in yachting and Barrie Neilson records that he once owned *Stormvogel*, the 73 ft classic cold-moulded racing

12   Neilson *Sailing Holidays* p 12

yacht built by Bruynzeel in South Africa. Or perhaps he just wanted to give his two sons, David and Tom, Jr., something to occupy them. However it happened, in 1975 Tom ordered twelve Jaguar 27s and had them trucked down to Ancona in early 1976 from where they were sailed down to Corfu.

The Jaguar 27 was originally the Catalina 27 and was an inspired choice for a flotilla boat. It had a large sliding hatch leading from the cockpit into an airy and spacious interior and was well suited for living aboard in the hot Mediterranean climate. For the lead crew, Tom managed to employ Janet Green who had been the first skipper for YCA on the Snapdragons in 1974. His son David went along as engineer. The flotilla quickly filled up

Jaguar 27 – an inspired choice for a flotilla boat at the time.
Photo Sailing Holidays Ltd.

with bookings for 1976, so Tom ordered two more fleets of Jaguar 27s for 1977 that would arrive in dribs and drabs from Brindisi as and when they were built and trucked down.

Martin and Sue Evans on the Jag 27 lead boat.
Photo Sailing Holidays Ltd.

One of the lead crews for 1977 was the brother and sister team of Martin and Sue Evans who had sailed down from Suffolk to Greece in a converted lifeboat. In 1977, I arrived in Greece from the UK in *Roulette*, a 20 ft ply boat built in the 1950's. With me was Bridget, my girlfriend, and an empty kitty. At the time we were living on something like £2.50 a day and when the chance of work with FSC came up, we jumped at it.[13] Martin and Sue Evans had some Jaguar 22s in their fleet and these could not keep up with the Jaguar 27s. Our job was to look after this mini-fleet and do a bit of cleaning and repair work on turn-around days. Our combined wage was around £100 a week, a fortune. At the end of the season Tom Keen suggested I run a new fleet of Jaguar 27s he was buying – we would meet at the London Boat Show to sort things out.

We returned to England that winter with the promise of a job from old Tom Keen. It's difficult to describe the wonderment of many of the lead crews on flotilla that they were being paid real money to sail a flotilla around the Greek islands. It was hard work, 24/7, keeping the boats maintained and the customers happy, but it was a once in a lifetime experience to be sailing in the Mediterranean and to get paid for it. At the London Boat Show in 1978 I met Tom again and he seemed to have trouble remembering who I was and the job offer. A series of other introductions led me to a job with another company which was going to put a flotilla down in Greece and so my time with FSC ended, though I still kept in contact with the crews on the FSC fleets.

Through 1978 to 1980 FSC grew to become the dominant player in the Ionian. Extra boats were ordered, and the sailing area extended from Corfu down to Zakinthos with some fleets based in the north at the half-completed marina in Gouvia on

Some 'one design' racing on the Jag 27 flotilla. Photo Sailing Holidays Ltd.

Corfu and others in the inland sea, predominantly in Levkas. Other fleets were springing up in the Ionian which was proving to be the ideal flotilla sailing area, with consistent prevailing winds from the northwest and lots of harbours and anchorages for a fleet of yachts to visit.

Ashore things were gradually changing and, although much of the maintenance was still ad hoc, with whatever spares were stocked by the company or could be jerry-built from whatever materials were available locally, some of the local operators were setting up yacht service facilities for the care and repair of yachts.[14] Yards that had formerly hauled out *caiques* on a sledge and runners modified the sledges so they could haul yachts for the winter lay-up. Taverna owners soon cottoned on to the fact that forty or so charterers who wanted to dine out represented a lucrative way of increasing their income if they could be attracted to their taverna.[15] In many ways this water-borne tourism reached places off the beaten track that didn't benefit from localised land-based tourism in rooms or hotels.

In 1980 Barrie Neilson, today the owner of FSC[16] re-branded to Sailing Holidays after he and his wife bought the company, arrived in Corfu to work as the engineer on the northern flotilla route. As more boats arrived he was promoted to skipper of the new flotilla. Barrie had set off from New Zealand, crewing on a ferrocement yacht, where the joint aim was to find paradise… oh, and some girls. They sailed the boat across to Australia, but Barrie felt he still hadn't found that 'paradise' place. It took until 1980 and sailing around the Ionian islands for him to finally declare he had found 'the place'.

Barrie returned to FSC in 1983 after running a flotilla in the Caribbean. Tom was by now expanding the operation and wanted to put a flotilla in Istria in the former Yugoslavia. He had also put a fleet in the northern Sporades, though the Ionian remained the focus of his flotilla operation. Tom seemed to be running out of steam with FSC. In 1983 and 1984 he franchised some of the fleet to the lead boat crews on the basis they would get a share of the profits at the end of the year. Sadly, the profits were close to zero.

In 1985 one of the flotilla skippers, David Lewis, had taken over in the London office and convinced Tom that the whole emphasis of the flotillas should be more singles-orientated so that the boats became 'head boats' with berths

---

14   Some of the flotilla crews remained in the Ionian and started up yacht service companies that still exist to this day. Joe Charlton, who arrived in the Ionian in 1979, set up Contract Yacht Services in Levkas, Sue Evans set up Sioux Sails when she finished her stint with FSC, and Brian Clarke, who began with FSC in 1976, set up his own business in Corfu and now skippers a large motorboat.

15   Neilson *Sailing Holidays* p 62

16   SH formerly FSC is owned by Barrie and Heidi Neilson.

sold off individually. The lead boat would have just the skipper on board and the rest of the berths on the lead boat would be sold to charterers. To this end he persuaded Tom to invest more than half a million pounds in a fleet of sixteen new Beneteau 345s.[17] David Lewis' concept soon failed and Tom got back in the harness to run the company. It was bleeding money by now.

Fiskardho in the 1970's.
Photo Sailing Holidays Ltd.

At the end of 1985 Barrie and Heidi moved into the office in London to run the company. In many ways they took it back to its roots, to the fundamentals of flotilla sailing where you could buy a holiday on a yacht and be looked after by a lead crew. Not having the money to deposit the £80,000 ATOL bond with the Civil Aviation Authority, they brought in an accountant who guaranteed the money – on the back of restructuring the company so he had a controlling share. Barrie and Heidi and the flotilla crews worked their socks off getting what was now Sailing Holidays Ltd back on the road to recovery. This worked for a while until their 'tame' accountant decided he and his wife would be better off running the company. Barrie bided his time, secure in the knowledge that the accountant didn't have much of a clue about running a flotilla operation. In December 1989 the accountant relinquished control of the company and Sailing Holidays was back in the hands of Barrie and Heidi.[18]

And Fiskardho today with the Sailing Holidays fleet on the quay.

Bit by bit Barrie and Heidi built up Sailing Holidays to the company they wanted it to be. The old Jaguar 27s were upgraded with new engines and the Beneteau 345s

17   Neilson *Sailing Holidays* p 161
18   Neilson *Sailing Holidays* p 203–204

got upgraded equipment. Because he felt the old Jaguar 27s were ideal for couples he fitted large beds and showers – and then in his own inimitable way nicknamed the boats 'Shaguars'. Barrie was emphatic that the boats needed to be reliable, the lead crews amenable, and everyone had to have fun learning to sail around the Ionian. His mantra is summed up in the introduction to his book.

Flotilla sailing holidays remain a classic avenue into keelboat sailing for the mainly English-speaking people. They have also become a popular way to accumulate 'on the water' practical sailing and boating experience. In addition, they take place in a kindly environment on yachts designed for the purpose. At the same time, flotilla sailing holidaymakers have brought income to formerly desolate Greek islands.

Without flotilla sailing holidays, many thousands of people would never have found the key to escaping the stresses of shore-based life. The advent of this type of holiday accelerated sailing as a pastime in a way never witnessed before.

Barrie Neilson *Sailing Holidays* p 10

The Sailing Holidays fleet was gradually expanded and older boats replaced with newer models. Barrie expanded to other areas of Greece, to the northern Sporades and the Saronic, but the Ionian remained his prime area for flotilla holidays. Today Sailing Holidays runs over 180 yachts in its various fleets and is the largest privately owned yacht charter company in the world. There were a lot of ups and downs along the way, but as Barrie puts it at the end of his book, it has all been worth it.

There have been challenges to cope with over the years, but we have chosen not to dwell on them. The focus is simply on the good times, the good people, without which none of this would have been possible. We have all been privileged to have been able to enjoy this era of carefree sailing in the sun. Long may it continue.

Barrie Neilson *Sailing Holidays* p549

CPT Sailing in Greece becomes Falcon, becomes Sovereign, becomes Sun World, becomes Neilson

When a job with FSC didn't materialise for me at the 1978 London Boat Show I was offered, through the kind offices of the FSC operations manager, an introduction to John Kaye, who was setting up a new flotilla operation in Greece. John and his partner, Richard Perry, ran a company called Crawford Perry Travel that had done very well organising skiing packages. They also organised the flights for FSC and no doubt poached the idea of flotilla sailing from Tom Keen's operation. In those days there was 100% capital allowances on exporting yachts, so it made good financial sense to start a yacht charter operation. For CPT, not very catchily titled CPT Cruising in Greece, the flotilla side would give them a summer operation to balance the winter skiing holidays.[19]

With my modest experience from the previous year I set off to help set up the new fleet. The first thing we had to get was some sailing boats, so we went to see Chris Freer who was building a 30 footer called the Europa 3000. John and Richard (who was large and not the most agile) were thrown around in the trial sail on the Solent and, probably more because of the weather than anything else, decided against the Europa. Meanwhile John Charnley, who had a small bareboat company called GreekSail, with Sabre 27s in Poros in Greece, had found a boat called the Cobra 850. The Cobras were designed by David Feltham who also designed the Mirages used by some other fleets, as well as a number of other production yachts.

John Charnley, who was still working for British Airways while setting up GreekSail, had few problems convincing John that the Cobra 850s were ideal for the job. The initial order was for nine Cobras for CPT and three for John Charnley's GreekSail. They would all be trucked down to Brindisi and from there we

CPT Cobras out in the Saronic.

would sail across to Greece and the Saronic. GreekSail was based in Poros and we were to be based in Spetsai where John Kaye knew the local Mr Fixit, Takis of Takis Tours, a.k.a. the King of Spetsai, as he liked to title himself.

19   Most of this history is from my own recollections of the period. I worked for CPT Cruising in Greece in 1978–1979 and again in 1981. Some of the history was written down and there are photos and odd documents including the 'guest' book in which charterers could write and draw what they wanted. Some is corroborated from others who were out there at the time, but most of it is my own recollections of the period.

I zoomed around the country exercising my newfound power, buying multiples of all the stuff you need to equip a charter yacht. I bought dinghies, sleeping bags, cutlery and crockery, lifejackets and flares, reels of rope and chain and anchors. The boats were trucked down to Brindisi and I arrived on the last truck. Here crew, largely from British Airways, sailed them across to Spetsai in the Saronic where we were to be based. I had never been there before.

In 1978 there was little to nothing in the way of backup. Half of the boats were not registered with the Greek authorities and we ran them illegally. Repairs were rudimentary: an alternator bracket made up of angle iron, sail repairs with tape, epoxy resin and glassfibre tape for patching and holding things together, engine repairs on the fly. When we lost a mast, it was replaced with the one off the lead boat and we motored everywhere until a new one was shipped out. There were no real chandlers to buy equipment from and most of the engineering work we did ourselves. Communications with London were from the local telephone exchange or by Telex from Takis at Spetsai Tours. Somehow it all worked, and for the second year there was an 80% return rate.

One of the problems encountered along the way was satisfying the Greek authorities that our charterers were qualified to sail the yachts. In London John got a designer to draw up an impressive 'Sailing Diploma' complete with a signature and seal from the president of the 'Fulham Road Sailing Club' – strangely enough with the same address as the CPT office. Over the next few years there was some competition between the different flotilla companies to produce the most overdone and impossibly Baroque certificates for the charterers, and they were preferred by the Greek officials to the somewhat plainer Royal Yachting Association tickets.

There were a few interesting episodes in that first year. We had a Frenchman and his girlfriend who disappeared with their yacht in the early hours of the morning. I put out a call to the port police to impound the boat wherever it turned up, though I eventually found him moored outside the port police office in Spetsai – they hadn't noticed. I took the boat around to our base, took the keys away and, against my better judgement, let him stay on board. He hot-wired the boat and disappeared again, although when we caught up with him (he hadn't gone far) I made sure he was off the boat, which by now had been scraped and bashed all along the topsides. We had a Canadian admiral who kept getting lost. At one point I got to him, only just in time, to stop him running the boat up on the rocks. On Hydra, I had to get a couple of heavy drinking lads out of jail for lewd behaviour – the police weren't specific, which was probably just as well.

By the end of 1978 CPT was running nearly twenty boats and for 1979 we planned to move half the boats to Levkas in the Ionian. This time I would be in an area I had some knowledge of. In the winter of 1978–79, through the kind offices of John Kaye, I had bought a Cobra 850 which was going to be the lead boat for the Ionian flotilla. I sailed it down from England to Greece that winter in company with another Cobra 850 for the fleet. It was a bit of a wild ride at times, with a couple of bad gales on the way, but eventually we arrived at Spetsai, loaded down with spares, in time to get the fleet together for delivery to the Ionian.

By 1979 fleets had multiplied in areas all around Greece. YCA had fleets in the Ionian, Saronic and Northern Sporades and had introduced one of the first fleets to Turkey. A company called Mirage Holidays had several fleets in the Saronic. FSC had fleets throughout the Ionian and Seascape had upped the stakes in the Ionian by introducing fleets of Sadler 32s, comparatively big flotilla boats at the time, with a Moody 40 as the lead boat. I based the new CPT fleet in Levkas town and ran the route around the inland sea, the sheltered body of water shielded from the long fetch of the outer Ionian by the islands of Levkas, Cephalonia and Zakinthos. I was back where I had started in 1977.

It's difficult to fit the inland sea of the late 1970's with the Ionian seascape we sail in today. Development has gone on apace and where there was rock and scrub-land, now there are villas and hotels. Even so it is all recognisable and the geography does not change: the silhouette of the mountains, the steep

Cobras at anchor in BBQ Bay in Porto Kheli in the Saronic.

cliffs of Sappho's Leap, the turquoise
and light blue of reefs and shallows
and that wine-dark sea all remains
the same. It is the landscape at
the bottom of the mountains and
around the bays that has changed.[20]

BBQ's were part of the deal. Here on
Meganisi in the Ionian.

In 1977 there were few private or
charter boats around. There were
a handful of flotillas in the Ionian.
Roulette, all 6.5 metres (20 ft) of her,
was the only yacht hauled out at
Christo's Boatyard on the canal bank opposite Levkas town. In Levkas town
there were two battered Mercedes taxis and a lot of Piaggio three-wheelers.
Outside of the towns, donkeys were still used to transport farm produce and,
occasionally, the farmer himself. His wife usually had to walk.

On the flotilla route there were only a limited number of tavernas to choose
from compared to today. In Nidri there were only three tavernas, including

On the island of Kastos in the Ionian there were no
tavernas at all in the 1970's.

Nic the Greek and Panorama.
In 1977 in Fiskardho there
were no tavernas at all and
with a bit of luck you could
get an omelette at Irini's
cafeneion. That was it.[21] Only
later did new tavernas arrive
on the scene, mostly to cater
for the flotillas that stopped
here. Today tavernas ring the
harbour at Fiskardho. On the
remote islands of Kastos and Kalamos there were no tavernas at all, whereas
today there are several. In most places you had to get fresh water for the boats
by jerry can, though it wasn't long before a few of the locals around the flotilla
route installed a tank on the back of a Piaggio three-wheeler and filled the
boats from that for a small charge.

20   For locations in the Ionian see Rod & Lucinda Heikell *Ionian* Imray 2017.
21   Irini is generally reckoned to be Pelagia in Louis de Bernieres' *Captain Corelli's Mandolin*.

In the early days, charterers flew into Corfu and then transferred to Levkas via the ferry from Corfu to Igoumenitsa and the ferry across the neck of water separating Preveza from the road to Levkas. On a good day it would take six

In Kastos today there are four tavernas, mostly relying on waterborne tourism.

hours. On a bad day it could be eight or more hours. The lead crew would be waiting anxiously for the tired travellers to arrive, hoping that most of them retained a sense of humour. In general, we gave charterers three days to become human and wind down from the everyday grind of their lives. In the meantime, we would need to feed them copious amounts of bad wine to salve their tormented souls. There were very few that didn't respond to the delights of sailing a boat around the islands and eating out in some of the most picturesque locations in the world; and if that didn't work there was always the wine.

When the airport at Aktio opposite Preveza opened, transfers became much shorter and less tiring. Aktio had been, and still is, a military airport that was opened to commercial flights in 1982. For many years it didn't even have a terminal building and passengers, once they had retrieved their luggage, simply walked to a gate in the perimeter fence and to the road where coaches, taxis and cars were waiting for them. While it was a bit primitive, it cut the transfer time to Levkas to thirty to forty minutes.

In 1979 Crawford Perry Travel joined forces with another travel company, Chancery Travel, to become Falcon. The flotillas now became 'Falcon Sailing in the 80's'. It seems none of the owners could resist making the brand name short and succinct. It soon became plain 'Falcon Sailing'. By 1980 the Saronic flotilla had been abandoned and there were now three fleets of Cobra 850s operating in the Ionian from Levkas town. Two of the fleets were standard two-week flotillas while the other smaller flotilla did a one-week flotilla and then one week in a villa – Villa-Flotilla Holidays.

Sometime in the early1980's Falcon merged with Dinghy Sailing in Greece and moved its operations to Nidri under the watchful eye of Jim Baerselman who was the owner of the dinghy sailing operation. It underwent several name changes, to Sovereign and then Sunworld, before it was bought by Thomas Cook and then Neilson Holidays who wanted a summer operation to balance their winter skiing programme. Along with running flotillas, the company expanded the original dinghy sailing holidays started by Jim Baerselman to other parts of Greece and continues to operate shore-based sailing holidays, mostly around Greece, but also in Italy and Croatia.

What goes around comes around and Neilson, like its previous incarnations, still run flotillas in the Ionian, though from their new base at Vounaki near Palairos in the inland sea. The old Cobra 850s were retired in the late 1980's, though you will still see some of them around the Ionian in private ownership. The modern Neilson fleets have new, larger yachts for the flotillas, though the flotilla routes remain much the same. Some of the old faces from those days have gone; you will likely find a son or daughter running one of the original tavernas or cafés. Despite it being busier and more sophisticated than in the early days – you can get your latte or freddo cappuccino in most places – it is still one of the most wonderful sailing areas in the world and one that many of us 'old hands' return to often.

GreekSail becomes Island Sailing, becomes Sunsail

When CPT bought the original Cobra 850s, John Charnley of GreekSail bought three for his bareboat charter company in Poros in Greece. He already had several Sabre 27s based there and through the late 1970's continued to build up a small but successful charter business. In 1980 GreekSail was sold to the Guinness group who wanted to get into the leisure business and thought sailing yachts in the Mediterranean looked an attractive proposition. The company was re-branded as Island Sailing and new flotilla fleets were introduced into Greece and later into Turkey.

The Guinness group soon decided to offload Island Sailing and in 1984 it was sold to Chris Gordon who ran the Emsworth Sailing School. He had big ideas for the company and it expanded to become a major player. In 1987 Island Sailing bought YCA to create the biggest charter and flotilla operation in the world with a combined fleet of 640 yachts. It was re-named Sunsail.

Mike Cox, who had been operations director at YCA, continued in this role for Sunsail and the company began an expansion programme to put yachts in other sailing areas outside the Mediterranean – principally the Caribbean.

The company prospered until the chill of recession affected the holiday market in 1989. Some of the older boats from Island Sailing and YCA were sold off and no new boats were bought to replace them. Financial difficulties saw a publicly listed tour operator, AirBreak, acquire Sunsail in 1990. AirBreak itself collapsed in 1992 and Sunsail was snapped up by Mercury Private Equity and ECI Ventures, with Chris Gordon still at the helm.

GreekSail moves up from the Sabre 27's. Cobra 850 in the Saronic.

Things weren't helped when war broke out in the former Yugoslavia in 1991. Flotilla and bareboat companies scrambled to get their boats out of the rapidly disintegrating country and away to safe havens in Italy and Greece. Mike Cox was asked to get a fleet of Sunsail Beneteau 25s out of Trogir, on what is now the Croatian coast, to safety in Italy. Somehow Mike had himself smuggled into the country from Trieste and organised the local fixer to employ fifteen young lads to get the boats across to Italy. The Croatian lads all had to sign a paper promising to return to Croatia when they had finished the job. Not surprisingly, none of them did.

The late 1980's and early 1990's marked a significant change in flotilla and bareboat charter. The companies running flotillas, and often bareboats as well, were not the small companies of old, working as best they could to maintain the boats and keep customers happy. They had turned into much bigger and slicker operations that attracted the attention of large corporate companies with an eye on a niche market to supplement their mainstream holidays. Yachts always look sexy in a travel brochure.

Attitudes and expectations towards flotilla sailing had changed as well. Yachting magazines and national newspapers often featured flotilla and barcboat holidays and invariably the write-ups were glowing. Sunsail's new yachts were creeping up in size and it was common to find flotillas running 35 ft and bigger boats by the mid-nineties. Most boats had roller reefing headsails, many had roller-reefing mainsails, and all now had fridges, VHF and some instrumentation. Sunsail's fleets of charter yachts, both flotilla and bareboat, increased at an exponential rate, both by acquisition of other companies and the introduction of new yachts. At the end of the 1990's Sunsail acquired the Moorings, the largest bareboat operator in the Caribbean, which also had operations in other areas like Tonga and French Polynesia. By 1999 Sunsail had over 900 yachts operating from thirty-seven bases in nineteen different countries and was ripe for plucking.[22]

One of the major innovations Sunsail made was the introduction of a leaseback scheme whereby individuals could put a down payment on a yacht and, over a three- to five-year charter period, the balance of the value of the yacht was paid off by leasing it back on charter with Sunsail. They were not the first company to do this. Back in 1977 Mediterranean Charter

Small tavernas soon realised that 40 or 50 hungry charterers represented a significant boost to their balance sheets

Services operated a similar scheme in the northern Sporades.[23] There are variations on the scheme, but in essence it allowed an individual to purchase a yacht over time and at the end of the leaseback period sail away in their own yacht. The scheme also had the further inducement of allowing leaseback owners to use other Sunsail yachts in other locations for a certain number of weeks of the year.

In 1999 the First Choice Group bought Sunsail in a move which has a strange congruence to it. First Choice had evolved from the Falcon Holiday group which was then owned by Owners Abroad, that in embryonic form all those

22   www.ybw.com/news-from-yachting-boating-world/sunsail-under-new-ownership
23   See below for Mediterranean Charter Services.

years before had started CPT Cruising in Greece. Sunsail was now part of a group which had an airline and the financial muscle to finance the charter group. Things didn't stop there. Sunsail was now part of a corporate pass-the-parcel and in 2007, when First Choice amalgamated with the giant TUI group, it became part of TUI UK and then TUI AG. As part of that group it was parcelled up under Travelopia until that company was sold to the US private equity firm KKR & Co for a reputed $400 million.[24]

Sunsail today occupying a fair chunk of Levkas Marina.

If this litany of the evolution of Sunsail seems somewhat torturous – that's because it is. What it does illustrate is how flotilla sailing and yacht charter in general has radically changed over the years as charterers' expectations have risen and yacht design and equipment has moved on. Sunsail are a good example of a small company starting out on a wing and a prayer and becoming the biggest charter company in the world. In the Ionian, YCA used to haul their yachts in Sivota on an improvised gantry system that looked like it would topple over if you gave it a shove. Today Sunsail is based in Levkas Marina with all the facilities you expect in a modern marina and yacht service companies on hand to maintain and solve any mechanical issues the yachts might have. The Sunsail staff are all neatly kitted out in crisp whites and if you break down there is a chase boat that will come and sort problems out. It is a long way from the humbler beginnings of the flotilla story told above.

24   *Trade Only Today* February16, 2017

Other players who came and some who went

OCC Yachting A Dutch company that started operations in the Ionian in 1977. They ran flotillas with Aloa 27s and later with bigger boats. For a period, they built the Aloa 27 in Holland and shipped the boats down to Greece. Their clientele was largely Dutch and the company continues to this day operating in the Ionian and in Turkey.

Mediterranean Charter Services Operated from 1977 in the northern Sporades using the comparatively big Maxi 95s. Tony Nielsen can pretty much be credited with introducing the owner leaseback system. Through his company, owners put a deposit on the boats and income earned from them paid off the balance so that the boat became the outright property of the investor at the end of the termed period. Unfortunately, the company went bust after five or so years and most of the owners had problems getting their boats back.

Yacht Tours Tony Nielsen surfaced again and started a flotilla and bareboat company in Bodrum in 1980. The same leaseback system operated with these boats which were a fleet of Maxi 95s and some larger Maxi yachts. The company again went bankrupt in 1983 or 1984.

Mirage Holidays Operated in the Saronic in 1978–1980 using Mirage 26s and 28s.

Odysseus Sailing Started in the Ionian in Gouvia in 1980 and now runs a flotilla out of Gouvia and another out of Palairos in the inland sea.

Kiriakoulis Yachting Operate flotillas in the Saronic and 'sailing in company' in other areas. The company has charter yachts, mostly bareboat, in most of the countries around the northern Mediterranean. It also has a major share of the marinas at Gouvia, Levkas and Zea.

Greek Sails A family-run flotilla operating out of Poros in the Saronic that started in 1983 when Sottos Kouvaras bought two Hummingbird 30s and brought them out to Greece. I've known Sottos since that time and his two sons, Richard and Andreas, who now run the business. They operate flotilla and bareboat charter around the Saronic.

Seafarer Offers flotillas around the Mediterranean but concentrates on Greece.

Port Leucate. In the south of France in the Languedoc-Roussillon area the *étangs* were dredged and huge marinas carved out of the coast.

13 THE 1960's TO THE 21st CENTURY

With the 1960's came increased prosperity and leisure time for yacht ownership and going sailing. There were numerous reasons: a decrease in the length of the working week and an increase in leisure time from paid holidays to public holidays; a rise in real incomes and secure employment; and the arrival of package holidays that were affordable for many. For some this leisure time was directed towards yachting.

In the United Kingdom small, affordable boats were being built, both professionally and by amateurs in their backyards, enabling the less affluent to participate in the sport of sailing, whether racing or just cruising, along with the entitled who had long dominated the sport. Numbers of smaller, more humble yacht clubs, without the appellation of 'royal' in their names, sprang up around the coast and on any inland body of water big enough to sail a dinghy on. While the 'blazer and slacks' crowd still made the rules and dominated the sport, there was an upspring of more down-to-earth converts to this sailing lark, and for some of them there was a desire to sail off into the sunset.

Much of this desire was fuelled by books about the cruising life and, not least, by the publicity generated by the *Sunday Times Golden Globe Race* of 1968–1969 in which the competitors had to complete a circumnavigation alone and unassisted.[1] Earlier, the *Observer Single-handed Trans-Atlantic Race*, or OSTAR, first run in 1960 and the first single-handed race ever to have been staged, was won by Francis Chichester in his 40 ft (12 metre) *Gipsy Moth III* – the largest yacht among a fleet of modest cruisers in the race. He became a celebrity in Britain and was feted for efforts that lead him on to further sailing adventures.[2] On the *Sunday Times Golden Globe Race* all of the yachts were cruising yachts of one sort or another: Robin Knox-Johnson in his 32 ft (10 m) Atkins designed ketch *Suhaili* was the only yacht to finish and Bernard Moitessier in his 39 ft (11.5 m) steel ketch *Joshua*, named after his hero Joshua

1   Peter Nicholls *A Voyage for Madmen* Profile Books,2002
2   Derek Wilson *The Circumnavigators* Constable, 1989, Chapter 12

Slocum, bailed out once he got back to the Atlantic and continued on sailing a second time around until he got to Tahiti.[3]

Bernard Moitessier had already been cruising in the south of France where, prior to the *Golden Globe Race*, he had a sailing school that he ran in his own eccentric way. On *Joshua* he would take the students out and, once out of the sight of land, would remove the compass and charts and get them to use the sun, moon and stars to navigate. His own years of sailing had given him an almost sixth sense about the sea and he tried to get his students to understand his own personal philosophy and develop the sort of seamanship skills he had acquired. In his book he describes the rhythm of the sea in almost poetical terms.

Bernard Moitessier. Photo from the flyleaf of *The Long Way*.

Nearly midnight. I slept a few hours, as usual. The rhythm of the sea is not the same as that ashore. At sea I wake up almost automatically around midnight, feeling fresh, and go back to sleep an hour later. This gives me plenty of time for a turn on deck to feel the heart of the night and sense what is around. Then I roll myself a cigarette at the chart table, dreaming before the Damien globe.

Bernard Moitessier *The Long Way* Sheridan House 1971/1995 p 61

On the strictly cruising front, Eric Hiscock's *Cruising Under Sail*, first published in 1959, and his later *Voyaging Under Sail*, became the bibles of anyone thinking of going cruising.[4] Eric, along with his wife Susan, first went cruising around the coast of France and to the Azores in the 21 ft Laurent Giles-designed *Wanderer II*. Soon after they had Laurent Giles design their famous 30 ft *Wanderer III* in which they spent seventeen years cruising around the world. Another inspiration to thousands of sailors was Alec Rose, who completed a solo circumnavigation in 1967–1968 in his modest 36 ft ketch

3   In 2018 on the 50th anniversary of the *Golden Globe Race*, seventeen yachts set out to re-run the race. The yachts all had to be designed before 1988 and be of a retro design. No modern aids that were not carried by Robin Knox-Johnson in the original race are allowed. https://goldengloberace.com/ggr/. Only five yachts completed the race.
4   Eric Hiscock *Cruising Under Sail* A&C Black 1950/2002; *Voyaging Under Sail* Oxford University Press 1959/1977. Numerous reprints of both titles.

Lively Lady. Without brouhaha or sponsorship and on a modest budget, the greengrocer from Southsea showed dreamers everywhere that it was possible for 'ordinary' people to set off on an adventure in a small yacht.[5]

The publicity that these early exploits engendered in the general population spurred some to think about sailing around the Mediterranean. At this time the Mediterranean was still thought of as an exotic destination. While the coastal strip of the Riviera in France and Italy had long been colonised by tourists, other areas were now becoming the destination for the nascent package holiday industry. Parts of coastal Spain and parts of France and Italy outside the Riviera were seeing the first vestiges of tourism, as holiday companies flew people in. In the western Mediterranean new hotels were built to accommodate the new breed of tourists and often a marina was built as well to add a little class and improve the view for land-based tourists – a sort of window-dressing for the bland concrete on the shoreside.

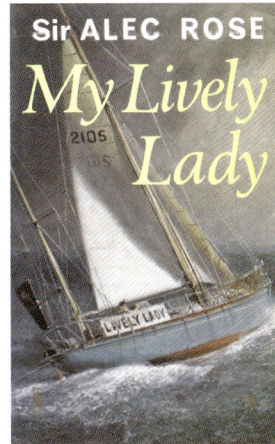

Alec Rose in *Lively Lady* demonstrated that in a modest boat on modest means you could sail long distances. Cover of Alec Rose's *My Lively Lady.*

Malta was considered a very 'British' sort of place in the 1960's and 1970's and consequently a safe haven for cruising yachts. Malta Tourism Authority.

The eastern Mediterranean was, by comparison, largely unknown. A few holiday companies flew tourists into Greece and that was about it. For the sailor, the waters of the Aegean and the Adriatic were off the beaten track in the 1960's and few ventured past the Tyrrhenian Sea off the western side of Italy. The one exception here was Malta, which up until 1964 had been a

5   Alec Rose *My Lively Lady* Nautical, 1968

British Crown Colony and was a popular place to base a yacht. The locals all spoke English and even after independence it remained a very 'British' sort of place.

1960's

In the Second World War the coastal infrastructure around the shores of the Mediterranean had been blitzed by both the Allies and the Axis powers and any initial re-building concentrated on the large commercial harbours so that trade could continue. The scenes described by George Millar after the war are of devastation and almost a despair that things might never get back to normal for those left behind in the bombed cities and towns.[6] Understandably it was to be some time before thoughts turned to building a pleasure boating infrastructure and to the promotion of the sport.

Cap d'Agde, one of the huge complexes with a marina developed on the coast of Languedoc-Roussillon.

6   See Chapter 10.

The development of the Languedoc-Roussillon coast around the Golfe du Lion in the 1960's and 1970's by the French government was one of the biggest tourist projects ever attempted in the Mediterranean to this day.[7] The coastal littoral of the region was underdeveloped compared to the coastline further to the east and had long been a lost place of swampy *étangs* and a dangerous shore with few natural indentations. Right up until the 20th century this was a lost and hostile coastline. There were a few old established coastal towns at Port Vendres, Port La Nouvelle, Agde, and Sète, but apart from that there was little along the coast except long sandy beaches and a few ramshackle *cabanes* used by the locals for fishing and a bit of relaxation in the summer months.[8] Government ministers must have looked at the sandy beaches and the increased prosperity of the French middle class with increased leisure time, and put two and two together to form a plan to radically transform the coast to accommodate the new mass tourism. And it included yacht marinas.

Six purpose-built tourist cities, or *unités*, were planned, strung along the coast from the Pyrenees to the Rhone delta. All the *unités* were planned to have apartments, hotels, shops and restaurants and huge purpose-built marinas that would be dredged out of the coast and be part of the tourist complexes. This was a huge undertaking that required some of the *étangs* to be opened up, a new trunk road to be built, fresh water and electricity to be introduced to the coastal littoral where there was none, and the pesky mosquitoes that lived in the stagnant lagoons and plagued the area had to be sprayed to get rid of them. The yachting infrastructure required a huge dredging operation and the construction of massive breakwaters at the entrances to the dredged marina basins.

Today five of the *unités* have been built and one, L'Embouchure de l'Aude, has been abandoned. From the west the five are:

- St-Cyprien (Argelès-Plage, St-Cyprien-Plage and Canet-en-Roussillon)

- Leucate-Barcarès (Leucate-Plage and Port Barcarès)

- Gruissan (Gruissan-Neuf, Narbonne-Plage and Valras-Plage)

- Cap d'Agde (Cap d'Agde, Ambonne and Marseillan-Plage)

7   The region was re-named Occitania (Occitanie) in 2016.
8   Rod & Lucinda Heikell *Mediterranean France and Corsica* Imray, 2017, Chapter 2.

- La Grande-Motte (Frontignan, Carnon-Plage, La Grande-Motte and Port Camargue).

All in all, there are now over 16,000 yacht berths dotted along this coast in the new marinas, along with huge numbers of holiday homes and apartments ashore.[9]

While the development of the Languedoc-Roussillon region was aimed at the masses, in Sardinia the development of Porto Cervo by the Aga Khan was aimed at the very rich. The Aga Khan, with others in a consortium, began development in the early 1960's of an up-market marina with villas and apartments ashore, with prices that made other resorts look like a bargain. The northeast corner of Sardinia was re-christened the Costa Smeralda and today Porto Cervo is still one of the most expensive marinas in the Mediterranean. The real estate prices ashore outstrip anything in the rest of Europe and several of the most expensive hotels in the world can be found here.[10]

In Genoa, the first international boat show was held in 1962 with exhibits ranging from small dinghies to larger wooden cruisers from the likes of Baglietto and Sangermani.[11] Fibreglass boats were just making an appearance and there were several plastic dinghies at the show. Fibreglass was not new, it had been around since the Second World War, but it was only in the 1960's that its use in production yachts became widespread and boatbuilders across Europe started turning out affordable small sailing and motor yachts.

The history of the yacht builder Jeanneau is typical of many, although few companies were as successful or as big as the French yacht builder. Henri Jeanneau built his first wooden motorboat in 1957 and soon after, in 1958, he was building his motorboats in fibreglass – he even called his first model the Sport Polyester. Jeanneau kept building powerboats until the first sailing yacht,

The Alize, Jeanneau's first GRP sailing yacht, was built in 1970.

9   Figures from Rod & Lucinda Heikell *Mediterranean France and Corsica* Imray, Chapter 2.
10   Rod & Lucinda Heikell *Italian Waters Pilot* Imray 2015 pp 290–294
11   Luisa Piccinno and Andrea Zanini *The Development of Pleasure Boating and Yacht Harbours in the Mediterranean Sea: The Case of the Riviera* Ligure International Journal of Maritime History June, 2010 p 91

the Alize, was built in 1970. In the same year they built the Sangria, a small sailing yacht with accommodation that went on to sell over 3000 boats. They have now become part of the Beneteau Group, the largest yacht builder in the world and one which would have a significant impact on yachting in the Mediterranean.[12] Along with Jeanneau, other yacht builders were turning to fibreglass in Scandinavia, Britain and France; large numbers of yachts ranging from sailing dinghies to cruising yachts and motorboats were coming on the market. Boatbuilding had moved on from small builders working on a custom-built wooden yacht to production line methods whereby a standard hull and fit-out was produced more cheaply in fibreglass.

1970's

The 1970's are often remembered as the decade in which doom and gloom settled over the world economy. Forget the fashions that now look faintly ridiculous, the haircuts and the sideburns, and the Austin Allegro, this was the decade commonly remembered for the oil crisis, for petrol and food shortages, for the three-day working week and the miner's strike in the UK. And yet, while it seemed like there was plenty of doom and gloom around, in fact living standards went up and more people than ever wanted to go on holiday to exotic destinations, most of them in the Mediterranean.

This was the decade when in 1974 Eric Richardson started flotilla sailing in Greece and his yachts were soon booked up for the entire year. More and more people were booking package holidays in Spain where bigger and more luxurious hotels were being built and tourist resorts were spreading like a rash along the coast. Other Mediterranean countries were also getting in on the package holiday business and Italy, Greece and Cyprus jumped onto the Spanish bandwagon and started building large hotels to cash in on the tourism business. None of this would have been possible without a rapid expansion of charter airlines and bigger planes like the Boeing 737 and 747 that could transport more people, more cheaply, than the older planes. All over northern Europe sun-starved northerners beat a path down to the sunny Mediterranean.[13]

---

12   www.jeanneau.com/en-gb/jeanneau/history
13   See Chapter 4 of Dave Richardson's *Let's Go: A History of Package Holidays and Escort Tours* Amberley, 2016.

The construction of large hotels and resorts on the seafronts of Spain and Italy invariably led to the addition of yacht marinas as part of the resort. It added caché and a touch of class to a package holiday destination. In Phillip Bristow's guide to sailing the Spanish coast, first published in 1973, he lists sixty harbours suitable for yachts.[14] Most of these are fishing harbours, with just a few purpose-built marinas scattered along the coast. Many of the marinas like Puerto Jose Banus at Marbella were attached to a large onshore holiday resort.

Likewise, Bristow's guide to the French Mediterranean coast includes details of numerous new harbours in addition to the old established yacht meccas of the French Riviera.[15] In his introduction Bristow has this to say:

> No other coast that I know has changed in recent years more than the French Mediterranean. New yacht harbours have appeared, little harbours have become big harbours, pontoons have sprouted everywhere, all in the last five – ten years? It all seems to have happened so quickly, before one's very eyes as it were. And all this quite apart from the ambitious new development in the Languedoc-Roussillon.

Phillip Bristow *French Mediterranean Harbours* Nautical 1974 p 11

The oil crisis which affected the whole of the western world and dented the economies of nations that had previously seen an ever-increasing prosperity, seemed to affect the Italian economy more than most. The rapid expansion of marinas and older harbours adapting to the new yacht tourism in Spain and France was not reflected in Italy, where the numbers of registered boats were much the same in 1979 as in 1970.[16] The Italian Riviera was still popular as was the area around Venice and Naples, but there was little development elsewhere. When I cruised down the western Tyrrhenian coast of Italy in 1977 it was apparent that the numbers of yacht marinas declined rapidly as you went south, so that by the time you got to Calabria and Sicily there were really only fishing harbours and a

Old harbours on the Riviera still accommodated yachts, but little new infrastructure was built. Menton on the French Riviera.

14   Phillip Bristow *Down the Spanish Coast* Nautical 1973
15   Phillip Bristow *French Mediterranean Harbours* Nautical 1974
16   Piccinno and Zanini T*he Development of Pleasure Boating* p 95

few commercial and ferry ports for yachts to berth in.[17] You were more likely to rub shoulders with a tuna fishing boat than with another yacht.

In the Adriatic, the former Yugoslavia under Tito was being opened up to yachts, although the paperwork was endless. There were few yacht facilities and dedicated yacht harbours, but a multitude of anchorages and enough fishing and commercial harbours to make it worthwhile for H. M. Denham to write a cruising guide to the Adriatic.

> ... this book is intended to help those cruising in small to medium deep-keel yachts, and motor cruisers, it is also hoped that it may be of some service to those who now trail their small 2- or 3-ton vessel across Europe by car and then hoist her into the sea to spend a month's holiday in Yugoslav waters.

H. M. Denham *The Adriatic* John Murray 1967/1977, preface

In the eastern Mediterranean there was next to no yachting infrastructure in most places. In Greece the old harbour at Zea was converted to a yacht marina in the 1960's and, along with Mikrolimani (Mounikhias), was largely for local yachts. While Zea could accommodate superyachts, including Stavros Niarchos' *Creole*, Mikrolimani was a much smaller harbour and the home of the Yacht Club of Greece. The Yacht Club of Greece was formed in 1933 and had even enjoyed some royal patronage between 1940 and 1973, during the reign of King George II and later Kings Paul and Constantine, who were dedicated yachtsmen and admirals of the club. At this time, it was known as the Royal Yacht Club of Greece. In the 1960 Olympics Crown Prince Constantine won a gold in the Dragon class.[18]

Down the coast from Athens, Vouliagmeni Marina, the first purpose-built marina in Greece, was constructed in the early 1970's, although it was designed for the rich to keep a yacht outside of the hustle and bustle and the nefos of Athens.[19] In northern Greece on the Khalkidhiki, John Carras built Porto Carras Marina, completed in the mid-1970's, and to an extent modelled on the sort of developments being built around the shores of Languedoc-Roussillon in France.[20]

---

17   Heikell *The Accidental Sailor* Chapter 9
18   www.ycg.gr/index.php/en/ycg
19   *Nefos* refers to the pollution that hangs over Athens, much like the smog in Los Angeles.
20   For details on these marinas in 1980, see Rod Heikell *Greek Waters Pilot* Imray, 1982.

When I arrived in Greece in 1977 there was little in the way of yachting infrastructure. In Gouvia near Corfu town there was the exoskeleton of a marina project, allegedly dreamed up by the colonels during the Greek Junta, and presumably abandoned when the Junta ended in 1974. In Levkas, where I hauled my 20 ft yacht *Roulette* out for the winter, it was the

Christo's boatyard in Levkas where *Roulette* was the sole yacht amongst the caiques.

only yacht sitting amongst local caiques and a couple of cigarette-smuggling boats in the boatyard. Hauling was done on a sledge and runners and at the time there were no travel hoists in the whole of Greece.[21] It was a Greece unrecognisable today when just up from Levkas town where I hauled *Roulette*, in present-day Preveza, there are three boatyards adjacent to each other on the Aktio peninsula that haul out an estimated total of 3500 yachts a year with travel hoists and hydraulic trailers.

The same boatyard today, now run by his son, Adonis.

In Turkey, the heads of the tourism office had evidently been looking across the Aegean to Greece and had started a project to build a number of marinas for the nascent yachting tourism that was creeping ever eastwards from the western Mediterranean. At least, so they hoped. Altin Yunus Marina near Cesme was built privately and was really aimed at a few wealthy Turks who wanted to keep their yachts in the Aegean. Kusadasi Marina and Bodrum Marina were projects funded by the government's Turizm Bank and

21   Heikell *The Accidental Sailor* Chapter 11

built at the end of the 1970's. At the time these were the only two Turkish marinas in the Aegean where visiting yachts could find a berth.[22]

In Cyprus construction began on the marina at Larnaca and by 1976 it was operational. In the intervening period the colonels in Greece had backed armed action by EOKA[23] on the island and Turkey had invaded Cyprus in 1974 in retaliation. The marina was allegedly built with UN funding to ease tensions between Greek and Turkish Cypriots on the island – something it signally failed to do given the subsequent events.

The existence of numerous yachting guides, especially by Phillip Bristow and H. M. Denham, to the various countries around the Mediterranean, is evidence that a certain number of yachts must already have been cruising around these areas and using these published guides. Bristow's guides to Spain, France, the inland waterways of France and Italy were all published in the early 1970's. In Italy a series of six guides, the *Navigare Lungocosta*, described the coast and islands of Italy for yachtsmen. The guides, researched and published in the late 1960's to early 1970's by a journalist, Mauro Mancini, had wonderful hand-drawn charts and reflected a deep love of sailing and of the Italian coast.[24] H. M. Denham's guides to Italy, the Adriatic, Greece and Turkey were researched and written in the late 1960's to the 1970's and were widely available and found on board most yachts cruising these areas at the time. I deal with these sailing guides in a later chapter and mention them here as a

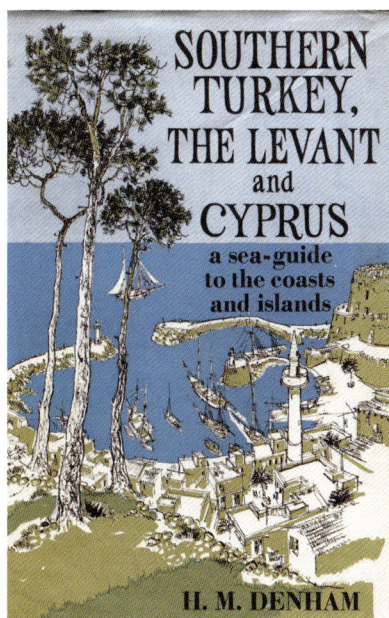

---

22 For an idea of what the Turkish coast looked like in the early 1980's, see Rod Heikell *Turkish Waters Pilot* Imray 1984.

23 Ethniki Organosis Kyprion Agoniston, a guerrilla organisation.

24 I had most of his volumes in the early 1980's and later communicated with him. Sadly, they were lost in storage in Greece. Mauro Mancini Navigare Lungocosta Vols 1-6 Class Editori.

substantive indicator of the growing numbers of yachts beginning to cruise far flung parts of the Mediterranean.[25]

Some of those cruising the Mediterranean were well known sailors who had 'retired' to the inland sea after sailing exploits elsewhere. One of these was Humphrey Barton, 'Hum', the founding father of the Ocean Cruising Club, known for his various passages in small yachts across the Atlantic. In 1977 I was alongside Hum's *Rose Rambler* in Corfu. *Rose Rambler* was in many ways a stretched *Vertue*, the 25 ft class he had first sailed across the Atlantic.[26] The designer, Laurent Giles, drew a 38 ft yacht that mirrored many of the features of the *Vertue*, only bigger. It looked big to me in the 20 ft *Roulette* berthed alongside her. At some point Hum leaned over and asked me where I had sailed from. I told him England and he stroked his chin before enquiring, in

the direct way he had, if I knew of anywhere in Corfu where he could buy epoxy primer. I assured him that it was highly unlikely they had even heard of epoxy here in 1977, but he was in luck. In Southampton I had sheathed the bottom of *Roulette* using nylon cloth and epoxy paint, for which I had needed epoxy primer and, as it so happened, I had a spare tin in the bilge. So started a relationship that meant, whenever we met, Hum would proffer the whiskey. I never did tell him I didn't like whiskey.

Humphrey Barton's *Rose Rambler*. National Historic Ships archive.

Hum and Mary Barton were part of an annual migration that you could almost set your watch to in the eastern Mediterranean. Quite a lot of yachts wintered in Malta, a few in Majorca and the south of France and, in the spring, set off for the eastern Mediterranean. In early spring we would keep an eye out for *Rose Rambler* and, sure enough, one day she would turn up ready for the summer's cruising before setting off in the autumn back to Malta. Hum could be quite laconic in his conversations. In Argostoli on Cephalonia I was anchored off in the bay in the approaches to the harbour when *Rose Rambler*

25   See Chapter 18, From the Periplus of Skylax to the Digital Age..
26   For a detailed history of the OCC, see Tony Vasey's *The Ocean Cruising Club: The First Fifty Years* OCC Publication 2003.

came trundling around the corner. Hum came over and asked how deep it was where I was anchored. I replied that I was in five metres to which came the reply: 'Metres eh?' In 1978 Hum was awarded the Cruising Club of America's Blue Water Medal, though unusually it was not for any specific passage but 'For a lifetime of cruising, racing, twenty or more Atlantic Crossings, founder of the Ocean Cruising Club and promoter of long-distance cruising.'[27] When I met up with Hum the following year, Mary prompted him to tell me what his reply to the Cruising Club of America was on being notified of the award. 'They wanted me to go to America in July,' Hum told me. 'I telegrammed back to say: "July is no month to be crossing the Atlantic in a small boat."' Sadly, he died not long after.

1980's and 1990's

In the decade up to 1990, yachting in the Mediterranean became a mainstream pastime and the numbers of yachts increased dramatically, as did the yachting infrastructure ashore. Just as with the charter fleets in Greece and Turkey, the size of yachts being sailed to the Mediterranean and available for charter went up to 35 ft, and at the end of the decade it wasn't unusual for the average bareboat to be over 40 ft. By now companies like Jeanneau and Beneteau were making 35–40 ft boats with three cabins and two heads for the charter market and for privateers as well. In 1982 Jeanneau introduced the Sun Kiss 47 and the year after the Sun Kiss 45. These boats and similar from Beneteau, whose Oceanis range started with the 405 and 430 in 1986, went on to be popular charter boats

While the Mediterranean-style yacht was derided by some, the French and German builders just kept making them and taking orders. Photo Sailing Holidays Ltd.

around the world. Not surprisingly, lots of private owners wanted one as well – so much so that both companies offered a charter and private version for

27   Vasey *The Ocean Cruising Club* pp 162–163

sale, the charter version having more cabins and the private version more room in fewer cabins.[28]

In many ways the French boatbuilders stole a march on boatbuilders in Britain and Scandinavia, and not until the arrival of the German-built Bavarias on the scene was the hegemony of the French builders dented. These boatbuilders not only developed economies of scale that smaller builders couldn't compete with on price and marketing, but also closely followed trends in yacht design, especially in the growing Mediterranean market. The development of a certain style of boat for the charter market with plenty of sun-bathing space, a large cockpit with table for al fresco dining and an open stern with a swimming ladder resulted in the phrase 'Mediterranean-style' being applied to certain

In the more popular anchorages in Turkey, makeshift restaurants were built on the shore and rough catwalks built for visiting yachts.

28   Data on commercially built yachts can be found on www.sailboatdata.com/.

boat designs in a sort of mealy-mouthed way that implied this style of boat might be suitable for the Mediterranean, but not really anywhere else. Still the French boatbuilders just rubbed their hands, ignored the yachting press, and kept taking orders for more boats.

While the numbers of yachts based in the Mediterranean grew throughout the 1980's, so too did the infrastructure ashore for yachts. I started writing yachting guides at the beginning of the 1980's and as new editions came out it was necessary to update the books with details of new marinas and facilities. In this sense, the books chart the history of yachting in some of the countries around the Mediterranean. Turkey is an instructive example.[29]

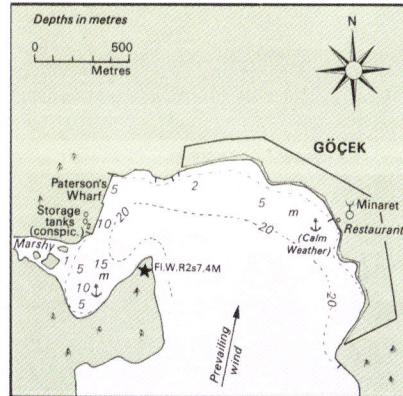

Gocek 1983 from *Turkish Waters Pilot* 1st edition. Note that there are no marinas in the bay.

In 1980 Turkey had just three marinas along the Aegean coast. Yachts visiting the country mostly anchored off in some of the idyllic bays around the coast or used fishing harbours where the locals were more than happy to make space for the few yachts that cruised the coast of Turkey. By the time of my third edition of the book, published in 1989, there were six dedicated yacht marinas and at least four more in the pipeline. In many of the fishing harbours quay space was now allotted for yachts and in some of the more popular bays little restaurants had been built, often no more than shacks with an outside kitchen, to cater for the new water-borne visitors.

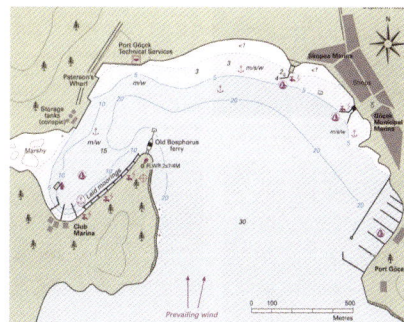

Gocek 2001 from *Turkish Waters Pilot* 6th edition. There are now four marinas and more in the pipeline.

---

29   See Rod Heikell *Turkish Waters Pilot* Imray 1984 and later editions by the same publisher.

Often the restaurants would put down moorings or construct rickety catwalks for yachts to berth at.[30]

The Turkish Tourist Board in Ankara actively promoted this new tourism and the government converted old military runways to take commercial flights from Europe.

The new destinations that started coming up in the 1990s were Turkey and Egypt, both known only as cultural destinations but with big ambitions to attract the 'fly and hop' holidaymaker. Turkey took advantage of the latest trends by developing all-inclusive hotels from scratch along its Mediterranean coast, becoming so successful that Thomas Cook was selling more holidays there than any other country by the mid-2000s. Prices were keen, quality was good and it soon came to rival Greece, while the rise of Egypt was equally striking.

Richardson *Let's Go* p 53

The converted military airport at Dalaman near the resorts of Marmaris and Gocek opened in 1982 and, while principally for package holidays in hotels around the nearby coast, it nonetheless encouraged charter companies to open bases in Turkey and provided easier communications for private yacht owners. By the 1990's the Turkish coast was a popular cruising area for yachtsmen and new charter companies seemed to pop up everywhere. By the turn of the century there were fifteen yacht marinas around the Turkish Mediterranean coast with more planned or partially under construction.[31] In the major centres, dedicated boatyards had been established and yacht service agencies had sprung up. Yacht spares and equipment were easier to find and the local work force had adapted to the standards needed for the care and repair of yachts.

By the turn of the century boatyards in Greece were doing a roaring business and the hauling and care of yachts was as good as anywhere else in the Mediterranean.

Next door in Greece just a handful of marinas were built compared with Turkey, as well as some white elephants that were partially built in unlikely locations

30   See Heikell *Turkish Waters Pilot* Imray 1985 and the revised 1989 3rd edition of the same book.
31   Heikell *Turkish Waters Pilot* Imray 6th edition, 2001

and have not found anyone to take them on to provide the infrastructure of a modern marina. In the Ionian, the rapidly increasing numbers of charter and private yachts provided the impetus for the development of the large marinas at Gouvia on Corfu and Levkas town. Around Athens several marinas were built and rapidly filled up with local and charter yachts. Like Turkey, many of these started out as government projects with additional European Union loans and were later leased to private companies. Greece had joined the EU in 1981 and joined the Euro currency countries in 2001 which gave a significant boost to the economy.

The increasing numbers of yachts needing spares and repairs had a knock-on effect on shore-side economies. Local car mechanics became marine engine specialists, sailmakers morphed out of upholstery shops, hardware shops started stocking basic chandlery items, import-export companies offered transit facilities for European nautical equipment, and agencies for marine engines and other yacht equipment were set up in Athens and Piraeus.

While the Greeks had been building wooden boats for centuries, it took a little while for them to get into modern yacht construction. At Gaidhouromandra, just outside of Athens, the Olympic Yard had been constructing yachts from the late 1970's on. At first they built the Peter Ibold designed Endurance range in ferrocement and later a series of Dick Carter designed yachts in GRP, principally the Carter 33 and 39. Later they built the Ted Brewer designed Olympic 42 before going bankrupt in the 1980's.[32] In the late 1980's, with the growth of charter fleets, a number of Greek yards jumped on the yacht-building boom and very soon a number of companies were building the sort of yachts that charter companies used. Many of them were built using older Beneteau and Jeanneau moulds with some modifications to bring them up to date. Companies like Dromor and Atlantic produced significant numbers of yachts through this period and could compete with the large French yards, though things came to a standstill after the Greek economic crisis.

While Greece and Turkey were riding on the back of increasing numbers of yachts in the eastern Mediterranean and establishing the infrastructure to support them, in the Adriatic things turned sour in the 1990's. With the

---

32   Chris Freer, who designed a number of 12-metre yachts for the America's Cup, was in charge at Olympic Yachts for a while in the 1970's. See Chris Freer *Twelve Metre Yacht: Evolution and Design 1906–1987* Adlard Coles Nautical 1986.

death of Tito in 1980, the different ethnic groups that made up the former Yugoslavia began to unravel and by 1991 war had broken out between the different secessionist movements. Up until then increasing numbers of yachts had started to cruise the coast and islands of the former Yugoslavia and charter companies were operating from several bases around the coast.[33]

Those who were there at the beginning of the wars that divided Yugoslavia into separate states talk of escaping with yachts under gunfire and military bombardment, and of yachts sunk in harbours from artillery shells and

In Italy it took a while for local authorities to cotton on to the value of a marina. Porto Azzuro on Elba was originally a high security prison called Longone. A change of name and the construction of the marina transformed it.

mortars. Mike Cox relates how in Dubrovnik the old town and the harbour was regularly shelled by the largely Serbian army from the heights above the city, sinking large numbers of yachts and causing many of the local inhabitants to flee.[34] The wars that caused the breakup of Yugoslavia into Croatia, which garnered the lion's share of the coast and islands, and Montenegro, Serbia and Kosovo, damaged not only the yachting infrastructure, but also the confidence

33   See Chapter 12, The Flotilla Story.
34   Conversations with Mike Cox who was operations manager for Sunsail at the time.

of charter companies and private yacht owners, and it would take years before yachts again returned to the waters of Croatia and Montenegro.[35]

In Italy, infrastructure and boatbuilding seemed to take two steps forward and three back. Boat builders would start to prosper and then falter at the next economic hurdle. The increase in oil prices in the 1970's and hence the increase in resin costs for the builders crippled Italian yacht builders. In the 1980's business was back up again, only to see it collapse again with the economic woes brought on by the Gulf War in the early 1990's. In the decade from 1990 to 2000, boat production tumbled by over 20% and a number of boatbuilders went bankrupt.[36] The problem was further exacerbated by high taxation on pleasure yachts and the lack of new marinas to provide berths for Italian-owned yachts. Many Italians re-flagged their yachts to a flag of convenience and kept their yachts outside of Italy.

In France, yacht construction continued apace with both Jeanneau and Beneteau building new factories and introducing stream-lined construction methods along the lines of car assembly plants. The country had taken yachting to heart and the singlehanders and those on crewed races were household names. Numerous new trans-ocean races were introduced, like the *Vendée Globe* (1989) and t*he Route de Rhum* (1978), and in the Mediterranean there was a spinoff with numerous coastal races. In France and Spain, in Malta with the *Middle Sea Race*, in Greece with the Aegean series, yacht racing was returning to the Mediterranean. The *Solitaire du Figaro*, a race open to both professionals and amateurs, is raced around different ports in France and in 1991 the race became a one-design event with the Figaro Beneteau chosen as the one-design for the race. [37] In 1996 Jeanneau and Beneteau amalgamated to form the largest commercial boat-building company in the world.

France was buzzing with the new-found sport and the new marinas in the Languedoc-Roussillon were soon being expanded to cope with the demand for yacht berths. The expansion of harbours and marinas to the east of the Languedoc-Roussillon developments was slower and relatively few new

35   Montenegro has a small piece of the coastline in the Adriatic, including the Gulf of Kotor. See T. & D. Thompson *Adriatic Pilot* Imray 2016.

36   Piccinno and Zanini *The Development of Pleasure Boating and Yacht Harbours* p 96

37   The *Figaro* was originally called the *Course de L'Aurore*. In 1980 *Le Figaro* newspaper bought *L'Aurore* and it became the *Solitaire du Figaro*.

marinas were built. Mediterranean France has a relatively short coastline and most of the infrastructure development was the construction of a few new marinas and a lot of expansion in existing marinas and harbours.[38] In Corsica several new marinas were built, and others expanded to promote tourism around the island. Ashore, yacht service companies and specialist builders using exotic new materials like carbon fibre boomed and many of these specialist builders still exist along the coast. There was also a boom in providing yacht equipment and big chandlers supplying yacht equipment like Plastimo were built up on the back of the new French passion for yachting, before spreading to other parts of Europe.

I lived on and off in France in the 1990's and it's hard to describe just how enthusiastic the French were about going sailing and about the evolution of yacht design to produce faster racing boats, particularly multihulls. If a big yacht race was taking place, the major television channels and the national papers would often start with the yacht race or some maritime disaster on a yacht race as the lead item, whereas in Britain it would hardly be mentioned, if at all, despite British entrants in the races and a few newsworthy catastrophes along the way. The elevation of yachting in France to near the level of popularity enjoyed by football and tennis gave a boost to yachting in the Mediterranean, with French yachtsmen spreading their wings and sailing outside their native country. Magazines devoted to yachting flourished with more glossy yacht magazines published in France than in Britain – a surprising number given the smaller French readership compared to English speakers.

In Spain, progress was a lot slower building the infrastructure for yachts and, although a few marinas had been built, including Ampuriabrava along the style of the French Languedoc-Roussillon developments next door, and a number of marinas on the Costa del Sol where hotels had been built for package holidays, most of the harbours were fishing harbours and you berthed wherever you could find a spot. Even in Palma Majorca, now a hub of expensive marinas and the port of choice for many superyacht owners, you

---

38   Rod and Lucinda Heikell *Mediterranean France and Corsica* Imray 2017, introduction. Mediterranean France has around 918miles/1700km of coastline, of which around half is Corsica.

still had the Paseo where you could turn up and go stern-to in the middle of town – right up until 2000.[39]

For obscure reasons, yacht construction did not get off the ground in Spain and just a few small companies like Rodman motorboats, Belliure, and North Wind sailing yachts built small numbers of yachts for the pleasure market. Compared to the mighty French companies next door, relatively few homegrown yachts were produced and Spanish yachtsmen tended to buy yachts built elsewhere.

The situation was the same in Britain, where yacht building companies declined significantly through the 1980's and 1990's. The builders of quality yachts like Oyster, Southerly and Rustler yachts survived, building relatively expensive, and to some extent hand-crafted, yachts that appealed to those with the money to buy them. Companies like Marine Projects that built the more affordable Moody and Westerly yachts did not survive, and Westerly was in and out of bankruptcy in the 1980's until its final demise in 2000.[40] The only competition to the large French builders was from Germany, where Bavaria and Hanse produced models similar to Beneteau and Jeanneau and could compete on style and price. Many of these yachts in the so-called 'Mediterranean style', designed for al fresco living and with numerous cabins tucked into the hulls, were snapped up by charter companies in the Mediterranean and in the late 1990's you could find nearly as many of the German models in charter fleets as you could French models.

The new century would see some remarkable changes to yachting in the Mediterranean, with a huge development in the infrastructure to support what has been a huge increase in the numbers of yachts sailing the sea. The great recession of 2008 would severely affect the economies of countries around the Mediterranean, though less than you might think. What it did not affect was those with large amounts of money who could afford to ride the recession out and even make money out of it and, at the other end of the scale, the passionate and committed individuals who tightened their belts and kept on sailing on diminished budgets.

39   I visited here several times in the late 1990's and tied up on the Paseo. Today that is impossible with expensive concessions where pontoons have been installed with gated entrances and a berthing fee that makes your eyes water.
40   Mike Bender *A New History of Yachting* Boydell 2017 p 362

Steve's Clarke-Lens' Wayfarer *Leon II* hauled up on the beach in Crete.
Photo Steve Clarke-Lens.

14 DOING IT ON A SHOESTRING: SMALL YACHT EXPLOITS IN THE MEDITERRANEAN

It can be easy to get the impression that to sail a yacht in the Mediterranean requires a substantial bank balance. Some, the rich and the super-rich, do have substantial amounts of money inconceivable to ordinary mortals, and I describe them in a later chapter.[1] To some extent I include this chapter for its righting moment in describing small boat voyages in the Mediterranean on modest sums and a pinch of daring-do. In fact, it never has cost substantial amounts and, even in an age where we are plagued by struggling economies and the awful world of 'austerity', it is still possible to escape in a yacht to the sunshine and different cultures scattered around the shores of the Mediterranean. In this chapter I look at a number of small, read very small, boat voyages made in the Mediterranean, though relating the stories is more in admiration than as a rallying call for anyone to emulate these voyages. Even the two small-boat voyages I made to the Mediterranean were of a more modest nature than the other voyages described here, and I won't dwell too much on those as I've written about them elsewhere.[2]

The first voyage described here is probably the most daring. It was made by Steve Clarke-Lens in an open Wayfarer dinghy from the Ionian Sea in Greece, down around the Peloponnese to Crete, and across to the Nile Delta. Here, Steve sailed up the Nile and then back down again before setting off for Turkey. He then sailed back across the Aegean and through the Corinth Canal to his starting point – all in all a voyage of some 4000 miles.[3]

Steve sailing *Leon II*.
Photo Steve Clarke-Lens.

1   Chapter 15, The Rich and the Super-rich, Part II.
2   Heikell *The Accidental Sailor* 2013
3   From conversations with Steve Clarke-Lens and his film of the trip at www.youtube.com/watch?v=Kuy4goz3stl

Two other voyages are coincidentally in the same sort of boat: a Drascombe Lugger. In the early 1970's Ken Duxbury trailed his Drascombe Lugger, *Lugworm*, down to Greece and then set about exploring the Greek islands. In the following year he and his wife set off to sail *Lugworm* back to England. They coasted

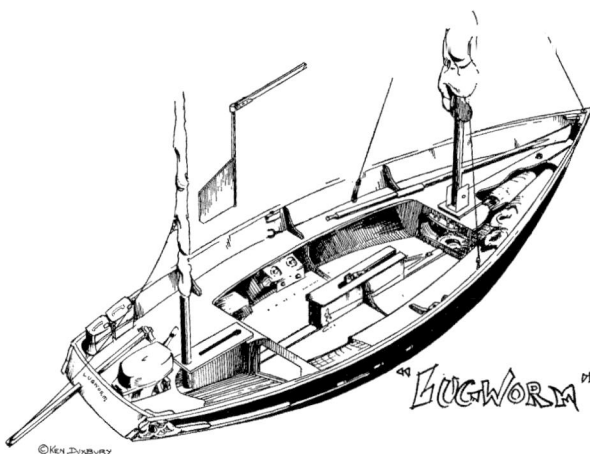

The layout on *Lugworm*. Drawing in *Lugworm Homeward Bound.*

around Italy and France and then cut through on the French waterways to Bordeaux where they coasted up to the English Channel and back home.[4]

The other voyage was by Webb Chiles in an open Drascombe Lugger from the Red Sea across the Mediterranean to the Atlantic. Webb had already sailed most of the way around the world in *Chidiock Tichborne* when it was seized by the Saudi authorities in the Red Sea. Undaunted he got another Drascombe Lugger, *Chidiock Tichborne II,* shipped it to where it would cross his track in the Red Sea, and sailed it up to and across the Mediterranean to where it was sadly lost in the Canaries in the Atlantic. Webb Chiles didn't think much of the Mediterranean as a place to sail, but then after much voyaging he was probably more used to the lonely spots in the world. I include him, partially because I encountered Webb in Malta after he had sailed there non-stop from Egypt, so his voyage has some plagency for me, and because he represents the sort of sailor who just needed to get across the inland sea rather than exploring its shores.[5]

The last voyage I describe took place in 1969 and 1970 from an account of a trip in an open dinghy from Ischia in the Gulf of Naples to Greece, and

4   Ken Duxbury *Lugworm on the Loose* Pelham Books 1973 and *Lugworm Homeward Bound* Pelham Books 1975.
5   Webb Chiles *A Single Wave* Sheridan House 1999 and *The Ocean Waits* Norton 1984

of cruising around the Greek coast and islands with friends and his young brother. The account makes for wonderful reading and is peppered with the folly and enthusiasm of youth and with the curiosity of a wondering mind.[6] The young Chris Geankoplis set off in *Vayu*, an old Lightning dinghy that he had bought from another American family who were leaving Italy to return home.

The boat was made of Mahogany in Genoa, Italy shortly after the war, in 1948, so it was a bit older than I was. It was 19 feet long, 6 ½ feet wide and had 24 inches or less of freeboard. Even though it was wooden it was not too heavy, old and waterlogged it didn't weigh even 800 lbs. It had a very tall mast and carried 177 square feet of sail. It had a large open cockpit and leaked consistently; and we loved that boat.

Chris Geankoplis *The Story of the Vayu*

The story makes light of the travails they encountered along the way and features on the joys of following in the wake of Odysseus around the Italian coast and home to Ithaca. The voyage all those years ago has come full circle, and Chris is back in the Mediterranean to follow that voyage of long ago. Not in a super-sized yacht, but in his beloved Rhodes 22 *Enosis* that he had shipped over from the USA to retrace his route in *Vayu*.

You might ask why these intrepid sailors didn't set off in something more comfortable, a small yacht with a cabin and sleeping berths below, and a few amenities like a cooker and a bookshelf. For Steve Clarke-Lens in his Wayfarer dinghy, it was what he could get hold of from the dinghy sailing holiday company he worked for and because he was familiar with the boat and young and fit enough to sail it offshore. Likewise, for Ken Duxbury, the Drascombe Lugger was the boat he had, and he felt the urge to go on an adventure before he got too old '…wouldn't it be a marvellous adventure before I actually fell to bits?' For Webb Chiles there was the ambition to sail an open boat around the world because it was the sort of challenge he liked to set out on where he '… sought an even greater challenge, qualitative rather than merely quantitative, with even greater reliance on myself than on the boat'.

There are other advantages to a small open boat. The Wayfarer could be hauled up on a beach and with a tent rigged over it there was shelter from the elements, even if rudimentary. Ken Duxbury's Drascombe Lugger also had a tent that could be rigged over the hull and two inflatable mattresses provided

6   Chris Geankoplis *The Story of the Vayu* Unpublished manuscript from the log of the *Vayu*

berths for the two of them. Ken had sorted out a pulley system so he could drag *Lugworm* up on the beach out of the sea. Likewise, Webb Chiles could beach his Drascombe Lugger and turn it into tented accommodation. On the *Vayu*, Chris would anchor or beach the boat and often put a tent up ashore or slept on the boat. He had a little stove to cook on and there was the never-ending search for good restaurants and bars ashore.

The ability to beach these craft and not be reliant on finding a safe anchorage or harbour gave all of them a lot more freedom about where they could go and cut the number of miles they needed to sail along a coast. All of them had little stoves stowed along with cooking utensils and basic provisions and a few luxuries in watertight lockers and barrels. As has been mentioned often, food, even a simple meal, somehow tastes better after a passage at sea and you don't need all the bells and whistles of a gourmet kitchen to appreciate the smells and tastes of simple fare. Ken Duxbury warmed to the task of describing how everything worked to a curious retired sea captain when they first arrived in Greece.

He was genuinely interested so I pulled *Lugworm* on to the beach and proudly explained our portable stainless steel two-burner alcohol stove, the chartboard that also served as a table and writing desk, the steering and hand-bearing compasses, and how the clock and barometer slotted into special brackets on the forward bulkhead. I explained how our bedding and change of clothes stowed in the large forward locker while the food and cooking gear went into one of the after lockers. 'And when it rains,' I enthused, warming to the subject, 'both masts quickly unship. The mainmast then rests on two light crutches to form a ridgepole and a waterproof tent fits over the whole boat lapping over the rubbing strake so that we have eighteen feet of space.'

Ken Duxbury *Lugworm on the Loose* p 25

Steve Clarke-Lens and *Leon II*

In 1991 and 1992 Steve Clarke-Lens sailed his Wayfarer dinghy, *Leon II*, from the Greek Ionian to Egypt, up the Nile and back down again, and then across to Turkey and back to the Ionian – a voyage of some 4000 miles in an open boat.[7] The Wayfarer was sponsored by Falcon Sailing, using what was available from the dinghy sailing company that Steve worked for at the time. In the 1960's Frank Dye made some epic trips in a Wayfarer, including a voyage from Scotland to Iceland and a later voyage across the North Sea to

7   Most of this tale is from conversations with Steve Clarke-Lens and from his film of the trip at www.youtube.com/watch?v=Kuy4goz3stl.

Norway. In many ways he was the pioneer of cruising long distances in the Wayfarer and became well known through his books on his exploits and an annual seminar on the hows-and-ways of cruising in an open dinghy.[8]

Steve was not unfamiliar with the virtues of the Wayfarer for cruising long distance. It was designed in 1957 by Ian Proctor and originally built in plywood, later in fibreglass, and proved a hit from the beginning. Frank Dye modified it so it had a cockpit tent and dry stowage and was soon off cruising far and wide. Steve Clarke-Lens had been teaching sailing using the Wayfarer in the Ionian and in 1981 took his *Leon I* around the Peloponnese to research possible new base areas for Falcon Sailing. This trip set him thinking about a more ambitious voyage, this time to Egypt.

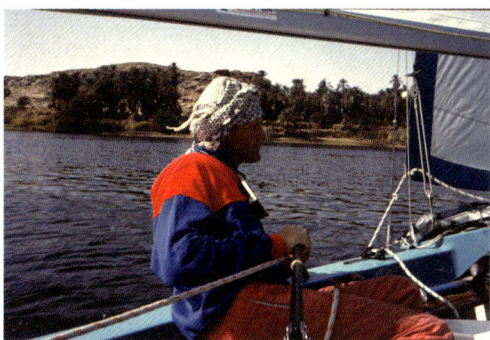

Steve Clarke-Lens on the Nile.
Photo Steve Clarke Lens.

With a few modifications to *Leon II* that Steve had garnered from his earlier trip on *Leon I*, he launched the boat in Levkas in 1991. For the first part of the trip he sailed solo down through the Ionian islands and across to the western Peloponnese where he coasted down to the bay of Finakounda just around the southwest corner of the first finger of the Peloponnese. Steve seemed quite at home with this solitary life on *Leon II* and while the weather held he would sail down the coast for ten or twenty miles to a bay or a harbour where he either anchored the boat off the beach or, if the anchorage was exposed, hauled the boat up onto the beach. The Wayfarer drew just 8 inches (20 cm) with the centreboard up so it could get into shallow water where even a small keel-boat could not.

Like Frank Dye, he had a cockpit tent and an inflatable mattress that fitted down one side of the dinghy and a little gas stove to cook on. All his water, food, charts, clothes and safety equipment were stored in watertight containers and stowed securely forward or aft in the boat. When you see all the bits and pieces out of the boat it's difficult to imagine where it all went in a 16 ft dinghy.

8   Frank Dye *Ocean Crossing Wayfarer: To Iceland and Norway in a 16ft Open Dinghy* Adlard Coles Nautical 1977/2006

In Finakounda Steve had arranged to meet Jules Glibbery to accompany him down to Crete. They sailed down to the island of Kithera and on to the isolated island of Andi-Kithera where bad weather held them up for a few days. When the forecast looked good, they set off for the island of Gramvousa just over twenty miles away. A trip which should have taken around six or

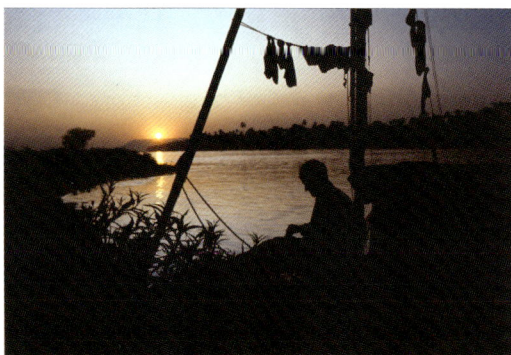

Steve and *Leon II* tucked up for the night on the way to Crete. Photo Steve Clarke-Lens.

seven hours turned into a marathon row all the way when the wind didn't materialise. Sometimes too little wind can be as trying as too much when your only auxiliary power is a pair of oars.

Steve and Jules continued around the south side of Crete to Matala where Jules had to leave and go back to work. Steve continued coasting around the south side of Crete until he got to Ierepetra close to the eastern end of Crete. It is no small feat to sail along this coast, where the gusts of wind off the

Steve on Crete checking the gear over before setting off for Egypt. Photo Steve Clarke-Lens.

high mountains that run along the spine of Crete scream down onto the sea with some ferocity.[9] At times Steve had to haul *Leon II* up the beach and sit out the weather for days at a time.

In Ierepetra a fellow dinghy sailing instructor, Laurie Campbell, joined Steve for what was to be the most audacious part of the adventure: the voyage from Crete to Alexandria in Egypt. The duo checked and re-checked their equipment and then sailed to the island of Chrysi lying just eight miles off Ierepetra. This would give them a bit of a head-start on the longer voyage and test how prepared they were.

9   See Rod and Lucinda Heikell *Greek Waters Pilot,* Chapter 10.

The voyage to Alexandria, some 300 miles, took just three days and nights with two young and fit dinghy sailors helming *Leon II* across this open stretch of water. The weather was settled and they ate well, even had a tumbler of wine at times, and arrived off Alexandria with so much water to spare that they washed and shaved, donned clean clothes, and arrived looking as if they had just been out for a daysail. When they told the yacht club guard they had sailed from Greece they were immediately whisked up to the commodore of the yacht club who made them welcome and plied them with 'tea and cucumber sandwiches'. Laurie returned home and Steve, still not quite believing he had got this far, prepared for his trip up the Nile.

In the yacht club Steve encountered a young Egyptian lad, Sameh Moneim, who was enthusiastic about sailing with him for part of the trip, so he invited him along. From Alexandria they set off along the coast to the mouth of one of the tributaries of the Nile. When they arrived off the entrance Steve couldn't see exactly where to head for, so he got Sameh to ask directions from a nearby 20 ft fishing boat. 'Follow us,' they said, and headed in. Steve followed the fishing boat which all of a sudden disappeared from view. In an

Leon II on the Nile. Photo Steve Clarke-Lens.

instant *Leon II* was rearing up on the back of a breaker and surfing down into the trough of the wave breaking over the shallow bar at the entrance to the Nile. He watched as the fishing boat came up on the crest of another breaker and tried, as best he could, to keep *Leon II* aimed in the right direction so she didn't turn side-on and capsize. As it was, the dinghy surfed down the waves well and in no time at all they glided into the relative calm of the river.

At Cairo the Nile divides into two main tributaries flowing down to the Mediterranean and, as it turned out, the one Steve had chosen was choked with water hyacinths that completely blocked any progress up to the main body of the Nile. Undaunted, he got Sameh to arrange transport overland and when the flat-bed truck pulled up, the locals in the café trooped out and bodily picked *Leon II* up and plonked her on the back of the truck. Steve and *Leon II* were bound for Cairo and the Nile proper.

Steve spent most of the winter sailing up to Aswan and back down to Cairo before re-entering the Mediterranean. He fell in love with the upper Nile and with the lateen-rigged *feluccas* that sailed up and down this stretch of the river. At some time, the germ of an idea hatched in his head and he drew up a set of plans for a 30 ft *felucca* while in Aswan. He even had a name for this project boat: *Ayesha* – 'She-who-must-be-obeyed', from the Rider Haggard novel.[10]

Getting out into the Mediterranean through the breakers at the entrance to the tributary he was on proved as dangerous as getting in, and again he was lucky not to lose the boat as he was swept out on the current through the surf over the bar. Although he made it safely out, *Leon II* was swamped and it took him a few hours to bale her out and re-stow things before he could get on his way back to Alexandria. From Alexandria he sailed with Jo Rothwell to Paphos on Cyprus and then to Alanya in Turkey. Here he sailed solo up the

Homecoming in Nidri after 4000 miles. Photo Steve Clarke-Lens.

10   Rider Haggard's novel is called *She* and sub-titled *A History of Adventure*. An apt sub-title for Steve on his adventure and for his yet-to-be-built boat.

Turkish coast to Bodrum where, he decided, he would go for broke and build his *felucca*, *Ayesha*.

Ayesha was built at Icmeler near Bodrum where the old skills of shaping wood with an adze, of laying heavy planks and caulking them, of heavy solid spars, of red lead primer and galvanised rigging, are still part of the boat-building ethos that lends itself to the building of a *felucca* like that envisaged by Steve. By the end of the summer of 1992 *Ayesha* was launched and now Steve had two boats miles from where he wanted to be. With a friend, Mike Gregson, he sailed the Wayfarer back across the Aegean and then, from the Corinth Canal, solo to the Ionian. Once he turned the corner from the Gulf of Patras he 'could smell home' and was soon back in Levkas after 4000 miles.

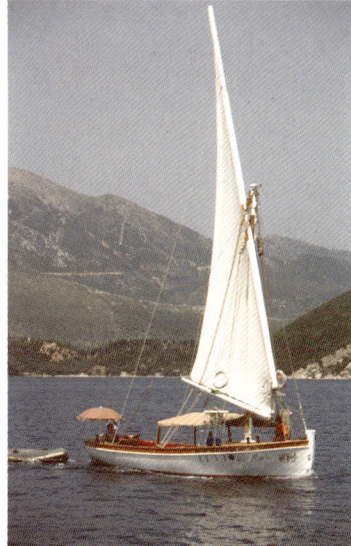

Ayesha, the lateen-rigged *felucca* Steve had built in Turkey.
Photo Steve Clarke-Lens.

He still had *Ayesha* in Turkey and so he returned with Jo (now his wife) to sail his *felucca* to Levkas. Steve used the *felucca* for several years to take people on snorkelling, sailing and star-gazing trips where he would guide them around the inky skies of the Mediterranean. He still lives in Levkas.

Ken Duxbury and *Lugworm*

In spring 1971 Ken Duxbury and his wife 'B' and two friends drove across Europe and down to Greece trailing *Lugworm*, their Drascombe Lugger, behind them to Volos, in the Aegean. The idea had been brewing in Ken's mind for a while as he became increasingly unhappy with how his boat-building business was going and how his life now seemed to be confined to sitting at his desk shuffling paper. He looked out his office window.

Out there, the first gold tinges of the rising sun had caught the edge of a cloud beyond the windmill. As I watched it grew steadily in brightness and with it, on that cold winter morning four years ago, my spirit seemed to burn with a challenging new certainty. I'D HAD

ENOUGH!

Ken Duxbury *Lugworm on the Loose* p 12

It took him three years to put that plan into action and extricate himself from his former life; it took him a little while to persuade his wife 'B' to come with him, but in the end, they loaded *Lugworm* on a trailer. The plan was to launch *Lugworm* and then his two friends would drive the car back to England. Ken and 'B' would spend the summer cruising around the Aegean and then the next year sail her back.

Ken Duxbury, the Author

'B', the Crew

They launched *Lugworm* in Volos near a seaside taverna.[11] As with all of us who have experienced the exuberant kindness of Greeks, the taverna owner soon had matters in hand, fed them, plied them with retsina, and when the wind got up organised his clientele to bodily haul the boat out – the vision of customers in the taverna taking off their shoes and socks, rolling up their trousers, and wading into the water to lift *Lugworm* out is resonant with those of us who have

Lugworm under sail. Ken Duxbury and 'B' in insets.
Photo in *Lugworm Homeward Bound.*

sailed small boats in these waters. For Ken and 'B' it was the beginning of acts of kindness that would follow their journey throughout the Mediterranean.

So, it was that we had our first practical example of this predominant characteristic of the Greek people: a willing kindness and hospitality which on occasions could be carried to an embarrassing stage… We were far from home maybe – but here in Greece we felt we were already among friends.

Ken Duxbury *Lugworm on the Loose* p 29

11   For the location of the places they visited in Greece see Rod and Lucinda Heikell *Greek Waters Pilot* Imray 2018.

Ken first sailed *Lugworm* around to the northern Sporades, the chain of islands scattered across the sea in the northern Aegean. Most of the trips were in the order of ten to twenty miles and they relied mostly on the wind as their budget didn't allow for a lot of petrol for the small outboard. They refined life on the Drascombe Lugger, learning where to put things so they didn't roll off when at sea, how to read the weather and pick safe havens to shelter in when it turned bad, how to efficiently get *Lugworm* up on a beach with the purchase Ken had rigged, how to meld into the life of roving sailors in a strange land. In that strange land the locals were endlessly curious, sometimes infuriatingly so, though ever kind to the couple on this madcap voyage.

It wasn't always easy for them to adapt to life as sea gypsies. At first they had an agenda, a plan that dictated they move on to the next destination and an irritation when bad weather held them up. They found it difficult to immediately shake off how life had been, '… the conditioned compulsive haste, the hysteria in the soul resulting from twelve years' business pressures', and learn to live and cruise in a more relaxed and carefree way. It wasn't until they left the Sporades and headed back down the Evia Channel that they started to unwind and enjoy the adventure in a looser and more confident way, though they still had to contend with the meltemi, the roaring tumultuous wind that blows over the Aegean in the summer.[12]

By the time they got to Andros, the northernmost of the Cyclades, the incessant shriek of the meltemi howling over the sea gave them pause to think about the next part of their adventure. The meltemi can come up quickly and blow for days on end. It can easily reach Force 7–8 (30–40 knots) and sometimes more. Along the coast of Andros they encountered the full force of the meltemi blasting down off the hills and ricocheting through the valleys, and they very nearly lost the boat when trying to find shelter. Given the longer distances they would have to

Lugworm at anchor.
Photo in *Lugworm Homeward Bound.*

12   See the section on weather in the introduction to Rod and Lucinda Heikell *Greek Waters Pilot.*

sail between the islands, Ken and 'B' reluctantly decided to leave *Lugworm* in Batsi on Andros and explore the Cyclades on local ferries.

They returned to *Lugworm* at the end of August when the meltemi becomes less frequent and set off for the Ionian and places in between. Many people think of the Mediterranean as a big lake with a few gentle zephyrs wafting over it when, in fact, the average wind strength is higher than the English Channel. It can blow, and it can blow old boots, as Ken and 'B' were finding out. The meltemi wasn't the only thing that plagued the voyage. Mosquitoes and gnats were a constant in the evenings and when they got to the Saronic it was wasp season. Small things you might think, but small things can add up and it was time for them to think of the winter and some sort of accommodation ashore. By October they had reached Corfu and in the small village of Kassiopi on the northeast corner of the island they struck lucky and found a house to rent.

The winter was not entirely idyllic, but Ken and 'B' had somewhere to stay and he had time to work on his book. When they came to leave in the spring to sail back to England it was a wrench to leave the village and village life. They had come to love the kindness of the Greeks and the anarchic culture that spiked life here, the beauty of the landscape and the uncertainty of the seascape.

As we walked down to the boat, a sound – far away and hauntingly familiar – came floating from the hills and caused us to turn again. It was music which for us will ever bring with it the overpowering essence of Greece… elusive, hidden, seldom located but always there and half-heard… the voice of the very hills themselves; the distant trembling of goat bells…

Ken Duxbury *Lugworm Homeward Bound* pp 16–17

They sailed *Lugworm* up to the small islands north of Corfu, and here Ken had his own moment of uncertainty about the whole undertaking, the butterflies that any thinking sailor has before beginning a voyage. Sitting under a tamarisk tree on the beach he mulled it all over and then, when 'B' came out to find him, asked her if she wanted to go on. She did.

Once they got across to Otranto they had the boot of Italy in front of them and could hop around the coast clear to France – with a few detours to places like Sicily and the Aeolian islands. There were highs and lows along the way, storms and calms, isolated anchorages and crowded harbours, but always the kindness of strangers. In the south of France they entered the French waterways at Grau du Roi and pottered through the Canal du Midi and the

Lateral a la Garonne to Bordeaux. Now there was just the Bay of Biscay and the English Channel to cross. *Lugworm* finally nosed into Fowey in Cornwall and home at the beginning of November. As Ken Duxbury says, this was no 'Do or Die' voyage but…

… it had its moments, and really I know we were very lucky to get Lugworm back more or less intact. A thousand ill chances might have resulted in complete disaster.

Ken Duxbury *Lugworm Homeward Bound* p 180

Le Somail on the Canal du Midi – *Lugworm's* shortcut to Biscay.

Webb Chiles and *Chidiock Tichborne*

Webb Chiles is hard to pin down and that is as it should be. When I met him in Malta it was his birthday and he sadly looked me in the eye and told me he was happy to be alive because none of his family had lived to be more than forty – he was forty-two. He had just sailed direct from Egypt in *Chidiock Tichborne II* and it had been a slow old trip that took him two weeks. His story then and now is extraordinary.

Chiles had previously circumnavigated single-handed in *Egregious*, an engineless stock model Ericson 37. In 1978 he set out in *Chidiock Tichborne*,[13] a Drascombe Lugger like Ken Duxbury's *Lugworm*, to sail single-handed around the world in an open boat.

CHIDIOCK TICHBORNE was a stock English-built Drascombe Lugger. 18' long, 6' wide, unballasted, and with a draft of 4' with the centreboard down, 10" with it up. She weighed less than 900 pounds.

Using the EGREGIOUS circumnavigation as a baseline, I sought an even greater challenge with even greater reliance on myself than on the boat. Not at all incidentally I needed to do this in a boat that did not cost much. In 1978 CHIDIOCK TICHBORNE cost $5000.

Webb Chiles *A Single Wave* Sheridan House 1999 p 46

Webb Chiles set out from San Diego and, after reaching the Marquesas, island-hopped down to Fiji where he laid *Chidiock Tichborne* up for the cyclone

---

13   Chidiock Tichborne was an English poet who was hung for sedition in 1586. Webb Chiles much admired his elegy to his wife before he was hung, drawn and quartered.

season. The Pacific is a big ocean and these passages covered thousands of miles alone in an open-decked boat just 18 ft long. It's difficult for most of us to imagine these long passages in a small boat and, even though you get some idea of the scale of the boat and voyage from the photos along the way, you cannot imagine the mental tenacity and emotional rigour needed to single-hand over these distances unless you have some similar experience yourself.[14]

In 1979, once the cyclone season was over, Webb returned to the boat and set off to cross the rest of the South Pacific on his way to the Indian Ocean. It was nearly his undoing. Three hundred miles west of Fiji he was pitchpoled and *Chidiock Tichborne* was swamped. She floated with just her gunwales above the water and away floated all sorts of equipment and a few luxuries: an oar, lines, a bag of books.

CHIDIOCK TICHBORNE felt as though she were sinking. Except for a few inches at the bow, she was completely below the water. With each wave, she dropped from beneath me and I thought that she was gone. But each time she came back.

Webb Chiles *A Single Wave* p 63

After two weeks drifting on the water he washed up on an islet in Vanuatu. He managed to get *Chidiock Tichborne* repaired and set off to close the loop

*Chidiock
Titchborne.*
Photo in
the presentsea.com.

across the Indian Ocean and up the Red Sea to the Mediterranean. Halfway up the Red Sea he put into a port in Saudi Arabia and was arrested as a spy. The boat was impounded. When he was released Webb went back to the builders of the Drascombe Lugger in England and was given another identical boat: *Chidiock Tichborne II.* This he had shipped to the Red Sea and once again he set off from his last position to sail up to Port Suez and through the Suez Canal into the Mediterranean. Much of this might seem peripheral to a history of yachting in the Mediterranean, but it gives a measure of the man and contrasts with what he found in the Mediterranean – he was not as enamoured of the sea as many of us so evidently are.

From Port Said Webb sailed directly to Malta. As far as the Mediterranean was concerned, he reckoned the sea '… is for power boats and always has been, even when the power came from men at oars.' It took him two weeks to

14   See Webb Chiles web site www.inthepresentsea.com/the_actual_site/webbchiles.html

get to Malta and here he hauled *Chidiock Tichborne II* out and went to Britain where he had bought a She 36, a boat with a good deal more accommodation and some home comforts – and a deck. He returned in August and sailed *Chidiock Tichborne II* directly to Vilamoura in Portugal. His description of the voyage is brief and pointed.

Again the wind was fluky and the sailing slow, boring and uneventful until I reached the exit. After the events of the preceding year, I could live with boring… About noon half-way through the strait and a half-mile off sheer Spanish hills, a wind that I later learned is called a "levanter" because it blows east from The Levant came up as suddenly and unexpectedly as any wind I have known.

Webb Chiles www.inthepresentsea.com/the_actual_site/chidiocktichborne2.html

The disaffected perspective of a voyager like Webb Chiles in the Mediterranean is a useful counterpoint that illustrates the difference between sailors who pine for the trades and the long rolling swell of the open ocean and those of us who like tinkering around the edges of the inland sea. I've known numbers of ocean voyagers who have a dislike for this sea and its history because it presents a seascape so different from something like an Atlantic crossing. In the Mediterranean it is impossible to sail in a straight line for a thousand miles without bumping into the land, whereas on an Atlantic trade wind passage you sail 2800 miles from the Canary Islands to the Caribbean on a clear and uncluttered sea.

This dichotomy between the ocean voyager and those of us who have an affection for the Mediterranean, with all its wiles and moods, is a curious one that may hide more than it reveals. In 1976–77 I sailed the 20 ft *Roulette*, an old hard-chine plywood boat with a dodgy engine and little else down to Greece. No electrics, a steering compass, a few charts, cotton sails and a certain naivety about wind, weather and sea. *Roulette* sailed to St Malo and then through the Brittany canals to the Bay of Biscay where we coast-hopped down to Bordeaux. The Garonne Canal and Canal du Midi provided a short-cut to the Mediterranean coast of France and a lot of sight-seeing along the way in a reverse route to that taken by Ken Duxbury in *Lugworm*. From here *Roulette* crossed to Corsica, Italy and finally to Greece.

The second small boat voyage I made was in 1987 in *Rozinante*, a Mirror Offshore 18 that, like *Roulette*, was also minimally equipped. The voyage down the Danube started in Regensburg in Germany and continued downstream through the eastern bloc to Constanta on the Black Sea. Being unable to get fuel in Romania, the 200-mile passage to Istanbul took four days under sail. After a breather in Istanbul we sailed *Rozinante* on through the Marmara Sea to the Aegean and down to Bodrum on the Turkish coast. This voyage was made before the Iron Curtain tore and the former satellites of the USSR broke free from their communist masters.[15]

Subsequent voyages I've made have included a circumnavigation and various ocean passages in other yachts I've owned, so I get the idea of an ocean passage and the rewards it gives. But it is the pull of the Mediterranean I feel the most and it is passages across its waters that please me more than an ocean passage. There are no landfalls like a landfall in the Mediterranean and, at the risk of sounding churlish, I have dreamed of gunk-holing in the Mediterranean when I've been in the South Pacific or the Indian Ocean or any of the other wonderful places I have sailed to.

I'm never going to make the sort of gutsy circumnavigations that Webb Chiles has made, though I love reading his accounts of them. And in many ways his writing is as much an impetus to his sailing as the boats he sails in. On the introduction page to his website, 'In the Present Sea', he writes this:

People who know of me at all probably do so as a sailor; but I have always thought of myself as an artist, and I believe that the artist's defining responsibility is to go to the edge of human experience and send back reports. Here are my reports.

Webb Chiles www.inthepresentsea.com/the_actual_site/introduction.html

Chris Geankoplis and *Vayu*[16]

In 1969 a young student who was working in the language lab for the American army in Naples decided he would like to sail down the Italian coast and maybe, just maybe, across to Greece in his 19 ft open dinghy. He was at a time in his life when the contract for working in the language lab was coming to an end and the possibility of being conscripted and sent off to Vietnam loomed over him. Time to strike out on an adventure. First of all, he needed a friend to go sailing with and secondly, he needed to somehow persuade his father of the merits of the trip and how it wasn't really going to be all that dangerous.

---

15   See Heikell *The Accidental Sailor* and *The Danube: A River Guide* Imray, 1991.
16   *Vayu* is a Sanskrit word meaning 'wind'.

He enlisted his friend Doug Hayes to go with him and they both approached their fathers to get permission. They got a resounding 'NO'. With the tenacity of youth they nagged their fathers until they caved in.

Now Dad being of open mind and familiar with the winds in the Tyrrhenian Sea gave me a simple and straight forward answer: absolutely no. For the next three weeks Doug and I shuttled back and forth between parents, pleading, coercing, making all sorts of promises, showing our charts and explaining how careful we would be. I even showed them the international orange survival canister that was used by ejecting pilots that had an emergency radio, various flares and other supplies sealed in the canister. (The fact that it was only an empty canister which we had filled with peanut butter, jars of spaghetti sauce, books, and a "radio", a transistor AM/FM receiver, was something we forgot to mention). Impressed and overwhelmed, they finally gave in and we could really start our preparations.

Chris Geankoplis *The Story of the Vayu*

They caulked the old dinghy to stem the leaks, packed up food for the trip which mostly seemed to involve *ziti*, a pasta similar to *penne*, jars of *ragu* sauce for the *ziti*, and jars of peanut butter, and modified the floorboards so they could be raised to make a sleeping platform on either side of the centreboard case.

In the summer they set off down the Italian coast towards the Strait of Messina.[17] They would sail, motor with an ageing Seagull outboard when it worked, or row if they had to. In the evening they would anchor off close to the shore or beach the boat if they could, and cook dinner, *ziti* and *ragu*, or if a nearby restaurant beckoned, go there for a change of diet. The insouciance of youth runs in and

Vayu alongside in Italy 1969.
Photo Chris Geankoplis.

out of the account of their voyage. In the Strait of Messina they got caught in one of the whirlpools that develop there and, once they figured how to get out

---

17   For the places visited in Italy see Rod & Lucinda Heikell *Italian Waters Pilot* 2015, Chapters 3 and 6.

of it by running the outboard flat out and sheeting the sail in tight, they dipped back into it again just for the fun of it.

It would be foolish to succumb to the notion that it was a wild and carefree trip. Sandwiched into the text there are thoughtful observations on looking after the boat under sail and at anchor. Chris makes light of some of the problems along the way, keeping the leaky *Vayu* a going concern and meeting up with crew mates. Scattered through the text are paeans to the kindness of strangers along the way and an admiration for the landscape and the culture.

On the insole of the boot of Italy they nearly lost the boat when a southerly gale sprang up and *Vayu* was tossed about at anchor in the breakers. Fortunately, there was road repair crew with a tractor nearby and the boys persuaded them to haul the boat up the foreshore to safety.

I swam out to the boat; it was bucking widely with the bow submerged then the stern. I timed my attempt and pulled myself up on the stern that was almost submerged. The next second I was flipped out of the water and landed upside down in the cockpit. I grabbed our two spare anchor lines and tied them together and made a bridle around the whole boat because the bow cleat wouldn't hold. I then jumped back overboard and swam through the breakers to the shore; the line just barely reached the tractor. One last trip back through the waves with the adrenalin waning, I flopped back into the boat and struggled to attach the rudder. With that done and a quick and frantic bail to lighten the boat I signalled to the tractor all was ready and cut the anchor line. The tractor surged ahead; the boat spun around and surfed down the breakers to the beach. At the last possible moment I pulled up the rudder and the boat hit the beach. There was a pause as the lines stretched, and then with a jerk the Vayu slithered up the beach above the breaking waves, the boat was saved! We thanked the driver and offered to pay but he refused. I jumped back into the beached boat and pulled out our last complete carton of Winston's and gave it to him, he certainly earned it and even then he was reluctant to take something.

Chris Geankoplis *The Story of the Vayu*

Chris and Doug set off again in *Vayu* when the weather moderated and sailed across the Gulf of Taranto to Gallipoli where Doug got the train back to Naples and Chris settled down to wait for his dad and his twelve-year-old brother to arrive. They were to be the crew for the voyage across to Greece.

Chris and younger brother Brad sailed *Vayu* down to Santa Maria de Leuca where Chris's father joined the boat. The plan was to set off for the northern end of Corfu island in the afternoon, sail through the night, and then make landfall the next day on Corfu, so avoiding the Albanian coast still under the communist control of the hard-line leader Enver Hoxha. Between fickle winds and the south-going current it took them three days before they sighted land, though it was not Corfu but Levkas some seventy-five miles south of their intended destination. Their father left them in Levkas and returned home, while Chris and Brad set off to sail up to Corfu.[18]

Unable to stand the constant ribbing about his navigational skills from his sons, (and seeing them safely in Greece) Dad decided to fly back to Italy. After a day's rest and some good Greek cooking, Brad and I sailed north to the town of Preveza 8 nm away. Since it was the official port of entry we had to do so in a "timely fashion". I found that I had been processed in by customs as an "International Yacht" and was entitled to duty free fuel just like an ocean liner! Cool!

Chris Geankoplis *The Story of the Vayu*

The duo sailed up to the west side of Corfu to Palaiokastrita where they had been on holiday before and a place that Chris's dad described as the most beautiful place in the world. They stayed several days waiting for a break in the weather before sailing around to Corfu town. On the way they managed to hit an 'uncharted reef', though later when 'Chris scraped the spaghetti sauce off the chart he found the "uncharted" shoals.' In Corfu they found a friendly fisherman, Michale Bouas, who agreed to look after the *Vayu* while Chris went off to university in Munich and Brad went back to school in Naples. Both of them were already dreaming of the next summer and where *Vayu* would take them to.

The young Chris at the 'chart table'. Photo Chris Geankoplis.

In June 1970 Chris returned with a friend, Paul Clapp, to get *Vayu* ready to go sailing. They had a lot to do: one of the planks needed replacing; the deck needed new canvas; and everything needed painting and primping for the new season. They sailed south from Corfu through the night straight down to Levkas, and almost ended the voyage before it had begun.

I woke up around 1 a.m. to find the seas breaking and confused around us, and I felt the same way. I could see through the dark that

18   For the places mentioned in Greece see Rod & Lucinda Heikell *Greek Waters Pilot* Chapters 1, 3, 4 and 6.

we had just passed a large above-water rock by less than 20 feet. It seems that Paul took a shortcut through some "fly specs" on the chart, those black crosses represented an extensive shoal with rocks awash! He didn't even have the spaghetti sauce excuse. After much tacking and dodging in the dark, in desperation we tied up to a huge light buoy, to sit out the rest of the night. We had sailed 55nm, which almost ended up being the total of all our sailing that summer.

Chris Geankoplis *The Story of the Vayu*

The next day they pottered down the canal to Levkas town and found that Chris's father had brought the family boat, an old motorboat called *Caribbee*, to Levkas and there it was tied up to the dock with all the family on board. From Levkas they headed down into the inland sea and island-hopped down to the Gulf of Patras. At times the sailing was good, but a lot of the time they had to row in the morning calm as the outboard wasn't working, and from Ithaca ended up rowing the twenty-eight miles to Oxia Island off the entrance to the Gulf of Patras.

In the Gulf of Patras the prevailing winds are from the west and they made good progress towards the Corinth Canal. This stretch of water, hemmed in by mountains on either side, tends to channel the wind and it can get quite boisterous by the afternoon. On *Vayu* things went well until a big blow nearly put them on the rocks. Somehow the *Vayu*'s rudder had broken off as they surfed down the waves and they only just managed to round a rocky cape and find shelter of sorts behind the cape. They were both so exhausted they drifted off to sleep and *Vayu* drifted gently into a vertical cliff. The close call was an adrenalin shot for them and they rowed to the village of Andi-Kiron. The crew were chastened by the experience, but their appetite was not.

We woke up around noon, had a huge meal to celebrate our good fortune, followed by a siesta, a late afternoon meal, a nap and finally a complete dinner late that evening. It is strange how much you appreciate food after a close call with death.

Chris Geankoplis *The Story of the Vayu*

With the rudder repaired they set off for the Corinth Canal. Here they had a small problem as you are not allowed to sail through the canal; you must motor. They had abandoned *Vayu*'s ancient Seagull in Levkas. They found a French yacht to give them a tow, although as it turned out the yacht could only run its motor for ten minutes before it overheated and needed to be turned off. With the *Vayu* in tow, ten minutes was enough to get into the canal and then the French yacht raised a spinnaker and sailed down the canal to the Aegean with *Vayu* still in tow. Once through the canal Chris sailed down to the island of Salamis and then onto Zea Marina in Piraeus. This was to be the end of this trip until the next year when Chris would return for one final voyage in the Aegean.

In 1971 Chris returned from Munich and travelled back to Athens to reacquaint himself with *Vayu*, and to make *Vayu* seaworthy, or as seaworthy as you can make an old open dinghy, for his forthcoming voyage up to the northern Sporades. This time his crew was just fourteen-year-old Brad. They hadn't gone far down the Attic coast before the tiller broke and Chris left Brad on the boat while he returned to Piraeus to get a new one built. He needn't have worried too much about his little brother looking after himself, as later events proved.

Once around into the southern Gulf of Evia they encountered the meltemi blasting down from the north and northeast – just the direction they were headed in. They battled against it, spent time holed up waiting for it to die down, and when a southerly blew tried to get as much distance in as possible. Eventually Chris was wondering if he had bitten off more than he could chew.

The boat was leaking like a sieve, the repaired motor had not been tested and proven reliable and the constant wind was wearing on my nerves. And I missed my girlfriend. It was Brad who suggested that we not give up, but at least try for one more point on the coast and see how that went. It was dark and overcast that morning of the 30th when we left and headed to Porto Buphalo, 9 nm away.

Chris Geankoplis *The Story of the Vayu*

Once they had got to Khalkis Chris's sister Nikki joined them. Now there were three of them on the dinghy, Brad was demoted to sleeping on the foredeck. In the night Chris realised the boat was sinking and tracked the problem down to loose caulking in the bows. With Brad's weight on the foredeck, the bow had been immersed enough for water to leak though the gap in the planks. Undaunted they sailed a short way up the coast and Chris got a bus into town to get materials to effect a repair. Chris sailed *Vayu* up the northern Gulf of Evia and across to the northern Sporades. There were incidents along the way and lots of running repairs to the boat were made, including hauling it out in the north of Evia to re-caulk and repair some planks that were threatening to let in more water than was good.

In Skiathos Chris heard he had the chance of a job on a charter boat for ten days, something that would substantially top up the boat kitty. He left Brad with five dollars, a bag of rice and some 'mystery' cans of food.

What happened during those 10 days only Brad knows for sure. What I do know was when I returned at the beginning of September, with the "Big Bucks" (about $50.00) that I had earned, I did not find a slimmed down version of my little brother. He wasn't at the boat, but as I was passing one of the more exclusive tourists' restaurants, I heard someone call to me. "Hey hippie, you want something to eat?" There was Brad seated at a table with all sorts of food and wine looking well fed and very smug. He ordered a meal for me and paid the rather large bill from a fat roll of Drachmas… It seems he opened up a charter boat business. He would take the girls on tours of the small island near the village and over to Koukounaries beach and when requested to more "secluded" beaches. For this hazardous and difficult labor he often made as much in a day as I had made in the whole charter.

Chris Geankoplis *The Story of the Vayu*

Chris sailed back down to Piraeus with assorted crew, nursing the *Vayu* most of the way as she had begun to leak badly when driven hard by the meltemi. The journey home almost ended in disaster. On rounding Cape Sounion again and heading for Piraeus he put into a cove on the northeast corner of the island of Patroklou. With his crew he set up camp on the island and, exhausted, they both went to bed. In the night a vicious squall came through and the strong northerly blew the *Vayu* onto the rocks and up onto a gravel beach, springing several planks in her hull. Chris and his crew, Susan, were now marooned on the island with little in the way of food or water.

They explored the island to see if anyone lived there and finally found a rough hut by the shore. When Chris tapped on the window a young Greek, incongruously dressed in a suit, looked like he would hightail it out the back window until Chris assured him they meant no harm. We are in 1971 and the right-wing colonels are in power and imprisoning anyone who gets in their way. Nikko, the young, suited Greek, was a socialist who had escaped to the island when the police had come for him.[19] His cousin had brought him over by boat and dropped by every now and again to deliver supplies to him. When he came by after a couple of days he motioned for Nikko to hide and heaved the sack of supplies ashore and then gunned the motor to get away. Minutes later a naval cutter appeared around the corner shadowing his cousin.

---

19   In fictional form based on the coup of the colonels, see J. C. Graeme *To Ithaca* Taniwha Press 2016.

After five days Chris managed to repair the *Vayu* sufficiently to get them the short distance across to the mainland. Susan cadged a lift on a tour bus and once in Athens phoned Chris's dad. He put out the next day in the *Caribbee* to tow *Vayu* back to Piraeus. It didn't go well. Chris had taken two towing lines to the stern quarters of the *Caribbee* and when one broke the *Vayu* careened sideways, filled with water, and sank. In the three years of *Vayu*'s voyage she had never capsized or sunk until nearly at the end of her voyages.

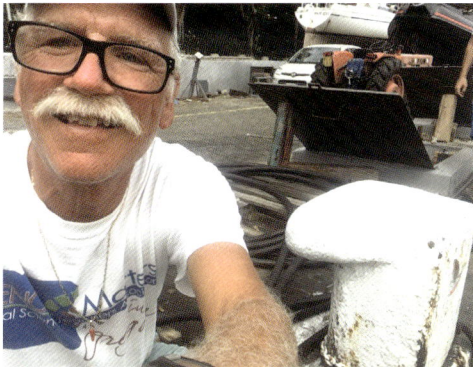

Chris on the quay in Ischia where he set off from in *Vayu* 50 years ago. Photo Chris Geankoplis.

By inserting fenders under the thwarts of the boat they somehow raised her to the surface and then free-dived to collect all the gear that had been in *Vayu*. She was then lashed to the side of the *Caribbee* and ignominiously towed to Zea Marina. Chris went back to the USA after being away for eight years. The *Vayu* remained in Piraeus and his dad and younger brother fixed her up again. The experience stayed with Chris all his life. In a recent letter he had this to say:

They say you can never "go home" after 50 years. In the broad sweep of things, the sea and the Islands, the waves and the wind are the same. Individually, each single wave, day, sunrise and sunset is everchanging and new. Yes, much change has occurred over the last 50 years, I certainly have changed too. I accept the change (something I learned from sailing so long ago) and I adjust, I still can appreciate the experience, I explore the new, and embrace the old. I can think of nothing better than sailing the Med with my wife in a small boat.

And that is exactly what he is doing. In the ensuing years he has cruised around much of North America in his Rhodes 22 *Enosis*. Still, the voyage of the *Vayu* all those years ago was seared on his memory, and what better thing to do than ship *Enosis* to the Mediterranean and retrace that youthful voyage. So he has.

Chris back in the Mediterranean in the 22 ft Rhodes *Enosis* to retrace his voyages in *Vayu* some 50 years on. Photo Chris Geankoplis.

The Perini Navi *Is a Rose*. Photo Chris Blunt..

15 THE RICH AND THE SUPER RICH, PART II: SUPERYACHTS GALORE

At the end of the 20th century the overall trend in yachts was the rapid increase in what were called 'Mediterranean-style yachts' that were more affordable and offered a degree of luxury – yachts built largely by big European builders like the Beneteau group and Bavaria. Other builders were also getting into the action and companies like Hanse were producing relatively affordable yachts for the mass market, or at least that part of the mass market that had the time and the money to go yachting. While this was happening there were other players afoot that wanted very large and luxurious yachts to cruise in different parts of the world, as long as part of that cruising was in the Mediterranean.[1]

With the break-up of the Soviet Union in 1991 many of the national assets were acquired by a small number of Russians and, almost overnight, a small band of oligarchs joined the wealthiest people in the world. According to *Forbes Magazine* there are today seventy-seven Russian billionaires we know of.[2] By the early 2000's many of these oligarchs were popping up on superyachts in the Mediterranean and doing it on yachts that have become bigger

Little and large.

and more luxurious over the last two decades.

Along with the Russian billionaires, the very rich from other countries also invested in mega-yachts and based them in the Mediterranean. The Royals from Middle East countries had based superyachts in the Mediterranean in

1   In Alberto Cappato FEMIP paper *Cruises and Recreational Boating in the Mediterranean* 2010 p 43. Super Yacht Intelligence evaluations state that 50% of the global fleet spends eight months out of twelve in Mediterranean waters. The same report also underlines that 76% of yachts tend to stay in Europe.
2   *Forbes Magazine* 2018 billionaires' list: www.forbes.com/billionaires/list/2/#version:static_country:Russia

the late 20th century and in the 2000's they were joined by billionaires from southeast Asia and those who had been in on the IT revolution in the USA. All of them invested large amounts of money building increasingly bigger superyachts, most of them motor-yachts, although the term 'motor-yachts' hardly describes what are effectively small private ships.

In the 125 years before 1992 just nineteen superyachts over 260 ft (80 metres) were built, whereas in just over a decade, from 1992 to 2005, 20 superyachts over 260 ft were built.[3] Part of the reason for this can be attributed to advances in the technical construction and fitting out of large yachts, though commercial ships much bigger than this were being built at the time. So, a more likely reason is the large number of wealthy individuals when compared to the past who want to exhibit their wealth through ownership of a superyacht in the Mediterranean.

It's instructive to take a look at the costs involved in building and running a superyacht. The terms for what constitutes a 'super' or a 'mega' and now a 'giga' yacht are not fixed and to an extent are interchangeable. A superyacht is generally defined as any yacht over 78 ft (24 metres) and up to 200 tons, at which length a professionally certified skipper and crew are required.[4] A mega-yacht is loosely defined as around 130–140 ft (over 40 metres) while a giga-yacht is over 330 ft (100 metres plus). Any yacht over 200 tons requires additional MCA qualifications and over 3000 tons requires a commercially endorsed master and deck officers.[5] For convenience I'll refer to all categories as superyachts.

According to *Forbes Magazine* there are nearly 4500 superyachts in the world with around 455 more in build.[6] This represents a staggering number of large yachts and the rate of growth is exponential – literally. To the initial cost of

3   Yachtharbour, *How Russian oligarchs shaped the yachting industry* June 8, 2016 www.yachtharbour.com
4   For example, RYA Yachtmaster Ocean Certificate of Competence with the commercial endorsement.
5   These are British qualifications from the Royal Yachting Association and the Maritime and Coastguard Agency. Other countries have equivalent qualifications, although the RYA qualifications are highly regarded outside Britain. www.rya.org.uk/courses-training/careers-advice/Pages/skippering-commercial-yachts.aspx
6   Doug Gollan *The Superyacht Industry is Poised for Growth* Forbes Magazine, 13th April, 2016. Other figures quoted say 10,000 superyachts are afloat, but I suspect the Forbes figure is the more accurate.

a superyacht, anything from a modest few millions to hundreds of millions for the largest, must be added the annual cost of running a superyacht which typically is around 10% of the initial cost.[7]

Gas prices, general maintenance, taxes and crew salaries are typically the biggest sources of added expenditure for owners. Towergate estimates that annual dockage fees run for $350,000, insurance averages $240,000 and maintenance and repairs can be in the millions, as can crew salaries. Overall, the owner should expect to spend about 10% of the yacht's initial cost on annual upkeep.

Towergate Insurance: www.towergateinsurance.co.uk/boat-insurance/the-cost-of-maintaining-a-super-yacht

If it cost 25 million dollars to buy then it will cost around 10% annually of that to run it. That rules most of us out.

The number of superyachts around and the cost of running one, in the Mediterranean and elsewhere, reflects the disproportionate rise in the wealth of what are called ultra-high-net-worth individuals (UNHW), which usually means those whose assets are greater than US$30 million.

So that rules most of us out. The surprising thing is that this group of people are growing at a rapidly increasing rate – in 2018 the numbers of UHNW in the world grew by 12.9% to a staggering record of 255,810 people.[8] The astonishing statistic here is that, while the real incomes of the working and middle class have declined in the last two decades, the divide between the uber-rich and the rest of us has increased exponentially.[9] The large number of UHNW individuals is the principal reason for the renaissance of superyachts in the 21st century. After all, once

---

7   The 10% figure is typically used for a yacht of any size and is often quoted by brokerage companies.
8   Rupert Neate *Booming global stock markets swell ranks of the super rich* The Guardian, 5th September, 2018
9   David Leonhardt *Our Broken Economy* New York Times 7th August 2017. According to the New York Times only those in the top 1/40th of income distribution have seen an increase in wealth in the last decade. When shown on a graph, a typical hockey-stick increase is shown.

you have apartments in London and New York, a few villas scattered around the world, and a garage full of expensive motor cars, what is it that you need next to impress friends and business colleagues and the odd mistress or two – a superyacht.

The rapid increase in the number of superyachts, many of them based full or part time in the Mediterranean, prompted a scramble to provide the infrastructure for servicing and repair facilities for these expensive acquisitions.[10] Such is the increase in these numbers that there are now a number of publications like the annual superyacht directories, magazines like *Boat International* that publishes a glossy magazine and books on superyachts, and numerous websites for everything from crewing jobs, crew training courses, to where to find the perfect flower arrangement for the aft deck.[11] Even the academic world has cottoned on to just how big this industry is and you can now do a whole variety of courses at the Warsash Superyacht Academy attached to Solent University.[12]

Superyacht infrastructure in the Mediterranean

In the past the much smaller overall numbers and the smaller size of superyachts in the Mediterranean meant that they could be accommodated in the long-established harbours that had traditionally served this purpose. Harbours like Monaco, Cannes, Antibes, Barcelona, Genoa and Livorno had the slipways and skills to carry out refits and install new equipment. If the workforce skills were not up to a job, then these harbours had good communications to bring the skills and equipment in. Once the yachts were ready

Cannes. While the old ports on the Riviera have adapted to the increasing size of superyachts, there are still only so many big yachts you can fit in.

10   Estimates are that 50% plus of superyachts are based in the Mediterranean. Alberto Cappato FEMIP Trust Fund paper *Cruises and Recreational Boating in the Mediterranean* 2010 p 35
11   www.boatinternational.com/ and www.superyachtservicesguide.com/.
12   www.warsashsuperyachtacademy.com/home.aspx

to go for the Mediterranean summer season there were sufficient harbours and refuelling and reprovisioning stops for a cruise around the eastern Mediterranean before returning to the western Mediterranean or crossing to the Caribbean for the European winter.

With the rapid rise in the numbers and size of superyachts, some of these old haunts fell out of favour, others were revamped to provide the facilities needed, and new hubs for superyacht maintenance developed in harbours that could accommodate the bigger superyachts. Palma Mallorca is a good example of how an old commercial harbour is now almost entirely populated by yachts. In 1972 the Club de Mar Marina opened in the port with the express intention of attracting superyachts as well as the bread-and-butter of smaller yachts. It has berths for yachts up to 400 ft plus (135 metres) and currently has plans to increase the marina berths by 61% for yachts over 59 ft (18 metres).[13]

Across the other side of the harbour at Palma is the yard of Astilleros de Mallorca that can handle the refit and repair of superyachts up to 230 ft (70 metres). Any superyacht home port needs a berth and the repair facilities of a yard as a minimum. Other requirements are good communications and the airport for Majorca is fifteen minutes away for the owner's private jet. There are other requirements too; one of the most important is security and privacy. Unlike the Victorians who promoted the yacht and its travels through a book, or in more recent times courted publicity like Aristotle Onassis, most of today's superyacht owners want to stay out of the limelight. Most of the larger superyachts have high-end security systems and cameras covering everything on board and in the immediate environment. If you have enough money, like Roman Abramovich, you can even lease a fenced-off section of a harbour as he does in Barcelona for the refit and repair of his fleet of superyachts.

It's hard to pin down exactly why somewhere like Palma Mallorca has become a superyacht hub, apart from the provision of a good infrastructure. Other reasons can be that the capital of the Balearics is on an attractive island in the Mediterranean, and so the skippers and crew of superyachts are kept happy as well. There are a lot of good restaurants and bars in Palma and most owners want to look after and retain the skipper and crew once they have been on the yacht for a while. A lot of superyacht skippers have made Mallorca their

---

13   Club de Mar Corporate Dossier 2016.

home base and have bought property there.[14] In many ways a place like Palma acquires its own momentum once things are set in motion, and superyacht numbers increase as much by word of mouth and the availability of facilities and, not least, that crew live there, as by anything else. It has become the 'new' place to be seen.

Along with the berthing and repair facilities come lots of shoreside amenities. Owners may have a good chef on board, but he needs to obtain the best ingredients for the owner and lay down a stock of good wine and champagne. Not surprisingly, provisioning services have been established that can get the finest Grade 10+ Kobe beef, sashimi grade tuna, fresh truffles and Beluga caviar, organic fruit and vegetables and organic anything else, along with the best Chateau Latour and Grand Cru Chablis and the odd Mathusalem of Dom Perignon. Eating out is catered for by nine Michelin-starred restaurants on the island and a whole host of other restaurants and fashionable cafés.

For those who can't get a berth in Palma itself, there are now several other marinas around Mallorca with superyacht capacity where specialised repair and refit facilities have been established as well as all those ancillary services ashore. Port Adriano, Andratx and Puerto Portals are home to the superyachts who prefer somewhere out of town but no less luxurious. Success begets success and so Mallorca, and to a lesser extent Minorca and Ibiza, now attract the large number of superyachts looking for a home in the Mediterranean. It's difficult to work out what the superyacht industry is worth to a place like the Balearics, but in 2017 the industry injected nearly 13.5 million Euros into the local economy.[15] You could hazard a guess that the figure is actually higher than that, and this amount represents a substantial part of the local GDP, and it follows that other countries are looking to emulate the Palma Mallorca model.

While Palma Mallorca is the superyacht hub of the western Mediterranean, a number of the older established superyacht harbours have developed facilities to compete for the market. Monaco's Port Hercules has been substantially enlarged and its facilities improved. Barcelona on the mainland opposite the Balearics is home to significant numbers of superyachts. Likewise, Cannes

14   I know a good number of superyacht skippers and crew who have settled down here in preference to returning to their home country.
15   www.abc-mallorca.com 18/06/2018

Calvi on Corsica. In many harbours only 'modest' superyachts will find a berth. Anything bigger must anchor off.

and Antibes have dedicated superyacht berths and services to match. As the size of superyachts has stretched to somewhere near the size of a small cruise ship, so the yards that can provide lifting and repair facilities have increased. Commonly, this has been in yards where previously shipbuilding went on, such as at La Ciotat on the French Mediterranean coast. The proposed yard in Marseilles will be capable of taking superyachts up to 425 ft (130 metres) and 6000 tons.[16]

In Italy much of the superyacht construction has historically been based around Viareggio on the Tuscan coast, with the likes of Azimut who own Benetti, Perini Navi and San Lorenzo building superyachts here. In the case of Benetti there is a 200-year-long history of building boats and the yard morphed into the superyacht market in the 1960's and 1970's – though a large yacht in those days was fifty or sixty ft long, not hundreds of feet. The success of Benetti building large motorboats attracted other boatbuilders, and so a cluster of skills and resources built up around what is essentially a little seaside town that today builds a remarkable 20% of Italian superyachts.[17] Given that Italy accounts for more superyacht production than anywhere else, at 32% overall, the volume of superyacht construction in Viareggio turns out to be very big indeed.[18]

Not all superyacht infrastructure development is successful. In Valencia a dedicated superyacht dock was built with facilities ashore for the America's Cup in 2007. It can accommodate superyachts up to 490 ft (150 metres) and, though it was built to cater exclusively for superyachts with all services to hand, it just hasn't proved as popular as Mallorca. The allure of an island like Mallorca has a lot to do with it; there is a cache to island life, and when an

---

16   Monaco Marine plans to open the yard in 2022.
17   Katie Hope *The City that Makes the Most Expensive Boats in the World* BBC 24 July 2017
18   Alberto Cappato FEMIP paper *Cruises and Recreational Boating in the Mediterranean* 2010 pp 32 ff

individual can afford a superyacht, a very expensive 'toy', he will want to be somewhere he likes and somewhere his crew likes as well.

In the eastern Mediterranean there has been much development of infrastructure to attract superyachts. Turkey is the country where the building and repair of superyachts has gone on apace and near Istanbul there are several yards producing superyachts that have turned heads in some of the older European yards. Some superyacht companies in Europe have sub-contracted to yards in Turkey for the building

Superyacht construction in Turkey has moved on apace. The innovative *Maltese Falcon* was largely built in Tuzla near Istanbul.

of superyachts, the most notable being the Perini Navi 280 ft (88 metres) square-sail *Maltese Falcon*. This revolutionary three masted yacht uses dyna-rig technology, originally developed for sail-assisted cargo ships, and all the sails are computer controlled so the yacht can be sailed by a small crew.

The dyna-rig technology was originally developed by Wilhelm Proelss so that cargo ships could be sail-assisted with steel tripod masts. For *Maltese Falcon*, free-standing carbon fibre masts with load sensors embedded in them were developed with the squaresails controlled by computer from the helm.[19] The result is a remarkable boat, like no other, that I have seen sail in and out of coral atolls in the Pacific with ease, belying its superyacht size. The factory that developed the rig and sensors was gifted by the first owner of *Maltese Falcon*, Tom Perkins, to the yard in Tuzla where the yacht was built. Recently the *Black Pearl* was launched with a three-masted dyna-rig and, at 350 ft (106.7 metres), she is bigger and faster than *Maltese Falcon*.[20]

Apart from Perini Navi, other prominent yards have based themselves in Turkey. Oyster Yachts for a time built its 100 ft (30 metre) and 125 ft (38 metre) yachts here. There are also Turkish-owned yards building large superyachts,

19   www.compositesworld.com/articles/megayacht-composite-masts-get-smart
20   www.boatinternational.com/yachts/
news/106m-sailing-yacht-black-pearl-delivered-by-oceanco--31765

with Bilgin Yachts constructing motor yachts to 262 ft (80 metres) and CBK Superyachts building motor yachts up to 138 ft (42 metres). Overall Turkey ranks fourth in the Mediterranean for the construction and repair of superyachts.[21] The yards developing these boats are modern and well-run affairs with covered hangars for construction and a labour force increasingly well-skilled in modern yacht design and composite construction methods. In the past, construction techniques may have been somewhat unrefined and some even questionable, but today Turkey has a young and well-educated work force and a manufacturing base that turns out quality yacht equipment with labour costs generally less than the old established yards in Europe.

While Turkey has capitalised on superyacht construction and maintenance, nearby Greece has struggled. There is limited superyacht construction and maintenance in the old shipyards at Perama near Piraeus, but little else.

In Mikonos superyachts shunned the new marina and opted for the old harbour in the middle of town. Photo Harry Potts.

The shipyards here used to build commercial ships and, while some of the local workforce have the skills for superyacht construction and repair, many of them do not and there is little training available to develop these skills.[22] Nor are there sufficient marina facilities for superyachts. Around Athens, Zea Marina, Faliron, Flisvos and Vouliagmeni marinas provide berths for superyachts, though demand for berths, especially from local superyachts, is high.[23] There are superyacht berths in a few other marinas as well, notably Corfu and Porto Carras on Khalkidhiki, but these are limited and superyacht facilities are few and far between.

21   Cappato *Cruises and Recreational Boating in the Mediterranean* pp 34 ff
22   Peter Beaumont *Greek shipyards kept afloat by luxury yachts for the super-rich* The Guardian Thursday 4 Aug 2011
23   See Rod and Lucinda Heikell *Greek Waters Pilot* Imray 2018 for details of marinas and the max LOA they can take.

Sometimes, in an attempt to cater for superyacht berths, while the intention seems logical, in practice mistakes are made over what an owner or charter guests want. On Mikonos a large new harbour was built some miles outside Mikonos town. It has large quays for berthing and good shelter from the meltemi that howls down over the island. It is also an ugly reinforced concrete monstrosity in the middle of nowhere. For a while, Mikonos old harbour was reserved for a few tripper boats and local ferries until it was pointed out that superyachts no longer turned up on the island because the new harbour was too far away from Mikonos old town and its location was 'drab'. So the old harbour, which is right in the middle of Mikonos town, was re-opened to superyachts and they again visit the island. Cruise boats and small yachts use the new harbour. Again, like the success of Palma Mallorca in attracting superyachts, the sense of place can be as important as shoreside facilities for the fastidious owner.

While you might hope that the sheer scale of costs involved in the superyacht world would result in a degree of philanthropy by the owners, when it comes to infrastructure, a recent report from the lifeboat station in St Tropez seems to give the lie to the notion. When the St Tropez branch of the Société Nationale de Sauvetage en Mer (SNSM), the French national lifeboat association, wrote to the owners of superyachts berthed in the harbour and nearby for funds to complete the purchase of the new lifeboat, they were roundly ignored. Around €200,000 was still needed to pay the balance on the €1.4 million cost of the lifeboat and it is now on hold. Not a sous was received from the superyacht owners and so far, only small yacht owners have contributed. It seems that largesse for these owners is confined to their own world, so you have to hope no superyachts catch fire or need the services of the lifeboat in the area.[24]

Superyacht sailing yachts

The majority of superyachts are motor yachts, with just 20% of the total being sailing yachts.[25] Despite the relatively small ratio of sailing to motor superyachts, there is something of a movement to convert from motor yachts to sailing yachts, though the figures are still small. At the 2018 Monaco Boat Show there were only eight sailing yachts out of 120 superyachts on display, though this figure

24   Henry Samuel in *The Telegraph* 31 July 2018.
25   Alberto Cappato *Cruises and Recreational Boating in the Mediterranean* p 32

does not necessarily represent the ratio of sail to power superyachts around.[26] Many of the superyachts at the show are for charter and the Monaco Boat Show has always had a leaning towards motor yachts. Other shows at Genoa and Cannes have a bigger ratio of sail to power.

Part of the move is a perception that the sailing yacht is somehow more 'green' than a motor yacht and, perhaps more importantly for the owner upping the status stakes, that a sailing yacht is an object of taste and has an aesthetic appeal that trumps a motor yacht – no matter how many helipads and swimming pools the motor yacht boasts. In conversation with a superyacht skipper who worked for an Italian owner who migrated from a motor yacht to a sailing yacht, the prime reason for the move was that he felt better, felt more at home with the sea, and also his friends approved of his transition from motor to sail.[27]

There is the perception that a sailing superyacht is somehow more tasteful than a motor yacht, no matter how many helipads it has. *Marie Cha III*.

One of the things that characterises sailing superyachts over motor yachts is that a number of rallies with some competitive racing is organised for sailing superyachts and there does seem to be more camaraderie around sailing yacht owners than with motor yachts – you just don't see motor yachts getting together to race around the cans like sailboats do. In Palma Mallorca, the Superyacht Cup has attracted large numbers of sailing yachts since its inception in 1996. The race is held over four days in early summer and features some of the most exciting superyachts around including the huge J-Class yachts. On the Costa Smeralda on the northeast coast of Sardinia, the Superyacht Regatta emulates the Palma event with the yachts racing around the azure waters of Sardinia and in the evenings reliving the races in the swanky clubs

26   Sam Fortescue *Yachting World Supersail* supplement October 2018.
27   The skipper is still working and prefers to be anonymous.

and restaurants of Porto Cervo. The Costa Smeralda also runs the Rolex Swan Cup that attracts some of the bigger Swans to Porto Cervo as well as a number of other regattas that include superyachts.[28]

If there is one category of sailing superyacht that has expanded and has a dedicated following, it is the classic class.[29] Regattas are held all over the Mediterranean and elsewhere for the sort

There is something about the grace of a yacht under sail.

of superyachts that draw the eye even if there are other bigger and more extravagant superyachts around. I well remember for the America's Cup 2003–2004 in New Zealand that Patrizio Bertelli trumped everyone who had arrived on their superyachts by living on a modest 55 ft classic yacht in the Auckland Viaduct. It was the ultimate triumph of taste over glitzy excess.

Perini Navi Cup in Porto Cervo.
Photo Chris Blunt.

Italy has been in the forefront of resurrecting classic yachts in the Mediterranean. Around the creeks and backwaters of northern Europe, numbers of classic yachts had been left to rot in muddy estuaries and forgotten harbours. Some had been sailed to the Mediterranean and left to decay in the unforgiving sun. Many of these have been lovingly and expensively restored, often by Italian owners who wanted a

sailing yacht that exuded class, and that 'something' you don't get from a

28   Yacht Club Costa Smeralda: www.yccs.it/en/
29   A veteran yacht is one built of wood or metal prior to 1950. A classic yacht is one built prior to 1976.

modern yacht. The restored yachts are not all in the superyacht class though many of them are, especially old Fifes and other wooden classics built in Britain. *Creole*, described in Chapter 11, is one such classic abandoned after the Second World War and restored by Stavros Niarchos. It is now kept in the Mediterranean and regularly seen cruising there.[30]

There are major classic yacht regattas around the western Mediterranean: in St Tropez, Palma Mallorca, Costa Smeralda and around Monte Argentario on the Tuscan coast. This last regatta, based in Santa Stefano, is a tribute to the yard there, Cantiere Navale dell'Argentario, which for decades has restored classic yachts and is renowned as one of the leading artisanal boatyards for the care and repair of vessels in need of loving care. None of this comes cheap, and the work that goes into restoring a classic yacht is often greater than that for building a new one.

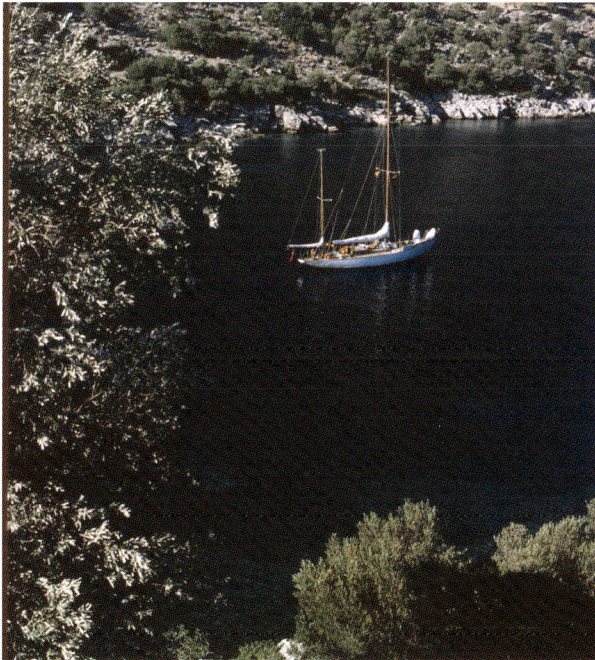

Classic yachts draw the eye like few modern yachts can. Photo Chris Blunt.

And new ones are built. The Spirit of Tradition class has flourished in recent years, with most of them built in Holland and Britain. Some of them, like marine architect Andre Hoek's Truly Classic range, are graceful representations of early classics with the twist of a modern underwater body and carbon masts and rigging. They look like an elegant old lady but go like a modern racer – or very nearly so. Others, like Spirit Yachts based in Suffolk in England, build their Spirit of Tradition yachts in wood epoxy

30   Chapter 11, The Rich and the Super Rich, Part 1: Greek Tragedy

composites so that you get that shimmering varnished appeal without as much traditional varnishing as in times past. Like Hoek's designs, these are graceful yachts with modern underbodies and rigs. While many are built in northern Europe, most migrate to a home base in the Mediterranean and most of the literature on these yachts imagines them there.[31]

Of all the classic yachts around, it is the J-Class that impresses most of the people most of the time. These 120 ft plus arrows were built to a rule devised by the American designer Nathanael Herreschoff in 1903 which effectively defined the rule for eligibility to sail the America's Cup up until the Second World War. These are the sort of yacht that even non-sailors declare to be the most beautiful thing they have seen on the water. After the war the rule changed to the 12-metre rule and J-Class yachts were left abandoned or broken up. Only three survived to be restored: *Endeavour*, *Velsheda* and *Shamrock V*, all of them designed by Charles Nicholson. Since the restoration of the surviving three, another six have been built to original J-Class designs and now race with them in regattas around the world.[32] Many of them will be found in the Mediterranean racing in the classic regattas before crossing to the Caribbean for the winter season.

Is the Mediterranean passé?

In recent years there has been a trend for superyachts to be built as expedition yachts that have long-range fuel tanks and are tough enough to take on cruising areas like the Arctic and the Chilean fjords. They are easily recognised, being more like a large tug or ice-breaker than the conventional sleeker look of a superyacht. These boats are built to standards close to that of an icebreaker, have ecological treatment tanks for black water treatment, and just about everything else you need to get away from it all for months at a time.

The impetus for all this is said to be the desire to reach the sort of remote places in the world that other superyachts do not reach – though not in a way where you would be roughing it. The fashion for explorer yachts is said to have been started by Paul Allen, one of the founders of Microsoft, with the construction in 2003 of the 414 ft (126 metres) *Octopus*. The yacht is equipped with seven tenders including a landing craft, a submarine and a

31   www.hoekdesign.com/sailing-yachts/truly-classic and https://spirityachts.com/
32   Toby Hodges *Yachting World* March 2017

remote-controlled vehicle that can go down thousands of metres, and two helicopters. *Octopus* was rarely chartered, but Paul Allen did lend her out for scientific purposes and also liked to investigate historic naval wrecks around the world. Although the boat spent some time in the Mediterranean and was sometimes used for Paul Allen's legendary parties at the Cannes Film Festival, she was mostly out and about doing what she was designed for.

Since the appearance of *Octopus*, numerous other expedition yachts have been built and there are said to be more explorer superyachts in build now than at any other time. [33]While some of them, as *Octopus* did, roam far and wide, many end up back in the Mediterranean, or at least do the summer season there, before heading to the Caribbean for the winter season. To some extent these expedition yachts are more of a fashion statement, though they do have an advantage over many of the superyachts in that they have an extended fuel range in comparison to more conventional superyachts. I have consulted on Mediterranean itineraries for several superyachts where the principal worry was getting in somewhere to take on fuel and where to head for if there were mechanical issues. There is also the matter of picking up and dropping off guests and taking on provisions and other sundries.

I have already alluded to the fact that superyachts are constrained by length and draught to those harbours and anchorages that can accommodate them. Most of the harbours and many anchorages in the Mediterranean, especially the eastern Mediterranean, are just too small for superyachts to get into. Consequently the owners and guests miss out on some of the most enchanting spots in the Mediterranean. Many of the harbours were built as fishing harbours that have subsequently been modified to take modestly sized yachts and, though they might have a few berths for smaller superyachts, often on the outside of a breakwater or mole and often in an exposed position, these are few and far between.

There does seem to be a scramble to build or acquire a superyacht that somehow stands out from the crowd. The old classics and the new Spirit of Tradition sailing yachts fit into this bracket and to an extent, the new expedition yachts do as well. If you look around the superyacht quay in Cannes or Antibes it can be difficult to determine the aesthetic sensibility of the yachts lined

---

33   Gavin Haynes, The Guardian Wednesday 1 August 2018, quoting Stewart Campbell, editor of *Boat International*.

up there, no matter how big or glitzy. But let the eye roam over the classic lines of a sailing yacht in the Spirit of Tradition class, or a true classic, even an expedition yacht, and your gaze will be held by something that is truly beautiful and shows what money cannot buy – a dash of style.

Something like this Spirit of Tradition yacht stands out from the other glitzy boats on the quay.

Levkas. In 1978 there was one small charter company and the marina had not been built. Today it is one of the busiest charter bases in the Mediterranean.

16 THE YACHT CHARTER SCENE TODAY

Flotilla You sail in company with a group of yachts, typically between ten and twelve, and a lead boat on which there is a skipper and hostess and sometimes an engineer.

Bareboat You charter a boat and sail independently in a given area.

Skippered Skippered charter encompasses everything from small bareboats where a skipper is engaged to look after the boat up to superyachts with not only the skipper but a full complement of crew.

The rise and rise of the charter scene is one of the reasons for the increased numbers of yachts in the Mediterranean when in other countries, like Britain and Scandinavia, there has been a steady decline in yacht ownership and participation in yachting activities.[1] The Mediterranean is indisputably the biggest yacht charter area in the world; only the Caribbean can come close in numbers of charter yachts. In places like the Ionian and the Saronic in Greece there are the greatest concentrations of charter yachts anywhere in the world. It is difficult to work out exact numbers of charter yachts, but if we look at the numbers of flotillas alone, each flotilla normally consisting of ten to twelve yachts, then flotillas in Greece or Croatia far outnumber flotillas in the Caribbean by around ten to one.[2] Bareboat numbers have also increased markedly with many of the flotilla companies now offering bareboat charter as well as flotilla sailing, and there are now a whole host of companies that only do bareboat or skippered charter yachts.

It's difficult to know what is cause and what is effect. Do the increased numbers of charter boats reflect an increased demand for them or did would-be charterers respond to companies getting more boats and the inevitable price-cutting that this caused? In all likelihood it was a bit of both, combined with cheaper airfares to Mediterranean destinations and more flights. Old military airports have been revamped to take civilian flights and increase the number of destinations that European airlines serve. The populations of the better-off

1   Mike Bender *A New History of Yachting* Boydell Press 2017 pp 367–379
2   Rough estimate, counting up flotillas advertised in yachting magazines for Greece and the Caribbean.

countries now feel that it is a 'right' to have a holiday in the sun, and that includes those who go sailing in the Mediterranean.

Ashore, charter base operations are a lot more polished than in the previous century. Transfers from the airport to the charter base are on coaches that are a good deal more comfortable than some of the buses used in the past. You can pre-order provisions to be delivered on board and upgrade the equipment on the boat to include toys like paddle-boards and sea kayaks. Many of the bareboat companies have a powerful chase-boat and guarantee they will be with you in four hours or so to fix mechanical and equipment problems within the charter area. Other companies employ reliable yacht service companies with a RIB or breakdown van to fix mechanical or other problems on their charter boats. This sort of service is a good deal more sophisticated than the make-and-do approach, however charming it may have been, of the past, and charter clients now expect that the boat will be ready and waiting, positively gleaming, when they arrive.

Today charter yachts are a lot bigger than 40 years ago and 40–50 ft yachts are not uncommon.

The most noticeable aspect of yacht charter has been the increase in the size of the yachts available for charter. In the 1980's 28 ft (8.5 metre) was an accepted size for a flotilla yacht. By 2000 the average size had increased to around 35 ft (10.5 metre) and today there are flotillas where you have the option of a 40 ft (12 metre) or bigger boat to go on flotilla. Bareboat and skippered charter yachts have also increased in size. In the 1980's 40 ft was a big bareboat and also used for skippered charter with the skipper sleeping in the cockpit. Today bareboats up to 50 ft (15 metre) and more are not uncommon and on average are probably around 45 ft (13.5 metre).[3]

Just as the average size of yacht for ordinary mortals has increased, so has the size of superyachts available for charter. Figures vary, but in 2016 *Forbes Magazine* reported that there were 4,476 superyachts in the world with around a quarter of those available for charter.[4] The majority of these superyachts are based in the Mediterranean with an estimated 70% of the superyacht charter fleet based there, mostly in the western Mediterranean.[5] A number of superyachts still do the Mediterranean in the summer and the winter in the Caribbean, but many are now based exclusively in the Mediterranean.

Bareboat and flotilla

While it might seem that flotilla holidays have been eclipsed by the bareboat market, this is not so. Flotillas have adapted to the needs of charterers with newer and bigger yachts that are better equipped and lead crews who are experienced at gauging the wants and needs of their charterers.

There are two principal reasons that people go back again and again on flotilla holidays. The first is the social aspect, where you sail with a group of people and you

Flotilla remains a popular option for many charterers despite the rise of bareboat charter.

3   A quick search through the internet for yachts for charter will reveal these figures from the major charter companies.
4   Doug Gollan *The Superyacht Industry is Poised for Growth* Forbes Magazine April 2016.
5   Alberto Cappato *Cruises and Recreational Boating in the Mediterranean* EU paper Plan Bleu 2011

will inevitably link up with the crew on another boat or two. Evenings ashore turn into social occasions with the day's waves getting bigger, winds increasing to way above gale force, and a few confessions of tangled kedge warps with every glass downed. A fleet of identical boats means there are lots of opportunities for a bit of impromptu one design racing and if you are beaten ... well, you weren't really racing anyway. Families with young

With a lead crew around to help when mooring up in harbours much of the stress of getting into a strange harbour is removed. Photo Sailing Holidays Ltd.

children will likely be on holiday at the same during the summer or on a mid-term break, so there are other children to mix with and flotilla companies will often organise group activities for youngsters, leaving parents a bit of time to do their own thing.

If there is one thing that has changed with flotilla holidays, it is the number of one-week flotillas now running. In the past there were villa-flotilla options with one week in a villa and one week on flotilla, but the preponderance of flotillas were two weeks. Today there are as many one-week flotillas as two-week flotillas, somehow mirroring the popularity of short break holidays on land.

Flotilla sailing has a definite social edge to it. Photo Sailing Holidays Ltd.

Although yachts sail together as a fleet, this doesn't mean you have to sail in line astern behind the lead boat. A number of companies advertise 'sailing in company' to avoid the perceived stigma of the idea of flotilla sailing, though in practice it is much the same as flotilla sailing. On flotilla you leave a harbour or anchorage in your own time, stop off for lunch in a bay somewhere if you are so inclined, and finally end up in the next bay or harbour for the evening. Depending on the area on a two-week flotilla you could get anything from three to eight days independent sailing where you can go off and explore an area before re-joining the flotilla towards the end of the cruise. Flotilla options with a lot of independent sailing days are effectively a fifty-fifty mix of flotilla and bareboat, though with the added advantage that when you are off sailing independently, you can always call up the lead crew should you have any problems.[6]

On a bareboat charter you don't have the guidance of the flotilla skipper and hostess so some extensive preliminary research is necessary. Most companies will provide a briefing at the charter base about the area you are going to sail in and recommend lunch stops, harbours and places to eat. A number of companies also offer a service where you get a skipper on board for a day so you can practice stern-to berthing and get a feel for systems on the yacht under expert guidance. After that you are on your own.

Many will go on a bareboat holiday with the family cajoled into going along as crew, cook and deck-washer. Others will convince friends that sailing your own boat in a foreign place is the perfect antidote to work, lost loves and manic depression. Since you are all going to be not just living together in a small space, but also sailing the boat, navigating in strange waters, wondering if the wind and sea are going to get worse, and socialising ashore, it is important that you all get on together. This aspect is probably most important for bareboat charter over and above flotilla and skippered charter where there are possibilities to ease tensions that may arise. On a bareboat charter you are on your own with the maximum of freedom and also the maximum responsibility for each other and the boat.

On a bareboat charter you get to do your own thing and explore places off the beaten track.

6   For more on charter see Rod Heikell *Sailing in Paradise* Adlard Coles Nautical 2009.

One of the distinguishing characteristics of bareboat charter in the 21st century has been the introduction of catamarans into the Mediterranean. Catamarans have long been used for charter in the Caribbean and places like French Polynesia and the Whitsundays in Australia for charter but are comparatively new arrivals in the Mediterranean. In the Caribbean catamarans make a lot of sense: you are more often tied up to a mooring buoy or at anchor than in a harbour or marina; at anchor you tend not to roll around as much when any swell curves around into a bay; catamarans don't heel like a monohull and tend not to roll when going downwind making life on board a lot more comfortable and, for the idle, has the advantage that you don't need to run around stowing things when you go to sea, at least in a moderate breeze;

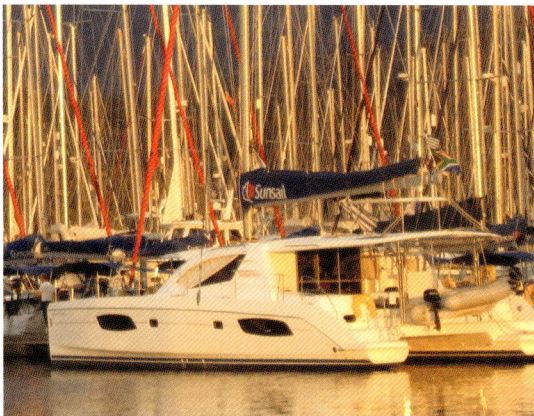

One of the distinguishing characteristics of bareboat charter in the 21st century has been the introduction of catamarans into the Mediterranean.

there is a lot of space for lying around on deck and a spacious cockpit for the al fresco life; and a modest 40 footer has a lot more accommodation than the equivalent-length monohull. It is no wonder that they are a popular option in places like the Caribbean and charter fleets there have a high proportion of catamarans in them.

In the Mediterranean they make less sense. The big disadvantage of catamarans is their beam. Not all marinas will have berths that a catamaran can fit into and those that do will charge somewhere between one-and-a-half to two times the normal berthing rate for a particular LOA (length overall) compared to the equivalent LOA for a monohull. In smaller harbours when berthed Mediterranean style it is a common sight to see a number of free berths sufficient for a monohull, but which will not accommodate the beam of a catamaran. If you do find a berth big enough a catamaran can be difficult to berth stern-to if there is a cross-wind. It has little 'grip' in the water which means it will tend to be pushed sideways more easily than a monohull, though with twin engines this can be overcome. One of the appealing aspects of a catamaran over a monohull, namely the large amount of space on board, can also be its downfall. Multihull performance is more susceptible to loading than the equivalent monohull and most cruising catamarans carry so much weight that their performance is impaired.

Despite the drawbacks of a catamaran in the Mediterranean, they have proved popular enough for charter companies to invest in them and there are now significant numbers around for charter. To an extent, catamarans in the Mediterranean are a fashion that may or may not prove enduring. It's important not to confuse the sort of catamarans from Fontaine-Pajot or Leopard Yachts used by the charter companies with sleeker and faster catamarans from the likes of Outremer. These charter catamarans feature space and the al fresco life and are not as nimble as some.

Superyacht charter

A superyacht owner may have gazillions to spend on a yacht and can probably afford the running costs as well, but for many of them putting the yacht out to charter helps defray expenses. All of these superyachts, sail and power, cost a small fortune to run and even if you are uber-rich, many owners keep a close eye on the account books. Apart from the income derived from charter, which is considerable, charter also keeps the crew and yacht in good shape rather than slowly decaying in harbour. It's an old adage that 'men and ships rot in port' and for an owner there is a need to keep crew working and on the move some of the time or they invariably get bored being in one place and start looking around for another yacht to work on.

When you see something like a 200 ft (60 metres plus) Perini Navi sailing yacht for between ten and twelve guests for charter at something like €200,000 a week, that is just the starting price. Yacht charter prices normally fall into high and low season and the difference between the two can be substantial. If you want the charter at a specific time, say for the *Monaco Grand Prix* or for the *Superyacht Cup* in Palma, the charter fee will be loaded for that event. Then again if your yacht is famous or stands out for some reason, think *Maltese Falcon* or one of the J-Class yachts, then the charter fee will be higher than a yacht of similar size that doesn't have the cachet of the unusual or of fame. To that you need to add the costs of food and beverages, fuel, docking fees and a tip, all of which comes under the Mediterranean Yacht Brokers Association

Superyacht charter is usually to the Mediterranean Yacht Brokers Association (MYBA) charter contract which is generally reckoned to add 25% to 50% to the charter cost depending on the services requested.

(MYBA) charter contract. This is generally reckoned to add 25% to 50% to the charter cost depending on the services requested and whether you charter a sailing yacht or a motor yacht.[7]

The charter itinerary depends to an extent on where the yacht is based and where the charterer wants to go. There is an irony here that escapes many superyacht charter guests in the Mediterranean and some of the owners as well. In the past when the numbers and size of superyachts was a lot smaller than in the present, there was the space to get a 100 ft yacht into the likes of a Saint Tropez, Portofino, Capri, Amalfi, Corfu, Mikonos or Bodrum. These were places the rich and eccentric visited in years gone by because they had the charm of a small fishing village and a bit of history attached. With increasing numbers of larger superyachts there is neither the space nor the number of superyacht berths to get into the harbours that charter guests might want to go to. Increasingly superyachts must anchor off outside these harbours and guests go in on the yacht's tender to visit and relax ashore. While this may suit some who want the ultimate in privacy, it is a disappointment to those guests who want to be in the thick of it berthed in the middle of historic harbours where everything is going on. There is an allure to past images and accounts of certain locations around the Mediterranean that, whether true or not, still have a siren call for most people.

This jostling for a berth in smaller harbours only makes the skipper's job that much more difficult. He needs to give charter guests paying large amounts of money for the charter the sort of experience they expect, and that is not always possible because superyachts have got so big. One important addition to the superyacht armoury is to have as many 'toys' on board as possible so

7   www.boatinternational.com/charter/luxury-yacht-charter-advice/
charter-costs-explained--1753

guests will be happy playing around on a jet-ski, sailing dinghies, water-skiing, snorkelling and scuba diving and, on larger superyachts, even a small submarine and, of course, a helicopter. This way any disappointment from not being berthed outside the pastel-hued buildings of Portofino or under the cliffs of Capri can be ameliorated somewhat and the practice of being anchored off is not too much of a drawback.

There is one case I know of where the owner of a 100 ft yacht traded down to a 50 ft yacht and sailed it himself with just one crew member.[8] That way, he said, he could get into all sorts of places that he hadn't been able to in his bigger yacht. Moreover, he felt happier in a yacht that was not as ostentatious as his 100 footer. That is hardly going to satisfy the rich owner who wants an offshore palace with all services on tap, but it does give some insight into the drawbacks of chartering and owning a superyacht with the intention of visiting all the old haunts in the Mediterranean that smaller yachts used to, and still do, visit.

Gulets

The minute you arrive in Turkish waters you will see lots of the traditional wooden sailing boats lined up on the quay or ploughing their way up and down the coast. These boats, that go under the general title of '*gulet*', are built in yards around the coast and with an elegant clipper bow and a broad round counter-stern, convey the charm of traditional yachts much removed from the bland designs that seems to make so many modern yachts look alike. The word *gulet* is a corruption of the Italian goelette, which itself comes from the French *gouelette*, referring to a type of schooner-rigged craft.[9] It is known as a *karavoskaro* in Greece and related to the Arab *baggala*. They have been used for trading in the Aegean for several centuries, though the hull and rig has evolved considerably in that time and today's *gulets* used for yacht charter are a different beast to those early trading vessels.[10]

One other traditional hull shape has been used for charter *gulets*, though less so today than in days past. The *tirhandil* is closer to the traditional boats of the

8   In conversation with the previous skipper of the 100 ft yacht who still works on superyachts so I won't identify him.
9   *Oxford English Dictionary*. Also conversations with boatbuilders in Icmeler, Bodrum.
10   See Kostas Damianis and Tasos Leontidis *Greek Wooden Sailing Boats of the 20th Century* Gavrielides 1993 pp 34–40 & 99–100.

area. This double-ended sweet hull form is found throughout the Aegean and the Turkish name is almost identical to the Greek name for it, the *trehandiri*. It is a more seaworthy boat than the *gulet* and properly rigged it is a better sailing boat. It is not as popular as the *gulet* for charter simply because it is difficult to distort the hull lines too much to get more deck space and volume down below.[11]

Typical *gulet* on the Carian coast in Turkey.

The evolution of the modern *gulet* began in Bodrum some time in the 1970's. In 1980 when I first sailed in Turkey there was little local boat-building going on except for a few boats for private owners and a few new fishing and sponge boats. With the arrival of tourists in Bodrum and elsewhere local entrepreneurs saw an opening for charter *gulets* and for tripper boats to take land-based tourists out for the day. Most were built at Icmeler, on the outskirts of Bodrum, where there were several boatyards and people with boat-building skills. The boats were built using traditional methods which were often a bit rough and ready in the early days. Some were built using plans, but the majority were built by eye using forming pieces to get the shape

11   See Damianis and Leontidis *Greek Wooden Sailing Boats* pp 13–18 & 97–98.

of the hull right. The keel is laid first and then the ribs are attached to give the skeleton of the boat. It is then planked up, the cabin built and the deck laid, before the interior is completed. The hull is then caulked and painted and varnished. Many of the metal fittings on these first *gulets* were made up locally and, in a country where yacht fittings were few and far between, ingenuity was the keyword.

Though the finished article tied up on the quay looked impressive with gleaming brightwork and polished fittings, the timber used was often of poor quality and the wood-working skills that put the boat together were not always what they should have been. Most of the boats were built of local pine that had not been properly seasoned and was full of knots. This was reflected in the life expectancy of these boats which was reckoned at best to be thirty years and for many not much more than twenty years. A properly constructed yacht built of quality hardwood has a life expectancy three times this.

In earlier designs the counter was not as large, nor did it overhang the stern as much as it now does, on modern *gulets*. The reasons for making it larger was simply to get more room on deck and to accommodate a permanent table on the aft deck for that all important 'al fresco' life. The beam of the boats increased considerably as well, again an expedient measure to fit more spacious accommodation into the traditional hull shape. The rig has changed as well. Originally a low-aspect lateen rig, later a gaff rig, was used when these boats were trading around the Aegean. Most are now rigged with high aspect Bermudan rigs. A few have gaff rigs, though today few *gulets* rely on sails for motive power when there is a big diesel below.

From these early days of utilising formers to get the hull shape and an adze to shape the wood, things have moved on. Modern materials and techniques have been adopted and yacht fittings are often imported for the *gulets*. Designs are CAD-CAM-aided and a number of well-known European yacht designers have been employed to design *gulets* with modern underwater profiles and better sail plans. Above the water the traditional look of the *gulet* is retained. Although some *gulets* are still carvel built, many of the newer *gulets* are strip-planked or cold moulded using epoxy resins. The wood used has improved, and iroko and other hardwoods are imported to build the hulls. Down below they are fitted out in quality hardwoods like mahogany and cherry. *Gulets* have also been built in steel and aluminium and fitted out below in hardwoods.

These new *gulet*s are much removed from the older-build *gulet*s and private individuals looking for something a little different in the superyacht world have been drawn to modern *gulet*s which often rival the look and finish of superyachts built in Europe in the old established yards in Italy and Britain.

From those early days in Bodrum yards have been set up around Tuzla near Istanbul, in Bozburun, Marmaris and around Antalya. The new techniques have led to bigger *gulet*s being built and 140 ft (42.5 metre) *gulet*s are not uncommon. In 2020 the largest wooden yacht in the world is set to be launched from a yard in Mugla in Turkey. The 480 ft (147 metre) *Dream Symphony* is a four-masted schooner designed jointly in Britain and Holland for a Russian owner.[12]

The look and style of these *gulet*s has not gone unnoticed in other Mediterranean countries and in Greece and in the Adriatic *gulet*s are often employed as tripper boats and for superyacht charter. The design is not only ideal for a charter boat, with lots of space above and below deck, it is aesthetically pleasing as well. In Turkey many of the charter skippers are great characters and the crew look after your every need

Gulet under sail in the Gulf of Gokkova in Turkey.

including preparing meals. For those who enjoy gin and tonic cruising it is hard to beat a charter on one of these local boats.

To encourage more sailing and less reliance on the engine, the Bodrum Cup started in 1989 to get classic wooden yachts, principally the local charter *gulet*s, to put some sail up and, well, sail. There was a proviso that boats

12 www.dailysabah.com/turkey/2016/05/12/worlds-largest-schooner-being-built-in-mugla

could motor and log their engine hours whereupon time would be deducted, but after accusations and near fisticuffs this proviso was dropped and boats had to stop motoring after the five-minute gun and sail the whole course. Paying guests are taken on most of the *gulets* and can actively participate or sit back and watch the crew race. The race

Gulets do battle in the Bodrum Cup.

is over four days around the Turkish coast in mid-October. Over the years the Bodrum Cup has attracted more and more *gulets* and true to the initial aim, better sailing performances. New *gulets* have been built with sailing performance in mind and older *gulets* have ordered proper sails, attended to standing rigging to cut down on mast losses, and educated the crews into the black art of sail performance rather than engine performance. Prizes are awarded for all categories, but the coveted trophy is the Bodrum Cup awarded to the overall winner in the traditional category.

The race is every bit as good as a tall ships' regatta for the spectacle and excitement of ninety-odd boats, most of them *gulets* upwards of 18 metres, under full sail and not always strictly in control. The parties afterwards are dangerous affairs with calculated *raki* poisoning directed at winning skippers to handicap them the next day. The competition on the water is fierce but don't expect normal racing rules to be obeyed even if they are known – a 30-metre *gulet* is a difficult beast to tack. The organisation is first class with referees on the water, a medical team following the race, and a quite spectacular prize-giving at the end complete with certificates, plaques, cups – and of course, *raki*.

The Millennial World

There are few of us who don't consult the internet when we want to book a flight, a hotel or a hire car. And there are myriad sites to do this on. Yacht charter companies of all sizes from one-man bands to Sunsail with some 6000+ charter yachts have web sites on which you can watch videos and photos, look at the type of yachts and equipment levels for charter, check different charter areas and pricing levels, and book online. The availability of online platforms to communicate on has led to new ways of going on charter and, not surprisingly, peer-to-peer groups have appeared on the market.[13]

Peer-to-peer (P2P) markets basically put people in touch with one another, for a fee, so they can charter a yacht directly from the owner. The charter can be for a day or for a week or more. The difference with P2P is that you are not dealing with a charter company or an agent, but directly with the owner who sets the fee and the rules for the charter. In a way it is not dissimilar to Uber taxis or Airbnb with the P2P site providing the platform and access to a charter yacht. There are various P2P sites to pick from and the bigger sites have lots of yachts for charter in the Mediterranean.[14] The yachts themselves can be anything from a small runabout to yachts in the 60–70 ft (18–21 metre) size and available for anything from a day-trip to charter for a week or more.

Like Uber and Airbnb, the fee you pay the platform includes things like third party insurance, safety checks and often reviews of the boats and owners. I suspect that a lot of P2P boats are small charter companies putting their boats up on this platform as another way of getting business. Like Airbnb and other hotel booking sites, picking a yacht can be a bit like picking a room or an apartment off a website and the pictures and description won't always match up with what you get – at least in my experience of Airbnb and I'm not overly fussy.

Apart from P2P sites there are also companies offering a share in a yacht where you pay 'X' amount and get a portion of time to use the yacht. Multiple owners of the yacht will usually have time slots that change so that everyone gets a fair share of the sailing season and school holidays so the kids can come too. In the early days, timeshare companies gave this sort of arrangement a bad name with substantial management fees and lack of maintenance on the yachts. Most of these companies went bankrupt, leaving part-owners with little or nothing for their money. These days the companies operate as a platform to bring owners

---

13   Toby Hodges *Borrow Any Boat* Yachting World December 2018
14   A company like GetMyBoat claims to have 63,000 boats in 171 countries www.boats.com/resources/peer-to-peer-boat-rentals-a-brave-new-world/.

together who own and operate the yachts. Yacht share syndicates have been around for a while on an informal basis and work well, with shares advertised in the yachting press and an annual get-together to sort out boat maintenance and allot sailing periods.[15]

So far so good. With the advances in increased bandwidth and the almost ubiquitous use of smart phones to access data, it is not surprising that yacht charter has moved into the digital age. Despite this, I wonder if it has had any real impact on old-fashioned ways of going about chartering a yacht. Boat shows still have a significant number of charter companies taking stands. There does seem to be something about talking face-to-face with a charter operator and, likely, some of the lads and lasses who work in the charter areas. Sitting down with someone who knows about the area you are going to or who can make a recommendation of a charter area suited to your needs has a lot going for it over looking at a drop-down menu. It may be that yacht charter will become a part of the digital world and, like Uber and Airbnb, become the dominant way we go on charter. Somehow like other aspects of the digital world, I doubt it is that straightforward and the sort of choices we make about our leisure activity often need more than an online video and a review on TripAdvisor.

15   See Rod Heikell *The Adlard Coles Book of Mediterranean Cruising* Bloomsbury 2018 Chapter 3

Port Gocek Marina in Turkey. In Gocek there were no marinas as such in the early 1980's. Today there are five marinas and other dedicated yacht berths dotted around the bay at Gocek. Photo Kadir Kir.

17 THE MEDITERRANEAN TODAY: 2000 TO 2019

The years immediately after the turn of the century were the good years for economies around the world and it seemed prosperity was assured for everyone. The European Union added new members to its number and the implementation of the Schengen agreement made travel through EU countries seamless. The introduction of the Euro solved the problem of carrying multiple currencies around and non-EU countries around the Mediterranean adopted it as a de facto currency. No-frills budget airlines like Easyjet and Ryanair slashed the cost of flying to and from countries around Europe and the numbers of tourists visiting the countries around the Mediterranean increased markedly. In 1970 58 million tourists visited the Mediterranean. By 2014 this number had increased to 314 million and by 2016 an estimated 355 million tourists were visiting the Mediterranean, around half of this number in coastal areas.[1]

These good years were reflected in the pronounced increase in the numbers of yachts in the Mediterranean and the scramble to improve the infrastructure for the increasing numbers of yachts. When I first sailed down to the Mediterranean in 1977 there were few other yachts cruising around and most of them, like mine, were small compared to today. When I hauled the yacht out in Greece in Christo's boatyard opposite Levkas town, *Roulette* was the only yacht in the yard amongst the Greek *caiques*.[2] Some 40 plus years later that same yard hauls around ninety yachts up to 50 ft, depending on draught, and there are just one or two local caiques sitting forlornly amongst all the yachts. In the nearby town of Preveza, three boatyards that barely existed before the turn of the century now haul over 3000 yachts between them.[3]

There were other political changes that influenced yachting in the Mediterranean. The collapse of the Soviet Union in 1991 and the carving up of the riches of the new Russia provided oligarchs and middle-class Russians with the freedom to pursue travel in Europe, and this inevitably swelled the

1   Kristian Petrick, Jérémie Fosse, Heloïse Lammens and Fabio Fiorucci *Blue Economy for the Mediterranean Union for the Mediterranean*, EU paper prepared under the supervision of Raffaele Mancini and Alessandra Sensi, 2017. https://ufmsecretariat.org/wp-content/uploads/2017/12/UfMS_Blue-Economy_Report.pdf
2   Heikell *The Accidental Sailor*
3   Rod and Lucinda Heikell *Greek Waters Pilot* p 75

numbers of yachts sailing around the Mediterranean.[4] Likewise the collapse of the Eastern bloc in the late 1980's would eventually swell the numbers of yachts from the former Communist countries sailing in the Mediterranean in the 2000's. The slice and dice of the former Yugoslavia in the early 1990's resulted in Croatia getting the lion's share of the Mediterranean coast and in the 2000's the country set about building a whole string of marinas around the coast.

In the Ionian there are three boatyards adjacent to each other that haul a combined 3500 yachts for the winter – easily the biggest combined yard(s) in the Mediterranean.

In Turkey the development of marinas went on apace and the numbers of middle-class Turks buying yachts increased exponentially.

Working out just what the increase in numbers of yachts actually is that we are talking about is fraught with difficulties. Yachts come in all shapes and sizes and the difficulties of counting them up depends on what you include in the figures. We are, to some extent, back to the problem of defining just what a yacht is, the problem of definition I looked at in the Introduction and to which there was no really satisfactory answer. Here I will go with a definition that includes yachts, sail or power, that cruise around the coast of the Mediterranean whether that is just ten or fifteen miles down the coast or from one end to the other. For small runabouts and dayboats there are no reliable overall figures at all. To add to the imprecision of overall figures is the problem of comparing like with like, and it is a nonsense to talk about a 10 ft (3 metre) dinghy with a small outboard that is used for a bit of coastal fishing with a 40 ft (12 metre) motor or sailing yacht cruising from place to place.

Given this obvious problem, one I have already referenced in trying to define just what a yacht is, I will exclude small open boats that go out for a day's fishing or a spin around the bay. With the exception of the small boat

---

4   On the rise in numbers of superyachts see Chapter 14, The Rich and the Super Rich Part II: Superyachts Galore.

exploits I've written about, that means a yacht, whether motor or sail, needs a few rudimentary comforts to qualify for inclusion – basically a cabin and somewhere to sleep.[5] I will mention a few figures on yacht numbers in this chapter to try and put some perspective on things, but these figures need to be used with the proverbial grain of salt and in some cases are patently not correct. One of the major problems with the statistics gathered for yachts in a particular country is that often everything from small runabouts used for the occasional daytrip are lumped in with bigger yachts that cruise more extensively. It is the latter I'm interested in.

Looking at yachting infrastructure is more revealing than trying to count yachts, as these developments have been more closely documented and, in the cumulative editions of yachting pilots for the Mediterranean, the numbers of yacht berths of all sizes can be reliably charted.[6] Likewise the development of yachting services gives some idea of the changes and of the numbers of yachts based in an area. To an extent the Mediterranean can be divided into the western half, including Spain, France and Italy, and the eastern half, comprising Croatia, Greece and Turkey. It is estimated that the western half accounts for 80% of yachting in the Mediterranean and the eastern half for 14%, though these figures should be regarded with some scepticism.[7] The balance is made up of the North African countries, Malta and Cyprus.

One of the immediate conclusions we can make is that countries like Turkey, Croatia and Montenegro developed marinas and services at an accelerated rate compared to the western Mediterranean where there was already a good deal of yachting infrastructure in place and most development has been in expanding existing marinas and harbours and building a few new marinas. Greece is a special case where there has been some development of marinas and refit and repair facilities in scattered areas, but not the concentrated development of Croatia and Turkey.

The global financial crash of 2008, the worst downturn since the Great Depression of the 1930's, brought austerity measures to Europe and elsewhere.

5   See Chapter 15, Small Boat Exploits in the Mediterranean
6   In the biennial *Imray Mediterranean Almanac*, editor Lucinda Heikell, the development of marinas and yacht harbours can be tracked from the 1st edition in 1995 up to the present.
7   Jamie M. Chen, Chrysanthi Balomenou, Peter Nijkamp, Panoraia Poulaki and Dimitrios Lagos *The Sustainability of Yachting Tourism: A Case Study on Greece* International Journal of Research in Tourism and Hospitality (IJRTH) Vol. 2, Issue 2, 2016, p 44

The middle class, which up until the crash had been doing well, suddenly found their income flat-lining and declining in real terms. The downturn and the austerity measures that followed affected the countries in the EU and those outside it in different ways, and so had variable effects on the development of yachting. In Britain there was a dramatic decline in the numbers taking part in yachting, in yacht building and yachting infrastructure.

Something was happening or about to happen, and the signs in all areas of yachting activity were there for some years before 2008, just as the late Victorian boom in yachting finished some fifteen years before the outbreak of the First World War. British yacht building, yachting publishing, and yacht club memberships were all in sharp decline. Long before the 2008 crash, British yachting, along with much of British industry, was being eviscerated, a hollowed shell, a shop front for imported goods.

Mike Bender *A New History of Yachting* Boydell Press 2017 p 364

Countries around the Mediterranean also experienced a decline in the income and leisure spending of the middle class. Greece had to be bailed out by loans from the European Central Bank to keep it afloat and experienced, and still does in 2019, a dramatic decline in income and high unemployment rates. Spain and Italy looked shaky for a while, and only now in 2018–2019 are coming out of the recession. France is still in the throes of austerity measures and all of these countries have seen a surge in right-wing populist politics that threatens the fabric of the EU itself. Emerging countries like Croatia and Turkey initially fared well, though the omens for Turkey in the near future are not so good.

The one group who have not been affected by the global crash are the super-rich. While the crash has meant austerity and a decline in real incomes for most people, the super-rich have profited off the back of the recession and their incomes have increased exponentially. In 2017 almost 30,000 people joined the ranks of Ultra High Net Worth (UHNW) individuals, those worth more than $30 million US, off the back of profits on the stock market and property assets.[8] This has led to a rapid rise in the number of superyachts on the water and in build, more than 50% of them based in the Mediterranean. I've already dealt with the superyacht phenomenon in a previous chapter and I only mention it here to contrast it with the gloomier picture, at least

8   Rupert Neate The Guardian 5 September 2018

asset-wise, of the majority, the middle class, to provide some elucidation for the rapid rise of the numbers of superyachts in the Mediterranean.[9]

The increase in numbers of yachts cruising the Mediterranean today for those who do not have elastic wallets in our lean economic times is intertwined with a number of factors and changes in how people take up yachting. It has to do with the changing demographics of populations, especially the expansion of the middle class in countries like Croatia and Turkey. There may also be something less tangible but still evident, a return to the idea of the romance of sailing in such austere times that can be compared to the passion and determination of those who, after the Second World War, wanted to escape the drab life of post-war Europe and head for the azure seas and blue skies of the Mediterranean. There are no figures for this sort of sentiment.

Greece and Turkey

In 2013, in Rocella Ionica on the boot of Italy, I met a Turkish skipper delivering a brand new 45 ft Beneteau yacht to Turkey. After we had been talking for a bit, he told me he and others were doing these deliveries all the time, and that Turkey was the second biggest market for Beneteau yachts after the USA. I have no figures to back this up, but there are an awful lot of new Turkish-owned Beneteau, Jeanneau, Hanse and Bavaria yachts in Turkey. While yacht ownership declined in parts of Europe, in Turkey a newly wealthy and emboldened middle class were buying yachts and putting them in the new marinas around the Aegean coast. In 1980 there were three marinas around the Turkish coast. By 2000 the number of marinas had grown to eighteen and by 2018 there were thirty-seven marinas around the coast, another two in Turkish-controlled Northern Cyprus, and plans to build more around Istanbul and the Aegean and Mediterranean coasts.[10]

In 1980 in Greece there were just three marinas around Athens and a few others in the rest of Greece. By 2000, there were fifteen marinas operating around the Greek coast and islands, and in 2019 the figure was still only twenty-five, though we are not comparing like for like when comparing these marinas to

9   See Chapter 14, The Rich and the Super Rich Part II: Superyachts Galore.
10   See Rod Heikell *Turkish Waters Pilot* Imray 6th edition 2001 and Rod & Lucinda Heikell *Turkish Waters and Cyprus Pilot* 10th edition 2018.

the Turkish marinas.[11] Many
of the Greek marinas are
relatively small and generally
do not have the standard
of facilities found in their
Turkish counterparts. It may
seem fatuous to compare
toilets and shower blocks
in marinas, but it's a useful
measure to compare the
differences between the two
countries that illustrates the
five-star standard of Turkish
marinas compared to the
often two- or three-star
Greek marinas. In Turkey

In Turkey there has been a steep rise in yacht
ownership in the 2000's and a consequent increase
in marinas to keep them in. Yacht Marine in
Marmaris. Photo Kadir Kir.

most of the marinas have marble-lined edifices housing toilets and showers
that would not be out of place in a swanky hotel. In Greece the facilities are
often inadequate prefabricated blocks that seem to have been erected as an
afterthought. In the Turkish marinas you will often be met by a RIB with
marineros to help you in. In Greece that is rarely the case.[12]

There has been an effort by various governments in Greece to increase the
numbers of marinas, and around the coast and islands you will often see the
skeletal structure of a breakwater and piers where the government, with EU
funding, has built the basic structure with the hope that a private company
will take the lease on and develop the infrastructure. Sadly, many of these
projects seem to have been designed by bureaucrats with no knowledge of
how a marina works and how big a modern yacht is, so it is not surprising
that many of these proto-projects to develop marinas in Greece have been
abandoned, though they do make useful harbours for local fishing boats.

11   See Rod Heikell *Greek Waters Pilot* Imray 1st edition 1982, *Greek Waters Pilot* Imray 8th edition
2001 and Rod & Lucinda Heikell *Greek Waters Pilot* 13th edition 2018.
12   In the EU report, *Blue Economy in the Mediterranean*, the figure given for Greek marinas is 135.
This is patently wrong and is likely a reported figure from a Greek government office that counted
up any harbour that had yacht berths. Many of the figures for other countries are also patently
wrong, though bizarrely the figure for Turkey is pretty much correct at thirty-seven.

In Greece many of the old harbours have had new pontoons with laid moorings installed to increase the number of berths available to yachts and shore facilities like water and electricity boxes have been installed. In many ways the Greek model, more by accident than design, has a more compelling allure to many of us who sail the Mediterranean than the Turkish model. Swanky marinas surrounded by concrete infrastructure and boutique shopping are not what many sailors are looking for in the eastern Mediterranean. Once you have seen one or two, the marinas look much the same.

In Greece progress has been slower though some projects have finally matured. Gouvia in the early 1980's and now. Pictures taken from approximately the same place.
Photos Sailing Holidays Ltd.

Small harbours where the village ashore has grown organically seem more convivial, more 'real' in many ways, with a sense of place that cannot be created by pouring concrete and adding trendy fashion boutiques. While the Greek coast has not escaped the concrete blight altogether, there are rules and regulations that mostly curb unbridled development. Moreover, tiny Greece, once you unravel the gulfs and bays of the mainland and the coast of the myriad islands, has the longest coastline in the Mediterranean at some 7385 miles (13,676 km) compared to Turkey, with a coastline of 3888 miles (7200km).[13]

One of the manifest differences between the coasts of Turkey and Greece has been the development of houses and apartments along the shores of the Mediterranean and the urban sprawl of coastal cities. In 1983 when I first cruised the Sea of Marmara that connects the Mediterranean to the Black Sea, it was dotted with small villages along its coast until you got to the magnificent sight of Istanbul straddling the Bosphorus. On a recent cruise there in 2015

13   Rod Heikell *Mediterranean Cruising Handbook* Imray 2012 p 219 and p 226

I sailed along a coast that is now mostly built up from the Dardanelles to Istanbul, an urban sprawl of concrete suburbs extending for nearly sixty miles on the northern side and around the Gulf of Izmit and as far as Çinarcik on the southern side, a vast concrete coast that has grown over the last thirty years to accommodate the suburban populations who commute to Istanbul on highspeed ferries. The rash even continues down the Aegean coast where vast holiday villages have been built to accommodate the middle-class Turks who want a home near the sea and also to house tourists, both local and foreign.

While Athens sprawls around the Attic coast and has its own concrete satellite suburbs, there is nothing like the swathes of concrete construction around the Greek coast and islands analogous to that in Turkey. This again is where Greece has, at least so far, hit the sweet spot of serving tourist populations while keeping a hold on the natural beauty of the place. Yachts cruising in Greece can wend their way in and out of coves and bays and small harbours and still enjoy a relatively unspoilt seascape. In Turkey there has been unrestricted development of huge holiday villages along long sections of coast and, while there are still unspoiled areas in the deep gulfs cutting into the coast and around some of the wilder Carian and Lycian coasts, the omens are not all good for it remaining so pristine.

In 2011–2012 civil war erupted in Syria and this upheaval next to Turkey's southern border was to have a significant effect on tourism, including yacht tourism, in Turkey and the adjacent Greek islands in the Aegean. Prior to this, yacht tourism had been extending down to Syria and the Levant. From 1990 the East Mediterranean Yacht Rally, the EMYR, had cruised in company along the Turkish coast and in 1995 Syria, Lebanon and Egypt were added to the itinerary. At Latakia on the Syrian coast a makeshift yacht marina was established and EMYR participants enjoyed tours of sites in Syria and the sights and sounds of a new yachting destination for the adventurous. From just seventeen yachts in the first rally it expanded to over a hundred in later years until the civil war curtailed the EMYR route. Today it really only takes in the Turkish coast and Northern Cyprus.[14]

14   www.emyr.org

The large numbers of refugees fleeing the war in Syria and making their way to Turkey and across to Greece was to severely impact on yachting in Turkey and the adjacent Greek islands. In addition, the uncertain political situation in Turkey with the rise of the Justice and Development Party, the AKP, with an Islamic bent to its policies, further added to the rumour mill of troubles in the country, causing significant numbers of private yachts to leave Turkey as well as damaging the nascent yacht charter market. For anyone cruising this coast there was little difference to previous years, but the rumour mill powered by social media and internet forums can have a dramatic effect on the perception of what a country is like and can severely impact tourist numbers. Despite the fact that most of the places that yachts cruise around on the Turkish coast are 300–400 miles away from Syria, nonetheless the geography of the two countries being side by side signals danger to some people, and so the numbers of yachts have declined, with some yacht service companies quoting a 30–40% decrease in business.[15]

The downturn in yacht tourism was not confined to Turkey, as the media reported on the horror stories of migrants struggling to reach the adjacent Greek islands off the Turkish coast. I cruised up the Turkish coast from Bodrum to the Dardanelles in 2015 and back down through the Greek islands off the Turkish coast from Limnos to Kos. In 2015 it was estimated nearly a million refugees had entered Greece by boat from Turkey. Some 460 had drowned attempting to cross the short stretch of sea separating the islands from the Turkish coast, a truly horrendous and heart-breaking episode of human misery resulting from the war in Syria.[16] And yet sailing up the coast there was little to see, not a migrant boat in sight, which is hardly surprising when the boats leave at night and need to get to Greece undetected. The only tangible evidence along the shoreline of the Greek islands was piles of red lifejackets that had been discarded when the migrants arrived and the odd hull of a refugee boat that had been driven up on the shore.

None of this diminishes the tragedy of the migrant crisis in this part of the Mediterranean. It is more a pointer to how the perception of problems and the media coverage of real problems can lead to unintended consequences and spin-off into other spheres, in this case tourism and yacht tourism in

15   Conversations with various individuals in Turkey that run yacht service companies.
16   www.bbc.co.uk/news/world-europe-35854413

particular, where the perception becomes that it is dangerous to go there when really it is no more dangerous than in the past, and life for most goes on much as it always has. This impression of danger is reinforced by events in other Islamic countries, like the 2015 massacre at the hotel in Port El Kantaoui in Tunisia in which thirty-seven people were gunned down, most of them British, and the 2015 bombing of the Russian plane leaving Sharm El Sheikh in Egypt, in which everyone on board was killed. By association, Turkey, an Islamic country though constitutionally secular, is grouped with the terrorism in these other Islamic countries and it doesn't take long for tourists to start asking if it is a safe place to go.[17] Nor was it helped when a bomb killed ten Germans in Istanbul in 2016 and, after the failed 2016 coup in Turkey, the president, Recep Tayyip Erdoğan, imposed draconian measures on those he considered dissidents.[18] Though the country is by and large safe, questions are asked and the decline in tourist numbers can be catastrophic for the locals.

In the case of Turkey many private boats left the country and charter yachts, faced with diminished bookings in Turkey, migrated to the Greek Aegean and Ionian. The consequences in Greece were large numbers of yachts, private and charter, corralled into relatively small cruising areas. In the Ionian in the winter of 2018–2019 it was difficult to find places to haul out. With an estimated 5500 hard-standing places available and at least another 2500 berths in marinas and smaller harbours

In Turkey the yachting infrastructure and services ashore today are as good as anywhere in the Mediterranean.

around the coast, we end up with a total of 8000 yacht places in the Ionian, though the total is likely much higher than this.[19] In the Saronic around Athens and down through the home islands to the Argolic Gulf, the situation

17   Dave Richardson *Let's Go: A History of Package Holidays and Escorted Tours* Amberley 2016 pp 199–201
18   BBC fact sheet: www.bbc.co.uk/news/world-europe-36816045
19   See Rod & Lucinda Heikell *Greek Waters Pilot* Imray 13th edition 2018, Chapter 1.

is much the same with ever increasing numbers of yachts competing for space to berth and haul.

This skewing of yacht numbers between western Greece and the Turkish Mediterranean coast in response to perceived problems in Turkey will likely right itself in future years, though if there is one thing that you can never be sure of when it comes to transient populations of tourists like yacht owners and yacht charterers, it is that rumour and uncertainty can have an effect out of all proportion to the reality on the ground and there are no guarantees that things will revert to how they were. After all there are other parts of the Mediterranean you can sail in where you may feel safer than in a country like Turkey, however untrue that is in reality. The rumour mill is a powerful influence on behaviour even when the rumours are just that – rumours.

Western Mediterranean

Compared to the eastern Mediterranean, the development of marinas and yachting infrastructure has been comparatively laggardly in Spain, France and Italy. In places, new marinas have been built and there has been work enlarging older marinas and adding berths, especially for superyachts, and an attempt to build a number of marinas around the boot of Italy and Sicily to boost these poorer regions with some yacht tourism. In large part this is because large numbers of marinas had already been built prior to 2000 and there was the perception by local authorities that there were sufficient numbers of berths for yachts around the shores of the western Mediterranean. That yacht owners in these countries disagreed was neither here nor there when it came to obtaining the permissions for the construction of new marinas.

In France the Languedoc-Roussillon marinas have been enlarged to accommodate more yachts, construction work which usually involves dredging out another basin in the waters of the *etang* and so is easily achieved. Still there are insufficient berths and friends of mine who sail the eastern Mediterranean in the summer make the voyage back to their home port in France so that they do not lose their permanent berth there. Along the Cote d'Azur and Riviera there has been little development since the turn of the century and owners of yachts large and small compete for spaces in the summer. France has one of the shortest mainland coastlines of any of the major countries in the Mediterranean, discounting Corsica, at around 350 to 400 miles depending on how many bumps and bays you measure. Along this coast there are more marinas per mile than anywhere else in the Mediterranean and the longest distance between marinas is just over 30 miles. There are probably some 7000 to 8000 marina berths along this short coastline.[20] This concentration of marinas was largely already here in the last century and it's difficult to see how or where more marinas would go without totally cluttering the shoreline.

Tropea. Initially Italy was slow to build marinas in the south of the country compared to the north, but eventually marinas were built in Calabria and Sicily.

Along the coast of the nearby Italian Riviera and around to Tuscany the situation is much the same as along the French Mediterranean coast and, although the Ligurian coast is one of the most developed in terms of yachting infrastructure in Italy, still space has been found to build a number of new marinas and ease the berthing situation along the coast. Further south in Italy there has been an effort to develop yachting tourism and build new marinas, with varying amounts of success. In Calabria and Sicily organised crime has been involved with the planning and building of some marinas in impractical locations so that the harbours have soon silted and in some cases are totally unusable by craft of any sort. Organised crime in southern Italy and Sicily 'likes' concrete as a way of laundering money into an apparently legitimate business and some of the projects have been generously supplied with concrete ramps and edifices and approach roads that are not strictly

Almerimar in Andalucia on the Spanish coast was granted its concession in the 1980's but only really got going in the 2000's

20   Rod & Lucinda Heikell *Mediterranean France and Corsica* Imray 2017 p 1

necessary, a scam that is visibly obvious in all the unnecessary concrete motorway flyovers in Calabria and Sicily.

The coasts of Spain, particularly the Balearics, and the coasts of France and Italy are undeniably crowded in the summer months when the locals go on holiday en masse in July and August. The waters resound to the flapping of sails and the roar of motorboat engines and the desperate attempts to find a berth for the night. The crowded coasts have led to something of a change in yachting patterns, and significant numbers of yachts from the western Mediterranean, particularly from France and Italy, now trek over to the eastern Mediterranean, principally to Croatia and Greece, for the summer season and return in late August and early September to their home ports. The change in sailing patterns is partially to do with the crowded coasts of their home countries and a desire to explore new sea areas. The advances in yacht design, safety equipment and sophisticated weather forecasts, not to mention reliable diesel engines that ensure a steady passage speed, make voyages to and from the western Mediterranean a lot easier than in earlier days. In Greece, in the Ionian and Aegean, the migration patterns are so well known by the locals that they can just about set their clocks by them. By the end of September the summer migration is over.

The Adriatic

After the war between the states of the old Yugoslavia, Croatia ended up with the lion's share of the Dalmatian coast. The former Yugoslavia had started building marinas around the coast in the early 1980's under a state-owned company, Adriatic Club Yugoslavia (ACY). After hostilities were settled between the states of the former Yugoslavia, Croatia began expanding the chain in the 1990's. In 1994 the company was renamed Adriatic Club International (ACI). By 2016 the company had twenty-two

Opatija-ACI marina in Croatia.
Photo ACI Marinas.

marinas in operation.[21] In addition to the ACI chain of marinas there are numerous other private marinas that have been built around the coast, and in 2012 Croatia had a total of fifty-eight marinas with more under construction.[22]

More than any other country in the Mediterranean, Croatia has forced the development of nautical tourism around its coasts, building marinas and the infrastructure for services and repairs ashore at a pace not matched by any other country in the Mediterranean. Unlike most of the other countries, the marina berths are not for local private owners, but for the owners of yachts in nearby countries and also for charter boat fleets. The coastline and islands of Croatia are a deal more attractive to sail around than the straight coast of eastern Italy, so most yachts cruising the Adriatic will sail up through the Croatian islands and many of the Italian yachts on the opposite side cross to the Dalmatian coast for the summer. In addition, significant numbers of German and Austrian yachts are kept here as the owners can easily drive down to the coast, and in many ways treat the Adriatic as their own home waters.

South of Croatia, a short section of the Dalmatian coast is part of Montenegro and, with an eye on their neighbour, the country has also been busy developing marinas and yacht infrastructure around the coast. Montenegro is not part of the EU so non-EU flagged boats and nationals can berth their yachts here – an attractive proposition for some superyachts that would otherwise have to pay substantial taxes under EU VAT law and a refuge for non-EU nationals who otherwise are restricted by visa requirements. Duty-free fuel is another attraction for large motor yachts that can use hundreds of litres of diesel an hour when cruising. Adjacent to Montenegro is Albania which has also started to build marinas to attract nautical tourism to its shores, no doubt trying to emulate the Montenegro model.

How the EU made yachting easy in the Mediterranean

A long time ago, or so it seems, before the EEC became the EU, before the Schengen agreement made travel between EU countries seamless, before the euro was introduced, before there was a Customs Union, yachts sailing in the Mediterranean needed to clear out of one country and clear into the

21   www.aci-marinas.com/en/povijest/
22   In a paper by M. Kovačić et al *The scenario method of nautical tourism development – a case study of Croatia* Scientific Journal of Maritime Research 29, 2015.

next. I remember writing the early versions of some of my books detailing the paperwork for the countries around the Mediterranean and describing the sometimes laborious process of signing in and out of the countries.[23]

The whole process took time and a little effort: in Spain you had to go to a port with customs officials who would check the boat and note down particulars of the boat and crew, all of which needed to be repeated at the next port; in France you needed to go to the first major port and clear in with your yacht papers and passports; in Italy you needed to first go to a port of entry and obtain a *Constituto in arrivo per il naviglio da diporto*, usually just shortened to *Constituto*, which detailed particulars of the yacht and crew and which needed to be presented at all ports and handed in at the last port in Italy; in Malta you needed to go to customs and the port captain in Grand Harbour; in Yugoslavia you went first to a port of entry where a sailing permit would be issued and a little triangular sticker was provided to go on the boat that showed the permit fees for that year had been paid; and in Greece you went first to a port of entry where a Transit Log was issued after visits to the port police, immigration and customs, and which had to be presented at subsequent ports that were visited. The implementation of the Schengen agreement and ratification of the Customs Union effectively eliminated all this paperwork in the early 2000's and, although Croatia and Greece still require some paperwork to be completed, it is much less onerous than in days past. Yachts could now sail freely between one EU country and another without let or hindrance and this encouraged yacht owners, especially those from EU countries, to cruise more extensively around the Mediterranean EU countries.

Yachts can still be inspected in random customs checks, but in practice this happens infrequently, and you can often sail from one end of the Mediterranean to the other without encountering any officialdom at all. In non-EU countries like Turkey and the countries of the Maghreb, it is still necessary to clear in at a port of entry and obtain the requisite paperwork, though in places like Turkey even this process is relatively simple. For non-EU yachts the requirement in EU countries is much the same wherever you are, and non-EU nationals will get a ninety-day visa after which they must be out of the EU for ninety days before they get another ninety days. The yacht itself can remain within the EU for eighteen months before it must be imported

23   Rod Heikell *Mediterranean Cruising Handbook* 1st ed. Imray 1985

and pay the requisite taxes, though it only needs to leave the EU for a day to visit a non-EU country before it is eligible for another eighteen months' stay in the EU.

The introduction of the euro also simplified matters so that it was not necessary to carry multiple currencies within EU countries and exchange one currency for another when you travelled from one country to another. In adjacent countries that are not part of the euro group, like Turkey, Croatia and Montenegro, the euro became a de facto currency and marina fees and yacht services in non-EU countries are usually priced in euros. The Customs Union also meant that yacht equipment and spares could be seamlessly imported, and it is now possible to buy most yachting equipment off the shelf or get it quickly delivered in the EU countries around the Mediterranean.

This harmonisation of the regulations and the growth of budget airlines encouraged significant changes to notions of yacht ownership and use in the Mediterranean. In the previous century many of the owners of yachts in the countries of northern Europe, especially Britain, the Scandinavian countries, Holland and Germany, looked at sailing around the Mediterranean as a period when you took a year or two off work or had retired and set off in your own yacht to sail around the Mediterranean. While the idea of basing your yacht in the Mediterranean was not new, it was not commonplace.

Today there are a lot of yacht owners who keep their yacht in the Mediterranean as if it was their 'home waters' and fly or drive out to prep the boat, cruise around, and then winterise it – as if whatever patch of the Mediterranean they are in is their own backyard. Some will fly out for several weeks or a month before returning home – a bit like driving down to the boat in your own country. A lot of owners will come out in the spring for several months, return home in the hotter months of summer citing the heat and

Today there are a lot of yacht owners who keep their yacht in the Mediterranean as if it was their 'home waters'.

crowds as the reason, and then return in the autumn for several months and to pack the boat away for the winter.

The relaxed restrictions also encouraged new ways of owning a yacht in the Mediterranean. Syndicates have been set up to buy a yacht and allocate the sailing period into chunks for all the part-owners. In this way the expense of buying and running a yacht is divided, usually by four or six co-owners, into digestible fiscal chunks and individuals who may not have the money or time to buy and run a yacht outright get to go sailing in the Mediterranean. Often one of these syndicates will use a yacht service agency for *gardiennage* so the boat is not out of action for the members and any repairs can be quickly attended to in the sailing season.[24]

The proliferation of charter companies, particularly in Croatia, Greece and Turkey, led to other new ways into yacht ownership. Many charter companies offer a leaseback system whereby an individual puts a down payment on a yacht and the charter company leases it, usually for three to five years, feeding a percentage of the charter fees back to the owner who can use the money to pay off the balance of the yacht. The charter company maintains the yacht and the owner also gets the use of it for a number of weeks in the year.[25]

These changes in regulations and ownership patterns go some way towards explaining the decline in the numbers owning and participating in yachting in countries like Britain. In Mike Bender's *A New History of Yachting* he analyses the decline in the numbers taking part in yachting and the falling membership of yacht clubs in Britain.

The facts and figures available from yachting offer no comfort to an optimistic view... Arkenford, a social research company, provide a yearly market report on yachting. Between 2002 and 2012, the numbers taking part in yacht cruising went down from 433 to 333k; in yacht racing from 153 to 106k; in small boats from 606 to 388k; and small boat racing from 333 to 165k. In 2002, 154,000 people, according to an ABC audit, attended the London Boat Show. In 2016, the unaudited attendance was 90,328.[26]

Bender *A New History of Yachting* p 369

A number of factors are involved in this decline. Changing work patterns have meant that the middle class have less leisure time on their hands and

24   Rod Heikell *The Adlard Coles Book of Mediterranean Cruising* Bloomsbury, 2012 pp 34–36
25   Heikell *The Adlard Coles Book of Mediterranean Cruising* pp 38–39
26   The London Boat Show was abandoned for 2019.

work, courtesy of tablets and smartphones, pervades even our diminished leisure time. The income for everyone, except the very rich, has flat-lined since the slump of 2008 and so, in real terms, has decreased leaving fewer funds to spend in our leisure time. Yachts that were once affordable are no longer within the reach of average incomes and travelling on a yacht to the Mediterranean has become more expensive for the day-to-day expenses there. Social patterns have also changed so that retired parents who might have gone off sailing are now part of an extended family network looking after grandchildren and often funding their children.[27]

There are anomalies to these figures for the decline in yachting in Britain. The Cruising Association, which caters for cruising yachtsmen, has nearly 6000 members scattered around the world, with the majority in Britain. While the numbers belonging to yacht clubs in Britain have been steadily declining, the numbers joining the Cruising Association have been steadily increasing.[28] The association has various geographical sections and one of the largest is the Med section, predominantly composed of British members cruising in the Mediterranean. Other organisations like the Royal Cruising Club and the Ocean Cruising Club also have active Mediterranean sections.

Charter yachts lined up on the quay in Levkas have played a role in reducing outright yacht ownership in the UK and elsewhere in northern Europe.

The figures for the decline in British yachting are also, to an extent, masked by the changes in patterns of yacht ownership, with syndicates and leaseback schemes from charter companies likely not included in these figures. Add to this the increased numbers who choose to charter a yacht, often in the Mediterranean, instead of owning one, and the actual numbers of individuals going sailing is almost certainly higher than the base figures recorded

27   For a more detailed discussion see Bender *A New History of Yachting* pp 365–379.
28   www.theca.org.uk/

for Britain. Many of the flotilla and bareboat charter companies are British in origin and the majority of clients are British as well.

If there is an elephant in the room looming over all this, it is the Brexit question. While no one seems to know what exactly Brexit will mean for travel and residency in the EU as this is written in late 2018/early 2019, and perhaps well into the future if no agreement can be reached or a political fudge worked out, the current rules are those already in place for non-EU nationals and non-EU flagged boats. That means a non-EU national will get ninety days in every 180 days in the EU and non-EU flagged boats will get eighteen months in the EU before the requisite taxes like VAT are applied. If this applies to British nationals and British flagged yachts, then the situation will change radically for British nationals sailing around the EU countries in the Mediterranean. It is likely that some yachts will return to non-EU countries like Turkey and some may choose to go to Montenegro, Tunisia and Morocco.[29]

The rise of yacht clubs and youth training

While yacht clubs in northern Europe have always been a part of life and it was not unusual to see the younger generation out on the water in a variety of dinghies learning to sail and to race, in many countries around the Mediterranean it was unusual. Yacht clubs in countries like Spain and the countries in the eastern Mediterranean were as much a social club for the prestige of it as an institution involved with yachting. Many of the members didn't own a yacht or actively participate in the sport and membership was a mark of status and a convenient club for drinks and dinner.

While countries like France and parts of Italy have long had clubs and sailing schools, often partially funded by local government and the state, in many of the other countries these activities were restricted to a few enclaves of the wealthy or aspiring middle classes and it was rare to see dinghies out training in any organised or structured way. With the new millennium that has changed and there are now numerous clubs and sailing schools in places like Greece and Turkey where fleets of Optimists and Lasers are out on the water with a safety boat giving instruction on the basics of sailing. Ashore there are schools teaching the requirements of sailing larger yachts, of handling bigger

29   See Lucinda & Rod Heikell *Imray Mediterranean Almanac 2019–2020* Imray, sections 5.1, 5.2, 5.3 & 5.4 for EU regulations and a country by country round-up of national regulations.

gear than that on an Optimist dinghy, of navigation and the 'rules of the road', of safety requirements and the logistics and care of organising crew.

Most of these clubs have evolved in the last couple of decades and reflect the increased interest in sailing in these countries and also the increased yacht ownership. The sailing clubs have organised yacht racing regattas all around the coast and it is now not unusual to see some modern racing machines optimised to IRC (International Rating Certificate) and ORC (Offshore Rating Congress) rules racing in well refereed races around the coast and islands in the Adriatic and eastern Mediterranean. Some of these races, like Marmaris Race Week in Turkey, the Mrduja Regatta in Croatia and the Aegean Rally in Greece, have become firm fixtures in the Mediterranean racing calendar and reflect a rapid increase in competitive yachting as opposed to solely cruising around these areas.

The Autumn Race series in Gocek in Turkey.

In the western Mediterranean there have long been numbers of races with, amongst others, events such as the Middle Sea Race from Malta, Les Voiles de St Tropez, the Trofeo in Palma Mallorca, and the Rolex series from Porto Cervo that have proved increasingly popular. The numbers have swelled substantially in the new millennium, with significant numbers of international entrants taking part. While these are the well-known races in the Mediterranean, there are large numbers of more local regattas, including what is thought to be the largest sailing regatta in the world, the Barcolano, from Trieste in Italy, with around 2000 yachts taking part.[30]

As well as these more informal regattas, there are now an increasing number of fully professional races held around the Mediterranean. The TP52 series regularly races in Palma, Italy and Croatia. World series dinghy races have been held in all the countries around the northern Mediterranean and more are scheduled for future years.[31] For the forthcoming America's Cup

The Challenger of Record for the America's Cup, *Luna Rossa*, is based in Cagliari in Sardinia. Photo Portus Karalis.

in New Zealand the Challenger of Record, the Prada team with *Luna Rossa*, is based in Cagliari on the bottom of Sardinia. In any terms, the western Mediterranean is busier with a professional yacht racing circuit than it was in the late 19th and early 20th centuries when the big boat regattas were held around France and Italy and the rich and titled would travel down to take part in the summer racing series.

30 The course is a fifteen mile around-the-cans race and regularly attracts a huge shoreside audience as well as an awful lot of yachts.
31 www.sailing.org/regattas.php

The Mediterranean and the Environment

The enclosed nature of the Mediterranean with large populations around its shores presents particular and challenging environmental problems for the sea. In 2010, 466 million people lived in the countries around the Mediterranean, a figure expected to increase to 529 million by 2025. More than a third of this population live along a relatively narrow coastal strip around the shores.[32] The demands of this population on the sea and the effect of industrial and agricultural pollution is further exacerbated by the numbers of tourists that flock to the Mediterranean. In 1970 58 million tourists from other countries holidayed in the Mediterranean. By 2014 this number was 314 million and by 2016, 355 million.[33]

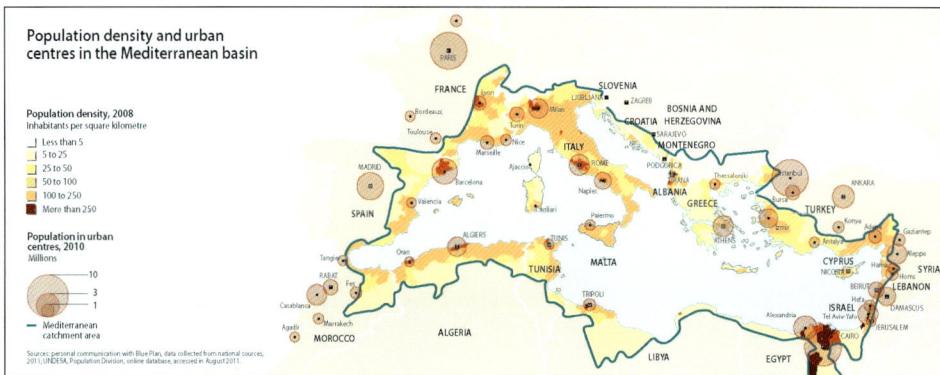

Population density in the Mediterranean. Source EU Blue Plan/UNDESA paper 2011.

In the past the Mediterranean has always had pollution problems resulting from the large population around its shores. Sewerage treatment has been rudimentary at best in the past and, while EU initiatives to build treatment plants have gone some way towards solving the problem, much remains to be done. Agricultural run-off of fertilisers that are brought down by rivers into the sea have caused algal blooms, the so-called red tides, especially in the Adriatic around the Po river. Excess nutrients in the water cause eutrophication, and the slow rate of water replacement has led to the appearance of these algal blooms

32   www.grida.no/resources/5900
33   Plan Bleu paper, August 2015 prepared for the EU by ECAP 3.3 *Tourism and Recreational Activities*

for half a century or more.[34] Industrial discharges, especially of heavy metals and chemicals, has also been a problem in this area and elsewhere along heavily industrialised coastlines like the Gulf of Fos on the French coast and around Piraeus and Perama in Greece.

One of the major sources of pollution in the sea and waterways, single-use plastic, has been in the spotlight for several years now. In the northern Pacific a gyre where the ocean currents meet has formed the great Pacific garbage patch, a huge plastic slick weighing an estimated 80,000 tons and covering an area of 1.6 million square kilometres.[35] While this visible plastic pollution is the most obvious, more dangerous is the microplastics which result from the breakdown of large plastic objects and which have been found to be present in marine life right up through the food chain from invertebrate filter-feeders to the sort of large fish we eat.

The Mediterranean suffers as much from plastic pollution as other seas and possibly more. In 2015 two French oceanographic students kayaked the length of the Mediterranean from Gibraltar to Istanbul. While they expected to find plastic pollution along the way, what they encountered was shocking. The endless urban sprawl along parts of the coast was a surprise, but even more of a surprise was the extent of plastic pollution off urbanised areas.

"We only had our eyes to witness pollution," said Couet. "But we were very impressed by huge coastal urbanisation. Close to big cities, we saw a lot of plastic waste in the water. At some point we could actually realise we were getting close to a big city or to a national park, depending on the amount of plastic in the water."

Stephen Starr *The Mediterranean's urban sprawl: 'You know a city's near by the plastic in the sea'* The Guardian January 20th 2015

In my experience, most thinking yachtsmen are aware of non-biodegradable rubbish on board and dispose of it responsibly. The problem does seem to be shore-based tourism where plastic is not disposed of responsibly and ends up in the sea. Countries like Greece and Turkey and the countries of the Maghreb do not have

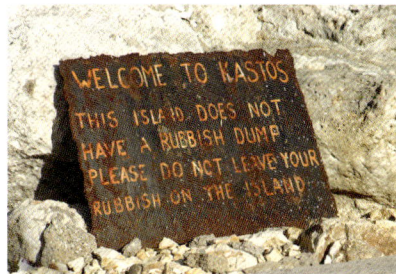

Please don't leave rubbish on the island.

34   Giovanni Nespoli *Eutrophication of the Coastal Waters of the North Adriatic Sea* Wiley Online 1988

35   www.theoceancleanup.com/great-pacific-garbage-patch/

sufficient recycling centres to deal with waste that can be recycled. In Greece many of the smaller islands cannot recycle plastics, or any recyclables, and it is simply burnt off in landfill dumps.

There are moves afoot to curb single-use plastics. In Britain legislation is planned to ban plastic straws and cotton buds. Large supermarkets have charged for plastic bags since 2015 and there are plans to extend the scheme to smaller shops. France has charged for plastic bags for decades and in 2016 introduced a total ban on plastic bags in supermarkets. In 2018 the EU passed a proposal and is planning to pass legislation banning plastic straws in the EU and to ban plastic water bottles by 2025.[36]

These measures by the EU, some of which have been adopted by non-EU countries, may at last address some of the environmental issues in the Mediterranean in an attempt to solve the pollution problems in the sea areas affected. Some non-EU countries like Turkey and Croatia have also implemented plans to clean up the seas. Some of the directives have been more successful than others and some of them affect yachting in the waters of these countries. There will doubtless be more legislation on environmental pollution in the Mediterranean as governments try to retain the seascape that attracts so many tourists, on and off the water, to its shores.

Sewerage

Sewerage has mostly been untreated until the last few decades and in some locations is still pumped untreated into the sea. The absence of tides in the Mediterranean means that, unlike the coasts of the tidal regions, the sewerage is not whisked away on the next tide. In most of the countries along the northern shores treatment plants for sewerage have been installed and this has gone some way towards solving the problem of untreated sewerage being pumped directly into the sea.

In most of the EU countries (in Spain, France, Italy and Greece) and in Turkey, new yachts and all charter yachts must have holding tanks for black water.[37] Older yachts are not required to have holding tanks, but under national laws

---

36   Arthur Neslen *European parliament approves sweeping ban on single-use plastics* The Guardian 24th October, 2018
37   Black water covers the waste from toilets. Grey water is the waste from showers and basins. Bilge water is self-explanatory.

cannot discharge black water within a certain distance, usually three to twelve miles, from the coast. Any thinking yachtsman should retro-fit a holding tank as no-one likes swimming or messing about in boats where waste is being discharged overboard in a harbour or bay. For the most part yachtsmen have a fairly good understanding of why holding tanks are necessary and discharge black water when out sailing, away from enclosed waters. Even if the yacht is not at the legal distance off the coast, the discharge of black water out at sea is an improvement on discharging it in a confined anchorage or harbour.

There has been an attempt to install pump-out stations in marinas. In my experience this has had only a limited success, with pumps regularly failing for mechanical reasons and operator difficulties – for the latter read incompetence. In Turkey, you are issued a machine-readable card, the infamous 'blue card', required to show that a certain number of pump-outs have taken place over the season. There are also laws governing the disposal of grey water in Turkey, though this requirement is pretty much impossible in most yachts for reasons of space and design, and so is almost universally disregarded there.[38]

Although the finger has been pointed at yachts as an important source of sewerage discharge, the overall impact of relatively small numbers of people on yachts makes this unlikely and I have seen no reliable data on the matter. Other sources of sewerage discharge into the sea involve significantly larger numbers of tourists and consequent sewerage discharge. Cruise ships are subject to national and MARPOL legislation, but

The average cruise ship is estimated to discharge 800 million litres of waste a year. Kusadasi cruise ship dock in Turkey. Photo Kadir Kir.

outside territorial waters can discharge waste.[39] The average cruise ship is estimated to discharge 800 million litres of waste a year. In 2013 there were

38   See the Introduction in Rod & Lucinda Heikell *Turkish Waters and Cyprus Pilot* 10th edition Imray 2018.
39   This is stated in the EU report below but appears to be in direct contradiction of MARPOL Annex iv/v which designates the Mediterranean as a Special Area.

136 cruise ships operating in the Mediterranean, principally on the northern side, carrying some 27 million passengers.[40] You can do the maths. As well as the cruise ship behemoths that can carry up to 8000 passengers, there are also smaller craft such as tripper boats carrying anything up to hundreds of trippers that ply the coastal waters daily. The waste from these boats is rarely pumped out at the end of the day and is usually discharged in coastal waters.[41] In addition there is the much bigger problem that land-based tourism around the coast often utilises sewerage systems which are discharged into the sea after no or little treatment and the numbers of tourists involved here make cruise ship numbers look modest.

It is likely that pump-out stations will be installed in more and more marinas and harbours in the future and that legislation on the rules for the discharge of black water from yachts will be more rigidly enforced. Legislation on grey water discharge is a good deal more problematic as the Turkish authorities have discovered. Yachts would have to have grey water tanks of a considerable

Marine Protection Areas in the Mediterranean.
Source *Mediterranean Cruising Handbook* 6th edition.

40   *Blue Economy in the Mediterranean*. Section 2.3
41   Observation by the author. In somewhere like Nidri in Greece there are four tripper boats, each licensed to take up to 250 passengers a day, but there are no pump-out stations anywhere along the route.

size, perhaps equivalent to the size of the fresh water tanks, and that is patently impossible in a modern yacht and it is unlikely further legislation or implementation will take place.

Marine Protection Areas (MPAs)

Marine Protection Areas are established in places where recreational, artisanal and fishing are having a detrimental effect on the sea. Generally, MPAs will have several sectors with different prohibitions on yachts and fishing vessels: no anchoring or navigation; MPA permit needed and mooring to buoys only; navigation but no commercial fishing; and navigation and anchoring permitted. In some countries, Italy in particular, there are also restrictions on fishing from private yachts whether by line or with a speargun.

The purpose of MPAs is to provide a habitat for marine life to regenerate. There are a number of misconceptions about marine life in the Mediterranean that need to be addressed. The Mediterranean has never been rich in marine life. It is a sea that has been written about, studied, fished and sailed on for thousands of years. Its marine life has long been described and illustrated, and the peoples around the shores have been experimenting with fish recipes for millennia. The Romans exalted in seafood and their descendants continue to produce fish dishes both novel and tasty. But that doesn't mean there is or ever has been much fish around, rather that it has always been prized. The Romans complained about the scarcity of good

Part of a fish mural in Pompeii (house no. 16, 1st century CE). While the Romans loved seafood, they still complained all those years ago of its scarcity in the Mediterranean.
National Archaeological Museum Naples.

fish stocks in the first century CE.[42] The abundance of fish in other seas make the Mediterranean look like a desert, which in a way it is.

The much-vaunted blueness and clarity of the Mediterranean results from it being poor in plankton, the basis of marine ecosystems. Plankton is scarcest in the eastern basin; the western basin is boosted by the inflow of less saline water and Atlantic plankton through the Straits of Gibraltar. In ecological terms it can be compared to semi-arid land regions like the steppes in Siberia or the prairies in Canada. A second important reason for the paucity of marine life is the relatively small area of continental shelf. Below 200 metres there is not the wealth of marine life that lives in shallower waters, and in most of the Mediterranean the depths drop away quickly to more than this.

The Mediterranean's weak fish population has also been harvested for thousands of years. Until recently some of the fishing practices were not exactly helping conservation. In Greece and Turkey, you may notice that a few of the older fishermen are minus a hand or an arm: it was probably lost dynamiting for fish, when the fuse was underestimated by a second or two and the dynamite exploded just before it was dropped into the sea. Today, the biggest problem is not dynamite but huge commercial trawlers with equipment capable of scouring entire areas, leaving almost nothing behind. The use of long drift nets has also caused the loss of species like the common dolphin, sunfish and loggerhead turtles, that get accidentally caught in them. Where the fisherman leaves off, the holiday diver with mask, snorkel and speargun who has sufficient time on his hands to go after almost anything that moves, and frequently does, brings in undersized fish and lobster.[43]

Posidonia beds are damaged by yacht anchors and MPAs are needed to restore the sea grass beds.

There are variations between the different EU countries on how MPAs are administered and even more so on whether some MPAs are policed at all in

42   Tony J Pitcher and Mimi E Lam *Fish commoditization and the historical origins of catching fish for profit* Maritime Studies (2015) 14 p. 2
43   Pitcher and Lam *Fish commoditization* pp 12–13

the summer. Despite the semi-arid nature of the sea there are fish in it and stocks need to be conserved. One of the reasons for installing mooring buoys in anchorages is to protect the sea grass beds, principally Posidonia nodosa, though there are other species, that regularly get rooted out by anchors and chain.

The sea grass is the habitat and nursery of numerous marine species and, as the numbers of yachts anchoring in the Mediterranean has grown, so has the destruction of the sea grass habitat and its ecosystem. It is likely that in the future the numbers of mooring buoys will increase so as to preserve the sea grasses and the marine ecosystem dependant on it. At present, the MPAs and Natura 2000 areas cover just 1.08% of coastal areas. The objective of the EU Convention on Biological Diversity is to reach 10% of coastal areas by 2020.[44] At present that seems unlikely, but it is certain that these areas will increase in the near future.[45]

Hydrocarbon pollution

The Mediterranean is one of the busiest seas in the world for commercial shipping. With ships transiting the Suez Canal, to and from the Black Sea, and from the Atlantic into and out of the Mediterranean, a huge armada of commercial ships criss-cross its surface. Many of these ships are oil tankers and the effects of a major oil spill would be catastrophic in the enclosed waters of the Mediterranean. Tankers frequently pump out their tanks, both legally and illegally, creating significant hydrocarbon pollution in the Mediterranean despite the fact this is illegal under International Maritime Organisation MARPOL rules.[46] Beaches frequently have remnants of tar balls scattered through the flotsam and jetsam on them and when sailing it is not unusual to see a slick on the water from refined oil discharges.

Not surprisingly the EU has implemented standards for yachts and their tenders. You can no longer buy a two-stroke petrol outboard in EU countries and all outboards for sale are petrol four strokes which are significantly less

44   Catherine Piante and Denis Ody *Blue Growth in the Mediterranean Sea: The Challenge of Good Environmental Status* WWF 2015 report

45   For MPAs currently in existence, see section 5.5 *Imray Mediterranean Almanac 2019–2020* ed. Lucinda Heikell.

46   The Mediterranean is a designated 'Special Area' under MARPOL. Piante and Ody *Blue Growth in the Mediterranean Sea* p 59

polluting. Inboard diesel engines must meet EU RCD II standards from 2016–2017 which mandate much lower emissions for yachts up to 24 metres (78 ft).[47] Yachts over 24 metres conform to EU commercial ship regulations.

While yachts do contribute to hydrocarbon pollution, like the sewerage problem, the emissions from yachts in no way approaches the emissions from commercial shipping. The principal culprits from commercial shipping are not just oil slicks from the legal and illegal washing of tanks, but also carbon dioxide, nitrogen oxides and sulphur contaminants. Cruise ships in small ports cause relatively large amounts of pollution and it is estimated that a cruise ship with 3000 passengers will cause as much hydrocarbon pollution as 12,000 cars in a day.[48]

There is also a divide between superyachts and the more run-of-the-mill yachts of around 40 ft or so. A 70 ft (21 metre) motor yacht will use around 200 litres an hour at cruising speed. A 230 ft (70 metre) motor yacht will use 500–750 litres an hour at cruising speed.[49] These are rough averages, but you can see that a superyacht can easily use twice the annual consumption of a small yacht in just one day and the concomitant increase in hydrocarbon pollution emissions is considerable. [50]And that's without factoring in generators and the petrol-powered toys on board larger yachts.

In recent years there have been attempts to introduce greener yachts running hybrid systems utilising solar panels and a generator to power electric drives. Some of these have been successful, others less so. In general hybrid motor yachts cruise at fairly low speeds and, while they have solar panels to charge the batteries, in practice most charging comes from plugging in to mains electricity or from an onboard diesel generator. While the first projects to go to greener propulsion systems have been mixed at best, later systems have more efficient solar panels and generators with sophisticated control systems. A company like Solarwave Yachts is claiming that its 54 ft model can cruise at

47   www.eucertification.com/ce-certification-2/rcd
48   Alberto Cappato *Cruises and Recreational Boating in the Mediterranean* Plan Bleu paper 2011.
49   Figures from various superyacht brokerage sites.
50   A 40hp engine in a 40 ft yacht will use around 2½–3 litres an hour at cruising speed. The superyacht will be going faster, but the overall use of fuel to cover the same distance is appreciably more.

ten knots using solar power alone, although there is a backup generator just in case.[51]

Hybrid propulsion is even catching on in superyacht circles. Admiral Yachts has researched hybrid systems and begun constructing superyachts with better fuel consumption than equivalent yachts of a decade ago. Their Momentum 50m Explorer (164 ft) has a quoted fuel range of 5000 miles. Another company, the Italian VSY Shipyard is building a 67 metre (220 ft) motor yacht that will also have a 5000 mile range from efficiencies of the hull and motors rather than the size of the fuel tanks.[52] Despite this the article goes on to say:

> The trend is clear and the environmental advances will have ramifications for future yachts in build, whether they are designed for long or short distance cruising. Of course, no-one can argue that the most fuel-efficient yachts are those that exploit the power of the wind and, as Oceanco's 106.7 metre Black Pearl proves, with the right sail plan – three 70-metre Dynarig carbon masts and 2,900 square metres of sails – fuel can be virtually left out of the equation entirely.

Superyachts.com article May 2018 *The Rise of Fuel-Efficient, Long-Distance Explorers*

Global Warming and the Mediterranean

Between global warming, global meteorological instability, climate change, the greenhouse effect and anthropogenic influences, it can get a little difficult to sort out what anyone is talking about. Global warming refers to an increase in the overall average temperature of the world that is at least partly the result of human activity (the anthropogenic bit). The big culprit in all this is carbon dioxide emissions which have increased significantly since the industrial revolution began in the middle of the 19th century. Carbon dioxide stays in the upper atmosphere and, while it lets light through, it does not let very much heat out. This is the greenhouse effect. It is just one factor in climate change, which can be affected by all sorts of things, but it is an important issue because of the catastrophic influence global warming could have on the world's weather in this century and indeed may be having on weather patterns today. Global warming and cooling have always been around, but what is significant here is the scale of the change over a comparatively short

---

51   www.solarwave-yachts-pacific.com/solar-hybrid-power-catamarans/
solarwave-cruiser-54-power-catamaran/
52   *The Rise of Fuel-Efficient, Long-Distance Explorers* Superyachts.com article May 2018

period of time and how that will affect the weather that we as sailors take to be the norm.[53]

Is global warming really happening? This is the really awkward question. There are a number of different models around for studying climate change, but for all of them the sort of variables needed, mostly gathered from satellite data, are not available over a sufficient period of time for the models to be 100% reliable. Most of the debate in scientific circles is about the interpretation of satellite data from the last ten to fifteen years. Without going into all the ramifications of the debate, it is possible to say that most climatologists believe that global warming is occurring and that some general conclusions can be drawn from the data that is available. The Intergovernmental Panel on Climate Change (IPCC) set up in 1988 by the UN and the World Meteorological Organisation had this to say in its 2018 report:

The world is currently 1°C warmer than preindustrial levels. Following devastating hurricanes in the US, record droughts in Cape Town and forest fires in the Arctic, the IPCC makes clear that climate change is already happening, upgraded its risk warning from previous reports, and warned that every fraction of additional warming would worsen the impact.

Jonathon Watts on the 2018 IPCC report *We have 12 years to limit climate change catastrophe, warns UN* Guardian 8th October 2018

In the last century the average global temperature rose by 0.5°C. A conservative estimate of the rise in global warming by 2100 is for temperatures to be 2°C higher than in 1990 and for sea levels to be 50 cm higher than present levels. This might not seem much, but small changes in temperature over a relatively short period of time can lead to dramatic changes in the weather. Some of the counter arguments to the global warming models which point to climatic temperature changes in the past are talking about time periods for these changes measured in thousands of years, not in the decades we are looking at now.

Competing against the global warming models are a range of counter arguments. Solar flares from the sun, mini climatic changes over a 400–500 year cycle, and the effects of other pollutants in the atmosphere which have a cooling effect, are all brought out to debunk the greenhouse effect and man's influence on climate change. Suffice to say that new models which concentrate on the world's air conditioning system, the very oceans we

53   www.metoffice.gov.uk/climate-guide/climate-change

sail upon and the polar ice caps, point to man and carbon dioxide as the significant factor in the increase in global temperatures in the last century. If anything, global warming is taking place quicker than previously predicted. Even more disturbing is the prediction that when the ocean's temperatures start to change, it takes a long time to stabilise them. Once started, global warming will be around for a long time to come even if carbon dioxide emissions are stabilised or reduced.[54]

What are the implications for the Mediterranean? While there is good evidence for some of the outcomes, other outcomes are less certain as the models used are complex and the inter-relationships of the atmosphere, air temperature, ocean temperature and currents and other variables are still not well understood. For some of us the anecdotal evidence is also compelling. With those caveats the following outcomes that will affect yachtsmen in the Mediterranean are likely.

Mid-latitude storms and 'Medicanes'

There are no clear predictions here. The simplistic model is that because tropical storms breed in waters with temperatures in the region of 26°C and above, an increase in sea temperature could mean that tropical storms will increase in number and affect areas not normally within tropical storm zones. This scenario is not completely ruled out, but the models need to take into account a lot of other variables like wind flows and different wind speeds in the atmosphere (vertical wind shear).

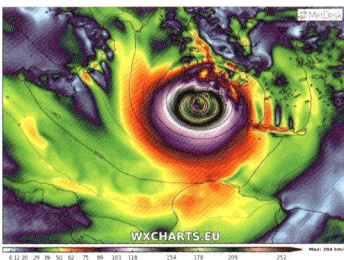

'Medicane Zorbas' in the Mediterranean late September 2018. WXcharts.EU.

Hurricanes and typhoons in the Atlantic and Pacific grab the headlines, but mid-latitude hurricanes or extratropical storms which originate outside normal hurricane breeding grounds are of more concern to the yachtsman as they affect seas and coasts not normally in hurricane areas. In the Mediterranean, hurricane-like weather systems have been dubbed 'medicanes': they have the same characteristics as a hurricane with a definite eye and winds circulating around the eye;

54   https://climate.nasa.gov/evidence/

winds up to and over 64 knots; and the development of the system and a track consistent with hurricanes in the Atlantic. In the past it has been said that the Mediterranean would not produce hurricanes as the sea temperatures are not warm enough and the Mediterranean did not have sufficient moisture in the atmosphere to feed a hurricane. With global warming the sea temperatures have risen considerably and in the autumn there is now the perfect storm combination of moisture-laden air over the Mediterranean and higher sea temperatures.[55]

There have been more medicanes and tropical storm systems in the Mediterranean than was formerly thought, but it is only really since satellite observations have been available that medicanes have been well documented. The first was in 1969 and since then there have been thirteen identified with the last, Zorbas, in late September 2018.[56] While these systems are now well forecast, nonetheless the damage to yachts in harbour can be severe, not only from the strength of the wind, but also the reversal of wind direction as the eye goes over. In Zorbas there was some damage to yachting infrastructure and significant numbers of yachts were damaged or sunk in Greece.

As elsewhere in the world, if sea temperatures keep rising we can expect to see more tropical storm-like systems and medicanes in the Mediterranean. Damage from hurricane-force winds and huge seas is one side of the coin as more damage results from the heavy rainfall associated with hurricanes. Flash floods wash debris down into harbours and the sea causing extensive damage to yachting infrastructure. During Zorbas there were flash floods in Greece

Storm damage at Rapallo Marina November 2018. Photo Shutterstock.

55   Nastos, Karavana-Papadimou and Matsangouras *Tropical-like cyclones in the Mediterranean: Impacts and composite daily means and anomalies of synoptic conditions* Proceedings of the 14th International Conference on Environmental Science and Technology Rhodes, Greece, 3–5 September 2015
56   en.wikipedia.org/wiki/Mediterranean_tropical-like_cyclone

and Turkey with the medicane dropping 20 cm (8 inches) of rain over several days. Mini-tornados and waterspouts also occurred, wreaking damage over a wide area.[57]

At the end of October 2018, a medicane looked to be forming between the Balearics and Corsica. Though it later lost its cyclic form, the front associated with it gave rise to hurricane-force winds and the west coast of Italy experienced exceptionally strong winds, heavy rainfall and tornadic activity.[58] The outer breakwater of Rapallo Marina at the head of the Golfo di Marconi was destroyed and large numbers of yachts were sunk or washed ashore. The marina looked like a bomb had hit it. In the thirty-eight years I have been describing the place there has never been this sort of damage to the harbour.[59]

The increase in numbers and the intensity of depressions crossing the Mediterranean is difficult to determine in the short term. However, given somewhere like Rapallo Marina has been around for more than forty years and has only now experienced the sort of catastrophic weather that can destroy the outer breakwater and sink and damage large numbers of yachts, it is likely there will be more extreme weather of this sort in the Mediterranean. Across from Liguria, Venice was flooded by the combination of high winds and high tide in an event said to be one of the worst in its history. On the other side of the Adriatic ferries were stopped from running in Croatia and marinas were buffeted by the last of the storm. If recent winters are anything to go by, it is likely that catastrophic storms will be a regular feature in the Mediterranean.

Disruption of normal weather patterns

One of the consequences of global warming is likely to be less settled weather in the summer season. Are the seasons becoming less settled or is the weather pretty much as it always was? The settled weather patterns of the Mediterranean have been observed and written about since antiquity. In the eastern Mediterranean the ancient Greeks observed the regularity of the *etesians*, modern day meltemi, blowing down through the Sea of Marmara and across the Aegean from the northeast, to north, to northwest in the

57   en.wikipedia.org/wiki/Mediterranean_tropical-like_cyclone
58   www.severe-weather.eu/mcd/enhanced-tornado-threat-western-coast-of-italy-ligurian-tyrrhenian-sea-plains-of-north-italy-north-adriatic-october-29-2018/
59   The first edition of my *Italian Waters Pilot* was published in 1983 with research from 1981–1982.

summer. In the winter southerlies often blow. The Romans also plotted the prevailing winds in the summer and winter seasons of the Mediterranean, and later the Venetians and Genoese were familiar with the prevailing winds of the Mediterranean. The Copts, the Christian minority in Egypt, even drew up a calendar of gales in the eastern Mediterranean.[60] These seasonal patterns have stayed much the same from the Graeco-Roman period to the present day. Only now is there some evidence that things may be changing.

At a gut level backed up by some forty years of observation in the Mediterranean, I and others do believe that weather patterns are shifting, although not to the extent some believe. It is always difficult to sort out the facts from the local lore, which invariably comes up with 'this is the worst year ever for sun/rain/wind' from the local Captain Kosta waving his seaweed in the air. Statistically there is little to go on. Coming up through the Red Sea to Egypt in late winter, the Arabian peninsula had its coldest winter for fifty years and it did seem odd to me to be freezing cold and pelted with hailstones next to the Sahara desert. The number of depressions passing through the eastern Mediterranean in the late spring and early summer also seems to be on the increase. The Azores high seems to take longer to stabilise. The trouble with all this is that it is short term and, statistically, means little over the longer period. Another ten years and we should know, but at a gut level and with some scribbled data I would plump for less settled weather patterns in the last ten years in the Mediterranean.

Some of this has to do with a shift of the old weather patterns so that the seasons seem to occur about a month later than they used to. Of importance to yachtsmen in the Aegean is the meltemi, the prevailing summer wind which normally blows predictably from the northeast through to northwest from mid-June to early September. It is a boisterous wind that often blows up to 30–35 knots. In recent years it seems to have moved its period to late July through to October and it now often blows at 40 knots or dies to a paltry 10 knots. At times there seem to be more southerlies than in previous years. Likewise, in the spring the unsettled weather caused by depressions passing through seems to go on longer than it used to. This is all personal observation of my and others' experiences, but there are enough people with relatively

60   See the Introduction of Rod & Lucinda Heikell *Turkish Waters and Cyprus Pilot* Imray 10th edition 2018 for details of the Coptic Calendar.

cool heads out there saying the same thing and, in the end, without recourse to statistics over a sufficient period of time, gut feelings mean a lot when you are caught out in bad weather at times you did not expect to be.

Waterspouts and tornadoes

Evidence for an increase in the numbers and intensities of waterspouts and tornadoes which hit coastal locations is difficult to find statistically. Anecdotally there are numerous reports on the web and social media. Waterspouts have always been around, but it is difficult to gather accurate data on numbers because the duration of a waterspout is normally only twenty minutes or so and they are localised phenomenons. Windspeeds are calculated to be in the 50–100 knot band. However, a new breed of waterspout, the 'water tornado' or double-funnel spout is more like a land tornado over the water with possible wind speeds up to 400 mph. A number of these have been recorded and studied, and their incidence in the Mediterranean does seem to be increasing.[61] These water tornadoes are significantly bigger and more violent than waterspouts and do not appear to break up when moving from the land to the sea or vice versa.

With the incidence of medicanes and violent storm fronts increasing there do seem to be an increased number of tornadoes reported. In the front that devastated Rapallo Marina in October 2018 tornadoes were reported in Naples, Rome and Terracina. Whether they are connected to global warming is difficult to know, but theoretically it would seem likely that localised patches of hot and cold air resulting from global warming could produce bigger and more violent waterspouts.[62]

Rainfall

One thing the models for global warming can predict with some accuracy is a disruption to normal rainfall patterns. Rainfall already appears to be conforming to predictions, with heavy precipitation over short periods becoming common and a shift in regional precipitation patterns occurring.

---

61   Nastos et al *Tropical-like cyclones in the Mediterranean*
62   www.severe-weather.eu/mcd/enhanced-tornado-threat-western-coast-of-italy-ligurian-tyrrhenian-sea-plains-of-north-italy-north-adriatic-october-29-2018/

Global warming means that there will be more rain overall and it will fall in different regions and in heavy downpours.

'So what?' the yachtsman says, 'how does that affect me?' In a number of ways, as it happens. Flooding of river estuaries will become more common and flash floods can cause a lot of damage to craft moored in an estuary and to marinas within rivers and estuaries. After a period of dry weather large amounts of rain inland can back up until a flood wave sweeps down the river carrying trees and other debris with it to an estuary where yachts may be moored. Already we have got used to news of flash floods around the shores of the Mediterranean in the autumn and winter, and it is predicted these rainfall events and flooding will get worse. In 2018 flash floods devastated Athens and parts of the Attic coast, northern Italy, southern France and the Balearics. The problem is compounded by the fact that torrential rainfall runs off too quickly to replenish reservoirs and ground water, so we end up in the paradoxical situation of droughts occurring despite earlier periods of heavy rainfall.

For yachtsmen cruising in lower latitudes water shortages are likely to become a problem. While global warming brings more rain, it will mostly be distributed in high northerly latitudes and in torrential downpours. Water shortages in the Mediterranean are a likely scenario, indeed are already a reality in some areas of the Mediterranean, and it will be more and more difficult to find good potable water.[63] There is a solution in the form of watermakers, but this is not an option for a lot of smaller yachts and, on larger craft, carry an environmental cost in as much as you need to run the engine or a generator, producing yet more carbon dioxide.

For users of inland waterways, short periods of heavy rain can close sections of a waterway where it is close to a river or where there is heavy run-off. Periods of prolonged drought mean that at other times waterways may be closed because there is insufficient water. This already occurs in the Canal du Midi in southern France which has been closed at certain times of the year because of lack of water and, ironically, in late 2018 was closed because of flood damage. Warmer temperatures also mean that the Alpine snows melt more quickly, producing strong currents in rivers like the Rhone.

---

63   www.nature.com/news/climate-change-could-flip-mediterranean-lands-to-desert-1.20894

And the future?

Going sailing is, for most people, as much about arriving at a quiet, beautiful place as putting up sails and pulling on ropes. That global warming threatens some of what we do is without question. There are a lot of 'ifs' and 'maybes', but that is the nature of the beast. Climatology is a complicated discipline with a lot of inadequate models, but also a lot of data that is hard to dispute, and the models are getting more and more accurate at predicting what is going to happen. The reports of various international and scientific bodies (such as the IPCC, the Intergovernmental Panel on Climate Change, and meteorological institutes like the UK Meteorological Office and NOAA, the US National Oceanic and Atmospheric Administration), and of the vast majority of meteorologists around the world, is that climate change is here already and affecting our weather and consequently the seas we sail upon.

It is all too easy for us to dismiss the arguments above as the ranting of a lot of crazy green activists, the sort of doom and gloom that the 'sandals and yoghurt brigade' have trotted out every few years. This is no longer a valid argument – not that it ever was. Most of the predictions on climate change are from panels of scientists who are experts in the field of global warming. The history of the Mediterranean has been determined by numerous factors that have impinged on the populations around its shores. Geographical, social, economic, cultural and technological factors have played their part in shaping the civilizations that have come and gone leaving their historical fingerprints on the fabric of the Mediterranean. These same agents have shaped the history of yachting in the Mediterranean that I have attempted to describe in this book. In the future we can be sure that man-made climate change will be a significant factor in the history of the Mediterranean and in the history of yachting on its waters.

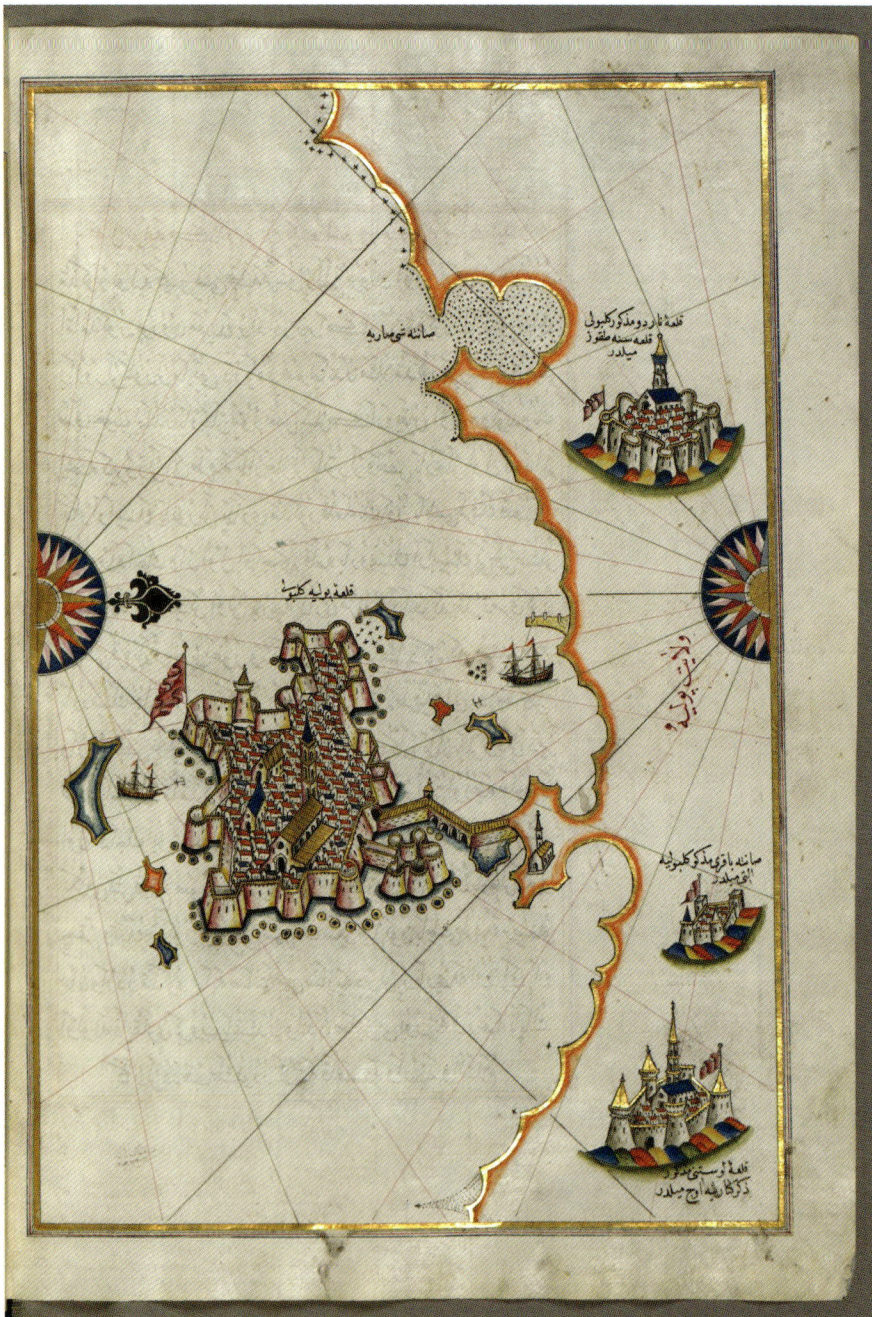

Piri Reis' map of the towns of Gallipoli and Nardo on the boot of Italy from his *Kitab-i bahriye*. Wiki Commons.

18 FROM THE *PERIPLUS OF SKYLAX* TO THE DIGITAL AGE

Using maps and pilotage directions arguably began in the Mediterranean long ago. In this age of electronic navigation it is easy to forget how this all happened and, despite our digital aids, how much we still rely on quite basic techniques and pilotage aids. We employ a huge range of modern technology to locate where we are, where we are going, at what speed, whether we are on course, and how long it will take at such and such a speed. Satellites beam down our co-ordinates and printed circuit boards process the information and display it on a screen to give us an apparent certainty as we navigate on the sea. And yet seemingly old-fashioned aids like yachtsman's guides to an area still thrive. I have a personal interest here and this history of the Mediterranean would not be complete without looking at the history of how we navigate this sea.

 Just a few decades ago we had no satellites beaming down our position and navigation was by dead reckoning and the stars along with pilotage skills when closing a harbour or anchorage. In the late 1970's I sailed the 20 ft *Roulette* from the UK down to the Mediterranean with a compass and some charts marked 'Not For Navigation'.[1] I'm not a Luddite and in truth love the certainty which the global positioning system (GPS) and the like give, but I do have a bit of a worry that all these black boxes and flickering displays have distracted us from the visceral experience of sailing and getting from A to B on our wits and a bit of fear.

The 20 ft *Roulette*, mostly sailed with little in the way of navigation equipment and a dollop of fear.

For the ancients, navigating around the Mediterranean was quite probably more sophisticated than is generally imagined. Some academic opinion is that there was little in the way of navigation equipment or information. This is not

---

1   Heikell *The Accidental Sailor*

true from an evidential point of view and more importantly from the natural instinct of homo sapiens to draw something to help our understanding: the 'picture is worth a 1000 words' perspective.

Mapping: A Human Imperative?[2]

The earliest maps we know of are prehistoric. One of these is of Catal Hoyuk near Konya on the Anatolian plain.[3] The town dates from around 7500 BCE and was an advanced Neolithic agricultural settlement. It is possibly the oldest known in the world. One of the finds at Catal Hoyuk is a map of the town showing the layout of the mud huts and streets and the profile of the Hazan Dag volcano behind the town. This map is dated to around 6000 BCE and is important because the painting – the 'map' – matches the layout of the excavated dwellings in the town.[4] There are other, older maps including one from the Ukraine from 11–12000 BCE showing dwellings along a river, but no settlement to 'match' to the map.[5]

The Catal Huyuk map. Wiki Commons.

Drawing a map involves a knowledge of perspective, of spatial arrangement,[6] the ability to translate a three-dimensional view to a two-dimensional view, and some basic geometry and mathematics. Drawing a map in the dust on the ground, on a dried skin or a piece of wood, on stone, on paper if you had it, is the most human of activities. It may be an old homily that tells us 'a picture is worth a thousand words', but that doesn't make it any less true.

---

2   Much of this section was published as Appendix IV in Rod Heikell *Sailing Ancient Seas*.

3   First discovered in 1956 and later excavated by James Mellaart in the early 1960's. The site has a large number of houses and apart from the 'map' there are many other spectacular paintings in the houses. The excavation is ongoing.

4   www.sci-news.com/archaeology/science-catalhoyuk-map-mural-volcanic-eruption-01681. html

5   The map was inscribed on a mammoth tusk found in Mezhirich, Ukraine.

6   One of the facilities of the human brain is the Gestalt function where the brain can make sense of apparently random dots. So, for example three dots at the corners of an imaginary triangle will be seen as a triangle.

Less developed societies, from the Australian aborigine to the Eskimo, all have a detailed sense of the geography around them. Some Australian aborigines chart the geography in songlines,[7] geographical reference points rich in detail, both of geography and culture, that are songs by which they can navigate areas of desert that Europeans would get utterly lost in without a paper map and some way of reckoning a position on that map. In the Pacific, Polynesian navigators could find their way across hundreds of miles of ocean from one island to another using the stars, the direction and shape of ocean swells, by watching sea birds and their flight path, and the shape and type of clouds and the time of day they appeared. These skills were passed on verbally from generation to generation, although some of the islanders made maps. The Marshall Islanders used shells and twigs to construct maps showing the position of islands and the prevailing direction of the ocean swell.[8]

Map-making is most likely a fundamental part of our cognitive world. The ability to organise the space around us into a two-dimensional form is one way of making sense of it, of understanding the spatial arrangement of the world, or at least the world that is known. Mapping the stars and mapping the planet go some way to understanding our place in it, at least our geographic place. Whatever else the priests, politicians and shamans derive from that map or add to it, the basic geography (and cosmology in the case of stars) does not overshadow the basic uses of a map for knowing where you are in the literal sense. In *The Nature of Maps* the authors conclude that:

Miletus was the hub of intellectual endeavour, including map-making, in the ancient world.

The reason for the common use of mapping as a metaphor for knowing or communicating has finally become clear: the concept of spatial relatedness, which is of concern in mapping

7   A theory popularised in Bruce Chatwin's readable *Songlines* Jonathan Cape 1987.
8   See David Lewis *We the Navigators* University of Hawaii Press 1972/1994 for details on Polynesian navigation.

and which indeed is the reason for the very existence of cartography, is a quality without which it is difficult or impossible for the human mind to apprehend anything.

Robinson and Petchenik *The Nature of Maps*[9]

By 500 BCE mapmaking was developing from a local scale to a world scale. Early cosmological maps from the Babylonian and Egyptian periods exist, but the first recognisable world map that survives is from Anaximander in the 6th century BCE. Anaximander lived in Miletus, a cauldron of intellectual endeavour in this period, producing some of the greatest Greek thinkers of the

15th century copy of Ptolemy's 2nd century CE map. British Library.

times. After Anaximander, Hecateus of Miletus produced a revised world map in the 5th century BCE. These maps probably survive because some versions of them were drawn on a wooden panel[10] in the case of Hecateus' map, or in the case of Anaxigoras of Miletus, Herodotus records that he took a bronze tablet showing a map of the world to Greece when he was seeking allies to fight against the Persians.[11]

Skylax

One of my pet projects has been to research the travels and endeavours of Skylax of Karyanda who wrote what we can call the first *Periplus* or sailing directions, assuming we discount the geography of Homer in *The Iliad* and *The Odyssey*. *The Periplus of Skylax*[12] was discovered, or more accurately, re-discovered in the 13th century CE and is basically a description of the Mediterranean proceeding clockwise around the sea.[13] The guide is usually

9   Quoted in John Noble Wilford's *The Mapmakers*, Pimlico 1981 pp 13–14
10   See Harley & Woodward *The History of Cartography* Vol. I, University of Chicago Press 1981 pp 134–135. This is a paper based on work by Germaine Aujac.
11   Around 500 BCE. *The History of Cartography* Vol. I and John Noble Wilford *The Mapmakers*, Chapter 1.
12   I use Graham Shipley's recent translation *Pseudo-Skylax's Periplous* Bristol Phoenix Press 2011.
13   The 13th century manuscript is located in Paris.

called the *Periplus of Pseudo Skylax* because the original has evidently been revised later on and includes some places and rulers who were not around in the earlier era.[14]

In the original it is described as the *Periplus of the Oikumene, A Circumnavigation of the World,* or at least the known or inhabited world. The *Periplus* describes cities, rivers, forts and harbours, with the distance in stades or number of days sailing between them. A stade was the length of a stadium, generally reckoned to be around 180 to 190 metres which happily works out to approximately a cable or one-tenth of a nautical mile, so we can just divide by ten to get nautical miles.[15] A typical daily voyage is reckoned by Skylax to be 500 stades or around fifty nautical miles.[16]

Skylax of Karyanda. The site of Karyanda, present day Salih Adasi, is still unexcavated to this day.

The *Periplus* is attributed to Skylax of Karyanda, and this same Skylax is mentioned briefly in Herodotus.

Darius, desiring to know where this Indus empties into the sea, sent ships manned by Skylax, a man of Karyanda, and others whose word he trusted; these set out from the city of Kaspatyros and the Paktyikan country and sailed down the river toward the east and the sunrise until they came to the sea; and voyaging ever the westward, they came in the thirtieth month to that place from which the Egyptian king sent the above-mentioned Phoenicians to sail around Libya.

Robert B Strassler, ed. *Histories*, Book 4.44: *The Landmark Herodotus*

From this mention of Skylax of Karyanda in Herodotus we would date the *Periplus* to around 530–500 BCE. Darius invaded north-west India in 521

14   I won't elaborate too much on the issue of Skylax and Pseudo Skylax as it would take up a considerable amount of space. See Shipley *Pseudo-Skylax's Periplous.*
15   Ten cables to one nautical mile. One nautical mile is the circumference of the earth at the equator divided into 360 degrees with a degree divided into sixty minutes. A minute of arc is one nautical mile.
16   Fifty miles would seem a reasonable average day's sailing for small coasting vessels, although there would be days when it was less.

BCE and the assumption is that Skylax was sent off to either chart the known boundaries of the Persian empire and what lay beyond the Indus River, or at an earlier date to scout out the territory for the coming invasion. It is likely that he got to Kaspatyros[17] on the Indus by voyaging up and into the Black Sea, though conceivably he could have travelled overland. Although there is not a lot of detail on the Black Sea in the *Periplus*, it does contain a list of ports and some detail on the Black Sea coast.[18]

So, did Skylax produce any maps to go with his *Periplus*? The likelihood that he produced sketch maps to accompany his notes is high, from the human imperative view, but no hard evidence exists. There are surviving frescoes which, while mainly ornamental, do have a map-like quality depicting coastline, a harbour and a village beside the sea. The Thira frescoes excavated at Akrotiri date from around 1500 BCE and, while obviously meant to be decorative, they point to map or plan-like depictions.[19] The journey-man jottings and scribbles of a Skylax or his contemporaries would be less likely to survive than a wooden or bronze pinax with the world map of Hecateus on it. In Aristophanes' play *The Clouds*, written in the 5th century BCE, there is obviously a map in the production which is mentioned in the text.[20] That Aristophanes could introduce a map on stage would indicate an audience familiar with the concept.

That there were maps of the world in different variations and interpretations and that they are mentioned by many of the writers of the time is interesting in itself. The known world is variously represented as a sphere, a cylinder, an oval and as an oblong.[21] Of all of these, the sphere was favourite for good empirical

17   In present day Kashmir. It may be Srinagar in present day Kashmir.
18   Shipley *Pseudo-Skylax's Periplous*, Periplus 67 The Black Sea
19   See *The History of Cartography* Vol. I, pp 132.
20   Mentioned in The History of Cartography Vol I. The following conversation takes place on stage:
Student (pointing to a map): Now then, over here we have a map of the entire world. You see there? That's Athens.
Strepsiades: That, Athens? Don't be ridiculous. Why, I can't even see a single law court in session.
Student: Nevertheless, it's quite true. It really is Athens.
Strepsiades: Then where are my neighbours of Kikynna?
Student: Here they are. And you see this island squeezed along the coast? That's Euboia.
Strepsiades: I know that place well enough. Perikles squeezed it dry. But where's Sparta?
Student: Sparta? Right over here.
21   See *The History of Cartography* Vol. I, Chapter 8

reasons that the Greeks understood.[22] Understanding the world in this way was considered a legitimate object of study for philosophers and so it is these cartographic reflections that were copied and passed on to future generations. The work of artisans copying the charts was beneath the dignity of philosophers and considered a lesser form of human activity.

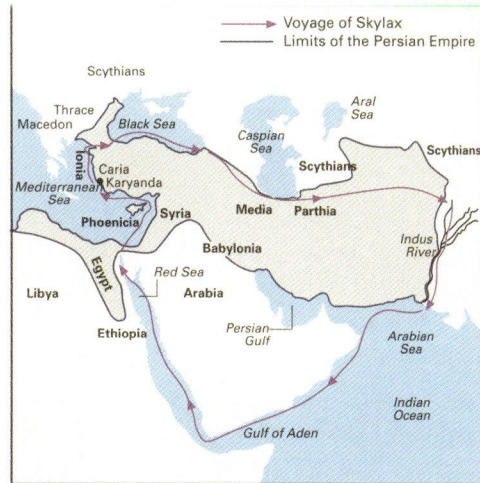

PERSIAN EMPIRE IN 490BC (Showing Skylax expedition)

Possible voyage of Skylax around the limits of the Persian Empire.

Any maps that Skylax produced would be considered journey-man banausic efforts, of little use to philosophers. Paradoxically the *Periplus of Pseudo-Skylax* was likely copied for its geographical data rather than its more prosaic use as a pilot for sailors. That the data for a philosophical idea of the world came from sailors like Skylax and his travels is likely. Herodotus who lived nearby to Skylax in Bodrum did not visit large parts of the world that he wrote about,[23] nor did earlier writers on the geography of the world, notably Anaximander and Hecateus. Likewise, Strabo and later writers can also be put in the category of 'encyclopaedists' rather than researchers out in the field, as it were.

Any cruising sailor sitting down with friends will soon resort to pencil and paper to scribble a rough map or diagram from memory to show what an anchorage looks like and the safe approach into it. To make a rough map of how to get from A to B works better than trying to put directions down in words, though combining a map with text is arguably the most useful. It's hard not to believe that 2500 years ago this imperative was not the same for

22   Aristotle, for example, noted that ships on the horizon were hull down as they got smaller, rather than disappearing as a smaller and smaller whole. Eratosthenes was a geographer in the 4th to 3rd century BCE who measured the circumference of the earth.

23   Though the assumption is sometimes made that Herodotus travelled widely, there is no good evidence for this and he likely used the information of Skylax and other fellow travellers to bulk out his *Histories*.

Skylax and his mates. Sadly, the mutability of wood and papyrus leaves us with no proof.

The authorship and origins of the *Periplus of Pseudo-Skylax* occupies a small corner of classical studies detailing the early geography and history of the Mediterranean. In the modern sense, a periplus could be described as a pilot or sailing directions for a sea area and would detail passage times, harbours, headlands, islands, forts, peoples and cities. Sailing directions like this have a long history, from Skylax[24] some 2500 years ago up to the present and, even in this age of electronic navigation, sailing directions still have a place on board boats little and large. Down the ages sailing directions have gone by different names starting with the *Periplus*[25] from the Greek era and up through the Roman era to the portolans of the Medieval period and the development of sailing directions or pilots by various hydrographic agencies around the world. I write sailing directions for yachts cruising around the countries of the Mediterranean and even in this age of instant communications sailors need a guide to harbours, sailing seasons, facilities and a brief summary of what the natives are like ashore.

Any periplus used as a sailing guide will be amended and corrected over time, even within the lifetime of the author. My sailing guides for a more pernickety group of yachtsmen cruising solely for pleasure go into new editions every three to five years and have supplements issued annually, noting changes and corrections. In the days of Skylax a captain would want to know how long a passage takes, where harbours and headlands are, and importantly whether the place he was headed for was friendly or not. City states frequently changed allegiances, waged war on other city states, or were taken over by a foreign power, which in the 6th to 4th centuries BCE meant not only the Persians,[26] but also city states that had decided to wage war on another city or region. Sailing around the Mediterranean involved not only pilotage to avoid the fixed geographical dangers, rocks and reefs, and headlands, but also pilotage around the ever-shifting political currents that swept back and forth over the sea.

24   Skylax was likely not the earliest. That title could go to Homer's *Odyssey*, to Hanno of Carthage, or to a number of logographers from Ionia.
25   *Periplus* from the Greek 'peri' and 'plous', a voyage through or around.
26   The Persians arrived on the west coast of Asia Minor under Cyrus around 546 BCE and were defeated by Alexander in 333 BCE.

None of this can be proved from the text itself, although what is assumed to be archaic or sloppy information about places from earlier dates used in a mid-4th century text, is likely original material from an earlier version marked up with later corrections. The *Periplus* is also assumed not to be the work of Skylax of Karyanda because it has nothing in it on India or the sea passage up the Red Sea mentioned in Herodotus. Yet Aristotle and other ancient sources mention Skylax as a source on India.[27] Given the few fragments we have of some ancient texts and the number of known texts mentioned by other ancient Greek writers, now lost over time, it is not entirely surprising that either a part of the original *Periplus of Skylax* or another complete periplus on India and the Red Sea have been lost to us. Interestingly there is a periplus from the 1st century CE on the Erythraean Sea[28] ascribed to an anonymous merchant. Perhaps this is a Skylax original amended through to the 1st century CE, though I'm sure few classicists would agree with that.

There is one classical scholar who puts the *Periplus of Pseudo-Skylax* at the earlier date and who has detected what he sees as an original 6th century BCE text amended and corrupted over time. In *The First Portulan*,[29] Aurelio Peretti argues that the *Periplus* was originally a portolan for working sailors that was later amended for scholars who had less use for it in a practical sense but valued its substantive knowledge. In this I concur, as to me it reads more like a set of sailing directions, a dry and tedious text that the navigator can consult quickly as he is blown down onto a strange coast. Scholarly expertise is a wonderful thing and gives us a detailed view of the world and special fields of interest, like the debate over just who Skylax was and when he wrote his *Periplus*, but like many I have a dilettante interest in things ancient and modern and a curiosity, some would say a pedantic turn of mind, over debates like this.

And something else. As a sailor who has sailed up and down and around the Mediterranean many times in a small sailing yacht, I recognise in the *Periplus* the embryonic sailing directions for this sea. In a way the writing is disappointing. It is a dull, purely technical exercise, that at times almost reads like a shopping list of ports and cities around the Mediterranean. It has

27   Shipley *Pseudo-Skylax's Periplous* p 5
28   *Periplus of the Erythraean Sea*. It describes ports and passages down the Red Sea and out to the western Indian Ocean. I use the translation by W H Schoff 1912.
29   Peretti *The First Portulan/Il Periplo di Scilace*

none of Herodotus' contemplation of different cultures and few interesting
asides about the places Skylax mentions. In this sense it matches the dull and
workmanlike prose of Admiralty Pilots and resembles them in a prototypic
way.

Portolans

Portolans, from the Italian *portolano*, meaning literally a collection or book of
sailing directions, a sailing pilot, first appeared sometime in the 14th century.
The importance of these early portolans has never been in doubt and they
are considered to be the forerunners of modern cartography in Europe. They
have been described as '...a unique achievement not only in the history of
navigation but in the history of civilization itself.'[30] These sailing directions,
complete with plans of islands, approaches to anchorages and harbours, and

Chart of the Black Sea and eastern Mediterranean from the *Cornaro Atlas* 1492.
British Library Digital Collection.

30   Tony Campbell *Portolan Charts from the Late Thirteenth Century to 1500* in *The History of
Cartography* Vol I, Harley & Woodward, University of Chicago Press 1981 p 371

detail of harbours along the way, were not for contemplation in libraries and monasteries, but were tools of the trade for craft working around the coasts and islands of the Mediterranean. For the captains and navigators on trading ships, portolans were essential aids, enabling them to navigate cargoes from one place to another as quickly and safely as possible.

As working tools, the portolans were a great deal more accurate than many earlier cosmographical maps. While the captain and crew may have prayed to this or that saint during bad weather or in calms, the portolans were gradually stripped of these saints and became more orientated to navigation details.[31] The portolans were also the most prized item a navigator had and as such were kept close at all times. If they were sold, they would have fetched a considerable price. Such was the value of the information in them that in the early 15th century the Portuguese under Prince Henry the Navigator and King Manuel decreed the death sentence for anyone betraying navigational information, principally charts and portolans, to other nations.[32]

Like modern pilots, they were no doubt annotated by the navigator to update them with new information discovered along the way and the plans modified with any new information obtained by the navigator. How this was done is obscure, though it is likely trusted scribes on the land were given the task. Few of the portolans that were around at this period survive and those that do were likely library copies or kept by the state. Most of them were hand-drawn and handwritten on vellum which was often re-purposed for other manuscripts, and so the original was lost. Still, the surviving copies show some quite incredible detail and even in the first known portolan, the *Carte Pisane* from around 1300, the shape and detail for the Mediterranean is surprisingly accurate.[33] Through the evolution of portolans over the next few centuries detail is added and the shape of the coastline and islands is changed so that the shape and dimensions are more accurate.

The portolans utilised rhumb lines to guide navigators. The eight cardinal points of the compass are used, indicating that the use of the compass for navigation was widespread by this time. Given rhumb lines to sail along to get to a destination, the Medieval navigator would use dead reckoning techniques

31   Campbell *Portolan Charts* pp 371–372
32   George Weissala *Contours of a Discipline European Studies in Asia* Routledge 2014 p 49
33   Campbell *Portolan Charts* p 380

to estimate position.[34] They may have had a simple Dutchman's log, a piece of wood tied to a long cord that was dropped overboard and timed over the length of the ship which, with an egg-timer or the simple expedient of counting seconds slowly, would give the speed of the craft. The sailor in tune with his craft can often guess the speed of a boat from its motion through the water.[35] With the portolan and a map of the sea area they could measure off their progress from one place to another.

The portolans also gave details of conspicuous objects on the shore like

Piri Reis' map of Europe and the Mediterranean in his *Kitab-i bahriye*. Wiki Commons.

castles and towers which could be ticked off on passage and sighted for the approach to a destination. This is navigation by the 'Mk 1 eyeball' that we still all use today. Sailors are also aware of the signs on the surface of the

34   The compass is generally thought to have been introduced from China in the 12th century, though the cardinal points of the compass were known much earlier. See Heikell *Sailing Ancient Seas* Appendix 5.
35   I sailed the diminutive *Roulette* from Britain to Greece without a log and could accurately guess its speed.

water indicating currents and possible dangers to navigation. Given you can often clearly see the bottom at ten metres in the Mediterranean, a lookout forward watching for dangers and shallows would be normal procedure to warn of reefs and shoal water.

Apart from the use of portolans and these new navigation techniques by ships engaged in commercial trade, the various nation states around the shores of the Mediterranean also had an interest in aids to navigation for their navies, none more so than the Ottoman Empire. In the early 16th century Piri Reis drew a chart of the world. He is best known for the portion of his chart showing the Atlantic; sadly

Segment of the Piri Reis' world map. Wiki Commons.

the rest of the chart has been lost, but from his notes we know it covered the Mediterranean and the Indian Ocean around to China.[36] Though the Piri Reis map is celebrated and also attracts a whole host of theories about extraterrestrial visitors or an early super-race who mapped the world before European cartographers,[37] it is Piri Reis' portolan, the *Kitab-i bahriye* (*Book of maritime matters*), that is most interesting. Like the Genoese and Pisan portolans and others, this shows in detail the Mediterranean with rhumb lines and plans of harbours and anchorages along with pilotage notes. The introduction to the *Kitabi* has detailed notes on navigation techniques and general advice on things like weather and currents, dealing with storms, the compass, the use of portolan charts and astronomical navigation. Various versions of the *Kitabi* have survived and it seems to have been much copied for the Ottoman fleet.

36   Svat Soucek *Islamic Charting in the Mediterranean* in *The History of Cartography* Vol II, Harley & Woodward, University of Chicago Press 1986 p 265 ff.
37   One of the first books on the Piri Reis map and a supposed super-race was Charles H. Hapgood's *Maps of the Ancient Sea Gods* Turnstone Books 1969/1979.

There is one other feature of the portolan maps that made them so successful. In order to have a rhumb line that works you need a map projection like the Mercator projection. Portolans did not have lines of latitude and yet they had a projection very close to a Mercator projection where the lines of latitude become increasingly further apart as you moved from the equator to the poles.[38] The Mercator projection with lines of latitude first appeared in 1569 and was soon adopted for marine charts. From the 17th century onwards marine charts became increasingly more sophisticated, with symbols used to depict things like suitable anchorages, churches and mosques on the shore, sandbanks, submerged rocks and reefs, and of course depths.

Paradoxically sailing directions contained pretty much the same sort of information over centuries. The sort of information I essayed in my early pilotage information for yachts was not so very different to that in portolans and the like: conspicuous objects in the approaches; dangers in the approaches, especially underwater rocks and reefs; depths and in particular shallows in a harbour or anchorage; where to berth or anchor; wind patterns and anomalies; and what to expect ashore. While these days we don't usually have to include information about whether the locals are friendly or not and where good drinking water can be found, most of the other information pertaining to pilotage has remained remarkably similar over centuries.

In the 19th century the concept of written sailing directions and charts or maps of the area being described in the same volume fell out of favour and in Britain the Admiralty published sheets of charts, including harbour plans, and volumes of written sailing directions containing only text and tables. This segmentation of charts and text by hydrographic departments would survive into the next century and into the 21st century. Paradoxically it was the yachtsman's pilot that carried on the conventions of the portolans and once again united charts and text.

Yachting Guides in the 20th century

Captain Henry Denham

At the age of sixteen H. M. Denham was on board HMS *Agamemnon* in the Dardanelles where he served as midshipman. Despite the disaster that was

38   Campbell *Portolan Charts* p 385

Gallipoli, the Mediterranean must have burrowed its way into Denham's being and when he retired from the navy in 1947, he sailed down to the Mediterranean and spent much of his time sailing there. He based his yacht, a beautiful 45-ft yawl called *Herald*[39] in Malta and every year set off to explore the eastern Mediterranean and research his series of cruising guides for yachts.

H. M. Denham was following a family tradition when he engaged himself to survey and write yachting pilots for the Mediterranean. He was named after his grandfather, Vice Admiral Henry Mangles Denham, who spent much of his career in the navy doing hydrographic research in different parts of the world, finally

H. M. Denham's yacht *Herald*. Photo on dust jacket of *Southern Turkey, the Levant and Cyprus*.

ending up as commander-in-chief of the Pacific Station.[40] After serving in the Dardanelles, Denham suffered damage to his ears from gunfire and consequently had shore jobs for most of his career, often as naval attaché in various countries, so it was not surprising that on his retirement he decided to combine his love of yachting and of the Mediterranean.[41]

His first book, *The Aegean*, was published in 1963, closely followed by *The Adriatic* in 1967, *The Tyrrhenian* in 1969, *The Ionian Islands to Rhodes* in 1972 and *Southern Turkey, the Levant and Cyprus* in 1973.[42] Some of the guides, like *The Aegean*, went into five editions. Denham's books were in many ways a throwback to the portolan style with added historical interest. Like many of his generation he had a wide education that pulled in the classics so that he was familiar with the ancient sites dotted around the coast and included brief details on them. Although the books were aimed at cruising yachtsmen, they contained much else besides.

---

39   The LOA is a guess on my part from a photo of *Herald*.
40   en.wikipedia.org/wiki/Henry_Mangles_Denham
41   Obituary in *The Independent* 23rd July 1993.
42   All his books were published by John Murray in London.

Beautifully presented with excellent and eloquent plans, photographs and sketches. In its own realms, Denham's Aegean is the best book since Homer. If you are to sail in the Aegean you must take this book with you; if you cannot sail in the Aegean you should read it at home, and in a trice you'll be there.

Lloyds List review

Denham's books were much loved by those cruising the eastern Mediterranean because they served as a general introduction to the culture and history of an area. Denham was also interested in the different types of local boat that sailed these seas and early editions of his books detailed the types of local boats you might see around the coast. In later editions he lamented the loss of these local sailing craft and removed the appendix relating to

Early edition of *The Eastern Medditeranean* by H. M. Denham.

different hull and rig types in the eastern Mediterranean. He also lamented the increase in tourists arriving in what were once lonely anchorages reachable only by yacht, and in his time in the Mediterranean between the Great War and later in the era after the Second World War, he must have seen huge changes in the populations and infrastructure in the countries he visited.

Denham decided to give up sailing when he fell from the mast of his yacht in a storm, saying '…that he must put an end to it; he did not believe it right to sail unless you could do so single-handed'.[43] His books might appear a little old-fashioned to some today, but they are emblematic of an era where the object of cruising was not just to find your way into a harbour and go ashore for a drink, but to explore interesting places and learn something about the culture and the people ashore. I have them all.

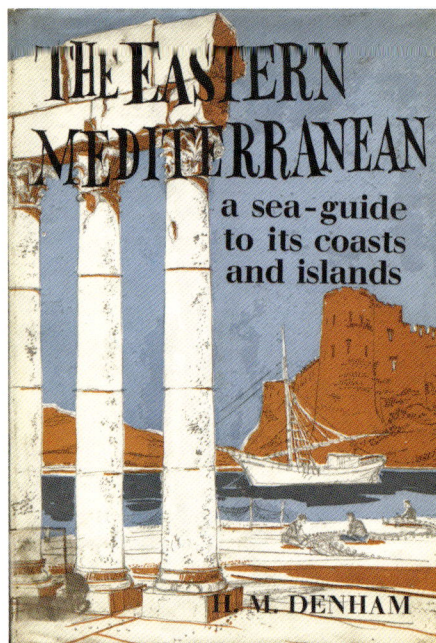

43   Quoted in his obituary in *The Independent* 23rd July 1993.

Philip Bristow

Philip Bristow was a prolific author who wrote a wide variety of books on matters nautical and is probably best remembered for *Bristow's Book of Yachts*, first published in 1963, which detailed production yachts down through the years and went into many editions. He also wrote a whole series of books on European waterways and his *Through the French Canals* is still in print, though not under the stewardship of Bristow.[44] In the early 1970's Bristow wrote a series of guides under the general title of *Mediterranean Harbours and Anchorages* describing the coasts of France, Italy and Spain.

These guides, illustrated with Admiralty plans and the occasional sketch plan, were very different beasts from Denham's guides with their sketch plans and pilotage details that somehow seemed more intimately experiential and more in tune with a place. Bristow's guides more resembled a catalogue of harbours along the coast which, while helpful, lacked the sense of place that was so evident in Denham's guides. While his series on European waterways went into several editions, his Mediterranean harbour guides were soon dropped with the appearance of the guides by Robin Brandon.

Robin Brandon and the RCC

When Robin Brandon retired from the army, he turned to writing yachtsman's pilots, starting in the south of England and proceeding down the Atlantic coast to the Mediterranean. He settled in the south of France and here he wrote the pilots he was best known for, on France and Spain, that have now been taken over by the Royal Cruising Club Pilotage Foundation. The pilots were initially loose-leaf affairs, which Brandon hoped would make updating them a simple affair of substituting sheets for any entries that required extensive corrections. Later editions reverted to normal, bound hardback books.

In exemplary army fashion the books were exhaustive and covered numerous volumes for France and Spain.[45] When the RCC took over Brandon's books they were gradually consolidated so that Spain had two volumes, one for the Balearics and one for the mainland coast, while for France only the volume on

---

44 David Jefferson *Through the French Canals* Adlard Coles Nautical 13th ed. 2014.
45 Mediterranean Spain and France eventually settled down into three hardbacks each for the two countries.

Corsica was maintained. Numerous authors from the RCC edited the books and they are still around today.

The RCC Pilotage Fund began in 1976 with a gift to the RCC by one of its American members, Dr Fred Ellis, who wished to commemorate his father and a number of other RCC members. A charity, the RCC Pilotage Fund, was formed and has gone from strength to strength in its objectives '...to advance the education of the public in the science and practice of navigation.'[46] The Pilotage Fund predominantly uses Imray to publish its books and also produces a number of short-run publications and e-books for cruising areas off the beaten track. For new editions, members cruising in an area volunteer their services and the appointed authors/editors get down to collating the information that has come in from their members.

Writing yachting guides – the inside view[47]

Like all good things that happen to us, it was an accident I started writing pilots for the Mediterranean. It began in 1978 when I was skippering a flotilla around the Saronic and eastern Peloponnese in Greece. On the first flotilla I had to take my little fleet around to harbours and anchorages I had never been to. Giving the morning briefing was a nightmare. From the old fathoms charts I gleaned enough information to suggest courses, bearings, dangers to navigation to be avoided and then announced I would definitely be in the harbour or anchorage I had never been to. The little engine on the Cobra 850 lead boat was red-lined so I could get in first and assume a pseudo-knowledgeable insouciance on the quay as I helped the flotilla to berth.

If I was a bit confused, I figured the charterers would be to, so I set to work writing a booklet with plans of the harbours, pilotage instructions and a bit on what to do and see ashore. An introduction detailed important stuff like how to operate the toilets and what not to put down them, basic engine checks, reefing the main and roller-reefing genoa, as well as important things like a bit on Greek cuisine and the history and culture of the region. The charter company had the booklets printed up and so began all those decades of my nerdy writing of these guides.

46   Quoted on the RCCPF web page https://rccpf.org.uk/About-Us.
47   Much of this section previously appeared as *How to Write a Pilot Book* in Marine Quarterly, Autumn 2014.

After several years working for the charter company I decided that I should write a yachtsman's cruising guide for Greece as an interesting diversion for a year or so before returning to life in New Zealand. Forty years later and I still haven't got back to life in NZ and the odds are stacked against it ever happening.

Starting out, I had no real training for surveying harbours. I taught myself the basics of triangulation to survey a harbour in the old-fashioned way with a hand-bearing compass and transits on known objects. Remember this was nearly forty years ago, so no GPS, no hand-held depth sounders, no laser distance measurer, and no CAD drawing programmes on your laptop or in the publisher's drawing department.

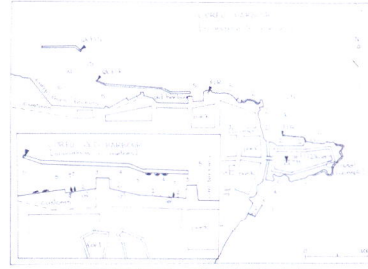

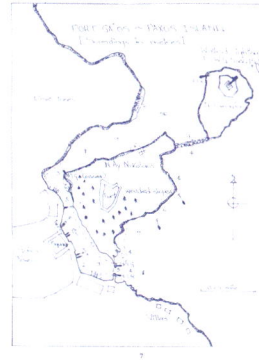

I set to work writing a booklet with plans of the harbours, pilotage instructions and a bit on what to do and see ashore. Early plans in the Ionian.

A bit of historical research soon flashed up some early surveyors who are still my heroes. Captain Graves and his able surveying lieutenant Spratt surveyed much of the eastern Mediterranean in the early 19th century on HMS *Beacon*. Even earlier, at the beginning of the 19th century, Beaufort, that same Beaufort of the wind scale, surveyed parts of Anatolia. As a consequence of being shipwrecked at age fifteen due to a faulty sea chart and in peril of starvation, Beaufort became obsessed with the importance of education and the development of accurate charts for those risking their lives at sea. When he was made hydrographer of the British Admiralty, he set

Francis Beaufort from a daguerreotype 1848.

about systematically getting parts of the world surveyed, converting the small collection of Admiralty charts into a folio covering most of the world.[48]

Prior to this era the principal chart maker was Imray, their Blueback charts being used by most merchant ships as well as the Royal Navy until the expansion of the hydrographic department by Beaufort. That same Imray became the publisher of most of my pilots.[49]

The thing that caught my imagination with these early surveyors – Graves, Spratt, Beaufort and a whole roll-call of others – is that they were Renaissance men. Not just versed in things nautical, but passionately interested in the history, natural history, culture, botany and geology of the places they visited. Of course, some of them were tyrants as well and at least one of them, Viscount Corry, was damned, literally, by his mapmakers art. On the island of Limnos in the northern Aegean there are a series of peaks around the natural harbour of Moudhros that are named: Yam, Yrroc, Eb and Denmad. Read backwards it tells you what the midshipmen and the sailors surveying the area under Viscount Corry thought of him: 'May Corry Be Damned'. Occasionally I get complaints that my pilots shouldn't stray into the history, geography and culture of the countries I cover and I always think back to these British adventurers exploring the landscape like eager kids on a treasure hunt. It is a long way to go just to go sailing in the Mediterranean without any knowledge of the place and a sense of where you are.

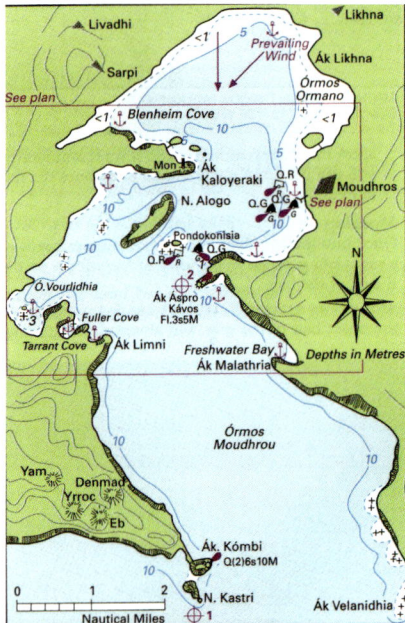

MOUDHROS - HARBOUR AND ANCHORAGES
⊕₁ 39°47'·13N 25°14'·17E WGS84
⊕₂ 39°51'·01N 25°13'·70E WGS84

You can be remembered for the wrong reasons. In the 19th century Commander Corry drove his surveying crews too hard, so they named four hills in the approaches to Moudhros on the Greek island of Limnos after him.

48   G. S. Ritchie *The Admiralty Chart* Pentland Press 1967/1995, Chapter 11.
49   Susanna Fisher *The Makers of the Blueback Charts* Regatta Press 2001

One thing those 19th century surveyors had was manpower. Typically, a couple of oared cutters, lead line, a midshipman and maybe a surveying officer in charge, if you could get him away from roaming around the countryside collecting ancient bric-a-brac and botanical specimens, would put out every day to survey a coast. Midshipman and mate would be taking sextant sights, for lat and long and elevation. I doubt many of us take sights anymore and even fewer in anger. I gave away my Tamaya computer that calculated sights in 1997. With air reduction tables you were lucky to get within a mile. These 19th century surveyors worked their sights using trigonometry and cosine tables where if you are good, very good, you might get an accuracy of 1/10th of a nautical mile. A lot of the time you might be lucky to get 2 cables or 0.2 NM.

So it was that, with hand-bearing compass, lead line (including a nylon fishing line knotted at half metre intervals and a decorative hook on the end), and of course camera and notepad, I sailed around Greece drawing harbours and anchorages. In a harbour or anchorage, I would find an elevated vantage point and make a rough sketch. At first these were not that accurate when checked by taking one point on the sketch and using bearings with a hand bearing compass to triangulate salient points of a harbour or bay; a bit like taking a cocked hat except salient points were 'moved' to conform to a bearing. Then I moved to another spot and continued the process until I got it right and the shape of the harbour or bay was as accurate as I could get it.

Depths were obtained using the depth-sounder in the boat or a lead line and positioned from transits within the sketch or simply in the corner or halfway along a quay or breakwater. Later I got my eye in and the sketches were a lot more accurate, but still checked with basic triangulation. And I got quite good at stepping out lengths and adjusting my stride to be a metre. Though what the locals would make of me striding up the quay mumbling numbers to myself I'm not sure. Still, in the Mediterranean there has always been a tradition of looking after the village fool as some sort of idiot savant.

In the early days I was obviously a spy. In Greece I was arrested four times, in Turkey twice, but I lied a lot to some very nice policemen about being an innocent tourist who liked to fish, (hence the nylon fishing line for depths). I soon learnt the Greek for a spy: *katascopos*. For much of this voyage around the archipelago I was on my own, sailing by day and heaving the dinghy into the water to sound a harbour or anchorage when I got to the next destination.

Things got tricky a few times. In Plomarion on Lesvos the situation got a bit sticky and I was thankful that for once I had crew. Dietrich, a German sailor I had met earlier in the year, came to my aid. After being trundled off on the back of a moped to the port police office (if I had been a spy I would have just bashed him on the head and escaped) and then held for several hours with phone calls to Athens and intimations of jail because I was obviously a Turkish spy, Dietrich, who had been off wandering around town, came to the police station to report me missing. I hadn't ever asked what he did, but it turned out he was an undercover policeman in Germany and he had a magic little police ID card with him. The day was saved, it was coffee and *cognaki* all round, and I survived to survey yet another harbour.

In Alexandroupolis near the border with Turkey I was woken at three in the morning by bright lights and someone banging on the boat. Two police cars and a van full of customs officers were parked in front of the boat with their headlights on. Several of the police and customs officers came on board and questioned me over what I was doing there. Mouthing 'tourism' late in the season with just me on board didn't sound convincing. They searched the boat, stripping the lockers of everything, and looked mystified when they found nothing. Luckily all my sketch plans were in the chart table where they neglected to look. On other encounters my passport was confiscated, the boat searched from top to bottom, and I was taken to the police station to be questioned.

For the first book, *Greek Waters Pilot,* I hadn't really looked at the coastline of Greece before I set out. If I had bothered to unravel the indented coastline of all those islands and the mainland and understood the huge extent of coastline this represented, I would have thought again. But after I'd signed the contract with Imray there were all those daunting legal clauses amounting to: 'major revisions will be at the expense of the author'; and 'manuscript not with the publishers

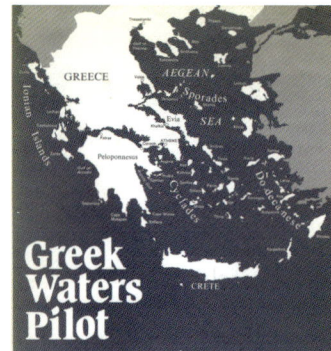

First edition of *Greek Waters Pilot* 1982.

at the date below then the author shall be liable for all expenses and the contract will be void', sort of stuff.

So, I spent one and a half seasons in Greece, adding to the knowledge I already had, sailing mostly alone and sitting up through the night typing. Oh yes, those were the days of typewriters and carbon copies and gallons of *Tippex*. I ended up with plans and pilotage notes and a very pruned down history and geography. At least I didn't suffer like those 19th century surveyors. Beaufort nearly died from a musket ball wound at Ayas in the Gulf of Iskenderun. Spratt nearly died of malaria or dysentery on one of his jaunts inland in the Aegean.

So now I have a portable depth sounder, a laser measuring device and a hand-held GPS to create reference points, but still use the lead-line or my trusty fishing line with metre and half-metre knots in it. It may surprise some that we still draw the plans by hand. These days we can do that a lot quicker than trying to draw it on a laptop, and in any case a pad and pencil is an awful lot easier to use in the dinghy when surveying a place than the laptop or tablet. After we have drawn the plans, they go to Imray's to be scanned and turned into a digital version with text and figures, contour lines and coloured depths and land, icons and features in a neat style now much removed from those early sketch plans in the first editions. It's still a nerdy, funny old business and I do feel like a bit of a dinosaur, but then the chuckle of water on the hull and the scratch of pencil on notepad pulls my gaze away and back to the sea.

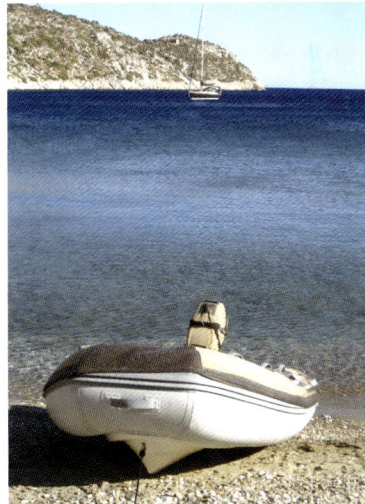

It may surprise some that we still draw the plans by hand – it is quicker than using a tablet and tablets don't much like sitting in a puddle in the bottom of a dinghy.

The Digital Age

Digital wizardry has transformed the way we navigate. Now we watch the boat gliding over an electronic chart on the multi-function display at the helm, we touch the screen and bring up information from the radar or AIS,[50] we get read-outs of our course and speed over the ground and zoom in or out on the chart, our eyes flicker up to take in the digital read-outs of speed and depth, we know our position and the estimated time to a destination. All of this is relatively new and, in my lifetime, navigation has gone from old-fashioned techniques of dead reckoning, fixes on terrestrial objects and an approximate lat and long from astronomical sights to digital displays that instantly tell the navigator what is going on.

I'm not going to dwell on the ins and outs of all these advances in the way modern electronics have transformed the way we do things. That would entail a book in itself. But I do want to dwell on some of the shortcomings that can lead to disaster when relying solely on electronic devices on board. One thing that does concern me in this age of chart plotters, GPS and people who trot out and buy a new yacht when they have hardly been sailing at all is the decline in seamanship and pilotage on our seas. There is a good reason that chart plotters and other devices come up with a warning to the effect that: 'These charts are an aid to navigation and should not be used as the primary source of navigation.' Navionics, one of the main players in electronic cartography, have this to say:

The principles of prudent navigation imply that skippers understand that electronic charts are an aid to navigation to be used in addition to official charts and multiple sources of information, including sailing directions, cruising guides, radar, sonar and most importantly, common sense and good eyesight.

www.navionics.com/usa/blog/post/proper-use-of-electronic-charts/

One of the principal problems with electronic charts is that they are not new surveys. With GPS and other satellite positioning systems we know what our position is to within around five metres or less on the earth's surface. What we do not have are charts of the earth's surface which are accurate to within five metres. Most of the charts we use were surveyed in the 19th century using celestial methods to determine latitude and longitude. Given the difficulties that many charts were surveyed under including bad weather conditions and hostile natives ashore, with just leadlines and sextants for equipment, the resulting charts are amazingly accurate. Many of them are beautifully detailed

---

50   Automatic Identification System that relays signals from ships and yachts giving position, speed and proximity to a boat.

affairs and, given the difficulties of standing in a small pinnace and taking sights to determine position, they are a tribute to the men who made them.

When surveying a chart there is the whole conundrum of datum points. A geodetic datum point is needed to establish just where you are on the ellipsoid surface of the globe. Every survey has to have a geodetic datum point and in the 19th century datum points for areas like the Mediterranean were not well established. Even longitude zero at Greenwich was not universally accepted until 1884. For many of these early charts the datum point is obscure and, in some cases, not known at all so the datum shift can vary: anything from a few hundred metres to miles in remote regions.

The charts could not possibly be consistently accurate compared to the repeatable accuracy of modern position finding equipment and so it is not surprising that in some areas there are errors of up to one nautical mile and more. The basis of the charts we use in the Mediterranean (and elsewhere) are these 19th century surveys. That includes all those lovely charts on our chart plotters and navigation software running on laptops and tablets. If you look at the attribution on any modern chart you will find that much of the survey is from quite old surveys and only commercial ports and channels will have been relatively recently surveyed. Although datum points have been matched as best they can, there are still considerable errors in latitude and longitude, mostly the latter.

What does this mean? It means we have an anomaly here wherein we have a satellite location system (GPS, Russian GLONASS, Chinese COMPASS and the soon-to-be Galileo) that can give a position to within plus or minus five metres or better, but we do not have charts accurate enough to plot that position on. That is why you will frequently find on your plotter that the position of the boat at anchor is halfway up a mountain, or that you really needed wheels where your track apparently crosses a headland or cape. It also accounts for those yachts that pile up on reefs and rocks that are clearly charted, just not in quite the right place on the earth's surface on the plotter display.

The appearance of certainty using modern electronic instruments and especially electronic charts belies the nature of navigating a small boat at sea. Before the advent of GPS, of electronic plotters, of sophisticated radar and reliable instruments, it was common-place to spend long periods of time familiarising yourself with the patch of water you were going to sail across. Mostly this involved sitting down with paper charts and pilots and going over the overall passage plan intended and over the tricky bits. The tricky bits mostly have to do with the hard bits along the way and the approaches to them.

This is a lot more than having a look at Google maps and putting a waypoint into the chart-plotter. It is a matter of forming a mental map of the passage, of the destination and of alternatives if things go wrong. That old-fashioned phrase, a 'port of refuge', springs to mind where, if for any reason you cannot get to or into your planned destination, you have somewhere else in mind. Researching where you are going to and how you are going to get there is a whole adventure in itself and it lays the basis for a more relaxed and enjoyable passage. That doesn't mean you aren't going to worry about stuff on passage, just that you have better knowledge of what to do and how to carry it out.

In our digital age the other major change to how we go sailing in the Mediterranean is the advances in communications. In the old days you could place a call using *jetons* from a landline or send text messages by telex. In the age of the smartphone and tablets connected to mobile signals that cover most parts of the Mediterranean coast and islands, people expect to constantly be in touch. You can often get phone signals thirty or so miles out to sea and given that a lot of the cruising in the Mediterranean is coastal, all you need is a mobile phone to be in contact with the outside world.

While phoning home from your yacht might seem miraculous when compared to the days of putting *jetons* in a public pay phone, even more astonishing is the ability to access the internet via a smartphone or tablet or by Wi-Fi from a café or restaurant or boatyard. The interconnected world brings the virtual world on board and using mobile data or Wi-Fi you can access weather forecasts from different agencies, phone home on Voice over Internet Protocol (VoIP), get the news, and even stream live video. Such is the pace of mobile communications that it is impossible to forecast how the future will affect the way we sail around the oceans of the world and just how future advances will change what we do at sea.

Or will it? I'm no Luddite and I welcome and use modern communications on board – to a point. In many ways we can be bombarded with too much information and getting a weather forecast can result in confusion over what might happen from computer generated GRIB files when different models throw up different wind speeds and direction.[51] It can result in confusion over pilotage information when opinions vary over how safe a harbour is and whether you can get a berth there. On social media it certainly results in acrimony over perceived insults and some trolling by bottom-dwelling internet users. It seems that some cruising sailors worry more about the loss of an internet connection than about the weather.

This is not the place to analyse the effects of technology on our everyday life – that would take a large volume in itself and I suspect most of us have a nagging worry about the subject anyway.[52] Like many debates it is often broken down into some Manichean debate about good and evil when in truth it is a lot more complex and embraces both sides of the argument. It is both good and evil.

From my perspective, after travelling through time for this history I can't help but feel a certain loss. Sailing off used to be seen as an escape from the drudgery of the everyday into a simpler life more in tune with the elements. That may sound like sloppy romanticism, and in a way it is. The denial of the romantic impulse is not a loss any of us should put up with. Before passages, before gunk-holing and pottering, I get the relevant charts out and let my eyes wander over the sea and land on my planned route. Where are the possible ports of refuge if things go wrong? Will I cross any shoal areas where bad weather could produce confused seas? How far off do I need to be to avoid that reef? And just as important, what does the land look like? What things will I see along the way and what do I know about them? And are there dragons here? It's romance, and we need to keep hold of that magic and not reduce what we do to some technical exercise.

---

51   For a good explanation of GRIB files and how they work see http://weather.mailasail.com/Franks-Weather/Grib-Files-Explained.
52   I'd suggest Nicholas Carr's *The Shallows: How the Internet is Changing the Way We Think, Read and Remember* Atlantic Books 2010 and Sherry Turkle's *Alone Together* Basic Books 2011.

'There be magic out there.'

BIBLIOGRAPHY

ABCMallorca www.abc-mallorca.com 18/06/2018

Abulafia, David *The Great Sea: A Human History of the Mediterranean* Penguin 2014

ACI Marinas Croatia www.aci-marinas.com/en/povijest/

Adrian, Jack *Obituary to Hammond Innes* Independent Saturday 13 June 1998

Afetinan, A. *Life and Works of Piri Reis* Turkish Historical Association 1975

Alberge, Dalya *Nile Shipwreck Discovery Proves Herodotus Right – After 2649 Years* Guardian March 19 2019

Alexander, W.D. *The Story of Cleopatra's Barge* Papers of the Hawaiian Historical Society No. 13 1906.

Anderson, Isabel *A Yacht in Mediterranean Seas* Marshall Jones Co 1930

Anderson J. R. L. *The Ulysses Factor* Hodder & Stoughton 1970

Apostolos, Delis *Mediterranean wooden shipbuilding in the nineteenth century* Cahiers de Mediterranee 84 2012

Atwood, Margaret *The Penelopiad* Canongate 2006

Bass G.F. (Ed.) *A History of Seafaring: Based on Underwater Archaeology* Omega 1972

BBC *Migrant crisis: EU-Turkey deal comes into effect* www.bbc.co.uk/news/world-europe-35854413 20 March 2016

BBC World Service *Remembering Maupassant* www.bbc.co.uk/worldservice/arts/highlights/000808_maupassant.shtmll

Beaumont, Peter *Greek shipyards kept afloat by luxury yachts for the super-rich* The Guardian Thursday 4 August 2011

Bender, Mike *A New History of Yachting* Boydell Press 2017

Bernières, Louis de *Captain Corelli's Mandolin* Vintage 1994

Boat International www.boatinternational.com/charter/luxury-yacht-charter-advice/charter-costs-explained--1753

Boat International www.boatinternational.com/yachts/news/106m-sailing-yacht-black-pearl-delivered-by-oceanco--31765

Boats.com www.boats.com/resources/peer-to-peer-boat-rentals-a-brave-new-world/.

Bradford, Ernle *The Journeying Moon* Grafton Books 1958/1987

Bradford, Ernle *The Wind Off the Island* Hutchinson 1960

Bradford, Ernle *Ulysses Found* Sphere Books 1963

Bradford, Ernle *The Mediterranean: Portrait of a Sea* Harcourt Brace Jovanovich 1971

Braudel, Fernand *The Mediterranean and the Mediterranean World in the Age of Philip II* BCA 1949/1992.

Bristow, Philip *Down the Spanish Coast* Nautical 1973

Bristow, Philip *French Mediterranean Harbours* Nautical 1974

Bristow, Philip *Round the Italian Coast* Nautical 1975

Brookes, Douglas S. *The Turkish Imperial State Barges* The Mariner's Mirror Vol 76 1990

Brotton, Jerry *A History of the World in Twelve Maps* Penguin 2012

Cappato Alberto [FEMIP paper] *Cruises and Recreational Boating in the Mediterranean* 2010

Cappato, Alberto [EU paper] *Cruises and Recreational Boating in the Mediterranean* Plan Bleu 2011

Carr, Nicholas *The Shallows: How the internet is changing the way we think, read and remember* Atlantic Books 2010

Carroll, Michael *The Gates of the Wind* Efstathiadis Group 1983

Casson, Lionel *Ships and Seamanship in the Ancient World* John Hopkins 1971

Cavafy, C.P. *Collected Poems*. Transl. Edmund Keeley and Philip Sherrard. Ed. George Savidis. Princeton University Press, 1992

Cavan, Earl of [Frederick Edward Gould Lambart] *With the Yacht, Camera, and Cycle in the Mediterranean* Sampson Low, Marston & Co 1895

Chatwin, Bruce *Songlines* Jonathon Cape 1987

Chen, J.M., Balomenou, C., Nijkamp, P. Poulaki, P., Lagos, D. *The Sustainability of Yachting Tourism: A Case Study on Greece* International Journal of Research in Tourism and Hospitality (IJRTH) Vol. 2, Issue 2, 2016

Chiles, Webb *The Ocean Waits* Norton 1984

Chiles, Webb *A Single Wave* Sheridan House 1999

Chiles ,Webb www.inthepresentsea.com/the_actual_site/webbchiles.html

Clarke, Lyndsey *The Return from Troy* Element 2007

Clarke-Lens, Steve www.youtube.com/watch?v=IuJ1gu2JotI

Club de Mar www.clubdemar-mallorca.com/home.php

Clyde Ships www.clydeships.co.uk/view.php?ref=15179

Composites World www.compositesworld.com/articles/megayacht-composite-masts-get-smart

Crace, John The Guardian archives May 2008

Crowninshield, Francis B. *The Story of George Crowninshield's Yacht Cleopatra's Barge. On a Voyage of Pleasure to the Western Islands and the Mediterranean 1816–1817*. Compiled from Journals, Letters and Logbooks by Francis B Crowninshield. Boston 1913 Hathi Foundation

Cruising Association www.theca.org.uk/home

Cunliffe, Barry *By Steppe, Desert, and Ocean: The Birth of Eurasia* OUP 2015

Cusack, Janet *Nineteenth-Century Cruising Yachtsmen in the Mediterranean* The Journal of Mediterranean Studies Vol. 10, No. 1/2 pp. 47–75

Daily Sabah www.dailysabah.com/turkey/2016/05/12/worlds-largest-schooner-being-built-in-mugla

Damianis, K. and Leontidis, T. *Greek Wooden Sailing Boats of the 20th Century* Gavrielides 1993

Denham, H. M. *The Aegean* John Murray 1963/1983

Denham, H. M. *The Eastern Mediterranean* John Murray 1964

Denham, H. M. *The Adriatic* John Murray 1967/1977

Denham, H. M. *The Tyrrhenian Sea* John Murray 1969/1978

Denham, H. M. *The Ionian Islands to Rhodes* John Murray 1972

Denham, H. M. *Southern Turkey, the Levant and Cyprus* John Murray 1973

Denham, H. M. *Dardanelles: A Midshipman's Diary* John Murray 1981

Dovkants, Keith *The Curse of Classic 63m Yacht Creole* Boat International 1 December 2015

Duck Design www.duckdesign.it/en/koniginii-2.html

Dumas, Alexandre *On Board the Emma* subtitled *Adventures with Garibaldi's 'Thousand' in Sicily* Transl. R. S. Garnett Fredonia Books 2002

Durham, Michael *Enigma of the Leader* The Guardian 9 June 2003

Duxbury, Ken *Lugworm Homeward* Bound Pelham Books 1975

Duxbury, Ken *Lugworm On the Loose* Pelham Books 1973

Dye, Frank *Ocean Crossing Wayfarer: To Iceland and Norway in a 16ft Open Dinghy* Adlard Coles Nautical 1977/2006

Eastern Mediterranean Yacht Rally www.emyr.org

ECAP 3.3 Plan Bleu paper prepared for the EU Tourism and Recreational Activities August 2015

EU RCD2 www.eucertification.com/ce-certification-2/rcd

Fawcett, N and Zietsman, J.C. *Uluburun – The Discovery and Excavation of the World's Oldest Known Shipwreck* Akroterion.journals.ac.za 2000.

Feifer, Maxine *Going Places* MacMillan 1985

Ferretti-Bocquillon Marina *Signac 1863–1935* The Metropolitan Museum of Art: Yale University Press 2001

Fisher, Susanna *The Makers of the Blueback Charts* Regatta Press 2001

Foot M.R.D. *Obituary George Millar* The Independent 26 March 2005

Forbes Magazine 2018 billionaires list: www.forbes.com/billionaires/list/2/#version:static_country:Russia

Fortescue, Sam *Supersail Supplement* Yachting World October 2018

France Today www.francetoday.com/archives/inventing-the-riviera/

Freer, Chris *Twelve Metre Yacht: Evolution and Design 1906–1987* Adlard Coles Nautical 1986

Gamm, Niki *Ottomans sail in style on the Bosphorus* Hurriyet 21 January 21 2012

Gamm, Niki *Sailing by the moon on the Ottoman Bosphorus* Hurriyet 23 August 2014

Geankoplis, Chris *The Story of the Vayu* Unpublished manuscript from the log of the Vayu

Get My Boat www.boats.com/resources/peer-to-peer-boat-rentals-a-brave-new-world/

Golden Globe Race https://goldengloberace.com/ggr/

Gollan, Doug *The Superyacht Industry is Poised for Growth* Forbes Magazine 13 April 2016

Gordon, Sophie, *Badr El Hage Cities, Citadels, and Sights of the Near East* American University in Cairo Press 2014

Graeme, J.C. *My Name is No One* Taniwha Press 2016

Graeme, J.C. *To Ithaca* Taniwha Press 2016

Grıd Arendal www.grida.no/resources/5900

Grosvenor, E.M. *Narrative of a Yacht Voyage in the Mediterranean during the years 1840–1841* John Murray 1842

Gulersoy, Celik *The Caique* Istanbul Kitapligi 1991

Haggard, Rider *She: A History of Adventure* 1886/1887 2016 Oxford Classics

Hapgood, Charles H *Maps of the Ancient Sea Gods* Turnstone Books 1969/1979

Harlaftis, Gelina *Cornerstone of Greek Shipping: 100 Liberties* Ekathimerini 19 August 2012

Harley, J. B. and Woodward, D. *The History of Cartography* Vol. I University of Chicago Press 1981

Haworth, Abigail *The Gucci wife and the hitman: Fashions darkest tale* The Observer 24 July 2016

Hay, Daisy *Young Romantics: The Shelleys, Byron and Other Tangled Lives* Bloomsbury 2011

Haynes, Gavin *Why the super-rich are taking their mega-boats into uncharted waters* The Guardian 1 August 2018

Heaton, Peter *Yachting: A History* Batsford 1955

Heikell Rod *Greek Waters Pilot* Imray 1st edition 1982

Heikell Rod *Turkish Waters Pilot* Imray 1st edition 1984

Heikell Rod *The Danube: A River Guide* Imray 1991

Heikell Rod *Sailing in Paradise* Adlard Coles Nautical 2009

Heikell Rod *Mediterranean Cruising Handbook* Imray 2012

Heikell Rod *The Accidental Sailor* Taniwha Press 2013

Heikell Rod *Sailing Ancient Seas* Taniwha Press 2015

Heikell, Rod *Adlard Coles Book of Mediterranean Cruising* Bloomsbury 2018

Heikell, Rod & Lucinda *Turkish Waters & Cyprus Pilot* 9th/10th edition 2013/2018

Heikell, Rod & Lucinda *West Aegean* Imray 2014

Heikell, Rod & Lucinda *Italian Waters Pilot* Imray 2015

Heikell, Rod & Lucinda *Mediterranean France and Corsica* Imray 2015

Heikell, Rod & Lucinda *Ionian* Imray 2017

Heikell, Rod & Lucinda *Greek Waters Pilot* 13th ed. Imray 2018

Henley, Paul *Denmark's Tvind* BBC Crossing Continents 21 March 2002

Herodotus (Ed. B Strassler) *The Landmark Herodotus* Quercus 2008

Heyerdahl, Thor *The Ra Expeditions* George Allen & Unwin 1971

Heyerdahl, Thor *The Tigris Expedition: In Search of Our Beginnings* Flamingo 1993

Hiscock, Eric *Cruising Under Sail* A&C Black 1950/2002

Hiscock, Eric *Voyaging Under Sail* Oxford University Press 1959/1977

Hodges, Toby Yachting World March 2017

Hodges, Toby *Borrow Any Boat* Yachting World Dec 2018

Hoek Design www.hoekdesign.com/sailing-yachts/truly-classic

Holland, Tom *In the Shadow of the Sword: The Battle for Global Empire and the End of the Ancient World* Little Brown 2012

Holmes, Nancy *The Dream Boats* Prentice-Hall 1976

Homer (Transl. E.V. Rieu) *The Odyssey* Penguin 1946

Homer (Transl. E.V. Rieu) *Iliad* Penguin 1949

Hope, Katie *The city that makes the most expensive boats in the world* BBC, 24 July 2017

Horden, P. and Purcell, N. *The Corrupting Sea: A Study of Mediterranean History* Blackwell 2005

Howarth David *The Greek Adventure* Collins 1976

Howarth, F. & M. *Fleurtje* Boat International February 2018

Howarth, Patrick *When the Riviera Was Ours* Century 1977

Inalcik, Halil *The Ottoman Empire: The Classical Age 1300–1600* Phoenix 1973/2003

Independent www.independent.co.uk/news/world/europe/venetian-dream-boat-ship-of-fools-sails-again-801237.html

Innes, Hammond *Sea and Islands* Collins 1967

Innes, Hammond *Levkas Man* Collins 1971

Islander *The Gucci's Creole* //theislander.net/gucci-s-creole/

Italian Event Planners https://www.italianeventplanners.com/blog/that-s-italia/item/262-historical-reenactment-that-features-colourful-16th-century-boats.html

Jacob, Getrude L. *The Raja of Sarawak: An Account of Sir James Brooke K.C.B. LLD. Given Chiefly Through Letters and Journals* MacMillan 1876.
Jakeways, Mike *From the Deck of Your Own Yacht* FloMo Publishing 2009
Jeanneau www.jeanneau.com/en-gb/jeanneau/history/
Jefferson, David *Through the French Canals* Adlard Coles Nautical 13th ed. 2014
Jenkins, Nancy *The Boat Beneath the Pyramid* Thames and Hudson, 1980
John, Noble Wilford *The Mapmakers* Pimlico 1981
Johnson, Peter *Yacht Clubs of the World* Waterline Books 1994
Johnstone-Bryden, Richard *The Royal Sailing Yachts* (PDF paper)

Kasten, Michael www.kastenmarine.com/25m_schooner_royalist.htm
Kavin, Kim www.boats.com/on-the-water/when-is-a-boat-also-a-yacht/#
Kemp, Dixon *A Manual of Yacht and Boat Sailing* H. Cox 1895
Kemp, Dixon *A Manual of Yacht and Boat Sailing* 1895/2018 Forgotten Books.
Kemp, Peter *The Oxford Companion to Ships and the Sea* OUP 1976
Kinglake, A.W. *Eothen: or Traces of travel brought home from the East* Century 1844/1982
Kovačić, M. et al *The scenario method of nautical tourism development – a case study of Croatia* Scientific Journal of Maritime Research 29 2015

Le Monde December 1864 www.centrefernandleger.com/47.html.
Lean-Vercoe, Roger and Boulton, Peter *Iconic Yachts: Christina O* Boat International 14 January 2015
Leonhardt, David *Our Broken Economy* New York Times 7th August 2017
Lewis, David *We the Navigators: Ancient Art of Landfinding in the Pacific* University of Hawaii Press 1972/1994
Little Ship Club littleshipclub.co.uk/little-ship-club-history

MacPherson, A.G.H. (Ed. John Scott Hughes) *MacPherson's Voyages* Methuen & Co 1946
MacTaggart, Ross *The Golden Century: Classic Motor Yachts 1830–1930* W.W.Norton 2001
Mancini, Mauro *Navigare Lungocosta* Vols 1–6 Class Editori
Mancini, R.and Sens, A. *Blue Economy For the Mediterranean* EU paper for the Union For the Mediterranean 2017
Maupassant, Guy de *Afloat: A Journal of His Days at Sea* [Introduction by Marlo Johnston] Peter Owen 1995
McMullen, Richard Turrell *Down Channel* Horace Cox Printers revised 1893 edition
Met Office UK www.metoffice.gov.uk/climate-guide/climate-change
Millar, George *Isabel and the Sea* Century 1948/1983
Millar, George *A White Boat from England* Heinemann 1951
Minney, Penny *Crab's Odyssey* Taniwha Press 2016
Moitessier, Bernard *The Long Way* Sheridan House 1971/1995
Monaco Marine https://monacomarine.com/en/
Monfried, Henry de *Hashish: True Adventures of a Red Sea Smuggler in the Twenties* Penguin 1985
Morris, Jan *The Venetian Empire* Penguin 1980

NASA https://climate.nasa.gov/evidence/
Nastos, Karavana-Papadimou and Matsangouras *Tropical-like cyclones in the Mediterranean: Impacts and composite daily means and anomalies of synoptic conditions* Proceedings of the 14th International Conference on Environmental Science and Technology Rhodes, Greece, 3–5 September 2015
Nature Magazine www.nature.com/news/climate-change-could-flip-mediterranean-lands-to-desert-1.20894
Neate, Rupert *Booming global stock markets swell ranks of the super rich*
The Guardian 5 September 2018
Neate, Rupert *Hundreds join growing list of Britain's ultra-rich* The Guardian
18 October 2018
Nederhof, Marc-Jan and Blackman, A.M. *Transliteration and Translation for Papyrus Westcar* 1988/2008
Neilson, Barrie *Sailing Holidays: A Pictorial History of a Unique Company* Sailing Holidays 2014.
Neslen, Arthur *European parliament approves sweeping ban on single-use plastics* The Guardian 24 October 2018
Nespoli, Giovanni *Eutrophication of the Coastal Waters of the North Adriatic Sea* Wiley 1988
New York Times 17 March 1901 New York Times Archive

Nicholls, Peter *A Voyage For Madmen* Profile Books 2002
Nicolson, Adam *The Mighty Dead: Why Homer Matters* William Collins 2015

O'Connor, David *Boat Graves and Pyramid Origins* Penn University 2005

Parry, Major Gambier *Sketches of a Yachting Cruise* W H Allen 1889
Pausanias *Guide to Greece* Penguin 1979
Pemble, John *The Mediterranean Passion* OUP 1988
Peretti, Aurelio *The First Portulan/Il Periplo di Scilace* 1979.
Phillips-Birt, Douglas *The History of Yachting* Stein & Day 1974
Piante, Catherine and Ody, Denis *Blue Growth in the Mediterranean Sea: The Challenge of Good Environmental Status* WWF 2015 report
Piccinno, Luisa and Zanini, Andrea *The Development of Pleasure Boating and Yacht Harbours in the Mediterranean Sea: The Case of the Riviera* Ligure International Journal of Maritime History June 2010
Pitcher, T. J. and Lam, M. E *Fish commoditization and the historical origins of catching fish for profit* Maritime Studies 14:2 2015
Pliny the Younger *Litterae* VIII-20 To Gallus 1900 Transl. J. B. Firth www.attalus.org/old/pliny8.html
Plutarch *Lives* 1859 Transl. Dryden/Clough
Port, Phillip *Pioneers Group* http://www.portphillippioneersgroup.org.au
Prell, Donald B. *The Sinking of the 'Don Juan' Revisited* Keats-Shelley Journal Vol. 56 2007
Pulak, Cemal *The Uluburun Shipwreck and Late Bronze Age Trade* Paper Institute of Nautical Archaeology cgs.la.psu.edu/documents/Pulak2008Reading.pdf

Ransome, Arthur *Racundra's First Cruise* Century 1956/1984
Rare Historical Photos https://rarehistoricalphotos.com/caligula-nemi-ships-1932/
Reuters report www.rt.com/search?q=mussolinis+yacht.
Richardson, Dave *Lets Go: A History of Package Holidays and Escort Tours* Amberley 2016
Richardson, Mary *Sunbeam Ahoy* Andrew Reid & Co 1932
Ritchie, G.S. *The Admiralty Chart* Pentland Press 1967/1995
Rose, Alec *My Lively Lady* Nautical 1968
Royal Cruising Club Pilotage Foundation rccpf.org.uk/
Royal Gibraltar Yacht Club site http://www.rgyc.gi/history.php
Royal Malta Yacht Club www.rmyc.org/about-rmyc/history/
Royal Naval Yacht Club rnyc.org.uk/historic-yachts/2013/06/sunbeam-ii/
Royal Yachting Association www.rya.org.uk/

Sadlier, M. *The Strange Life of Lady Blessington* http://extra.shu.ac.uk/corvey/database/authors/datab/blessington/aabless/aablessbio.htm#10
Sail Boat Data www.sailboatdata.com/
Sailing www.sailing.org/regattas.php
Samuel, Henry *St Tropez lifeboat appeal founders as luxury yacht owners 'too mean' to help pay for a new one* The Telegraph 31 July 2018
Scherer Jenna *The Fabulously Eccentric Life of James Gordon Bennett, Jr* mentalfloss.com/article/64130/fabulously-eccentric-life-james-gordon-bennett-jr
Schoff, W.H. (Tranls.) *Periplus of the Erythraean Sea* Longmans, Green 1912
Science News www.sci-news.com/archaeology/science-catalhoyuk-map-mural-volcanic-eruption-01681.html
Seven Seas Cruising Association ssca.org/#/history/
Severe Weather EU www.severe-weather.eu/mcd/enhanced-tornado-threat-western-coast-of-italy-ligurian-tyrrhenian-sea-plains-of-north-italy-north-adriatic-october-29-2018/
Severin, Tim *The Jason Voyage* Hutchinson 1985
Shelley, Percy Bysshe *Time* Poetry Foundation https://www.poetryfoundation.org/poems/45141/time-56d224858f450
Shipley, Graham *Pseudo-Skylax's Periplous* Bristol Phoenix Press 2011
Singleton, Frank http://weather.mailasail.com/Franks-Weather/Grib-Files-Explained
Slocum, Joshua *Sailing Alone Around the World* Epub Gutenberg Foundation. First published 1900
Smith, Helena *Aristotle Onassis heir sells private island to Russian oligarch's daughter* The Guardian 16 April 2013

Solarwave Yachts www.solarwave-yachts-pacific.com/solar-hybrid-power-catamarans/
solarwave cruiser 64 power catamaran/

Spectator http://archive.spectator.co.uk/article/2nd-august-1913/15/shelleys-yacht-the-ariel-or-the-don-juan

Spirit Yachts https://spirityachts.com/

Starr, Stephen *The Mediterranean's urban sprawl: 'You know a city's near by the plastic in the sea'* The Guardian 20 January 2015

Starkey D.J. and Jamieson A.G. *Exploiting the Sea* University of Exeter Press 1998

Strasser, Thomas F. *Location and Perspective in the Theran Flotilla Fresco* Journal of Mediterranean Archaeology 2010

Suetonius *The Lives of the Twelve Caesars/Caligula* Transl. Robert Graves Penguin 1957

Super Yacht Intelligence www.boatinternational.com/boat-pro

Super Yacht Services www.superyachtservicesguide.com/

Superyacht Fan www.superyachtfan.com/superyacht_octopus.html

Superyacht Times 15 October 2013 www.superyachttimes.com/yacht-news/the-resurrection-of-superyacht-southern-cloud

Superyachts.com May 2018 *The rise of fuel-efficient, long-distance explorers*

Tangoitalia http://tangoitalia.com/campania/historical-regatta-of-the-maritime-republics-of-italy-amalfi-genoa-pisa-and-venice/

Tennant, Peter *Obituary* The Independent 23 July 1993

The Ocean Clean Up www.theoceancleanup.com/great-pacific-garbage-patch/

Thompson,T. and D. *Adriatic Pilot* Imray 2016

Thomsen, Steen *Concerning Tvind* (Unpublished MA thesis)

Tilley, Alec *Seafaring on the Ancient Mediterranean* BAR International Series 1268 2004

Towergate Insurance www.towergateinsurance.co.uk/boat-insurance/the-cost-of-maintaining-a-super-yacht

Trelawney, Edward *Recollections of the Last Days of Shelley and Byron* Ticknor & Fields 1858

Turchi, Peter *Maps of the Imagination: The Writer as Cartographer* Trinity University Press 2004

Turkle, Sherry *Alone Together* Basic Books 2011

Tvind Alert www.tvindalert.com/ A website exposing the Tvind organisation

Vasey, Tony *The Ocean Cruising Club: The First 50 Years* OCC paper 2003

Verasanso, Janet *Tilman's Grace Darling* [Afterward to H.W. Tilman *Mischief Goes South: Every Herring Should Hang by its Own Tail*. New Edition 1966/2016]

Verasanso, Janet *The Med in the Fifties* Marine Quarterly Winter 2017

Violet, Charles *Solitary Journey* 1954/1962 Mariners Library

Warsash Super Yacht Academy www.warsashsuperyachtacademy.com/home.aspx

Watts, Jonathon *We have 12 years to limit climate change catastrophe, warns UN* The Guardian 8 October 2018

Wavetrain www.wavetrain.net/boats-a-gear/484-cruising-sailboat-evolution-cleopatras-barge

Weebly.com https://historybecauseitshere.weebly.com/roman-emperor-caligula-and-his-legendary-lake-nemi-ships.html

Weissala, George *Contours of a Discipline* European Studies in Asia Routledge 2014

Whigham, Peter *The Poems of Catullus* Penguin 1966

Wikipedia en.wikipedia.org/wiki/Mediterranean_tropical-like_cyclone

Williams, Eric *The Wooden Horse* Collins 1964

Wilson, Derek *The Circumnavigators* Constable 1989

Worth, Claud *Yacht Cruising* 3rd edition J D Potter 1926

Yacht Club Costa Smeralda: www.yccs.it/en/

Yacht Club de Monaco www.yacht-club-monaco

Yacht Club of Greece www.ycg.gr/index.php/en/ycg

Yachtevela www.yachtevela.com/konigin-ii-1516.html

Yachtharbour *How Russian oligarchs shaped the yachting industry* 8 June 2016 www.yachtharbour.com

YBW.com www.ybw.com/news-from-yachting-boating-world/sunsail-under-new-ownership 20.09.1999

INDEX

Colonna, Cardinal Prospero, 43
Communications, 350–351
  Mobile, 350–351
Communism, collapse of, 286
Compass, 345
Constantinople, 51, 101
Conversations of Lord Byron, 90
Coptic calendar, 320
Cordier, Emma, 74
Corfu, 154, 185, 188, 214, 236, 243
Corinth Canal, 155, 244–245
Cornaro Atlas, 334
Corry, Viscount, 344
Corsica, 152, 221
Corsica and Sardinia, 185
Costa del Sol, 222
Costa Smeralda, 208, 261
Cote d'Azur, 295
Cowes, 91, 95, 97, 104–105
Cox, Mike, 182–184, 197–198, 220
CPT Sailing in Greece, 191–196, 199
Crab, 140, 152–157
Crab's Odyssey, 152–156
Craxton, John, 147
Creole, 162, 163, 168–174, 211, 230, 263
  Cursed yacht, 172–174
Crete, 230
Croatia, 220, 286, 297–298
Crowninshield, Jr, George 112, 113–115
Cruise ships
  Numbers, 310
  Sewerage, 309–310
Cruising
  Cultural attitudes, 141–143, 149
  Early 20th C., 126–127
Cruising Association, 126, 142, 302
Cruising Club of America, 126
Cruising organisations and clubs, 126
Cusack, Janet, 97, 101, 120, 126
Cutter, gaff rigged, 107
Cyclades, 185, 235
Cyndus River, 28
Cyprus, 213, 232

Daily Express, 143
Dalaman Airport, 184, 218
Danube, 239–240
Dardanelles, 46, 97, 155–156, 292, 338, 339
Darius, 329–331
Davidson, Anne, 142
De Vries Lentsch, 174